Gentle Darkness

Gentle Darkness

MEDITATIONS AND PRAYERS
FOR ILLUMINATION

Edited by Rowland Croucher

AN ALBATROSS BOOK

© Rowland Croucher 1994

Published in Australia and New Zealand by
Albatross Books Pty Ltd
PO Box 320, Sutherland
NSW 2232, Australia
in the United States of America by
Albatross Books
PO Box 131, Claremont
CA 91711, USA
and in the United Kingdom by
Lion Publishing
Peter's Way, Sandy Lane West
Oxford OX4 5HG, England

First edition 1994

National Library of Australia
Cataloguing-in-Publication data

Croucher, Rowland
Gentle Darkness

ISBN   0 7324 1007 X (Albatross)
ISBN   0 7459 2431 X (Lion)

1. Meditations 2. Prayers. I. Croucher, Rowland

242

Cover photographs: John Waterhouse
Printed by Kyodo Printing Co. Ltd, Singapore

Contents

Theme: The gentle re-creation beyond darkness
Job 38: 2–12, 19–21, GNB

Theme: The gentle empowering through darkness
Job 29: 2–17, GNB

Preface

Louis Evely says contemplative prayer is 'opening ourselves to God so that he can open us to others'.

But in opening ourselves to God, we sometimes experience 'the loneliness of the night of God' (T. S. Eliot). All the Christian mystics testify to one or more 'dark night of the soul' episodes. They feel, frustratedly, that God has removed himself from their consciousness. The experience invariably includes self-condemnation, spiritual weakness and, sometimes, depression and moodiness.

St John of the Cross and others have helped us understand the purgative character of this experience and its divine source. God allows the 'dark night' to be endured by those he most desires to purify and draw into the light of his healing presence. . .

Like its threeb predecessors, *Still Waters, Deep Waters, High Mountains, Deep Valleys* and *Rivers in the Desert*, this book aims to be a devotional resource for the busy pastor or serious Christian. Besides their use in individual and couples' devotions and in preaching (from pulpits and radio), these chapters have proved useful for group devotions in many Christian churches, organisations — even touring parties!

All royalties go to John Mark Ministries, which seeks through counselling, consulting, seminars and writing to encourage pastors, ex-pastors, church leaders and their spouses. As a pastor, I know a little of the extraordinary — though somewhat intangible — pressures faced by this species!

Albatross Books is completing this series of five books with the next title, *A Garden of Solitude*. The complete series will be obtainable from your local Christian bookshop in Australia, New Zealand or the United Kingdom. For other overseas readers, you can buy any title, or the complete series, by writing direct to the nearest publishing address on the verso page (immediately after the title page).

Thanks to my wife Jan, at-home children Amanda and Lindy, and to Sue, Silvana, both Graces, Christine and David for their help and encouragement.

Rowland Croucher
John Mark Ministries
7 Bangor Court
Heathmont,
Victoria 3135
Australia

Theme: The gentle mystery of darkness

'I am not reduced to silence by the darkness'
(Job 23: 17)

My thoughts today are resentful,
　　for God's hand is heavy on me in my trouble.
If only I knew how to find him,
　　how to enter his court,
　　I would state my case before him
　　and set out my arguments in full;
　　then I should learn what answer he would give
　　and find out what he had to say.
Would he exert his great power to browbeat me?
No — God himself would never bring a charge
　　against me.
There, the upright are vindicated before him
　　and I shall win from my judge an absolute
　　discharge.
If I go forward, he is not there;
　　if backward, I cannot find him;
　　when I turn left, I do not descry him;
　　I face right, but I see him not.
But he knows me in action or at rest;
　　when he tests me, I prove to be gold.
My feet have kept to the path he has set me;
　　I have followed his way and not turned from it.
I do not ignore the commands that come from
　　his lips;
　　I have stored in my heart what he says.
He decides, and who can turn him from his purpose?
He does what his own heart desires.
What he determines, that he carries out;
　　his mind is full of plans like these.
Therefore I am fearful of meeting him;
　　when I think about him, I am afraid;
　　it is God who makes me faint-hearted
　　and the Almighty who fills me with fear,
　　yet I am not reduced to silence by the darkness,
　　nor by the mystery which hides him.

Job 23: 2–17, NEB

WEEK

1

Gentle darkness

You, O Lord, keep my lamp burning; my God turns my darkness into light.

My brothers and sisters, whenever you face trials of any kind consider it nothing but joy. . . the testing of your faith produces endurance.

I will give you the treasures of darkness, riches stored in secret places, so that you may know that I am the Lord.

He reveals the deep things of darkness and brings deep shadows into the light.

Even though I walk through the valley of the shadow of death, I will fear no evil.

If I say, 'Surely the darkness will hide me and the light become night around me,' even the darkness will not be dark to you; the night will shine like the day, for darkness is as light to you.

(Psalm 18: 28, NIV; James 1: 2–3, NRSV; Isaiah 45: 3; Job 12: 22; Psalm 23: 4; Psalm 139: 11–12 — all NIV)

Those of us who live in the city have nearly forgotten how to appreciate the dark. With the coming of artificial light last century, first by gas and then by electricity, life was radically transformed. Not only could the day's activities be extended into the evening, but it became normal to banish the darkness during waking hours.

The attractiveness of approaching darkness is rarely appreciated except when we are away from cities when the sun falls over the bush and the night life begins to become active. Then there is a delightful fascination about the change in tempo and the beauty of change from brightness through the muted shades to total blackness. At times like that we become aware of a whole range of animal and bird life that otherwise passes unnoticed.

So, too, with our clever civilisation; we have long since learned to minimise the times of darkness of the mind or soul. The 'dark night of the soul' is a mystical concept sought after by a few, but beyond the conception of many. Those who do explore it come away greatly enriched. The darkness of emotional depression is something for which early relief is sought, even though there is evidence that it can at times serve a positive function. And the dark world of bereavement is one we usually seek to leave as quickly as possible, even seeking to pretend that we never even entered it, lest we betray unseemly emotions.

Yet in times past, some of those who suffered most with depression were profoundly creative, not in spite of their experience, but by using it constructively. Poets like William Cowper have enriched hymnody out of their times of deep darkness. Bereavement used to be an extended process with clear rituals to identify the stages necessary to come through to a resolution of the pain. Seeking to short cut the process, or not being allowed to grieve, can often intensify and extend pain quite unnecessarily.

Few of us welcome such dark times, and yet intuitively we know that they are part of the rich texture of life. Without the darkness, we find it hard to appreciate the light and rejoice in it. But even the darkness itself can at times be welcomed when we banish fear of it. Some do their best thinking in the 'wee hours of the morning'. The emotionally dark times can be the opportunity for reflection, for meditation, for slowing down to move slowly enough to rediscover that there is beauty even in the shadows. We can really embrace the dark times when we can say, 'even though I walk through the valley of the shadow of death, I will fear no evil'.

To those accustomed to banishing the darkness, the light seems the only safe option. But for those who allow themselves to explore the darkness, its terrors can be dispelled. What seems at first fearsome can become an experience of personal reflection and discovery.

Psychologists in recent years have emphasised that we all need to be aware of our shadow side — that darker side of our nature which we are inclined to deny and yet has an authenticity as significant as the parts we embrace. Those who deny that part become lopsided and strangely lacking integration. It is the combination of dark and light which takes us into a sense of wholeness which we can only yearn for if we always seek to stay in the light.

True, in the spiritual realm, we are instructed to walk in the light and shun the darkness of evil, but there is a natural part of our earthly journey which takes us to darker moments where we gain a perspective, which then brings colour to all of life. The truth of this becomes more apparent as we move into the later years of life.

Finally, even the darkness of death need hold no terrors for the one whose life-friend is the Light of the world.

❧

God descends to re-ascend. He comes down from the heights of absolute being into time and space, down into humanity, down further still — if embryologists are right — to recapitulate in the womb ancient and pre-human phases of life. Down into the very roots and sea-bed of the nature he created. But he goes down to come up again and then bring the whole ruined world up with him. . .

One may think of a diver, first reducing himself to nakedness, then glancing in midair, then gone with a splash, vanished, rushing down into green, warm water, into bleak and cold water, down into increasing pressure, into the depth of ooze and slime and old decay. Then up again, back into colour and light. His lungs almost bursting, till suddenly he breaks surface, holding in his hand the dripping, precious thing he went to recover. He and it are both coloured now, but they have come back into the light. Down below, where it lay colourless in the dark, he lost his colour, too.

C.S. Lewis, *Miracles*

Day is dying in the west;
Heav'n is touching earth with rest;
Wait and worship while the night
Sets her evening lamps alight
Through all the sky.
Holy, holy, holy, Lord God of Hosts. . .

Mary Lathbury, 1877

A pastor responded to the words 'A dark tunnel is often the best way of getting round a hill' by writing: God used those words to show me that the darkness in which I was enveloped was really the prelude to the light. I had wanted to move on into something that I felt sure was the divine will, but every time I talked to God about it there was from his side nothing but silence. . . One day the light shone and with such radiance that I could never have believed it possible. In that moment there was enough light to compensate for every hour of darkness.'

Selwyn Hughes, *Every Day with Jesus*

Life is not always rainbows. Colours fade, and shades of grey — or even heavy tones of black — creep in. Perhaps right now your life seems 'black' and heavy, rather than cheerfully red and gold. If so, come with me to St Bride's Church in Fleet Street, London. . . down in the crypt in the rock face there is a thick, black line that speaks of the time when it was burned down. . . The Black Death in 1665 was followed by the Great Fire of London. The church was ultimately rebuilt and then, in 1940 during the London Blitz, 'St Bride's: a blackened ruin' mourned the papers. Yes, blackness, devastation, death — all three.

What about St Bride's today? It has risen again, more beautiful than ever, a church risen from the ashes like a phoenix. . . In the light of the history of this famous church, are you able to think back beyond your own 'thick, black line' to earlier times of joy and fulfilment? Is it safe for you to look ahead with confidence and say: 'Yes, for me the best is yet to be'?

John Court and Dorothy O'Neill,
Rainbows through the Rain

I call to you, O Lord, from my quiet darkness. Show me your mercy and love. Let me see your face, hear your voice, touch the hem of your cloak. I want to love you, be with you, speak to you and simply stand in your presence. But I cannot make it happen. Pressing my eyes against my hands is not praying, and reading about your presence is not living in it.

But there is that moment in which you will come to me, as you did to your fearful disciples, and say: 'Do not be afraid; it is I.' Let that moment come soon, O Lord. And if you want to delay it, then make me patient. Amen.

Henri Nouwen, *A Cry for Mercy*

Night-time sharpens, heightens each sensation;
Darkness stirs and wakes imagination.
Silently the senses abandon their defences;
Slowly, gently night unfurls its splendour.
Grasp it, sense it — tremulous and tender;
Turn your face away from the garish light of day,
Turn your thoughts away from cold, unfeeling light —
and listen to the music of the night.

Charles Hart, *The Phantom of the Opera*,
Act 1, Scene 5

Painting is about light. . . There are times when the strokes of colour don't produce that feeling of light. Then you look at the painting in dismay until you realise that the problem is a lack of contrast. The shadows aren't deep enough. The light tones don't register because the darks aren't there. The brilliance of the one depends on the depth of the other. And the feeling of light is produced by deepening the darks!

Even further, if you look closely at a landscape painted by a master, you'll see that in his lights there are subtle hints of the shadow colours; and to bring real unity and harmony the light colours have to be there in the deep shadows enriching them. It's not the case of either dark or light, but of both. And you begin to realise that the darkness and shade in a landscape are an indication, not of the absence of light, but of its presence.

Eddie Askew, *Many Voices: One Voice*

God of Light, Creator of a universe that combines both dark and light, I seek your strength to renounce the darkness of evil, yet embrace those dark experiences within which growth and maturation can occur. Help me resist the temptation to seek only the brighter side of life, like the moth that is eventually consumed by the very light it seeks, and be ready to embrace those times when shadows fall and darkness surrounds me.

May I be enriched by the contrast, nurtured in the slower pace of moving with few signs to guide. And when the darkness seems impenetrable, then lead kindly light, amid the encircling gloom, lead thou me on until the darkness once again retreats and I can walk again in the warmth of your light and love.

A Benediction
Let the Spirit of the Lord Jesus Christ guide your way.
Whether walking by night or by day,
Walk in the name of the Lord Jesus Christ,
Who rose from the dead to give you new life in him. Amen.

Jan Black

The cries wrung out of me!

I lived at peace until he shattered me, taking me by the neck to dash me to pieces. He has made me a target for his archery, shooting his arrows at me from every side. Breach after breach he drives through me, bearing down on me like a warrior.

Listen to me, all you inhabitants of the land! Has the like of this happened in your days or in the days of your forefathers?. . . What the locust has left, the swarmer devours; what the swarmer has left, the hopper devours; and what the hopper has left, the grub devours. . . A horde, vast and cunning, has invaded my land; they have teeth like a lion's teeth, they have the fangs of a lioness; they have laid waste my vines and left my fig-trees broken; they have plucked them bare. . . and all the people's joy has come to an end. . . food is cut off from the house of our God and there is neither joy nor gladness. Under the clods the seeds have shrivelled, the water-channels are run dry, the barns lie in ruins; for the harvests have come to naught. How the cattle moan! The herds of oxen are distraught because they have no pasture; even the flocks of sheep waste away. To you, O Lord, I cry out!

Up to the present, as we know, the whole created universe in all its parts groans as if in the pangs of childbirth. What is more, we also, to whom the Spirit is given. . . are groaning inwardly while we look forward eagerly to our liberation from mortality.

You must be vigilant at all times, praying that you be strong enough to come safely through all that is going to happen, and to stand in the presence of the Son of Man.

Then Jesus was led by the Spirit into the wilderness. . .
And the tempter came and said to him, 'IF. . .
Then the devil took him. . . and said 'IF. . .
Next the devil showed him. . . and said 'IF. . .
Then the devil left him,
and angels appeared and looked after him.

(Job 16: 12–14, JB; Joel 1: 2, 4, 6–7, 12 and 16–19, REB; Romans 8: 22–23, REB; Luke 21: 36, JB; Matthew 4: 1, 3, 5–6, 8–9 and 11, JB)

It's worth taking a good look at this word *anguish*.

The Latin and Greek roots of the word mean 'to squeeze' and 'to strangle'. The Gothic root means 'narrow'; in Old Norse it meant 'anger'; in Italian 'tight straits'. Today, it refers to 'severe suffering, trouble, affliction'. How can these ideas of continuing anguish connect with God's promises of liberation and freedom — especially if our experience of it is that it goes on and on, chaining us down with only occasional bits of relief?

Sometimes there is total healing — it's real and it lasts. So why isn't it always given? Why do some people have to know what it's like to be squeezed, to be pushed into tight straits, to feel strangled? What is it like when God chooses not to give total physical, emotional, mental and spiritual healing, here and now? What happens then? We cry out in exasperation — does God really care? Is he even there? Perhaps we could take it better if there was some *reason* to it all, if only there was some clear answer to our *whys*. . .

We are so reluctant to admit to mystery!

Most of our education is about de-mystifying things that we find confusing; most of our jobs are about finding solutions to things that are problems; much of our leisure is given to unwrapping different sorts of puzzles. Look at the popularity of spy stories, thrillers, science fiction, romances with happy endings — they all feed our intense need to find an answer and to know what's what.

We are taught to rationalise. Belief in a God who is all loving seems to be incompatible with our everyday experience of people who live with continuing anguish, so this becomes the greatest put-off of all. It has been called the strongest argument against Christianity. Something doesn't immediately tie up, it's not instantly subject to logic, so it had better be passed over.

There are so many theories. Could it be that when I suffer it is because:

* I have sinned? *OR*
* I haven't prayed hard enough? *OR*
* I enjoy suffering? *OR*
* I can somehow pay off the sins of someone else? *OR*
* I have been chosen to be one of the front-line warriors in the cosmic warfare between the Devil and God? *OR*
* I can be trusted with suffering, while others are left to be in the back-up positions? *OR*
* I suffer in order to discover that growth is possible as the result of suffering? *OR*
* I suffer because pain and hurt is a sort of currency that God uses to balance out the good and evil in the world?

All these are efforts to solve *whys*: to squeeze mystery into a solvable problem. But maybe continuing anguish is not so much about *whys*, but more about *hows*. Maybe, instead of using up so much energy in asking *why*, God wants us to embrace the experience and look at the *hows*.

God is not confined within reason. His creativity is not locked up in logic. He allows us to use every fibre of our being to know him — and not only with our minds. We learn with our total experience and we know, beyond reason, that the one thing we can be sure of is that God is there in all our experience of hurt and anguish.

Sometimes it's difficult to see him through the fog of puzzlement and confusion — and sometimes we can get so angry and frustrated, we try to push him out — but he's the Creator and he's still there.

❄❄❄

Take fright this night
For strangeness' sake,
Or glory in the tumult — Shout!
For all agree
'Tis small, and aching sweet,
This boy-king, gravely bundled.
We found out later what it cost;
All wealth in this and worlds beyond,
All wisdom deep and wide,
No weapons, only Love itself,
And the pain in Mary's side,
Allowed, as all his pain would be . . . for thee.

Thomas Turnbull, *The Birth*

When the discomfort has become so great that I can do nothing but lie down, and cannot think clearly, then I know my work has become prayer. . . This does seem a very churlish way to treat God. . . His humility appears endless. . .

It is very good to have something to try to do with the pain. While it remains an unmitigated evil, I can yet regard it somehow as a means to an end. I cannot describe the process very well, but I found it to be one of somehow *absorbing darkness* — a physical or mental suffering of my own or, worse, of someone else's into my own person, my own body or my own emotions. We have to allow ourselves to be open to pain. Yet all the while we must resist any temptation to assent to its being other than evil. If we are able to do this — to act, as it were, as blotting paper for pain, without handing it on in the form of bitterness or resentment or of hurt to others — then somehow in some incomprehensible miracle of grace, some at least of the darkness, may be turned to light.

Learning to live with the disorder as creatively as possible has in the end formed the person I am. I cannot, in the last resort, regret being the person I am.

Margaret Spufford, *Celebration*

There are still so many things left to say. But don't close this book and say, 'She lived happily ever after'. Instead, when you close this book, know that I am changing ever after.

. . .There is still crisis and hurt and pain, even in spring. There is still some loneliness and depression at times, even in spring. There are still some questions, even in spring. There is still, at times, frustration with God, myself and the world, even in spring. And sometimes I feel like giving up, even in spring. But I don't.

I want to share so much more, but some things are best understood by being experienced personally. . . Healing thrives in sincere desperation.

God bless those of you still in that place of barren winter. I pray the Holy Spirit will show you God's gutsy love. May you meet Jesus, who is dying to heal, and may you grow into spring.

Nancy Ann Smith, *Winter Past*

It is in the nature of things that we meet God in the desert, in sickness, prison, bereavement or some other desolation. As the philosopher puts it: 'Pain is a holy angel which shows treasure to men which otherwise remains forever hidden' (Adalbert Stifter).

Sheila Cassidy, *Good Friday People*

It's hard to believe the world is here just so I can party, when a third of its people go to bed starving each night. It's hard to believe the purpose of life is to feel good, when I see teenagers smashed on the freeway. If I try to escape toward hedonism, suffering and death lurk nearby, haunting me, reminding me of how hollow life would be if this world were all I'd ever known.

Sometimes murmuring, sometimes shouting, suffering is a 'rumour of transcendence' that the entire human condition is out of whack. . . [If] you want to be satisfied with this world and you want to believe the only purpose of life is enjoyment, you must go around with cotton in your ears, for the megaphone of pain (C.S. Lewis' phrase) is a loud one.

Philip Yancey, *Where Is God When It Hurts?*

God never would send you the darkness
If he felt you could bear the light.
But you would not cling to his guiding hand
If the way were always bright;
And you would not care to walk by faith
Could you always walk by sight.

Anonymous

In an imaginative reconstruction of Jesus' trial and execution, Cleopas is talking to a television interviewer.

Cleopas says, 'That's what his enemies in the Sanhedrin said. "If you are the Son of God, save yourself."

'He could've done that. No trouble at all. But it wouldn't have helped us, would it? I mean, when it came to die, the fact that he had arranged a last-minute rescue for himself last Friday afternoon wouldn't have made any difference to us then. You don't conquer death by avoiding it, Mr Tenel. You conquer death by accepting it and breaking through to life on the other side. Because he has done that, we don't need to be afraid of death any more.'

Stuart Jackman, *The Davidson Affair*

God weeps with us so that we may one day laugh with him.

Anonymous

Great Creator of the universe, all-wise God, there are so many theories we have concocted to answer our terrible question, 'Why suffering? Why me?'

All of them are part-answers, part-truths; there are circumstances in which each of them seems slick, pat, too easy.

Lord, please let me have the gut-knowing that there are answers; that they are in your hands and not ours; that you know the full value of suffering and that you give it full honour.

Help me to be prepared to accept it and act as a conduit, an unblocked channel, an unquestioning throughway for your purposes and your vision of the world that is yours. And yours alone. Amen.

A Benediction

For God loved the world so much that he gave his only Son that everyone who believes in him may not die, but have eternal life.

The blessing of the God of life be ours,
The blessing of the living Christ be ours,
The blessing of the Holy Spirit be ours,
To cherish us, to help us, to make us holy.

The Iona Community Worship Book

3

Wilderness

And. . . Moses and Aaron came and said to Pharaoh,
'This is the command of the Lord, the God of Israel,
"Let my people go so that they may celebrate a feast to
me in the wilderness."'

In their heart they put God to the test by asking for
food according to their unbridled craving. Then they
spoke against God. They said, 'Can God prepare a table
in the wilderness? Behold, he struck the rock so that
waters gushed out, and streams overflowed. Can he
give bread also? Will he provide meat delicacies for
his people?'

And a voice came out of the heavens, 'You are my
Beloved. You give me great pleasure.' And immediately the Spirit impelled him to go out into the
wilderness.

Behold, I send your messenger before your face, who
will prepare your way; the voice of one crying in the
wilderness. . .

He sent darkness and made it dark. . . He turned
their waters into blood, and caused their fish to die.
Their land swarmed with frogs. . . He spoke, and
there came a swarm of flies and gnats. . . He gave
them hail for rain, and flaming fire in their land. He
struck down their vines also and their fig trees. . . He
spoke, and locusts came, and young locusts, even
without number, and ate up all vegetation in their
land, and ate up the fruit of the ground. He also
struck down all the firstborn in their land, the first
fruits of all their vigour.

Then he brought them out with silver and gold; and

among his tribes there was not one who stumbled. . .
He spread a cloud as a protective mantle, and provided
fire to show the way by night. They asked, and he
brought quail, and satisfied them with the bread of
heaven. He opened the rock, and water flowed out; it
streamed across the land, turning dry places into raging
rivers.

I cared for you in the wilderness, in the land of
drought.

Nevertheless, he looked upon their distress when he
heard their appeal; and he remembered his commitment
to them and relented according to the depth of his
loving-kindness. He also had compassion on them in
the presence of their captors.

Save us, O Lord our God,
And gather us from among the nations,
To give thanks to your holy name,
And glory in your praise.
Blessed be the Lord, the God of Israel,
From everlasting even to everlasting.
And let all the people say, 'Amen.'
Praise the Lord!

John, the baptiser, appeared in the wilderness
preaching. . . And John's diet was locusts and wild
honey.

(Exodus 5: 1; Psalm 78: 19–20; Mark 1: 11–12; Mark 1: 2; Psalm
105: 28–41; Hosea 13: 5; Psalm 106: 44–48; Mark 1: 4, 6 — personal
translation)

The image of 'wilderness' can be a rich and profound one
for the enhancement of our spirituality.

It is tempting to pray that we might be preserved from
the 'wilderness': who wants pain, discomfort, poverty,
severe testing? Who embraces searing wounds of spirit
with ease? Or rejection, or misunderstanding? Who willingly would seek to be a victim in a success-orientated
culture obsessed with being the victor? (Sister Veronica
Brady, reflecting a belief of Patrick White's, says, 'History

is the story of the winners!')

There is a depth of spirituality found in the experience of the wilderness, the place of poverty of spirit, that is lost to those who don't have the nerve to accept the hard place. For the wilderness is offered to every pilgrim. All of us are given opportunities to taste the grit, feel the blast of the winds, glimpse desert where we hoped to see paradise.

Think for a moment of a 'wilderness' experience of yours, either from the past or in the present. Is it possible for you to trace a connection between that experience and the Holy Spirit? Jesus, we are told, was impelled into the wilderness by the Spirit. Could you have been similarly driven by the Holy Spirit into your 'wilderness'? It need not be the case that the Spirit directly placed you in your 'wilderness', but are you able to sense something of the presence of the Spirit in that experience?

Sometimes we rush to the conclusion that it is Satan who places us in the hard place of testing. Perhaps we need to be more careful: it may well be Satan who meets us there, but we also need to pray for eyes to see the Spirit in that hard place, too.

The 'wilderness' is a place of great value, as well as one of great pain. Alongside the tormenting of the 'wild beasts' which threaten destruction (Mark 1: 13) is the strong, gentle ministry of the 'angels'; in the stark wilderness, it is possible to have a festive celebration! John the Baptiser was nourished sufficiently in the wilderness for him to be formed according to the Lord's will and equipped for a powerful preaching ministry.

Sometimes the pain of the 'wilderness' is the pain of a new experience of the discipline of humility and of a deepening treasuring of the Divine — the agony of newly discovering the fragility of the earthen vessel of our own person, in which the Spirit is pleased to dwell. That fragility, that weakness, is penetrated in the 'wilderness' as with a laser.

Pause now and think for a few moments about your 'beasts' and your 'angels'. How attentive are you to the 'angelic' within you, ministering to your spirit? Be grateful to the Spirit for the presence of the Divine in your desert times. Put this book down for a few minutes, and take sufficient time to reflect and pray.

❧❧

Because the wilderness was seen as the place where the devil dwelt, the first Christians went there to take him on.

Wilderness. Wilderness means emptiness; the place where little grows; the place where survival is hard and where death is. You don't have to travel far to find wilderness.

George Carey, Archbishop of Canterbury

Gethsemane. . . Not just death, but the desertion of God the Father. The picture of anguish we have here should be enough to banish forever the easy triumphalism of much current commercial Christianity.

Virginia Stem Owens, *Christianity Today*

[Some people] want, and believe it possible, to skip over the discipline, to find an easy short cut to sainthood. Often they attempt to attain it by simply imitating the superficialities of saints, retiring to the desert or taking up carpentry. Some even believe that by such imitation they have really become saints and prophets, and are unable to acknowledge that they are still children and face the fact that they must start at the beginning and go through the middle.

M. Scott Peck, *The Road Less Travelled*

Everything may be very dark. The desert is dry and empty. Light has been eclipsed from everything and you feel that you have lost the way. It is in such spiritual ennui or despondency that you feel most your immobility, having been blocked at every exit. Confinement seems to press in from all sides to suffocate you. It would be so much easier to run away or to choose your own type of trial over those that are presented by the Spirit in your unique desert. No-one owns your desert! It is all yours and, in a way, you made it. . . You search desperately as you never did before when all was light. . .

George A. Maloney, *Broken but Loved*

We are never so near God as when we have to get on as well as we can without the consolation of feeling his presence. It is not when the child is with his/her mother that she is most anxious for the child's welfare. It is when the child thinks he/she is alone that the mother is most compassionate and thinks of her child most tenderly. It is the same with God and ourselves.

Abbe de Tourville, *Letters of Direction*

But one is least alone in the desert. Abraham was alone; Moses stood in solitude; and Elijah, too, took the lonely journey to the desert. Nevertheless, these and others were called to meet and speak to God. They are never less than when alone.

John Chryssavgis, *The Desert is Alive*

The desert Fathers see the divine flame in all things, the world as a burning bush of God's energies. In fact, their aim is to become fire: Abba Lot went to see Abba Joseph and said to him 'Abba, as far as I can, I say my little office, I fast a little, I pray and meditate, I live in peace and purity and purify my thoughts. What else can I do?' The old man stood up and stretched his hands towards heaven. His fingers became like ten lamps of fire and he said to him, 'If you will, you can become all flame.'

Joseph of Panepho, in *The Desert is Alive*

PANDANUS
  Ungainly pain
  Heat-snapped in the burning
  Agony beyond telling
  The twisted disjointed image
      of Nature's fiery crucifixion.

Form without form
As if created in fright.
Fits and starts of being
Hiroshima life print fragmented
Intended
Framed in delicate compassion,
  gentle breeze caressed
Full of promise yet hardly
  fulfilled
In black.
But higher
Miracle green shoots
Savage, wild beauty
Fire of life green-flamed
Ever burning
Firm flaring
Healing amid the brutal tearing
purging
Tears
White hot.

Ross Kingham, *Surprises of the Spirit*

Divine Lover, you are the Lord of life: all life, my life, our lives. And in you, pain and death find their rightful place.

Forgive me for the times I have wanted to go against your perfect will and tried to displace wilderness experiences from your place in my life — and in the lives of those I love.

Help me, in times of pain, to look for you above all else. And if it is hard to see you, help me to wait in the darkness.

In waiting, strengthen my so little faith, empower my pathetic dreams, slake my deepest thirst, and demolish the myths that slowly encrust my inner self and form a barrier between my spirit and your Spirit.

Give me a precious desert-glimpse of your kingdom, your love, your perspective.

Sustain me in the wilderness-waiting; carry me, when I have no strength left, on eagle's wings; and in your time, let me soar.

In Christ our Lord. Amen.

A Benediction

Lavishly generous God,
no human words or costly gifts
can ever adequately express our thanks and praise
  to you.
Grant that we may gladly give you
the one precious gift we have to bring,
the offering of our loyalty and love;
and enable us to walk in love for others,
  in Christ who walks the road with us,
  a fragrant offering,
  a rose in the desert,
  for you.
Amen.

4

Waiting for the sky to fall on me

Now Ahab told Jezebel everything Elijah had done and how he had killed all the prophets with the sword. So Jezebel sent a messenger to Elijah to say, 'May the gods deal with me, be it ever so severely, if by this time tomorrow I do not make your life like that of one of them.' Elijah was afraid and ran for his life. When he came to Beersheba in Judah, he left his servant there, while he himself went a day's journey into the desert. He came to a broom tree, sat down under it and prayed that he might die. 'I have had enough, Lord,' he said. 'Take my life; I am no better than my ancestors.' Then he lay down under the tree and fell asleep.

All at once an angel touched him and said, 'Get up and eat.' He looked around, and there by his head was a cake of bread baked over hot coals, and a jar of water. He ate and drank and then lay down again. The angel of the Lord came back a second time and touched him and said, 'Get up and eat, for the journey is too much for you.' So he got up and ate and drank. Strengthened by that food, he travelled for forty days and forty nights until he reached Horeb, the mountain of God. There he went into a cave and spent the night.

When we came into Macedonia, this body of ours had no rest, but we were harassed at every turn — conflicts on the outside, fears within. But God, who comforts the downcast, comforted us by the coming of Titus, and not only by his coming but also by the comfort you had given him. He told us about your longing for me, your deep sorrow, your ardent concern for me, so that my joy was greater than ever.

Do your best to come to me quickly, for Demas, because he loved this world, has deserted me and has gone to Thessalonica. Crescens has gone to Galatia, and Titus to Dalmatia. Only Luke is with me. Get Mark and bring him with you, because he is helpful to me in my ministry.

Create in me a pure heart, O God, and renew a steadfast spirit within me. Do not cast me from your presence or take your Holy Spirit from me. Restore to me the joy of your salvation and grant me a willing spirit, to sustain me.

To keep me from becoming conceited because of these surpassingly great revelations, there was given me a thorn in my flesh, a messenger of Satan, to torment me. Three times I pleaded with the Lord to take it away from me. But he said to me, 'My grace is sufficient for you, for my power is made perfect in weakness.' Therefore I will boast all the more gladly about my weakness, so that Christ's power may rest on me. That is why, for Christ's sake, I delight in weaknesses, in insults, in hardships, in persecutions, in difficulties. For when I am weak, then I am strong.

(1 Kings 19: 1–5; 1 Kings 19: 6–9; 2 Corinthians 7: 5–7; 2 Timothy 4: 9–11; Psalm 51: 10–12; 2 Corinthians 12: 7–10 — all NIV)

After great triumphs and victories, there often comes into the life of a Christian a dark moment of the soul. This happens so often in the biblical narrative and in the lives of great saints that it must be one of the cardinal spiritual principles about the Christian pilgrimage.

Elijah had just won a stunning victory over the prophets of Baal, and there came immediately a threat to his life from Jezebel. His victory should have confirmed for Elijah that God was able to do anything, but in a moment of weakness and under-confidence, he surrendered to abject cowardice and ran for his life.

He should so easily have perceived the nature of this temptation and should have counted on God to do another miracle in destroying Jezebel — which he did, incidentally — but instead Elijah scampered for the desert, found a broom (juniper) tree and asked for the sky to fall on him. 'I am no better than my ancestors,' he said, 'and I want to die.'

There is a tendency in all of us to collapse after the event, and feel sorry for ourselves. This is when people prone to migraines get them, when nervous exhaustion is experienced and when ulcers appear. So there should be no surprise when this occurs. The question is: do we just treat the symptoms when they occur, or are there spiritual principles which might prevent this happening?

In Elijah's case, God provided direct sustenance and encouragement while he was still alone. But more often comfort comes from a good friend who can pull us out of our slough of despair and self-concern and lift our eyes to the wider world around us and God's purposes for the next stage of our life. For the apostle Paul, Titus was such a friend, a younger man whose growth and development as a Christian he owed to Paul. Titus also found his opportunity for ministry by assisting Paul in his travels and in founding churches.

This is so often the way it works for us. I have found this to be true over thirty years of pressurised ministry, especially in social welfare and refugee work, where you feel the great weight of responsibility of supporting staff and at the same time identifying with the terrible problems of homelessness, abuse and human rights violations that people suffer. Friends are the best antidote against feeling weighed down and lonely.

Many friends are better than one friend. As Paul found, Demas, on whom he had relied in establishing one of the New Testament churches, had 'deserted' him and he had to call on other friends to fill in the gap. He was lucky: Luke the doctor and other friends quickly stepped in.

Some Christians worry that surrounding yourself with friends prevents you from ever finding those quiet moments with God. But it does not have to be like that. You can see from the life of Jesus that sometimes he wanted his disciples around him, and even great crowds, but there were other times he badly wanted to be alone with his heavenly Father, and people were getting in the way. Neither is better than the other; different times call for different approaches. But whatever happens, it is better not to be utterly alone. Everyone needs friends.

As David discovered, God's forgiveness is available. Instead of the victory such as Elijah experienced, what if it is a failure, a disaster of some kind? That's when we have to deal directly with God, be absolutely honest about what has happened and whose fault it is. The old-fashioned word is 'confession'.

Confession is confidence in God's willingness to forgive which enables us to keep going in periods of darkness and loneliness. For myself, working currently in refugee work in Asia in a religious environment which is quite different from the one I grew up in, I am learning how to admit weakness, to admit that I am not always right, even to acknowledge that conservative evangelical theology is not the only way to find truth.

It's the discovery that the apostle Paul stumbled across as the years of ministry rolled by — God's strength is revealed best through weak human beings. He can take me in dark moments, in weakness, in physical disability, and demonstrate his power and grace. While we are always 'winning', the credit goes to us. When we 'lose', when we feel weak, and yet God still works through us or speaks through us, then all the credit goes to him. And we can relax, because it no longer depends on us maintaining our adrenalin or our energy.

❧❧

'Spiritual desolation' describes our interior life when we find ourselves enmeshed in a certain turmoil of spirit or feel ourselves weighed down by a heavy darkness or weight; when we experience a lack of faith or hope or love in the very distaste for prayer or for any spiritual activity, and we know a certain restlessness in our carrying on in the service of God. . .

Often times in desolation, we feel that God has left us to fend for ourselves. By faith we know that he is always with us in the strength and power of his grace, but at the time of apparent abandonment we are little aware of his care and concern. We experience neither the support nor the sweetness of his love, and our own response lacks fervour and intensity. It is as if we are living a skeletal life of the bare bones of faith.

The important attitude to nourish at a time of desolation is patience. Patience can mitigate the frustration, dryness or emptiness of the desolation period and so allow us to live through it a little less painfully. We should try to recall that everything has its time, and consolation has been ours in the past and will be God's gift in the future.

David L. Fleming, *The Spiritual Exercises of Saint Ignatius*

I think of the times when I come alive,
and the times when I am dead.
I ponder on the features I assume
in moments of aliveness,
and in times when I am dead.
Life abhors security:
for life means taking risks,
exposing self to danger,
even death.
Jesus says whoever wishes to be safe will lose their life;
whoever is prepared to lose their life will keep it.
I think of the times
when I drew back from taking risks,
when I was comfortable and safe.
Those were the times when I stagnated.
I think of other times
when I dared to take a chance,
to make mistakes,
to be a failure and a fool,
to be criticised by others,
when I dared to risk being hurt
and causing pain to others —
I was alive!
Life is for the gambler.
The coward dies.

Anthony de Mello, *Wellsprings: A Book of Spiritual Exercises*

Australian poet Kenneth Slessor writes about Adam McCay, a very good friend:

Adam, because on the mind's roads
Your mouth is always in a hurry.
Because you know 500 odes
And 19 ways to make a curry.
Because you fall in love with words
And whistle beauty forth to kiss them,
And blow the tails from China birds
Whilst I continually miss them.
Because you top my angry best
At billiards, fugues or pulling corks out,
And whisk a fritter from its nest
Before there's time to hand the forks out,
Because you saw the Romans wink,
Because your senses dance to metre,
Because, no matter what I drink,
You'll hold at least another litre,
Because you've got a gipsy's eye
That melts the rage of catamountains,
And metaphors that pass me by,
Burst from your lips in lovely fountains,
Because you've bitten the harsh foods
Of life, grabbed every dish that passes,
And walked amongst the multitudes
With the curse of looking-glasses,
Because I burn the selfsame flame
No falls of dirty earth may smother,
Oh, in your Abbey of Theleme,
Enlist me as a serving-brother!

Geoffrey Dutton, *Kenneth Slessor*

Old men are in soul as stiff, as lean, as bloodless in their bodies, except so far as grace penetrates and softens them, for age is a frost upon them, chilling devotion and binding and hardening the heart. . .

O rid me of this frightful cowardice, for this is at the bottom of all my ills. When I was young, I was bold, because I was ignorant — now I have lost my boldness, because I have advanced in experience. I am able to count the cost, better than I did, of being brave for thy sake and therefore I shrink from sacrifices. Here is a second reason, over and above the deadness of my soul, why I have so little faith or love in me.

John Henry Newman

It is important to be in touch with our sorrows, to recognise them, to honour them even. So often we imagine there is virtue in pretending they don't exist. We treat them as Victorian *grandes dames* treated the wayward son, labelling him the black sheep and dispatching him to the colonies so that he could be forgotten or ignored until he returned home reformed, rich and famous. There is reason for that, of course. Having him around is painful, not least to the family pride.

In the same way, living in the presence of our sorrows is always painful, and one of the bits of us that is hurt most of all is our pride. I hate to acknowledge that I cannot love my mother; that I despise my brother; that I have made a mess of my career and my marriage. How much more comfortable to my self-esteem to push all those feelings away, to pretend to myself that everything in the garden is lovely, that summer will last for ever.

Charles Elliott, *Praying Through Paradox*

Lord, do not leave me desolate. Save me from the excesses of self-doubt and self-pity. Rescue me from faithlessness, from doubting your presence. If I look for a tree where I can sit down and feel sorry for myself, burn it up so I can sit under your withering gaze and examine my self-pity for what it is.

And as I feel the intensity of your eyes and hear you call my name, renew within me the certainty I once had of your continuing and eternal life within me. It does not depend on how I feel or whether the world outside praises me. It depends solely on your continuing love.

With love for you renewed within me, then give me friends again to share with, people I can open my heart to, my secret thoughts and fears spilling out to some who will not snigger or gossip. For true friends, Lord, I pray as I move forward in this pilgrimage. Through Christ who said, 'Call me not master but friend.' Amen.

A Benediction
May Christ the true friend befriend you. May Christ, who knew what it was to have his friends desert him, never desert you. May Christ in your moments of desolation give you his peace. Amen.

Still leading on

Who can discern his errors? Forgive my hidden faults. Keep your servant also from wilful sins; may they not rule over me. Then will I be blameless, innocent of great transgression. May the words of my mouth and the meditation of my heart be pleasing in your sight, O Lord, my rock and my Redeemer.

Great is the Lord, and greatly to be praised, in the city of our God, in his holy mountain. Beautiful in elevation, the joy of the whole earth, is Mount Zion on the sides of the north, the city of the great King. God is in her palaces; he is known as her refuge.

For a day in your courts is better than a thousand. I would rather be a doorkeeper in the house of my God than dwell in the tents of wickedness. For the Lord God is a sun and shield; the Lord will give grace and glory; no good thing will he withhold from those who walk uprightly.

Now when Daniel knew that the writing was signed, he went home. And in his upper room, with his windows open toward Jerusalem, he knelt down on his knees three times that day, and prayed and gave thanks before his God, as was his custom since early days. Then these men assembled and found Daniel praying and making supplication before his God.

So he said to me, 'This is the word of the Lord to Zerubbabel: "Not by might nor by power, but by my Spirit," says the Lord Almighty.'

And when you pray, you shall not be like the hypocrites. For they love to pray standing in the synagogues and on the corners of the streets, that they may be seen by others. Assuredly, I say to you, they have their reward. But you, when you pray, go into your room, and when you have shut your door, pray to your Father who is in the secret place; and your Father who sees in secret will reward you openly.

Now it came to pass in those days that he went out to the mountain to pray, and continued all night in prayer to God.

These things I have spoken to you while being present with you. But the helper, the Holy Spirit, whom the Father will send in my name, he will teach you all things, and bring to your remembrance all things that I said to you. Peace I leave with you, my peace I give to you; not as the world gives do I give to you. Let not your heart be troubled, neither let it be afraid.

Whatever is true, whatever is worthy of reverence and is honourable and seemly, whatever is just, whatever is pure, whatever is lovely and loveable, whatever is kind and winsome and gracious, if there is any virtue and excellence, if there is anything worthy of praise, think on and weigh and take account of these things (fix your minds on them). Practise what you have learned and received and heard and seen in me, and model your way of living on it, and the God of peace (of untroubled, undisturbed well-being) will be with you.

Set your mind on things above, not on things on the earth.

Psalm 19: 12–14, NIV; Psalm 48: 1–3; Psalm 84: 10–12; Daniel 7: 10–11 — all NKJV; Zechariah 4: 6, NIV; Matthew 6: 5–6; Luke 6: 12; John 14: 25–27 — all NKJV; Philippians 4: 8–9, AB; Colossians 3: 2, NKJV)

How easy to see life from the downside. How easy to let despair and disillusionment sweep over us. John Killinger, in his book *Christmas Spoken Here*, writes about a cartoon that depicted a business executive with a grouchy look on his face standing behind his desk reading a memo from his secretary. It said: 'While you were out, Mongol hordes swept across Asia, Jack Dempsey KO'd Firpo, the cow jumped over the moon, Montgomery landed at Normandy, they constructed digital computers and Neil Armstrong landed on the moon.'

When we get discouraged, we may have the feeling that the world has passed us by — that while we slept history was being made. There are those like Joseph, John Bunyan and Terry Waite who have had plenty of cause for having that sense of disillusionment descend on them. And yet in the final countdown, they rose above the dark times, the dark days, the black moments.

Perhaps the 'silent times' throw us most. When like Joseph, Bunyan or Waite we are in prison and our release seems as far away as ever, with tongue in cheek people can remind us that 'the mills of God grind slowly'. Such words only add to our despair.

And yet surely the key to our downtimes is in attempting to remember that God does not forget us and that in the silent times, when he seems as far away as ever, he is in fact giving strength to our sagging spirit. As Psalm 105: 18 reminds us regarding Joseph: 'His feet they hurt with fetters; he was laid in chains of iron and his soul entered into the iron' (Amplified Bible).

Joseph was in gaol, but God was not finished with him. We may slip down the chute of spiritual despair and yet God has not left us. He has, in fact, promised he will never ever leave us (Hebrews 13: 5). A tough lesson indeed, but we must learn to wait out God's will and trust him even when we cannot see the way ahead. John Newman wrote: 'So long thy power hath blessed me; sure it still will lead me on.'

So many things can make us look down instead of up. So often the sad events have the effect of dampening our enthusiasm for God. And always in the middle of events we feel so let down because people did not act as we expected.

We can easily forget what is promised for us in scripture. Note Paul's word in Romans 8: 37–39: 'No, in all these things we win an overwhelming victory through him who has proved his love for us. I have become absolutely convinced that neither death nor life, neither messenger of heaven nor monarch of earth, neither what happens today nor what may happen tomorrow, neither a power from on high nor a power from below, nor anything else in God's whole world has any power to separate us from the love of God in Jesus Christ our Lord' (J.B. Phillips).

And so even though we may sink from time to time into disillusionment, it will help if we can patiently trust at such times, knowing that along with the Psalmist we will yet praise our God.

❤️

Yet we cannot help feeling disturbed as well as moved, for this surely is the Church as it was meant to be. It is vigorous and flexible, for these are the days before it ever became fat and short of breath through prosperity, or muscle-bound by over-organisation. These [early Christians] did not make 'acts of faith,': they believed; they did not 'say their prayers': they really prayed. They did not hold conferences on psychosomatic medicine: they simply healed the sick. But if they were uncomplicated and naive by modern standards, we have ruefully to admit that they were open on the God-ward side in a way that is almost unknown today.

J.B. Phillips, *The Young Church in Action*

The Christly life as we first glimpsed it, as we set out to live it, as God meant that we should live it, was a splendid vision. But our minds are finite and we forget so soon. Sometimes the life journey is so beset with difficulties, we find ourselves bewildered and almost overwhelmed.

This interview is our daily opportunity of seeing the pattern of the splendid vision again. As we gaze upon it, we shall no longer want to grasp every material advantage for ourselves. In that beautiful presence we shall glimpse, and we shall keep, a true sense of values. We shall know why we were born: not for a meaningless and slave-driven journey through time, but for the adventure of free souls dedicated to the service of God and his universe for ever and ever.

Fay Inchfawn, *Having It Out*

I am therefore not really deeply worried by the fact that prayer is at present a duty and even an irksome one. This is humiliating. It is frustrating. It is terribly time-wasting — the worse one is praying, the longer one's prayers take. But we are still only at school. Or, like Donne, 'I tune my instrument here at the door.' And even now — how can I weaken the words enough, how speak at all without exaggeration? — we have what seem rich moments. . . But I don't rest much on that; nor would I if it were ten times as much as it is. I have a notion that what seem our worst prayers may really be, in God's eyes, our best.

C.S. Lewis, *Prayer: Letters to Malcolm*

Someone has said, 'Never doubt in the dark what God has taught you in the light.' That's good advice. Some of my friends find great comfort in prayer and studying the scriptures when they are going through a difficult time, but that isn't the way it works for me. When my rope breaks, the scriptures seem as dry as dust and my prayers never seem to get any further than my front teeth. I study the scriptures and pray when things are going reasonably well. Then, when the darkness comes, I remember the truth I discovered in the light, and I hang on to that with everything I've got.

In your dealing with discouragement, knowing Bible doctrine is essential because it gives you eternal truths, facts that are constant in spite of what your feelings are at any particular moment.

Sometimes I don't feel like a Christian; sometimes I feel that God could not possibly be [offering] any meaning in my broken rope; sometimes I feel that God has cast me aside and that my life has been wasted. But, you see, feelings are just that — feelings. They have no reality of their own. That is why I remember in the dark the truth that I learned in the light.

Stephen Brown, *When Your Rope Breaks*

Trials and temptations: yes, we are all in the same boat. The 'escape' that 1 Corinthians 10: 13 speaks of is not an escape from the temptation, that we may be able to dodge it, but an escape to him that we 'may be able to bear it'. He has pledged his very faithfulness that he will never allow the trials and sufferings of life to be too heavy for us.

A pair of little arms were one day stretched out while father piled up goods for his small son to carry to the other end of the shop. As the wee person still waited for more, an onlooker said, 'You can't manage any more.' To which the answer came, 'Father knows how much I can carry.' Substitute *the* Father for that father.

Guy H. King, A Belief that Behaves

How deeply does disillusionment dash to pieces our equilibrium of spirit and our expectation of heart! We all have suffered its sting. Our high hopes, like gallant galleons, have sailed afar, and returned not at all, or at best battered and broken. Our dreams, like high-blown cumulus clouds reaching to the very heavens, have vanished into thin air.

We had been confident beyond the slightest contradiction that the consummation of our heart's cry would be contentment; but contrariwise, there came crisis, chaos and confusion. Like disciples, we had built our life's expectations in the sunshine of Galilee, where crowds had applauded and multitudes had been fed; but there came Gethsemane's shadows, Golgotha's sorrow and the Garden's silent tomb.

Disillusionment, deep, dismal, disintegrating! . . .Disillusionment, designed by the Most High for our good, leads to delight, indescribable and enduring. It is a searching discipline of the soul. It leads to sorrow, suffering, silence and solitude, to the apparently utter loss of the cross; but beyond that cross it leads to everlasting gain and good, in time and in eternity. Therefore, let us follow him fearlessly, obediently, trustingly, until disillusionment is dissolved by delight.

V. Raymond Edman, The Disciplines of Life

I have a friend who says that the trouble with life is that it is 'so daily'. No matter who you are or where you are, trouble is inevitable. In Job, we read that 'we are born for trouble, as sparks fly upward' (Job 5: 7). Not one of us is exempt. Given that fact, we need to discover the truth about trouble. Our world likes to tell us that trouble is always unwelcome. In fact, we are told to do everything possible to avoid problems, pain or crises that might come into our lives. The darkness we live in is more than willing to break up a home just because it is 'troublesome' when life is not comfortable any more.

When the thought of children is 'troublesome', we simply abort them. . . But is that the way Christians should think? Admittedly, even Christians have been programmed to process trouble in terms of the priority of personal comfort at all cost. But if we are truly going to be set apart as unique lights in the ever-increasing darkness, we need to let God's wonderful, working, worthwhile Word change the way we think about and respond to trouble.

Joseph Stowell, *The Dawn's Early Light*

Having said that trusting God is first of all a matter of the will, let me qualify that statement to say that, first of all, it is a matter of knowledge. We must know that God is sovereign, wise and loving. . . But having been exposed to the knowledge of the truth, we must then choose whether to believe the truth about God, which he has revealed to us, or whether to follow our feelings. If we are to trust God, we must choose to believe his truth. We must say, 'I will trust you though I do not feel like doing so.'

Jerry Bridges, *Trusting God*

My heart is heavy as I pray and, Father, it seems that with ease I give way to despair and become downcast. I've been let down so often — even by your people. There are days, even weeks, when I find it so hard to shake my feelings of disillusionment.

And yet I find the Psalmists had the same trouble. Their faith was shaken, there were days when they were downcast and they did not know which way to turn. Likewise with me, Father, and so I ask that you might lift me out of this despondency and help me to realise that things are not as bad as they sometimes seem. In my heart of hearts, I know that things don't just happen. You are still on the throne and you do work 'all things' for my good. So please forgive me and help me to have a better outlook by focussing on your Son, my Saviour.

A Benediction

If you have been disillusioned with the world and the Lord's people, may you find a restored faith in the events and the people you daily interface with. May you be granted a better attitude and an ability to see the best rather than the worst in others. For the glory of Jesus. Amen.

The gentle darkness
of bereavement

But you do see! Indeed you note trouble and grief, that you may take it into your own hands; the helpless commit themselves to you; you have been the helper of the orphan.

Be merciful to me, O Lord, for I am in distress; my eyes grow weak with sorrow, my soul and my body with grief.

I went about mourning as though for my friend or brother, I bowed my head in grief as though I was weeping for my mother. But when I stumbled, they gathered in glee; attackers gathered against me when I was unaware. They slandered me without ceasing.

Although he causes grief, he will have compassion according to the abundance of his steadfast love; for he does not willingly afflict or grieve anyone.

In this you rejoice, even if now for a little while you have had to suffer various trials so that the genuineness of your faith — being more precious than gold that though perishable, is tested by fire — may be found to result in praise and glory and honour when Jesus Christ is revealed.

But now that he is dead, why should I fast? Can I bring him back again? I will go to him, but he will not return to me.

I tell you the truth. You will weep and mourn while the world rejoices. You will grieve, but your grief will turn to joy.

(Psalm 10: 14, NRSV; Psalm 31: 9, NIV; Psalm 35: 14–15, NIV; Lamentations 3: 32–33, NRSV; 1 Peter 1: 6–7, NRSV; 2 Samuel 12: 23, NIV; John 16: 20, NIV)

Our darkest times are those in which we suffer the pain of grief — and yet at the root of grief is blessing.

To grasp the positive side of sorrow we have to understand what is actually happening to us. First, we are reacting to our loss not perhaps *with* love, but *because* of love. The one we loved so much has left us and the loss seems to be intolerable; but the reason that it hurts so badly is love. If we did not love, we would not care and therefore would not hurt. Would we give up the joy of having loved to avoid the pain? No, we would rather love and lose than never love. We can learn to temper our grief with the knowledge and memory of that love which we shared.

For whom do we grieve? Not for the loved one. What greater joy could we wish upon them than that they live with Christ? No, we grieve for ourselves. We cry aloud about the unfairness of never seeing him/her again, never to touch or share again a gentle loving kiss. But it is our emptiness, loss and pain for which we are wailing. Thus grief which is inspired by love may become the pinnacle of self-pity and we may try to replace the love of our lost one with the attention and sympathy of others.

This is Satan's trap, his corruption of the great love, a mere shadow of God's love for us and a reminder of it. If Satan can twist our minds and hearts to make us believe that we deserved the love of our lost one and that God has unfairly taken him/her away, Satan has triumphed over us.

It is Satan who tries to turn our love for one another into idolatry; he tries to convince us that God has stolen what is ours by right. It is Satan who has inflicted grief upon us as the price we must always pay for love. We cannot, dare not, must not listen to him, for if we do we will find ourselves alone, blinded and deafened in a maze of pain; whilst all the time Jesus, whom we can neither see nor hear, shut as we are into our own prison of self-pity, is reaching out his hand and calling to us.

In the depths of grief — when we pause in our tears, in the stillness between our cries — if we listen hard we will hear a still small voice saying, 'I am here, and I love you.' God never deserts us. When we turn to him, not in tortured cries for help, nor angry demands for support (for these are born of pride), but in quiet resignation and loving humility, it is then that Christ gently lays his love upon our hearts and we know that we have not lost anything, but the one we love has gained eternity. This then is the blessing of bereavement, when all else is lost, and by agony the world is cast away. Then perhaps suddenly, we can know God.

❧

They weren't crying for Leslie. They were crying for themselves. Just themselves. . . He, Jess, was the only one who had really cared for Leslie. But Leslie had failed him. She went and died just when he needed her most. . . She had tricked him. She had made him leave his old self behind and come into her world and then, before he was really at home in it but too late to go back, she had left him stranded there — like an astronaut wandering about on the moon. Alone.

Katherine Paterson, *Bridge to Terebithia*

I sit down by the fire, thinking with blind remorse of all those secret feelings I have nourished since my marriage. I think of every little trifle between me and Dora, and feel the truth that trifles make the sum of life. . . This is not the time at which I am to enter on the state of my mind beneath its load of sorrow. I came to think that the future was walled up before me, that the energy and action of my life were at an end, that I could never find any refuge but in the grave.

David Copperfield, in Charles Dickens' *David Copperfield*, when David was grieving for his first wife.

It slowly began to make sense, the bits began to fall into place. Something was happening and it made me cry; for the first time in a long, long time I cried. I went out into the night and stayed out. The clouds seemed to be rolling back. It kept nagging at the back of my mind. Anna's life hadn't been cut short; far from it, it had been full, completely fulfilled. The next day I headed back to the cemetery.

It took me a long time to find Anna's grave. It was tucked away at the back of the cemetery. I knew it had no headstone, just a simple wooden cross with the name on it, 'Anna'. I found it after about an hour. I had gone there with this feeling of peace inside me, as if the book had been closed, as if the story had been one of triumph, but I hadn't expected this. I stopped and gasped. This was it. The little cross leaned drunkenly, its paint peeling off, and there was the name ANNA.

I wanted to laugh, but you don't laugh in a cemetery, do you? Not only did I want to laugh; I had to laugh. It wouldn't stay bottled up. I laughed until the tears ran down my face. I pulled up the little cross and threw it into a thicket.

'OK, Mister God,' I laughed, 'I'm convinced. Good old Mister God. You might be a bit slow at times, but you certainly make it all right in the end.'

Anna's grave was a brilliant red carpet of poppies. Lupins stood guard in the background. A couple of trees whispered to each other whilst a family of mice scurried backwards and forwards through the uncut grass. Anna was truly home. She didn't need a marker; you couldn't better this with a squillion tons of marble. I stayed for a little while and said goodbye to her for the first time in five years. . . I swung on the iron gates as I yelled back into the cemetery.

'The answer is "in my middle".'

A finger of thrill went down my spine and I thought I heard her voice saying, 'What's that the answer to, Fynn?'

'That's easy. The question is, "Where's Anna?"'

I found her again — found her in my middle.

I felt sure that somewhere Anna and Mister God were laughing.

Fynn, in *Mister God, This is Anna*,
describing how he came out of five years of grieving
for Anna who had joined Jesus at the age of seven.

Human beings can't make one another really happy for long. And. . . for your sake he wanted your merely instinctive love for your child (tigresses share *that*, you know!) to turn into something better. He wanted you to love Michael as he understands love. You cannot love a fellow creature fully till you love God. Sometimes this conversion can be done while instinctive love is still gratified. But there was, it seems, no chance of that in your case. The instinct was uncontrolled and fierce and monomaniac. (Ask your daughter or your husband. Ask your own mother: you haven't once thought of her.) The only remedy was to take away its object. It was a case for surgery. When that first kind of love was thwarted, then there was just a chance that in the loneliness, in the silence, something else might begin to grow.

C.S. Lewis, *The Great Divorce*

It [his marriage] was in fact the climax of everything his earthly life had led up to, and his life after her death was merely an exercise in patience and obedience.

D.H. Gresham about C.S. Lewis

Her death taught him something he had yet to learn: that in the very deepest despair there is hope and, when by grief the entire universe is suddenly emptied, there is God.

D.H. Gresham, in a letter about C.S. Lewis'
reaction to his wife's death

Father, forgive any self-indulgence in my grief. Forgive my shutting out those who would love me and my seeking of sympathy. Send me the warmth of your Comforter to fill the aching emptiness of my life with your holy peace.

When the darkness of loss and grief surrounds me, reveal yourself to me that I might have joy. Make my memories things of gladness rather than of pain. Lord, help me to see that my pain is a mere shadow of that which you bear for me. Show me the light of your living reality that I may love again without fear.

Grant me your peace, O Lord, that I might be able to praise and glorify you despite my sorrow.

These things I pray in Jesus' name.

Amen.

A Benediction

May the Lord of love be with us in our pain. May we hold in our hearts and minds that he knows our pain, shares our pain and takes our pain away.

May our souls rejoice and be glad again, knowing that those we have loved and lost would hurt to feel that they have caused us sorrow.

May the Lord of love be with us and in us, filling our souls with the luminescent peace and joy which drives out the darkness of sorrow and fear.

May we walk in the glorious light of the shadow of Christ.

In the name of Jesus the Lord of love.

Amen.

The God of all comfort

Blessed be the God and Father of our Lord Jesus Christ, the Father of all mercies and God of all comfort, who comforts us in our affliction, so that we may be able to comfort those who are in any affliction, with the comfort with which we ourselves are comforted by God.

In this you rejoice, though now for a little while you may have to suffer various trials, so that the genuineness of your faith, more precious than gold. . . may redound to praise and glory and honour at the revelation of Jesus Christ.

In everything God works for good with those who love him, who are called according to his purpose.

I know that you can do all things, and that no purpose of yours can be thwarted.

Though the fig tree does not blossom
nor fruit be on the vines,
the produce of the olive fail
and the fields yield no food,
the flock be cut off from the fold
and there be no herd in the stalls,
Yet I will rejoice in the Lord;
I will joy in the God of my salvation.
God, the Lord, is my strength.
I have loved you with an everlasting love.
Call to me and I will answer you, and tell you great and hidden things which you have not known.
The Spirit of the Lord is upon me,
because the Lord has anointed me
to bring good tidings to the afflicted;
he has sent me to bind up the broken-hearted. . .

to comfort all that mourn. . .
to give them a garland instead of ashes,
the oil of joy for mourning.
Know that the Lord is God! It is he who has made us, and we are his; we are his people and the sheep of his pasture.
Bless the Lord, O my soul!
(2 Corinthians 1: 3–4; 1 Peter 1: 6; Romans 8: 28 — all RSV; Job 42: 1, NASB; Habakkuk 3: 17–19, KJV; Jeremiah 31: 3, NIV; Jeremiah 33: 3, NRSV; Isaiah 61: 1–3; Psalm 100: 3; Psalm 103: 22 — all RSV)

It is now over a year since my husband died. The months have taught me many things about myself, about my faith, about the need to forgive those who mean well but who don't understand, and most of all about my Lord, who has become more truly my solace, my comfort, my guide and my friend. I have had deep questions, and I am grateful to the authors of the books quoted below, who have either answered my questions before I asked them, or who have provided confirmation after I have threaded my way through a morass of strange thoughts. I have gathered these thoughts together, hoping that someone else will be helped. After all, we all have to cope with bereavement sooner or later.

As is so often said, and I didn't believe it when I was warned, one of the deepest pains is of friends on whom one thinks one can rely who move away, generally through embarrassment. People do make empty promises and it is very hard not to be hurt. We have been taught by God to forgive and that prevents bitterness developing. But it needs to be worked at.

However, I have realised that new friendships begin. For one thing, you are united in a fellowship with others who have lost loved ones. You speak the same language! This can be very useful to one who wants to be used in the kingdom.

I have also learned the healing found in creative work, whether it is making a new garden, learning new skills or taking a course of study. I did all these things, and found satisfaction and a means of filling what would have been empty hours, later reading somewhere how therapeutic such work can be!

And when the lonelies strike, generally in the small hours of the morning, what can be done? Prayer, prayer, more prayer! Begin with adoration of God for who he is, then thank him for what he has done and for what he has given. Quiet humming of hymns seems to bring peace. My most used hymn sounds trite, but the last lines of 'What a Friend We Have in Jesus' — 'In his arms he'll take and shield thee, thou wilt find a solace there' — have been of enormous help to me.

I am grateful to the Lord for his cherishing during the last year. He has truly been my nearest kinsman, the one to whom I turn continually. May he also be to you the God of all comfort.

❧❀❧

In *Pilgrim's Progress*, Christian and Hopeful come to the river of death. They notice how deep, how wide, how swift it is, and they are afraid. Suddenly, two men with shining faces and clothes stand beside them. Christian and Hopeful inquire if there is a boat or bridge they can use to cross the river. The two men reply that there is no other way to the gate than through the river. When asked how deep the water is, the strangers say, 'You shall find it deeper or shallower as you believe in the King'. . .

The privilege of loving another person deeply involves the risk of separation. We cannot love richly without facing this risk. . . But though the parting is real and painful, we can count on the resources available to us in Jesus, to help us as grief does its slow work.

The resurrection of Christ can be a reality entered into by those who have physically died. And it can also be a sign of hope for those who have suffered bereavement. With Jesus' help, our life can be renewed and deep grief can give way to quiet acceptance and hope.

We know that, at our own death, we may share Christ's

resurrection and be united once more with those we have lost.

Harold Bauman, *Living through Grief*

They that love beyond the world cannot be separated by it.

Death cannot kill what never dies.

Nor can spirits be divided that love and live in the same divine principle, the root and record of their friendship.

If absence be not death, neither is theirs.

Death is but crossing the world as friends do the seas. They live in one another still.

William Penn

If we would really hearken to God, which means not only hearing him but believing what we hear, we could not fail to know that, just because he is God, he cannot do other than care for us as he cares for the apple of his eye; and that all that tender love and divine wisdom can do for our welfare must be and will be unfailingly done. Not a single loophole for worry or fear is left to the soul that knows God.

Hannah Whitall Smith,
The God of All Comfort

No-one ever told me that grief felt so like fear. I am not afraid, but the sensation is like being afraid, the same fluttering in the stomach, the same restlessness, the same yawning.

C.S. Lewis, in Donald Howard,
Christians Grieve Too

In God's word we read, 'We are surrounded by such a great cloud of witnesses'. I like to think of that special 'cheering squad' in heaven. . . all those who blessed and encouraged me on earth and who are now in their heaven-ly home. 'The communion of saints,' 'the prayers of all the saints' — these words have new meaning to me now. I am beginning to understand what my pastor said to me after Walter's death: 'You are separated from Walter physically, but you are closer than ever spiritually.'

Ingrid Trobisch,
Learning to Walk Alone

I was sitting, torn by grief. Someone came and talked to me of God's dealing, of why it happened, of hope beyond the grave. He talked constantly, he said things I knew were true. I was unmoved except to wish that he would go away. He finally did. Another came and sat beside me. He didn't talk. He didn't ask leading questions. He just sat beside me for an hour or more, listened when I said something, answered briefly, prayed simply, left.

I was moved, I was comforted. I hated to see him go.

Joseph Bayley,
The View from a Hearse

I was to be led by that Power outside myself into areas beyond my knowledge, along the path that leads through and out of the Valley of the Shadow of Death. There would be rocky ledges, steep slopes, slippery places, many a fork in the road where a clear-cut decision would be required. I knew none of the trails: the valley was untrodden country. Yet by sure steps I would be led through it. I was to discover the Lord as my Shepherd — quite literally and in many practical ways.

Catherine Marshall,
To Live Again

Let me say in a few words and, in very simple words, try to express what we are trying to do this morning. We are endeavouring to establish a new relationship. We have known Peter Marshall in the flesh. From now on we are to endeavour to know him in the spirit. . . The fellowship with him will be unbroken, and may God give us wisdom, grace and strength to join hands with him.

Eulogy at Peter Marshall's funeral,
in Catherine Marshall, *To Live Again*

Psychologists and psychiatrists consider that the matter of establishing new patterns of interaction with other human beings [is] one of the most important laws of recovery.

Catherine Marshall,
To Live Again

It was not that my adjustment to bereavement was complete.

In fact, it had scarcely begun. The great void was still there. Half of my personality was missing.

Catherine Marshall,
To Live Again

If they are with him,
and he is with us. . .
they cannot be far away.

Peter Marshall

My Lord and my heavenly Father:

You are my Lord and my God. There is no other for me to turn to in my loneliness and pain. But thank you that you do understand what it is like to be bereft of human and loving companionship. Lord, please meet me in my grief. Make it usable in the great mystery of your purposes. May this experience, too, bring good in your kingdom. Lord, I do not want to waste this sadness. I release it and myself for you to use as you choose, because I know your purposes are beyond anything that I could ever imagine.

Lord, may no root of bitterness be found in me. May I not be a weight or a responsibility to those around me, but seek you in the silences of the night, there finding the resources to reach out to others.

But Lord, I thank you for those who are in the fellowship of suffering, who know what it is to bear a deep weight of sadness in the heart. Thank you for their empathy and unspoken support. Thank you for the prayers of your people who even though they don't understand, still accept me as I am, not trying to hasten the healing, but staying with me through the dark places.

Lord, in all my pain and perplexity, I praise you that you have never left me, you have remained as my solace and have

continued to show your care in so many ways.
    I praise you that you are the God of all comfort. . .
    I pray in the name of the Father who loves and creates new life, in the name of Jesus, who bore all my griefs and sorrows, and in the name of the Holy Spirit, the Comforter.
Amen.

A Benediction

O Lord, support us by your grace,
until the shadows lengthen,
and the evening comes,
and the busy world is hushed,
the fever of life is over
and our work is done.
Then, Lord, in your mercy
grant us safe lodging,
a holy rest,
and peace at the last;
Through Jesus Christ our Lord. Amen.

(From a card printed by Palm Tree Press,
Rattlesden, Bury St Edmunds, UK)

In sickness and in health

But surely, God is my helper; the Lord is the upholder of my life.

Who has kept us among the living, and has not let our feet slip.

You brought us into the net; you laid burdens on our backs;

For with you is the fountain of life; in your light we see light.

You desire truth in the inward being; therefore teach me wisdom in my secret heart.

But the steadfast love of the Lord is from everlasting to everlasting on those who fear him, and his righteousness to children's children.

He brought them out of the darkness and gloom, and broke their bonds asunder.

For he shatters the doors of bronze and cuts in two the bars of iron.

He turns a desert into pools of water, a parched land into springs of water.

For the Lord takes pleasure in his people; he adorns the humble with victory. Let the faithful exult in glory; let them sing for joy on their couches.

O Lord my God, I cried to you for help and you have healed me.

So that my soul may praise you and not be silent. O Lord my God, I will give thanks to you forever.

For I know that my Redeemer lives, and that at the last he will stand upon the earth; and after my skin has been thus destroyed, then in my flesh I shall see God. . . my eyes shall behold, and not another. My heart faints within me!

I am about to do a new thing; now it springs forth, do you not perceive it? I will make a way in the wilderness and rivers in the desert.

But those who drink of the water that I will give them will never be thirsty. The water that I will give will become in them a spring of water gushing up to eternal life.

(Psalms 54: 4; 66: 9 and 11; 36: 9; 51: 6; 103: 17; 107: 14, 16 and 35; 149: 4–5; 30: 2 and 12; Job 19: 25–27; Isaiah 43: 19; John 4: 14 — all NRSV)

Is God suffering *with* us, or is he over against us?

Is God watching us in our pain, or is he in pain *with* us, *alongside* us?

It is totally inconceivable that the great Creator of love should sit back and watch his creation and his creatures suffer and not make use of this suffering. He could, if he wished, cure anybody of anything. The fact that he sometimes *doesn't* demonstrates incontrovertably that he has a use for the suffering.

What that use is is a mystery. Perhaps it is a moment in the good/evil continuing warfare? Perhaps it is an opportunity to live out our total dependence on God? Perhaps it is a time given to the bystanders, for them to grow in the honour of suffering? Maybe there are as many answers to the mystery as there are creatures, so no one person is likely to be privy to the whole answer. What is more important is that we acknowledge and offer our incomplete comprehension because, after all, if we understood everything there would be no need for faith.

Maybe sanctifying pain is something about being prepared to give up our clung-on-to desire for being in control. We are rightly keen on building up our own independence, our own space, our personal autonomy; we encourage people to be responsible for their own choices, their own decisions. How would it be if all these prized achievements had to be offered, even as they are gained, in order to become uncluttered for God?

Hildegard speaks of 'being open to emptying', so that God can flow through me, unobstructed by my will. If I can permit in my own body and mind that there is a need to give up some of my autonomy, will that make me more receptive to God, more receptive to others? Is there a vital difference between being a resigned receptacle of God's will, and wanting to be an *offered* receptacle?

God in his almighty ingenuity and contrivance and beneficence *can* and *does* bring all things together for good, if we will accept his purpose and his power to do so. I can either allow myself to be taken over by resentment and frustration, or I can try to put myself into God's capacity for caring. He will then flow into me, but also into the world and into the suffering of others.

So it's back to the basics of trusting where I can't see ahead and loving where I can't understand and hoping where the signposts are still secret. Flip and pat solutions are not good enough for the immensity of the mystery.

We, with Job, must learn the difference between the nature of love that is given because of gifts and favours, and the nature of love that is given in spite of being stripped and emptied. Living with unknowing, uncertainty, un-success, is the very ground of faith. If we knew it all, there would be no matrix for trust. And given that these are conditions in which our total dependence on God can be fully real, we also know that he is always right there with us.

When it came to the final crunch of personal ordeal, Christ resisted nothing, he rejected nothing, he absorbed it all. He let it take its course, not passing the evil on, but allowing it to flow through him and out again, defused. By his very choice of non-rejection, he transformed the evil coming at him and transformed it into power for good. Do we have the capacity to be converted into transformers?

❧❀❧

I began to understand that I had stumbled on a kind of miracle. These people [concentration camp survivors] had walked into the valley of death and out the other side

with their courage and their sense of humour intact. They
were rich human beings, with no bitterness left in them.
For years they had [suffered] starvation, torture, cold,
loneliness and agonising loss. . . Yet they seemed to be
beyond hatred. To me it was bewildering. In fact, I was
being shaken up and turned inside out.

One could live with pain precisely by not fighting it,
by not denying its existence, by taking it into oneself,
seeing it for what it was, going beyond it.

Mary Craig, *Blessings*

When we experience suffering, we are like a bear in bodily
pain. But it can teach us inner meekness, causing us to
walk along the right path by exercising patience like a
lamb and to avoid evil by behaving as cleverly as a
serpent. For through the distress of the body, we often
attain spiritual treasures through which we come into
possession of a higher kingdom.

Hildegard of Bingen, *Illuminations*

Christianity offers no supernatural remedy for suffering,
or indeed explanation of it, but supernatural *use* for it.

Lord Longford, *Suffering and Hope*

Lord, I come to your awesome presence,
From the shadows into your radiance;
Search me, try me, consume all my darkness —
Shine on me, shine on me.
Shine, Jesus, shine, fill this land with the Father's glory;
Blaze, Spirit, blaze, set our hearts on fire!
Flow, river, flow, flood the nations with grace and mercy;
Send forth your word, Lord, and let there be light!

Grahame Kendrick

I was sitting looking at the candle the other day and
thinking about the verse of the hymn, 'I will hold the
Christ light for you in the night-time of your fear'; I was
just thinking of the many people whose lives touch mine
and wondering who would hold for them the Christ light.
I prayed, and still do for you, that the light of the world

will garrison you around with his presence and power, that you might know the presence of the crucified as you hold the light for many, and that there may be those who will also hold it for you. Then I thought Jesus himself both holds us/you and the light for us/you and faith won't fail because he promised to keep us. . . I felt great joy and encouragement and, as I write this, it is still the same.

From a letter written by Rae, a young counsellor
with a severe spinal problem

Few of us have the luxury — it took me forever to think of it as that — to come to ground zero with God. . . Maybe God's gift to me is dependence. I will never reach a place of self-sufficiency that crowds God out. My need for help is obvious every day when I wake up, flat on my back. I can't even blow my nose on my own.

There's one more thing. The Bible speaks of our bodies being 'glorified' in heaven. That always seemed a hazy, foreign concept to me. But I now realise that I will be healed. I haven't been cheated out of being a complete person — I'm just going through a forty- or fifty-year delay and God stays with me even through that. I now know the meaning of being 'glorified'. It's the time, after my death here, when I'll be on my feet dancing.

Joni Eareckson

Another survivor of unimaginable deprivations and sufferings in a concentration camp is quoted as saying: 'I now have an innate advantage. I have learned to know the Who of my life. The Why doesn't then matter.'

Philip Yancey, *Where is God When It Hurts?*

All this is known to him,
And I am known to him,
And his eternal peace is known to him —
I will sleep.

Convent of St John Baptist, Windsor

All my hope on God is founded;
he doth still my trust renew.
Me through change and chance he guideth,
only good and only true.
God unknown,
He alone
Calls my heart to be his own.

Robert Bridges

Lord Jesus Christ, we know we have a sure hope and the promise
of an inheritance that can never be spoilt or soiled and can
never fade away, because you have told us it is being kept in
the heavens. Through faith, God's power will guard us until
the salvation which has been prepared is revealed at the end of
time. This is cause of great joy for us, even though we may
for a short time have to bear being plagued by all sorts of trials.
We know that, when Jesus Christ is revealed, our faith will have
been tested and proved like gold — only it is more precious
than gold, which is corruptible even though it bears testing by
fire — and then there will be praise and glory and honour.

adapted from 1 Peter 1: 3–7, JB

A Benediction

The God of life with guarding hold you,
The loving Christ with guarding fold you,
The Holy Spirit, guarding, mould you,
Each night of life, and day, enfold you,
Each day and night of life, uphold you.

Poems of the Western Highlands

9

Why the fullback panicked

Do not be anxious about tomorrow; tomorrow will look after itself. Each day has troubles enough of its own.

There was at that time a terrible famine in the land: and so Abram went on down to Egypt to live. But as he was approaching the borders of Egypt, he asked Sarai his wife to tell everyone that she was his sister! 'You are very beautiful,' he told her, 'and when the Egyptians see you they will say, "This is his wife. Let's kill him and then we can have her!" But if you say you are my sister, then the Egyptians will treat me well because of you, and spare my life!'

And sure enough, when they arrived in Egypt, everyone spoke of her beauty. When the palace aides saw her, they praised her to their king, the Pharaoh, and she was taken into his harem. Then Pharaoh gave Abram many gifts because of her — sheep, oxen, donkeys, men and women slaves, and camels. But the Lord sent a terrible plague upon Pharaoh's household on account of her being there.

Then Pharaoh called Abram before him and accused him sharply. 'What is this you have done to me?' he demanded. 'Why didn't you tell me she was your wife? Why were you willing to let me marry her, saying she was your sister? Here, take her and be gone!' And Pharaoh sent them out of the country under armed escort — Abram, his wife, and all his household and possessions.

(Matthew 6: 34, NEB; Genesis 12: 10–20, LB)

It was a good day. We had just celebrated my seven year old's first game of soccer and he made his father proud. In the opening seconds of the match, he was some thirty metres from goal — well, perhaps twenty — and, with great finesse, he put the ball between the posts. One-nil.

My mind drifted back to my own first game of soccer. Having played rugby all my life, I had no experience, so they put me in goal. On two occasions, our fullback had the ball with the opposition charging down on him. He panicked! He held onto the ball instead of passing it back, so I had no option but to race forward and take it off him, then he kicked it — straight past me. It happened twice, but somehow we still won three-two.

Why do people panic? In the fullback's case it was because of his uncertainty about my skills and that produced wrong options. It is the same in life, I find. When we are unsure about our health, employment, finances, family, church, gifts, retirement — even our relationship with God — we often panic and choose wrong options.

There are few Bible characters who motivate us more than Abraham. He certainly knew what it was to be confident. He heard the voice of the Lord to go into a foreign land and he did it without flinching. However, he was not always strong. There he was in Egypt, fearful of his own survival, and he made a frightful decision in passing Sarah off as his sister. Certainly, she was his stepsister, but his deception about their marital status embarrassed Pharaoh, compromised Sarah and could have led to the ultimate tragedy — his own death. Abraham panicked.

This human story reminds us of a number of truths. Like Abraham, most of us also know times of uncertainty. If in those times we panic and choose wrong options, there will be consequences. In Abraham's case, it included the father of the Jewish race being shown to have lower morals than Pharaoh, as well as setting a pattern for similar future failure for himself and his son.

However, it is not all bad news. There is a positive lesson to be learned from Abraham's impropriety. In times of uncertainty rather than panic, we should do what Abraham normally did: trust God, wait for God's voice and take actions that are consistent with the Lord's revealed general will for us. The message is really that simple. Panic cannot thrive when one is consciously resting in the Lord. We need to own our uncertainties and let the Lord guide us to the new day.

❧

Looking at ourselves and our certainty as *ours*, we discover its weakness, its vulnerability to every critical thought. . . But looking at God we realise that all the shortcomings of our experience are of no importance. Looking at God, we see that we do not have him as an object of our knowledge, but that he has us as the subject of our existence. Looking at God, we feel that we cannot escape him even by making him an object of sceptical arguments or of irresistible emotions. We realise that in our uncertainty there is one fixed point of certainty, however we may name it and describe it and explain it.

Paul Tillich, *The New Being*

Life from the centre is a life of unhurried peace and power. It is simple. It is serene. It is amazing. It is triumphant. It is radiant. It takes no time, but it occupies all our time. And it makes our life programs new and overcoming. We need not get frantic. He is at the helm. And when our little day is done, we lie down quietly in peace, for all is well.

Thomas R. Kelly, *A Testament of Devotion*

If Jesus knew nothing of self-interest, neither did he of self-sufficiency. He was dependent.

That was an important feature of our Lord's adjustment to life. He went confidently to every task in an attitude of dependence upon God, his Father. Such an adjustment inevitably lightened life's burden for him, for dependence is always restful.   When, by love and trust, we are able to place ourselves and our affairs in the hands of one who is entirely dependable, we at once find relief from the burden of responsibility. How much more restful is dependence when it leans upon the strength and loving care of the Almighty Father.   It proved to be so in the case of the Lord Jesus: so, also, it will prove to be in our case.

G.H. Morling, *The Quest for Serenity*

Some years ago, when my wife and I had a delicatessen, it seemed that everything was going wrong. We were low on stock. There were bills to pay. Then the deep freezer broke down and we lost a lot of frozen goods. A few other calamities happened as well.

I became really depressed. I went to bed miserable and woke up miserable. 'I wonder what will go wrong today?' I would think each morning.

One night, however, I did what we have been talking about. I turned the whole matter over to God and left it in his hands. For the first time for weeks, I went to sleep peacefully and easily. Next morning, I woke up happy and confident.

In fact, nothing had changed. The freezer still needed fixing. The stocks were still low and so on. But I had changed! I was different! I went about my duties that day singing. . .

We proved that you really can trust God in time of stress and it does make a difference!

Barry Chant, *How to Live the Kind of Life You've Always Wanted to Live*

I had family problems and ministry problems and I came very close to bailing out. I had thoughts not only of bailing out of the pastorate, but also out of my marriage. I wanted to bail out of being a father. I fantasised about riding freight trains and living the life of a railway bum. . .

I must admit, I have felt many times just like the people of Judah in Nehemiah 4: 10. I have often felt like screaming, 'There is just too much rubble. I can't keep on keeping on.'

Fortunately, each time I have become a rubble-gazer, I have gotten back on track and have been able to refocus on my faithful heavenly Father who never takes his eyes off me.

Frank R. Tillapaugh, *Unleashing Your Potential*

God knew where Paul was at in secret. And he knows *our* innermost thoughts; we cannot hide anything from him. We might be laughing and light on the outside, but all the time crying heavily on the inside. We wear masks: faces that we put on for different people and situations. These may convince other people, but they do not conceal our real selves from the living God, who sees all. . .

Suddenly, as Paul is travelling on the road to Damascus, a bright light from heaven flashes all around him. This is God meeting Paul where he is at and, in a real way, God will meet each one of us in our own place, in a way that is unique and personal. The common denominator will be an unmistakable encounter with the risen Jesus. Different sheep, one shepherd.

Kim Hawtrey, *Life After Debt*

Christian perfection is not the observance of a code of moral rules, or the avoidance of transgression, or an inner state of devotion — though all these things may enter into it. It is a manifestation of the conquering power of Christ in every situation and in every relationship of human life.

Stephen Neill, *Christian Holiness*

Father, Son and Holy Spirit: you are the one true God, the Almighty ruler of all the universe. Please, forgive me when I panic. Sometimes I take my focus off you and find myself immersed in a sea of uncertainty. I confess that what follows is often not pleasing to you or myself.

Lord, I know you as the rock. With your grace I now

offer to you the uncertainties, the panic in my life. God of Abraham, heal me, deliver me and give me your wisdom, strength and peace. Holy Spirit, indwell all of me. . . thank you, Lord.

A Benediction
Look to the Lord and his strength; seek his face always.

(Psalm 105: 4, NIV)

10

Unsurrendered things

O that I might have my request, and that God would grant my desire; that it would please God to crush me, that he would let loose his hand and cut me off! This would be my consolation; I would even exult in unrelenting pain; for I have not denied the words of the Holy One.

Besides this you know what time it is, how it is now the moment for you to wake from sleep. For salvation is nearer to us than when we became believers; the night is far gone, the day is near. Let us then lay aside the works of darkness and put on the armour of light; let us live honourably as in the day, not in revelling and drunkenness, not in debauchery and licentiousness, not in quarrelling and jealousy.

For everything that becomes visible is light. Therefore it says, 'Sleeper awake! Rise from the dead,
and Christ will shine on you.'
Here is my servant, whom I uphold,
My chosen, in whom my soul delights;
I have put my spirit upon him;
    he will bring forth justice to the nations.
He will not cry or lift up his voice,
    or make it heard in the street;
a bruised reed he will not break
    and a dimly burning wick he will not quench;
    he will faithfully bring forth justice.
He will not grow faint or be crushed
    until he has established justice in the earth;
and the coastlands wait for his teaching.
Happy are those whose strength is in you,
    in whose heart are the highways to Zion.

As they go through the valley of Baca
   they make it a place of springs;
the early rain also covers it with pools.
They go from strength to strength;
the God of gods will be seen in Zion.
(Job 6: 8–10; Romans 13: 11–13; Ephesians 5: 14; Isaiah 42: 1–4;
Psalm 84: 5–6 — all NSRV)

The Russian novelist Dostoyevsky depicts how, on a
beautiful sunny day, a farmer admires the quiet idyllic
scene on his farm — the cows chewing the cud, the hens
pecking away, the lizards lazing in the warm sun, the birds
chirping — altogether a picture of 'God is in his heaven'.
Suddenly a storm brews and the farmer is confronted
by dinosaurs instead of cows, frightening reptiles in
place of hens and lizards, vultures slip into the birds'
position — a darker, more threatening scene you can
hardly imagine. The eeriness prevailed, but in a flash
the farmer was quickly back in the former, more familiar
scene. All was back in place again, but the farmer from
that point onwards was never the same again. He knew
he had to account for the inner dungeon of his being
as well as those of the external world.
This story highlights the need for the close understanding and perception of the whole person — the
conscious as well as the subconscious and unconscious.
A good example of the power of such forces is found
in the Australian psyche. Australia has been founded
on unresolved grief. An eminent grief therapist maintains that we have never quite consoled that which is
left behind. The Isaiah image of the bruised reed and
the dimly burning wick portrays much of our spiritual
burden today. This leads to a sense of muddleheaded-
ness and powerlessness.
There is a very real connection between this kind of weakness and the first stage of the now well-established grief cycle
— denial. Paul Tillich spells out the extent and dynamic of
denial and the price we pay for too much denial:

Something in us prevents us from remembering, when remembering proves too difficult or painful. We forget benefits, because the burden of gratitude is too heavy for us. We forget former loves, because the burden of obligations implied by them surpasses our strength. We forget our former hates, because the task of nourishing them would disrupt our mind. We forget former pain, because it is still too painful. We forget guilt, because we cannot endure its sting.

Such forgetting is not the natural, daily form of forgetting. It demands our cooperation. We repress what we cannot stand. We forget it by entombing it within us. Ordinary forgetting liberates us from innumerable small things in a natural process. Forgetting by recession does not liberate us, but seems to cut us off from what makes us suffer. We are not entirely successful, however, because the memory is buried within us, and influences every moment of our growth. And sometimes it breaks through its prison and strikes at us directly and painfully.

As Nikos Kazantzakis put it so memorably: 'The only real death is the death we die every day by not living.'

ॐ

Often enough when we approach the altar to pray, our hearts are dry and lukewarm. But if we persevere, there comes an unexpected infusion of grace, our breast expands as it were, and our interior is filled with an overflowing love.

Bernard of Clairvaux

Some think, when they begin once to be troubled with the smoke of corruption more than they were before, therefore they are worse than they were. It is true that corruptions appear now more than before, but they are less.

For, first, sin, the more it is seen the more it is hated, and thereupon is the less. . .

Secondly, contraries, the nearer they are one to another, the sharper is the conflict between them: now of all enemies the spirit and the flesh are nearest one to another, being both in the soul of a regenerate person, and in faculties of the soul, and in every action that springs from those faculties, and therefore [it] is no marvel [that] the soul, the seat of this battle, thus divided in itself, be as smoking flax.

Thirdly, the more grace, the more spiritual life, and the more spiritual life, the more antipathy to the contrary; when none are so sensible of corruption as those that have the most living souls.

Richard Sibbes, *The Bruised Reed and Smoking Flax*

Since the communion of last Easter, I have led a life so dissipated and useless, and my terrors and perplexities have so much increased, that I am under great depression and discouragement; yet I purpose to present myself before God tomorrow, with humble hope that he will not break the bruised reed.

Samuel Johnson

God marched on to victory in those dark days. How many were praying for me I little realised. He began to show me something of what he was doing. I recall with great clarity sitting down in the corner of my room and following Jacob over the brook Jabbok in my mind's eye. The struggle of the angel with Jacob as a man walking in the flesh portrayed my state so perfectly. He had touched me in the seat of my natural strength and now, broken and shattered through solitary confinement with everything gone, my work, my liberty, my Bible, and now it seemed life itself, I could only cling to him for his blessing. I would no doubt never be the same again.

Then like a shaft of light in the mind, the relevance of Jacob's act of faith in Hebrews, where he is seen leaning on his staff in worship, to conflict with the representative of the camp of God, flashed into my mind. What does it matter if I come up from the waters limping? What does it matter if I am never the same again, provided my name is Israel? Then as a prince with God, having no confidence in the flesh, will I lean on my staff for my lameness and worship 'til the day dawn and the shadows flee away. Let that be my highest and final act of faith towards God my Strength and Redeemer.

I remembered that God's word said that, as Jacob passed over Penuel, the sun rose upon him. So after this I viewed everything as walking into the dawning, going on into the golden daybreak and the morning without a cloud.

Geoffrey Bull, *When Iron Gates Yield*

Lord, teach me now and every day that what the world calls failure is of passing value. Teach me only to care for that which brings me close to you. Amen.
    One moment of failure can be God's moment of grace.

Giles Harcourt

The Spirit's X-ray:
O Lord and Master, who dost know us more truly than we know ourselves: let thy Holy Spirit search out our weaknesses, our fears, the unsurrendered things within our souls, that we may be saved from denial, offence, disloyalty and betrayal, and be of whole heart in our commitment to thee.

George Appleton, *Journey for a Soul*

Penetrate these murky corners where we hide memories and tendencies on which we do not care to look, but which will not disinter and yield freely up to you, that you may purify and transmute them. The persistent buried grudge, the half-acknowledged enmity which is still smouldering, the bitterness of that loss we have not turned into sacrifice, the private comfort we cling to, the secret fear of failure which saps our initiative and is really inverted pride, the pessimism which is an insult to your joy.
    Lord, we bring all these to you, and we review them with shame and penitence in your steadfast love.

Evelyn Underhill

Dear God:
When we fall, let us fall inwards. Let us fall freely and completely: that we may find our depth and humility, the solid earth from which we may rise up and love again. Amen.

Leunig, *A Common Prayer*

O God, I am so very hurt. I don't feel I can pray or love.
I can feel nothing but anger, bitterness and fear.
Enfold me in your love and keep me until I can love again.
I am so full of hate; give me love.
I am so full of anger; give me peace.
I am so full of fear; give me trust.
I cannot go on. Lord, hold me.

Mother's Union Prayer Book

God did not say, 'You shall not be tempest-tossed, you
shall not be work-weary, you shall not be discomforted.'
But he said, 'You shall not be overcome.' God wants
us to heed these words so that we shall always be strong
in trust, both in sorrow and in joy.

Julian of Norwich

You are the God of every human being
and, too bright for us to look upon,
you let yourself be seen as in a mirror,
on the face of your Christ.
We are eager to glimpse a reflection of your presence
in the confusion of people and events:
open in us the gateway to transparency of heart.
In that place of solitude
which there is in each one of us,
come and refresh the dry and thirsty ground
of our body and our spirit.
Come and inundate us with your trust
till even our inner deserts burst into flower.

Brother Roger of Taizé

A Benediction
Blessed be thou, O Christ, my Master
*   never hurried, never worried,*
*   always trusting the goodness,*
*   the wisdom and*
*   the love of God.*

George Appleton

The agony and the idolatry

Thou shalt have no other gods before me.

Save me, oh God, for the waters have come up to my neck. I sink in the miry depths, where there is no foothold. I have come into the deep waters; the floods engulf me. I am worn out calling for help; my throat is parched. My eyes fail, looking for my God.

Listen to the voice of the people in all that they say to you; for they have not rejected you, but they have rejected me from being king over them. Just as they have done to me, from the day I brought them up out of Egypt to this day, forsaking me and serving other gods, so also they are doing to you. Now then, listen to their voice; . . .you shall solemnly warn them and show them the ways of the king who shall reign over them.

When I was a child, my speech, feelings and thinking were all those of a child; when I became an adult, I put an end to childish ways.

So I say live by the Spirit, and you will not gratify the desires of the sinful nature. For the sinful nature desires what is contrary to the Spirit, and the Spirit what is contrary to the sinful nature. They are in conflict with each other, so that you do not do what you want. But if you are led by the Spirit, you are not under law. The acts of the sinful nature are obvious: sexual immorality, impurity and debauchery; idolatry and witchcraft; hatred, discord, jealousy, fits of rage, selfish ambition, dissensions, factions and envy; drunkenness, orgies and the like. I warn you, as I did before, that those who live like this will not inherit the kingdom of God. But the fruit of the Spirit is love, joy, peace, patience, kindness, goodness, faithfulness, gentleness and self-control.

Set your affection on things above, not on things on the earth.

Blessed is anyone who endures temptation. Such a one has stood the test and will receive the crown of life that the Lord has promised to those who love him. No-one when tempted should say, 'I am being tempted by God'; for God cannot be tempted by evil and he himself tempts no-one. But one is tempted by one's own desire, being lured and enticed by it; then, when that desire has conceived, it gives birth to sin, and that sin, when it is fully grown, gives birth to death.

Fear not, for I have redeemed you; I have summoned you by name; you are mine. When you pass through the waters, I will be with you; and when you pass through the rivers, they will not sweep over you. When you walk through the fire you will not be burned; the flames will not set you ablaze. For I am the Lord your God, the holy one of Israel, your Saviour. . .

(Exodus 20: 3, KJV; Psalm 69: 1–3, NIV; 1 Samuel 8: 7–9, NRSV; 1 Corinthians 13: 11a, GNB; 1 Corinthians 13: 11b, NRSV; Galatians 5: 16–23a, NIV; Colossians 3: 2, KJV; James 1: 12–15, NRSV; Isaiah 43: 1b–3a, NIV)

What of the times when we feel that empty, aching void in our hearts, that emptiness which fills our chests with a pain we cannot understand? Throughout life we are prone to these feelings. They start with indefinable longings which deeply move us in our childhood years and we use romantic fantasies to combat them.

With puberty, the longings of the mind and heart can come masked by those of the body; often the three are confused within us and we think that we are experiencing one of them, when in fact it is another which we feel.

As we progress and all our environmental experiences and traumas roil and seethe within us, we begin to seek solace for the longings and the emptiness which we now perceive as pain.

Our agonies are not necessarily the result of great tragedies in our lives (though sometimes they are), but can be engendered by tiny rejections — the parental promise, forgotten or broken for reasons of grown-up expediency; the petty betrayal by the schoolyard friend; the arrogant injustice of one in authority over us; the special boy/girl who simply didn't turn up, leaving us waiting, alone and bereft. By fragments are the edifices of our pain constructed.

Then, in our years of maturity, we find this ache in our chests. We look at our lives and find that we have so much, and yet we live in pain. The guilt of feeling so sad amidst such plenty adds to our hurt. Then Satan crows as we turn in vain to the world for analgesia.

First, in youth perhaps, we take up smoking. Cigarettes make us feel one of the gang, they lend a spurious air of maturity and they give a false sense of belonging. Millions of dollars are spent every year to foster this illusion. But soon the feeling of emptiness returns and, instead of us smoking the cigarettes, the cigarettes are smoking us.

For some, social environments make the so-called 'soft drugs' necessary, if they want to be 'in'. A deep toke on the joint, and the longings and shortcomings in life fade away on the bittersweet smoke. Perhaps it is alcohol which ashes away longing and emptiness. A few beers, and everyone is a friend, and the false fear of social unacceptance dissolves into the fuzzy warmth of inebriation. Some of us fall longingly into the embraces of kindly and loving men/women and try to fill empty hearts with the ecstasies of sexual sharing.

When the high is gone, back comes the emptiness. When the hangover is all that is left, the pain and raw need floods back. After the orgasm is over, the vacuum of longing returns. When the coke wears off, when the heroin buzz dies, then we find ourselves right back where we started.

All these and many more like experiences are the traps which Satan sets to confuse us. As children, we often cannot see what is offered to us. As young people, Satan blinds us with peer pressure, fashion and the lie that we need to be 'in' and, when we glimpse the truth, he crowds us with cynicism so that we don't believe it. When we are young adults, Satan confuses us with the need to 'get ahead', concern for the welfare of our own new families and lies to us about what it is that we crave.

When our pain is such that we turn to the world for solace, when we stumble from our beds to the cigarette packet to start the day, when we shakingly grasp the bottle for a quick belt just to get the blood pumping, when we grit out teeth on the bitter-tasting leather of our belt wrapped tightly round our arm to raise the vein to our probing needle, when we run gasping with need to the arms of our lover — *then* is when Satan dances with delight, his laughter echoing around the halls of hell.

But here is the gentle glory in the darkness of addiction: when we are deepest in degradation, Satan's works confound themselves. For at the bottom of the trough of despair, we become disgusted with ourselves; we then see that we have been following a lie. When we peer out from beneath the pall of the darkness of our own sin, at last we can see Jesus waiting for us with his arms outstretched, and a smile of understanding and forgiveness on his face.

Now it is that the jolt from drink, the high from dope, the ecstasy of sexual self-gratification — these and all worldly pleasures pale into insignificance in the face of Jesus' all-embracing love.

❧

'No, the next car,' the conductor [the devil] murmured. 'I guess you're entitled to ride Pullman. After all, you're quite a successful man. You've tasted the joys of wealth and position and prestige. You've known the pleasures of marriage and fatherhood. You've sampled the delights of dining and drinking and debauchery, too, and you travelled high, wide and handsome. So let's not have any last-minute recriminations.'

'All right,' Martin sighed. 'I can't blame you for my mistakes. On the other hand, you can't take credit for what happened, either. I worked for everything I got. I did it all on my own. I didn't even need your watch.'

'So you didn't,' the conductor said smiling. 'But would you mind giving it back to me now?'

'Need it for the next sucker, eh?' Martin muttered.

'Perhaps.'

Something about the way he said it made Martin look up. He tried to see the conductor's eyes, but the brim of his cap cast a shadow. So Martin looked down at the watch instead.

'Tell me something,' he said softly. 'If I give you the watch, what will you do with it?'

'Why, throw it in the ditch,' the conductor told him. 'That's all I'll do with it.' And he held out his hand.

'What if somebody comes along and finds it? And twists the stem backwards and stops Time?'

'Nobody would do that,' the conductor murmured. 'Even if they knew.'

'You mean, it was all a trick? This is only an ordinary cheap watch?'

'I didn't say that,' whispered the conductor. 'I only said that no-one has ever twisted the stem backwards. They've all been like you, Martin — looking ahead to find happiness. Waiting for the moment that never comes.'

The conductor held out his hand again.

Martin sighed and shook his head. 'You cheated me after all.'

'You cheated yourself, Martin. And you're going to ride that Hell-Bound Train.'

Robert Bloch, *That Hell-Bound Train*

Nothing, not even the best and noblest, can go on as it now is. Nothing, not even what is lowest and most bestial, will not be raised again if it submits to death. It is sown a natural body; it is raised a spiritual body. Flesh and blood cannot come to the Mountains. Not because they are too rank, but because they are too weak. What is a lizard compared with a stallion? Lust is a poor, weak, whimpering, whispering thing compared with that richness and energy of desire which will arise when lust has been killed.

C.S. Lewis, *The Great Divorce*

There was a social gathering once, of Christians, that turned into one of those 'truth sessions'. It didn't start out to be, but somehow it just happened and everybody began to talk about their problems and temptations. The variety was endless; no two people had the same kind. But they all had one common denominator. None of these people blamed their dilemma on themselves. Every one of them was perfectly sure it had been caused by some other person or some set of circumstances beyond their control.

Because the evening had taken such a serious turn, they had a 'word of prayer' before they broke up. Then everyone went home, as confused as before, taking their problems with them. For everyone's greatest problem was themselves.

Ethel Barrett, *Will the Real Phony Please Stand Up?*

What shape is your idol, sister? Is it your house, or your clothes, or perhaps even your worthwhile and cultural club?

I worship the pictures I paint, brother. . . I worship my job; I'm the best darn publicity expert this side of Hollywood. . . I worship my golf game, my bridge game. . . I worship my comfort; after all, isn't enjoyment the goal of life?. . . I worship my church; I want to tell you, the work we've done in missions beats all the other denominations in this city and next year we can afford that new organ — and you won't find a better choir anywhere. . . I worship myself. . . What shape is your idol?

Joy Davidman, *Smoke On The Mountain*

It is so easy to become addicted to any of the myriad of traps which Satan lays for us: the adrenalin surge of crime and/or violence, the easy slip into all kinds of peer pressure-induced activities, then the long slide into emptiness and pain, and finally the sudden realisation that we have hit the bottom. Then comes revelation.

Now we know what it is that for all our lives we have been longing. Now the emptiness can be filled. If we turn to Jesus and welcome him as Saviour and Lord, never again need we be faced with that rawness, the burning cold vacancy in our chests which is the absence of God when we shut him out by listening to the lies of Satan.

D.H. Gresham

Lord, my soul cries out with remorse, for all my life I have longed so much to be happy and at ease, I have sought the acceptance and admiration of humankind, and have forgotten you whose love is perfect.

My heart has ached with emptiness and I have pursued fulfilment in the things of the world, never realising that your perfect love has been mine all the time.

I have lain with lovers, glorying in the physical demonstrations of their love for me, and in return have given to them the love I owed to you; forgive my foolishness, for I am weak and sinful.

I have loved so much — not in generous freedom, but demanding love in return. Forgive, Lord, my emotional greed.

I have misunderstood so much and yet have gloried in my understanding and in the intellect which you have given me. Forgive, Lord, my pride and arrogance.

In my unthinking conceit I have inflicted pain and guilt on those whom I loved. Forgive, Lord, my selfishness and lift away the burdens of guilt which my sins have inflicted on others.

Hear, O Lord, my cry of thanks for all the workings of my life, all the happenings which have led me to your side.

I am filled with sadness for all my misdeeds and the pain which I have caused others to bear; only you can ease those pains, dear Lord. I beg you to do so.

From this time forth, O Lord, lead me only in your path. Guard me from the temptations of the evil one. Guard me from the longings which have driven me for so long. Take away the fear of the world which so besets me and lead me to walk in inward peace.

I thank you, Lord, for the compassion you have placed in my heart; but guard me, Lord, from my tendency to twist it into what it should not be.

Grant me, I beg you: wisdom to add to intellect, peace to add to courage, and strength to add to effort. Lord, fill me with

your Holy Spirit that all that you have decreed I might become
may be realised in this weak and frightened servant.

    Lord, I bow my head in shame at what I have been and in
longing for what I should be.

    Lord, I make my plea in the name of your son Jesus Christ
whose holy death on the cross bought me the right to do so.

    Amen.

A Benediction

    May the Lord who walks beside you reach out and take
your hand;
May you hear his loving voice and feel his warmth.
May the heart which died and lives for you beat close to
yours this day
And the soul which starves within you now be fed.
May you see the shining glory which he showers all
around;
May his love restore the wounds which still you bear.
May your heart which pained and ached in you beat
wildly, glad with joy
And may you now see his presence in your life.
He is with you — may you know it.
He loves you — may you feel it.
He suffered and he died that you might not.
May you walk in peace and plenty,
In safety and in love,
Till you travel the final journey to him
Above.

    Amen.

12

Failure is not fatal

Who shall ascend the hill of the Lord? And who shall stand in his holy place? Those who have clean hands and pure hearts, who do not lift up their souls to what is false. This is my commandment, that you love one another as I have loved you. No-one has greater love than this, to lay down one's life for one's friends. You are my friends if you do what I command you. It is not enemies who taunt me — I could bear that; it is not adversaries who deal insolently with me — I could hide from them. But it is you, my equal, my companion, my familiar friend, with whom I kept pleasant company; we walked in the house of God with the throng.

Very truly, I tell you, if you ask anything of the Father in my name, he will give it to you. Until now you have not asked for anything in my name. Ask and you will receive, so that your joy may be complete. Now during those days he went out to the mountain to pray; and he spent the night in prayer to God. And when day came, he called his disciples and chose twelve of them, whom he also named apostles. . . and Judas Iscariot, who became a traitor.

You did not choose me, but I chose you. And I appointed you to go and bear fruit. My sheep hear my voice. I know them and they follow me, I give them eternal life, and they will never perish. No-one will snatch them out of my hand. What my Father has given me is greater than all else, and no-one can snatch it out of the Father's hand.

When it was evening, he took his place with the twelve; and while they were eating, he said, 'Truly I tell you, one of you will betray me.' And they became greatly distressed and began to say to him one after another, 'Surely not I, Lord?' He answered, 'The one who has dipped his hand into the bowl with me will betray me. The Son of Man goes as it is written of him, but woe to that one by whom the Son of Man is betrayed! It would have been better for that one not to have been born.' Judas, who betrayed him, said, 'Surely not I, Rabbi?' He replied, 'You have said so.'

When Judas, his betrayer, saw that Jesus was condemned, he repented and brought back the thirty pieces of silver to the chief priests and the elders. He said, 'I have sinned by betraying innocent blood.' But they said, 'What is that to us? See to it yourself.' Throwing down the pieces of silver in the temple, he departed; and he went and hanged himself.

I am grateful to Christ Jesus our Lord, who has strengthened me, because he judged me faithful and appointed me to his service, even though I was formerly a blasphemer, a persecutor and a man of violence. But I received mercy because I had acted ignorantly in unbelief, and the grace of our Lord overflowed for me with the faith and love that are in Christ Jesus. Grace to you and peace from him who is and who was and who is to come. . . and from Jesus Christ, the faithful witness, the firstborn of the dead, and the ruler of the kings of the earth. To him who loves us and freed us from our sins by his blood, and made us to be a kingdom, priests serving his God and Father, to him be glory and dominion forever and ever. Amen.

(Psalm 24: 3–4; John 15: 12–14; Psalm 55: 12–14; John 16: 23–24; Luke 6: 12–16; John 15: 16; 10: 27–29; Matthew 26: 20–25; Matthew 27: 3–5; 1 Timothy 1: 12–14; Revelation 1: 4–6 — all NRSV)

It was printed in block letters with a blue felt tip pen across the top of the mirror in the men's toilet in a restaurant in San Francisco: JUDAS, COME HOME — ALL IS FORGIVEN! I stood quietly, watching as several men came and went, some glancing at the carefully lettered graffiti, but then passing quickly on. I speculated on the source. Was it some young man who had become a prodigal, having run away from home now, in desperation trying to assure himself that his father might say these words to his own son who had become a Judas? Or was it some father searching for a son who had betrayed and fled into the city, hoping against hope that he might read these cryptic words and dare to believe that even betrayal can be forgiven?

JUDAS, COME HOME — ALL IS FORGIVEN! Could it be true? Would even Judas, the betrayer of Jesus, have found forgiveness if he had sought out the very One whom he had betrayed? Can God forgive anything and everything? Or does this bit of theological graffiti press beyond the limits of even divine love and grace?

We know that Judas was stricken with guilt and shame after having betrayed Jesus. Though he admitted his guilt and returned the money he had been paid to betray Jesus, he did not find forgiveness from others, nor in himself. The darkness of despair closed in upon him — a night where there was no gentleness to provide healing and hope.

Judas reminds us that to love others and to make promises to others is to risk betrayal. Even as we point to the betrayal of others, we know that the seeds of betrayal lie hidden in our own best intentions.

Why is it that betrayal seems to be a failure that is so fatal?

I think that betrayal is felt to be an unforgivable act because it exposes ambivalence at the deepest core of human relationships. When we cannot trust our own trust, and dare not be loyal to loyalty, we feel the cords that bind together our deepest and most precious moments slip out of our grasp. Perhaps this is why, if a devil did not exist, we would need to invent one. The defection of what once was good to become evil cries out for explanation. We can let neither God nor humankind bear the burden of introducing evil into what we all want to believe is essentially good.

Why is it that a single act of betrayal can destroy all of one's life? Why is betrayal such a devastating failure that it has the power to condemn the past and contaminate the future? Why, for some (as in the case of Judas) does suicide appear to be the only personal atonement for betrayal?

The act of the betrayer not only contains the power to destroy a relationship; it tears at the very fabric of human society. The very concept of betrayal is grounded in a structure of community based on loyalty, trust and commitment. A lie is not betrayal until it destroys the bond of friendship.

'It is not the fact that you lied to me that is so terrible,' Nietzsche once said, 'but the fact that I can no longer trust you.' Betrayal does more than deceive; it destroys trust in those who are deceived.

At the same time, if we are the betrayer of a confidence shared, of a promise given, of a vow made, we suffer a devastating loss to our own self worth. This reveals the difference between guilt and shame. When we break a rule or sin against God's commandments, we incur guilt against the law of truth and goodness. We stand objectively condemned before that law. The guilt is an offence for which we can be forgiven and even restitution made in some cases.

With shame, however, we have experienced a loss of being which cannot be restored by a quick word of forgiveness. This 'toxic shame', as John Bradshaw calls it, can only be removed by the living encounter and fellowship with people who are not shame-based.

The other disciples certainly failed Jesus as well. Peter denied Jesus three times during the crucial hours of his trial. Without the resurrection of the crucified Jesus, there would have been no power of forgiveness in the cross. Without a deep personal encounter with the living Christ following the resurrection, the disciples would not have experienced forgiveness and healing of their shame.

But what of Judas? I like to think that his repentance was genuine and I like to picture Jesus confronting him in the despair and desolation he chose for himself, saying:

'Judas, my choosing of you counts for more than your betrayal of me! Don't overestimate your power to cancel what God has chosen. Second, Judas, your betrayal did not put me on the cross; I went to the cross in obedience to my Father God. Don't claim through betrayal what I have gained through obedience. And finally, Judas, I have already died and behold I am alive! You can be forgiven — your death has already been overcome through my resurrection!'

And what of each one of us who harbour secret shame and long for a reassuring word from Jesus? Can we as children close doors that defy our attempts to open them as adults? I think so. I have such doors. I know they're there. Some of these doors are to keep me out rather than close me in. I no longer remember why they were closed, but only that they must be opened. Behind some doors lie undiscovered and unrevealed shame; behind others the bones of a child, who bears my name, buried in secret in order that the adult should live.

As I grow toward health and wholeness, I believe that the resurrected Jesus will explore with me the still un-opened doors and dispel unknown fears. He will give life to youthful dreams that perished in the anguish of failure and release the child within to become the health of my older years. Not all doors can be opened at once. And so I live with rooms not yet invaded by his presence, for I also have spacious rooms that open outward toward the green plains and undulating hills. And there are people in this landscape, moving toward me, and I am not afraid.

❧

A blur of romance clings to our notions of 'publicans', 'sinners', 'the poor', 'the people of the marketplace', 'our neighbour', as though of course God should reveal him-self, if at all, to these simple people, these Sunday school watercolour figures, who are so purely themselves in their tattered robes, who are single in themselves, while we now are various, complex and full at heart.

We are busy. So, I see now, were they.

Who shall ascend into the hill of the Lord? Or who shall stand in his holy place? There is no-one but us. There is no-one to send, nor a clean hand, nor a pure heart on the face of the earth, nor in the earth, but only us, a generation comforting ourselves with the notion that we have come at an awkward time, that our innocent fathers are all dead — as if innocence had ever been — and our children busy and troubled, and we ourselves unfit, not yet ready, having each of us chosen wrongly, made a false start, failed, yielded to impulse and the tangled comfort of pleasures, and grown exhausted, unable to seek the thread, weak and involved.

But there is no-one but us. There never has been. There have been generations which remembered, and generations which forgot; there has never been a generation of whole men and women who lived well for even one day. Yet some have imagined well, with honesty and art, the detail of such a life and have described it with such grace that we mistake vision for history, dream for description, and fancy that life has devolved. . . Who shall ascend into the hill of the Lord? Or who shall stand in his holy place? 'Whom shall I send,' heard the first Isaiah, 'and who will go for us?' And poor Isaiah, who happened to be standing there — and there was no-one else — burst out, 'Here am I; send me.'

Annie Dillard, *Holy the Firm*

There are dark times in everyone's life, times when the terror of being alive comes swooping down like an evil thing, compassing the poor mind with unimaginable tortures, shaking questions from its wings before which the established habits cower and shrink away, and leaving the victim exhausted and apathetic.

If these times come only once or twice in a person's life, then it is possible still to continue with the accustomed things, or if that time first breaks through the crust of routine at the crucial moment of death, it does not matter that the routine is smashed for ever. But to one who is studying for the ministry, these times come not once or twice, but again and again, storming like a black wave breaking on an island fortress, till his defences are battered in and he is utterly exposed to the mercy of the attack. . . it is a fight whose strength is weakness, whose life is the utter nonentity of the person. For the life of it is the Spirit, always and only the Spirit.

Ronald Gregor Smith, 'Preparing for the Ministry'

'My God, my God, why has thou forsaken me?' As Christ speaks those words, he, too, is in the wilderness. He speaks them when all is lost. He speaks them when there is nothing even he can hear except for the croak of his own voice and, when as far as even he can see, there is no God to hear him. And in a way his words are a love song, the greatest love song of them all. In a way his words are the words we all of us must speak before we know what it means to love God as we are commanded to love him. . .

This is the love that you and I are called to move toward both through the wilderness times on broken legs and through times when we catch glimpses and hear whispers from beyond the wilderness. Nobody ever claimed the journey was going to be an easy one. It is not easy to love God with all your heart and soul and might when much of the time you have all but forgotten his name. But to love God is not a goal we have to struggle toward on our own, because what at its heart the gospel is all about is that God himself moves us toward it even when we believe that he has forsaken us.

Frederick Buechner, *A Room Called Remember*

The paradox in the structure of community is that the very bonds of love and commitment that create and sustain our identities can also destroy us. This reveals how fragile even the strongest bonds between persons here on earth can be. Because we are not 'pure in heart' — each one of us carries within us the possibility of betrayal — our love can turn treacherous when betrayed. Yet we have no other choice but to risk this possibility. For 'it is not good to be alone', as God said of Adam before the creation of Eve (Genesis 2: 18). Created in the divine image and

likeness, we can experience and express that divine likeness only through the bond of social and community
relatedness. The only protection from betrayal is not to
love, never to trust. The only security against becoming
a Judas is never to become a disciple.

Ray S. Anderson, *The Gospel according to Judas*

Our believing is conditioned at its source by our belonging.

Michael Polanyi, *Personal Knowledge*

We have all experienced the bond of belonging. We have
all known the feelings. We believed the promises, we
danced at weddings, we cried for joy at a new baby's
birth. We were secure in the feeling of being at home.
But then the bond slips away from us so quietly that we
don't even realise that we've lost the connection. Or we
suddenly wake up to the fact that we've broken with the
past, and we have no confidence in the future. We know
too much of Judas, because we know too much of our
own desperate urgings and darkest fears. We're afraid
when we get too close to the failure of any relationship.
We keep our distance. Like the impulse to retreat from a
good friend who ends a marriage we had a stake in, we
fear it could happen to us.

But in our shared likeness there is also something com-
pelling about Judas. If there is a way back for him, then
perhaps there is for us as well — not in retracing our past,
but in discovering the love that comes to us from our
future.

Ray S. Anderson, *The Gospel according to Judas*

In a world of fugitives, one who moves in the opposite
direction will appear to run away.

Ronald Gregor Smith,
'J.G. Hamann and the Princess Gallitzin'

The Christian doctrine of forgiveness and reconciliation,
then, must deal with the social disgrace and exclusion
(objective shame) as well as the subjective feelings of
failure and unworthiness. . . The intention of forgiveness

is to nullify shame and guilt so that reconciliation and a new beginning become possible. The shamed person must find new identity and personal worth. And the guilty person must find expiation. Both objective alienation and hostility, which have been institutionalised in our social and legal systems, and the subjective remorse and blame that so inhibit personal fulfilment in human relationships must be overcome. . .

Only a forgiveness which covers the past and a genuine restoration of relationship can banish shame. What is needed is a restoration of communication. The rage which isolates and insulates must be overcome. Reconciliation and restoration of mutual intimate relationship through a loving open exchange is the only way to heal resentment and restore lost self-esteem.

C. Norman Kraus, *Jesus Christ our Lord*

Families are people who make *promises* to each other. When we see what these promises are, we see what a family is. . . It is not the failure to keep promises, in and of itself, that destroys family. Such failure happens in every family and can be expected. Family can remain family in the midst of unfulfilled promises. What destroys family is the collapse of promise-*making*. It is when the very making of promises is no longer believed and believed in that families die.

Craig Dykstra, 'Family Promises'

Stretched out on my cot, I stare at the grey wall.
Outside, a summer evening that does not know me
Goes singing into the countryside.
Slowly and softly the tides of the day ebb
On the eternal shore.
Sleep a little, strengthen body and soul, head and hand,
For peoples, houses, spirits and hearts
Are aflame.
Till your day breaks after blood-red night — Stand fast!
Night and silence. . .
I hear my own soul tremble and heave.
Nothing else?

I hear, I hear the silent night thoughts
Of my fellow sufferers asleep or awake,
As if voices, cries, as if shouts for planks to save them.
I hear the uneasy creak of the beds, I hear chains. . .
When luminous signs stand in the night sky,
And over the peoples new bells ring and ring.
I am waiting for that midnight
In whose fearfully streaming brilliance
The evil perish for anguish
And the good overcome with joy.
The first light of morning creeps through my window pale and grey,
A light warm summer wind blows over my brow.
'Summer day,' I will only say, 'beautiful summer day!
What may it bring to me?. . .'
Control yourself, brother; soon you will have finished it, soon, soon.
I hear you stride bravely and with proud step.
You no longer see the present; you see the future.
I go with you, brother, to that place,
And I hear your last word:
'Brother, when the sun turns pale for me,
Then live for me.'

Dietrich Bonhoeffer, 'Night Voices in Tegel'

Reach out to me, Creator God, for what is to me an unbridgeable chasm is but the span of your hand extended in mercy. Shade your glory so that it may cast moonbeams across my night, for I am blinded by darkness. Come beside me, Lord Jesus, and bathe my face and anoint it with oil so that my countenance may shine with an inner peace and radiance that comes from peace. Flood my soul, Holy Spirit, with an unquenchable fountain of healing love.

Remember my forgetfulness and rekindle in me the joy of being a child of God. Heal my memory of all self-incrimination for past failures. Give me permission to be angry when I have been betrayed and to grieve when I have suffered loss. Listen to me when I pour out my complaints and don't stop me until I am finished, and then ask, 'Is there more?' Let me get to the bottom of all sadness and the end of all bitterness. Make me relinquish all regrets, free all the emotional prisoners I have taken, and awaken me as from a deep sleep with the fever gone and a ravenous hunger for life restored.

Through the open door of the resurrection, Lord Jesus, I see the cross and the grave and they are empty!

I love you, Lord, and I lift my voice
To worship you — oh my soul, rejoice.
Take joy, my King, in what you hear.
Let me be a sweet, sweet sound in your ear.

Amen.

A Benediction
Now may the God of peace, who brought back from the dead our Lord Jesus, the great shepherd of the sheep, by the blood of the eternal covenant, make you complete in everything good so that you may do his will, working among us that which is pleasing in his sight, through Jesus Christ, to whom be the glory forever and ever. Amen.

13

Can we really call the darkness 'gentle'?

God is our refuge and strength, a very present help in trouble. Therefore we will not fear, though the earth should change, though the mountains shake in the heart of the sea, though its waters roar and foam, though the mountains tremble with its tumult.

What then are we to say about these things? If God is for us, who is against us? Who will separate us from the love of Christ? Will hardship, or distress, or persecution, or famine, or nakedness, or peril, or sword? No, in all these things we are more than conquerors through him who loved us. For I am convinced that neither death, nor life, nor angels, nor rulers, nor things present, nor things to come, nor powers, nor height, nor depth, nor anything else in all creation will be able to separate us from the love of God in Christ Jesus our Lord.

Even though I walk through the darkest valley, I fear no evil, for you are with me; your rod and your staff — they comfort me.

Blessed be the God and Father of our Lord Jesus Christ, the Father of mercies and the God of all consolation, who consoles us in all our affliction, so that we may be able to console those who are in any affliction with the consolation with which we ourselves are consoled by God.

The Lord is my rock, my fortress and my deliverer, my God, my rock in whom I take refuge, my shield and the horn of my salvation, my stronghold.

Break forth together into singing. . . for the Lord has comforted his people.

(Psalm 46: 1–3; Romans 8: 31, 35 and 37–39; Psalm 23: 4; 2 Corinthians 1: 3–4; Psalm 18: 2; Isaiah 52: 9 — all NRSV)

Two daughters spoke in whispers beside their father's hospital bed while their mother dozed in a chair nearby. The room was dark.

And then the daughters knew. They knew, even though they had not walked this path of sorrow before. His breathing was changing and it was time to wake their mother. Each long sigh allowed plenty of time for prayer. And then, very quietly, they found themselves singing to the father who would soon be leaving: 'Jesus loves you, this we know, for the Bible tells us so. . . Yes, Jesus loves you. . .'

And then, another gift of song, 'Amazing grace, how sweet the sound. . .', and they wept and sang him into heaven. And the mother and her daughters were surrounded by darkness. . . gentle darkness.

Is it possible to believe that the love of God surrounds us in our darkest moments? Can it be that the God of All Ages *is actually with us* when all the lights go out and the breathing ceases, and someone you have loved all your life is gone? Is God truly there when we need him most? Can we, with real integrity, call the darkness 'gentle' or is it merely playing with words?

If God is *not* with us, all is mockery. For Jesus gave his word that he would neither leave nor forsake us. *Can* I take Jesus at his word just as a child believes the word of her father, hidden in the darkness of the cellar below her, who says he will catch her when she jumps? Such a child does not find the cellar hard or harsh, but finds the gentle firmness of her father's waiting arms.

On that April Sunday evening, in the darkened hospital room, I did take Jesus at his word and found myself firmly caught in God's love. As Dad's final sigh was ending, I knew he had gone somewhere else to begin life again. I was there as he moved into a new dimension, where the life we are all created for was beginning for him — where all is sharper and brighter and clearer than anything Dad had ever imagined!

I can now go on in a new way, believing that the God of All Ages surrounds us during our darkest hours, gently firming up the darkness so that we are not harmed if we fall. On this Father's Day, I am filled with gratitude that God's loving, comforting presence *was* there that autumn evening as we sang my father out of our gentle darkness into the arms of his loving Father, where a new 'ten thousand years' of eternal moments were just beginning.

❧

The sun chased the darkness from the sky.
This day has come to claim its fractional share of
eternity — and so have I.
I want to say yes to new beginnings,
yes to the Comforter,
yes to the healing,
yes to the table of bread and of wine,
yes to songs and laughter,
yes to the Son of man,
yes to the challenges — YES TO LIFE!

Marilee Zdenek, God is a Verb

We must feel the need of comfort before we can listen to the words of comfort. And God knows that it is infinitely better and happier for us to need his comforts and receive them than ever it could be not to need them and so be without them.

Hannah Whitall Smith, The God of All Comfort

Ah, you little know my loss — indeed, it is great! It seems to include God! If you knew what he knows about death you would clap your listless hands. . . The knowledge of your own heart will teach you this — not the knowledge you have, but the knowledge that is on its way to you through suffering.

George MacDonald

We contemplate. . . a God who pursues us into our darkness and destructiveness and, entering and sharing it, brings life out of our death. Therefore we can take our own suffering, from whatever source it comes, whether physical illness, or bereavement, or the damage we have done to ourselves and the damage inflicted on us by others, or the pain we experience in letting God's pity, compassion and love act in us. In our pain we meet Christ in his passion, and know his presence and healing power that brings hope out of our despair.

Gerard W. Hughes, *God of Surprises*

O Love that wilt not let me go,
I rest my weary soul in thee;
I give thee back the life I owe,
That in thine ocean depths its flow
May richer, fuller be.

George Matheson

The very words *abiding Comforter* are an amazing revelation. Try to comprehend them. If we can have a human comfort to stay with us for only a few days when we are in trouble, we think ourselves fortunate; but here is a divine Comforter who is always staying with us and whose power to comfort is infinite. Never, never ought we for a single minute to be without comfort; never for a single minute ought we to be uncomfortable.

Hannah Whitall Smith, *The God of All Comfort*

Come, thou almighty King, help us thy name to sing,
Help us to praise!
Father all glorious, o'er all victorious,
Come and reign over us, Ancient of days!
Come, thou incarnate Word, gird on thy mighty
sword,
Our prayer attend;
Come, and thy people bless, and give thy Word success;
Spirit of holiness, on us descend!
Come, holy Comforter, thy sacred witness bear,

In this glad hour:
Thou who almighty art, now rule in every heart,
And ne'er from us depart, Spirit of power!
To thee, great One in Three, eternal praises be,
Hence, evermore:
Thy sovereign majesty may we in glory see,
And to eternity love and adore!
    Amen.

Anonymous

The letters of St Paul were written by a man who had
gone through imprisonment, stoning, shipwreck, sickness,
destitution, derision, inner uncertainty. St Paul's experience of consolation in the midst of affliction is not the
exception to a rule, though his expression of it is excep-
tionally forceful.

Another dimension of being consoled in the midst of
hurting can be illustrated from the life of American author
Margaret Prescott Montague, who died in 1955. A particularly instructive incident occurred one day. . . she was
permitted to sit out on the sun porch with other patients.
As she absorbed the scene around her — the people, the
sparrows chirping in the trees, the periodic splashes of
sunlight and the leafless trees moving with the wind —
she began to realise for the first time how wildly beautiful
and joyous all creation really is. She knew these moments
were a revelation of the meaningfulness of all reality. In
later years, as she went on struggling with her afflictions,
Margaret Montague recalled her experience at the hospital
and drew fresh strength from the goodness and validity
she had discovered at the heart of reality.

Charles Cummings, The Mystery of the Ordinary

---

*Dear loving God, you are a loving, comforting, caring Father
whose gifts include the courage to sing with creative joy even
in the midst of darkness. Gratitude cascades from our hearts
as we dare to believe Jesus' promises; and the harshness of your
feared absence is transformed by the gentle firmness of your
consoling presence. As a result, you enable us to rebuke and*

redefine old cliches that had imprisoned us, and you encourage us to refute and rewrite anonymous prophecies that had doomed us to despair.

We come, therefore, as grateful children to our loving Father, offering you a song of unending praise in Jesus' name.   Amen.

A Benediction

Go now with sure and confident knowledge that you do not go alone, for you are indwelt and surrounded by God's abiding presence. Go also with courage and the absolute conviction that not one single memory, thought, idea or action can remove you from God's amazing grace; grace that transforms dark doubts into firm hope, so that songs of joy accompany you this very day and on into eternity. Amen.

Theme: The gentle light in darkness

'. . .into thick darkness he brings light' (Job 12: 22)

In God's hand are the souls of all that live,
    the spirits of all human kind.
Wisdom and might are his,
    with him are firmness and understanding.
If he pulls down, there is no rebuilding;
    if he imprisons, there is no release.
If he holds up the waters, there is drought;
    if he lets them go, they turn the land upside down.
Strength and success belong to him;
    deceived and deceiver are his to use.
He makes counsellers behave like idiots
    and drives judges mad;
        he looses the bonds imposed by kings
        and removes the girdle of office from their waists;
        he makes priests behave like idiots
        and overthrows men long in office;
        those who are trusted he strikes dumb,
        he takes away the judgment of old men;
        he heaps scorn on princes
        and abates the arrogance of nobles.
He leads peoples astray and destroys them;
    he lays them low and there they lie.
He takes away their wisdom from the rulers of the
    nations and leaves them wandering in a pathless
    wilderness;
        they grope in the darkness without light
        and are left to wander like a drunkard.
He uncovers mysteries deep in obscurity
    and into thick darkness he brings light.

Job 12: 10–22, NEB

14

Light in the darkness

The earth was formless and empty, and darkness was over the face of the abyss. . . And God said, 'Let there be light!' and there was light.

God, who said, 'Let light shine out of darkness', has made his light to shine in our hearts to give us the light of the knowledge of the glory of God in the face of Jesus Christ. But we have this treasure in jars of clay to show that this all-surpassing power is from God and not ourselves.

For we who are alive are always being given over to death for Jesus' sake, so that his life may be revealed in our mortal body. So then, death is at work in us, but life is at work in you.

At the sixth hour, darkness came over the whole land until the ninth hour. And at the ninth hour Jesus cried out in a loud voice, 'Eloi, Eloi, lama sabachthani?' — which means, 'My God, my God, why have you forsaken me?'

The curtain of the temple was torn in two from top to bottom.

The Lord has caused the sun to shine in the heavens,
But has said that he would dwell in thick darkness.
I have built a royal house for you,
a place for you to dwell forever.
I form the light and create darkness,
I bring prosperity and create disaster;
I, the Lord, do all these things.
Truly you are a God who hides himself,
O God and Saviour of Israel.
All the makers of idols will be put to shame
and disgraced;

They will go off into disgrace together.
See now that I myself am he!
There is no god besides me.
I put to death and I bring to life,
I have wounded and I heal,
and no-one can deliver out of my hand.

And when the centurion, who stood there in front of Jesus, heard his cry and saw how he died, he said, 'Surely this man was the Son of God!'

And the Word became flesh and tabernacled among us, and we beheld his glory, glory as of the Only Son from the Father, full of grace and truth.

Jesus answered them, 'Destroy this temple and in three days I will raise it up.'

'. . .Father, the hour has come; glorify your Son so that the Son may glorify you.'

(Genesis 1: 2–3a; 2 Corinthians 4: 6–7 and 11–12; Mark 15: 33–34 and 38; 1 Kings 8: 12–13; Isaiah 45: 7 and 15–16 — all NIV; Deuteronomy 32: 39, NIV/RV; Mark 15: 39, NIV; John 1: 14; John 2: 19; John 17: 1b — all NRSV)

'There's glory for you!'

'I don't know what you mean by "glory",' Alice said.

'I mean, "There's a nice knock-down argument for you!"'

'But "glory" doesn't mean "a nice knock-down argument"', Alice objected.

'When *I* use a word,' Humpty Dumpty said in a rather scornful tone, 'it means just what I choose it to mean — neither more nor less.'

Lewis Carroll, *Through the Looking Glass*

What do we mean by 'God'? How may we use this most pervasive of words and yet the most slippery, too? To what — to whom — does it refer? If it does 'refer' at all. . .

Let us begin by using a relatively simple definition of 'God'. God is 'the name for that which concerns us ultimately' (Paul Tillich). But this business of 'ultimate concern' is itself rather slippery. For an ardent Leninist who is a passionate member of the Party would be just as ultimately concerned as, say, a Hudson Taylor or a David Livingstone, a Florence Nightingale or Mother Teresa of Calcutta. It's just that their objects of concern are somewhat different! And so, asking *human beings* how to define this 'religious feeling' is going to leave us merely with a list of competing claimants to deity — from our points of view.

While the Christian religion has often made use of this kind of approach, both in seeking a degree of self-understanding and in communicating to those outside the faith or of different faiths, in the final analysis things are rather different — or should be!

Eberhard Jüngel claims: 'The traditional language of Christianity insists that we *must have said to us* what we are to *think* of the word "God". It is thus presupposed that only the God who speaks himself can finally tell us what we are to understand or think by the word "God". Theology comprehends this whole subject with the category of revelation.' Revelation, it is claimed, authorises us to speak and think about God in a specific way.

Yet we need to ask: how does God reveal himself: through creation, moral conscience, ecstatic utterance, a mystical experience? Through certain key historical events (e.g. Israel's Passover, Buddha under the bodhi-tree)? The list could go on.

Christianity would offer us — and the world — what can only be called a scandalous answer to this line of questioning. As Martin Luther said: 'The true theologian is not the one who comes to see the invisible things of God by thinking about what is created; the true theologian is the one who thinks about the visible and "hinder" parts of God, having seen them in sufferings and the cross.' Here we have a deliberate contrast between 'seeing' and 'thinking about' or 'perceiving', and a play on the sequence in which these occur.

We do not transcend beyond creation as a supposed sphere of revelation to the Creator God as he really might be. Rather, there for all to see in our space-time concrete world is a broken body strung up on a Roman gibbet; and, having perceived this to be indeed nothing less than God-in-the-flesh, then we are to set about the task of pondering the radical significance of such a God who would do and be such a thing as this.

The 'darkness' motif has been used as a kind of shorthand in the history of Christian theology to refer to a cast of mind or a theological method which would employ *either* of these approaches. The first approach is 'dark' because it leads nowhere; the second approach is 'dark' because it centres on a 'dark' experience. But frankly this is rather confusing and not a little naughty, since they are so radically different — indeed contradictory, if one were to follow Luther, who himself is really only following St Paul (e.g. 1 Corinthians 1: 18–31).

Yet following Paul I guess is a tall order. For what are we to make of one whose self-confession of how he ticks spiritually is 'to know [Christ] and the power of his resurrection and the fellowship of his sufferings, being conformed to his death, in order that somehow I may attain to the resurrection from the dead' (Philippians 3: 10–11)? His 'straining forward' (verse 13) might have been interpreted by some in a mystical way as the disciple's walk of 'darkness' (so said Gregory of Nyssa in, for example, *The Life of Moses*).

While there may be some merit in this view of the Christian's spiritual ascent, one senses that Paul would have preferred to decry such 'ascents' to concentrate instead upon 'descending'. Just so, may we together with him ponder and practise Jesus' way of humility and the cross, which is 'glory' indeed, the true object of 'boasting' and the Christian's ultimate concern (Philippians 2: 6–11 and Colossians 1: 24–27).

❧❀❧

Then our good Lord put a question to me: 'Are you satisfied that I suffered for you?' I said: 'Yes, good Lord, all my thanks to you; yes, good Lord, blessed may you be.' Then Jesus, our good Lord said: 'If you are satisfied,

I am satisfied. It is a joy, a bliss, an endless delight to me if ever I suffered my passion for you and, if I could suffer more, I should suffer more.'

In response to this, my understanding was lifted up into heaven. . . What I am describing now is so great a joy to Jesus that he counts as nothing his labour and his sufferings and his cruel and shameful death. And in these words — 'If I could suffer more, I should suffer more' — I saw truly that as often as he could die, so often should he die, and love would never let him rest till he had done it. . .

And when he had died or would die so often, he would count it all as nothing for love, for everything seems only little to him in comparison with his love.

Julian of Norwich, Showings

The dove descending breaks the air
With flame of incandescent terror
Of which the tongues declare
The one discharge from sin and error.
The only hope, or else despair
Lies in the choice of pyre or pyre —
To be redeemed from fire by fire.
Who then devised the torment? Love.
Love is the unfamiliar name
Behind the hands that wove
The intolerable shirt of flame
Which human power cannot remove.
We only live, only suspire
Consumed by either fire or fire.

T.S. Eliot, 'Little Gidding'

The mystery of this passion, of the torture, crucifixion and death of this one Jew which took place at that place and time at the hands of the Romans, is to be found in the person and mission of the One who suffered there and was crucified and died.

His *person*: it is the eternal God himself who has given himself in his Son to be one of us and, as one of us, to take upon himself this human passion. His *mission*: it is the Judge who in this passion takes the place of those who ought to be judged, who in this passion allows himself to be judged in their place. . .

It is not simply the humiliation and dishonouring of a creature, of a noble and relatively innocent man that we find here. The problem posed is not that of a theodicy: How can God will this or permit this in the world which he has created good?

It is a matter of the humiliation and dishonouring of God himself, of the question which makes any question of theodicy a complete anticlimax; the question whether, in willing to let this happen to him, he has not renounced and lost himself as God; whether, in capitulating to the folly and wickedness of his creature, he has not abdicated from his deity (as did the Japanese Emperor in 1945); whether he can really die and be dead?

And it is a matter of the answer to this question: that in this humiliation God is supremely God, that in this death he is supremely alive, that he has maintained and revealed his deity in the passion of this man as his eternal Son.

We are not dealing with *any* suffering, but with the suffering of God and this man in the face of the destruction which threatens all creation and every individual. We are dealing with the painful confrontation of God and this man — not merely with any evil, not merely with death, but with eternal death, with the power of that which is not.

Therefore we are not dealing with any sin, or with many sins. . . We are dealing with sin itself and as such the preoccupation, the orientation, the determination of [people] as they have left their place as creatures and broken their covenant with God; the corruption which God has made his own, for which he willed to take responsibility in this one man. . . In the place of all humanity, he has himself wrestled with that which separates them from him. He has borne the consequence of this separation to bear it away.

Karl Barth, *Church Dogmatics*

Death be not proud, though some have called thee
Mighty and dreadful, for, thou art not so,
For, those, whom thou think'st, thou dost overthrow,
Die not, poor death, nor yet canst thou kill me.
From rest and sleep, which but thy pictures be,
Much pleasure, then from thee, much more must flow,
And soonest our best men with thee do go,
Rest of their bones, and soul's delivery.
Thou art slave to fate, chance, kings and
desperate men,
And dost with poison, war, and sickness dwell,
And poppy, or charms can make us sleep as well,
And better than thy stroke; why swellst thou then?
One short sleep past we wake eternally,
And death shall be no more; Death, thou shalt die.

John Donne

If God 'lets himself be pushed out of the world' (Bonhoeffer) and bears the world on the cross as the world which will not bear him, then the being of God is in fact to be thought of as a being which explodes the alternative of presence and absence.

This has its consequences. If God existed only in the sense of worldly presence, then he would be conceived of as a massive superlative of worldly presence, even if this presence were thought of fundamentally as superiority to the world and thus as worldly omnipresence. . .

But if God is present as the one who is absent in the world, if absence is not simply the alternative opposite to the presence of God, then what Bonhoeffer presented as the interpretation of the event of the cross actually expresses [the reality] of the divine being. . . The concept of the omnipresence of God must pass through the eye of the needle of the properly understood concept of the death of God. . .

Talk of the death of God means in its interpretation through the proclamation of the resurrection of Jesus:

(a) that God has involved himself with nothingness;
(b) that God has involved himself with nothingness in the form of a struggle;

(c) that God struggles against nothingness by showing it
   where its place is;
(d) that God gives nothingness a place within being by taking
   it on himself. In that God identified himself with the dead
   Jesus, he located nothingness *within* the divine life. . .

God is that one who can bear and does bear, can suffer
and does suffer in his being the annihilating power of
nothingness, even the negation of death, without being
annihilated by it. . .

As the one who suffers endlessly, God is the *one who
exists for others*. Being for others, he is identical with himself. The localising of nothingness within divine being is,
as an act of God, an act of divine being, an act of divine
self-determination. Whoever really is *for others* and seeks
to *be* himself in that always subjects himself immediately
to nothingness. . .

And so the actual meaning of theological talk about the
death of God is revealed as the most original self-determination of God for *love*, whereby this self-determination
of God itself already belongs to love. God defined himself
as love on the cross of Jesus. God *is* love (1 John 4: 8).

Eberhard Jüngel, *God as the Mystery of the World*

And can it be that I should gain
   An interest in the Saviour's blood?
Died he for me, who caused his pain?
   For me? Who him to death pursued?
Amazing love! How can it be
   That thou, my God, shouldst die for me?
'Tis mystery all: th' Immortal dies!
   Who can explore his strange design?
In vain the firstborn seraph tries
   To sound the depths of love divine.
'Tis mercy all! Let earth adore!
   Let angel minds inquire no more.

Charles Wesley

We shall not cease from exploration
And the end of all our exploring
Will be to arrive where we started

And know the place for the first time.
Through the unknown, remembered gate
When the last of earth left to discover
Is that which was the beginning;
At the source of the longest river
The voice of the hidden waterfall
And the children in the apple-tree
Not known, because not looked for
But heard, half-heard, in the stillness
Between two waves of the sea.
Quick now, here, now, always —
A condition of complete simplicity
(Costing not less than everything)
And all shall be well and
All manner of thing shall be well
When the tongues of flame are in-folded
Into the crowned knot of fire
And the fire and the rose are one.

T.S. Eliot, 'Little Gidding'

Heavenly Father, we praise and thank you for sending your Son our Lord to tread the way of the cross. May his compassion become our motivation, his gentle yet firm resolve the source of our determination. As he drew others after him, may we attract them, too, to share in the work of your loving, redeeming rule.

United, then, in your glorious life of sacrificial giving, may your people lift up Jesus in a world hankering after your powerful presence. May you touch this world afresh with the fire of your love that the Spirit's work to free creation might be advanced — yet not by clever schemes or in manipulative ways, but by the fruit of your enduring. So at the end may the nations of this world come indeed under the Messiah's just and peaceful sway and the whole created order reflect that awesome beauty which is yours alone — and yours alone to share!

Most high,
glorious God,
enlighten the darkness of my heart
and give me, Lord,

a correct faith,
a certain hope,
a perfect charity,
sense and knowledge,
so that I may carry out your holy and true command.

Francis of Assisi

A Benediction

May the God of peace, who brought again from the dead our Lord Jesus, the great Shepherd of the sheep, by the blood of the eternal covenant, equip you with everything good to do his will, and may he work in us what is pleasing to him, through Jesus Christ, to whom be glory for ever and ever! (Hebrews 13: 20–21). Amen.

Listening

Then the Lord answered Job out of the storm. He said: 'Who is this that darkens my counsel with words without knowledge? Brace yourself like a man; I will question you and you shall answer me.'

Then Job replied to the Lord: 'I know that you can do all things; no plan of yours can be thwarted.'

I love you, O Lord, my strength.

Listen and hear my voice; pay attention and hear what I say.

This is what the Sovereign Lord, the Holy One of Israel says: 'In repentance and rest is your salvation, in quietness and trust is your strength. . .'

Listen to me, O Jacob, Israel whom I have called: I am he; I am the first and I am the last.

He withdrew about a stone's throw beyond them, knelt down and prayed, 'Father, if you are willing, take this cup from me; yet not my will, but yours be done.'

Taking the five loaves and the two fish and looking up to heaven, he gave thanks and broke them. Then he gave them to the disciples to set before the people.

At that time Jesus, full of joy through the Holy Spirit, said, 'I praise you, Father, Lord of heaven and earth, because you have hidden these things from the wise and learned, and revealed them to little children. Yes, Father, for this was your good pleasure'.

(Job 38: 1–3; 42: 1–2; Psalm 18: 1; Isaiah 28: 23; 30: 15; 48: 12; Luke 22: 41–42; 9: 16 and 10: 21 — all NIV)

Talking and listening are two mutually dependent activities

and yet we often manage to separate them. We talk to our children, our friends or colleagues, yet frequently show little interest or courtesy in listening to their responses. Conversations with God are similar.

How often have we prayed for effect? Maybe it has been a grand, dramatic gesture with our body or voice or we've expected entertainment from someone else through prayer. The chaplain was asked to say grace. When his voice failed to carry to the president, Lyndon Johnson said: 'Louder, Bill, louder!' The reply came, low and firm: 'Mr President, I am not talking to you.'

Probably we've all prayed with added fervour when it's something we've really wanted — for example, promotion in our jobs, success in examinations or restoration to health. Our talking becomes a pouring out of words without pause or opportunity for reflection. While this type of prayer — asking prayer — is necessary, to receive benefits should not be the only reason for prayer. Talking with God should be an expression of love, of communication between friends at any time in any place, a time of listening as well as speaking.

Jesus prayed often: in different positions, in different settings, sometimes aloud, sometimes alone, sometimes in groups, when he was in anguish, when he was full of joy. His communication with his father was multifaceted. Times set apart for listening as well as talking are essential. If we pray only with busy minds, God may be denied entry and we may fail to hear his words spoken to us. Busyness may be detrimental to our fellowship with God. Jung is said to have remarked that hurry is not of the devil; it *is* the devil.

In the Old Testament story in 1 Kings 20, the person who was asked to look after a prisoner captured in battle allowed him to escape. When called to explain, the excuse was, 'While your servant was busy here and there, the man disappeared.'

The essence of communication and friendship is knowing when to listen and when to speak. The essence of prayer includes the same elements.

The opening verse of the Bible, 'Now the earth was a formless void, there was darkness over the deep, and God's spirit hovered over the water', is describing a present state of affairs, not a past event, and when I pray from the scriptures, I am letting the Spirit of God hover over the chaos and darkness of my being.

When I allow the word of God to hover over my preoccupations, then anything can happen, for he is the God of surprises.

Gerard W. Hughes, *God of Surprises*

He [Eric Liddell] seemed to get his strength and self-discipline and his air of quiet serenity from his early morning sessions of prayer, meditation and Bible study. He would come out from that and stride through the rest of the day as though the Sermon on the Mount was still ringing in his ears. . . Somewhere in this daily discipline of faith lay the secret of the man, perhaps the secret of how he ran.

Sally Magnusson, *The Flying Scotsman*

Through the discipline of contemplative prayer, Christian leaders have to learn to listen again and again to the voice of love and to find there the wisdom and courage to address whatever issue presents itself to them. . . When we are securely rooted in personal intimacy with the source of life, it will be possible to remain flexible without being relativistic, convinced without being rigid, willing to confront without being offensive, gentle and forgiving without being soft, and true witnesses without being manipulative.

Henri Nouwen, *In the Name of Jesus*

It was one of those moments of blinding and yet frighteningly calm insight when the thought goes so deep that it passes beyond reality. The tangible world is no longer seen; all that we see, as though from outside, is the world of our own spirit.

Thus he [Jean Valjean] contemplated himself, as it were, face to face and there arose in his vision, at some mysterious depth, a sort of light resembling that of a torch. But as he looked more closely at this light growing in his consciousness, he saw that it had a human form and that it was the bishop. . .

How long did he stay weeping? What did he then do and where did he go? We do not know. But it is said that on that same night the stage-driver from Grenoble, passing through the Cathedral square in Digne at three in the morning, saw in the shadows the figure of a man kneeling in an attitude of prayer outside the door of Monseigneur Bienvenu.

Victor Hugo, *Les Misérables*

To begin with, we must learn silence — to be still, until we consciously know that God is God and that he is with us at this moment, both as a loving Father and as a mighty God. We must train ourselves to listen to him, to be led by his Spirit in prayer, to be sensitive to his guidance, to understand his will.

David Watson, *Discipleship*

The basic form of divine guidance, therefore, is the presentation to us of positive ideals as guidelines for all our living. 'Be the kind of person that Jesus was. . . know your responsibilities — husbands, to your wives; wives, to your husbands; parents, to your children; all of you, to all your fellow-Christians and all others; know them and seek strength constantly to discharge them' — this is how God guides us through the Bible. . .

J.I. Packer, *Knowing God*

It was, he said, enormous self-deception to believe that the time of prayer must be different from any other. We are equally bound to be one with God by what we do in times of action as by the time of prayer at its special hour. His prayer was simply the presence of God, his soul unconscious of all else but love.

Brother Lawrence, *The Practice of the Presence of God*

He was a very simple old sailor, the skipper of the small boat that was taking them to the Shetlands, and they were a young, lively party, actors and actresses from London on tour, going to do a night or two on the Islands. They were not above 'taking the mickey' a bit and they thought his way of saying grace before meals very quaint and old-fashioned.

However, before long a storm blew up, a really severe north-easter and, as the little ship began to pitch more and more violently, morale among the visitors got lower and lower. A small deputation went up to ask the captain's opinion. 'Well,' he said, 'maybe we'll get through and maybe we won't. I never remember such a storm.'

The news was greeted with dismay down below and finally another deputation went up to the bridge to ask whether perhaps the captain would be so good as to come and say a prayer with his terrified passengers. His reply was simple: 'I say my prayers when it's calm and when it's rough, I attend to my ship.'

Anonymous

Open my eyes that I may see your glory,
Open my ears that I may listen to you speaking to me;
Open my heart that I may love you more perfectly;
Open my mind that I may understand your truth.
Forgive me where my life has been so busy that I've failed to take time to pray;
Forgive me where my mind has been so concerned with my own problems that I've failed to listen to others and especially you.
Thank you for the company of other people — but also for time to myself;
Help me to find solitude to draw closer to you and to use it to listen to you;
Never let me think that I can exist without you,
But draw me closer to you in love. Amen.

A Benediction
May the Lord lead us when we go, and keep us when we sleep, and talk with us when we wake, and may the peace of God which passes all understanding keep our hearts and minds in the knowledge of Christ. Amen.

16

The eloquence of silence

One day Jesus said to his disciples, 'Let us go over to the other side of the lake.' So they got into a boat and set out. As they sailed, he fell asleep. A squall came down on the lake, so that the boat was being swamped, and they were in great danger.

The disciples went and woke him, saying, 'Master, Master, we're going to drown.'

He got up and rebuked the wind and the raging waters; the storm subsided and all was calm. 'Where is your faith?' he asked his disciples.

In fear and amazement they asked one another, 'Who is this? He commands even the winds and the water, and they obey him.'

The Lord said, 'Go out and stand on the mountain in the presence of the Lord, for the Lord is about to pass by.'

Then a great and powerful wind tore the mountains apart and shattered the rocks before the Lord, but the Lord was not in the wind. After the wind there was an earthquake, but the Lord was not in the earthquake. After the earthquake came a fire, but the Lord was not in the fire. And after the fire came a gentle whisper. When Elijah heard it, he pulled his cloak over his face and went out and stood at the mouth of the cave.

For God alone my soul waits in silence.

(Luke 8: 22–25, NIV; 1 Kings 19: 11–13, NIV; Psalm 62: 1, RSV)

The fear of the disciples is the hub of this Gospel event.

They were fishermen who had a natural fear of the sea. They knew that this storm was life-threatening and that no amount of experience would automatically keep them safe.

But there was another fear. In the front of the boat lay Jesus — someone for whom they had been prepared to leave their nets and accept his simple but far-reaching invitation, 'Follow me.' They had remained with him because, in their understanding, he was unique. He was a man of God; no, that definition was inadequate and loose. Later, his disciples would come to say, 'He was fully man and yet fully God in a unique way.' In the early days, they were convinced enough about his uniqueness to remain with him.

But now this man-God lay in the prow of the boat undisturbed while a storm was threatening to end their lives. He seemed oblivious to their needs, indifferent to the storm, so silent. That was the crunch: how can he be God and yet indifferent and silent when all around is disturbance and agitation? One disciple, probably Peter, said, 'Wake up, don't you care that we perish?'

These disciples were not the first to feel the silence of God. Job complained, 'I cry out to you, O God, but you do not answer. I stand up, but you merely look at me.' One of the Psalms begins with 'Why, O Lord, do you stand far off? Why do you hide yourself in times of trouble? (Psalm 10); and the Preacher noted: 'I saw the tears of the oppressed — they have no comforter' (Ecclesiastes 4: 1).

We fear a silent God; but isn't God telling Elijah that silence and stillness are part of his *modus operandi*— maybe even more his style than wind, earthquake and fire? Doesn't God elsewhere suggest that stillness is the right environment for divine knowledge? 'Be still and know that I am God' — like is known by like. Certainly the response of Christ to the disciples when he awakes is 'Where is your faith?' Faith needs to develop as much with the silence of God as it does with his interventions into history.

In the dialogue between God and Job, forty chapters deal with the questions we would like to ask. Most questions challenge the concept of a silent heaven. God's answer was to take Job on a quick tour of the universe to see him at work. He makes Job look at his work in nature and, in most examples, the work of God is performed without noise.

❄❄

We need to find God, and he cannot be found in noise and restlessness. God is the friend of silence. See how nature — trees, flowers, grass — grow in silence: see the stars, the moon and sun, how they move in silence. . . the more we receive in silent prayer, the more we can give in our active life. We need silence to be able to touch souls. The essential thing is not what we say, but what God says to us and through us. All our words will be useless unless they come from within — words which do not give the light of Christ increase the darkness.

Mother Teresa

I believe in the sun even when it is not shining. I believe in love even when I don't feel it. I believe in God even when he is silent.

Words found penned on a prison cell wall in Europe

To preserve the silence within — amid all the noise. To remain open and quiet, a moist humus in the fertile darkness where the rain falls and the grain ripens — no matter how many tramp across the parade-ground in whirling dust under an arid sky. . .

Dag Hammarskjold

Silence is the element in which great things fashion themselves together, that at length they may emerge, full-formed and majestic.

As the Swiss inscription says: 'Speech is silver, silence is golden'. Or, as I might rather express it: 'Speech is of time, silence is of eternity'.

Thomas Carlyle, *Sartor Resartus*

What do I believe? I'm accused of not making it explicit.

How to be explicit about an overreaching grandeur, a daily wrestling match with an opponent whose limbs are never material, whose blood and sweat are scattered on the pages of anything the serious writer writes? Whose essence is contained less in what is said than in the silence?

Patrick White

Not as the songs of other lands
Her song shall be. . .
Her song is silence; unto her
Its mystery clings.
Silence is the interpreter
Of deeper things

George Essex Evans, *An Australian Symphony*

Standing in a karri forest is an experience that every Australian deserves. It may not be as awesome as it was when it was first discovered as all the big trees have gone — the standing trees are all second generation. Fortunately some areas have been set apart as National Park and one day we may see the 'big fellas' again.

The best time in the forest is autumn when the old bark falls off to reveal a beautiful fresh skin of salmon pink wood. It also needs a recent shower to augment the beauty of the trees with the effect that rain and light have in forests. And the smell of eucalypt — the aroma of freshness.

Mostly, the karri forest is still, apart from the sound and sight of the small fantail warbler whose continual nervous movements raise sympathetic thoughts for the workaholics of the world. The karri forest feels like a cathedral and it's easy enough to make the comparison. The large trees look like pillars of pure pink marble rising forty to fifty metres of unbroken bole before the first branch is reached. The smaller trees look like huge organ pipes and at any time you expect to hear the best of Bach.

Both column and organ pipe draw the congregation in an involuntary upward gaze — it can't be helped: everything points upwards to the canopy of karri leaves. Mostly, they hang still in an eloquent silence.

Silence is something we enjoy and fear. We welcome

the occasional quiet that comes, but fear too much quiet. We fear the silence of God. We sympathise with those who feel the silence of God. And we know in truth that God is often silent: in fact, he is mostly silent — but it is easy to mistake the meaning of silence.

In the karri forest, while listening to the silence, you are completely unaware that, while it is a cathedral, it is also a processing factory. Each tree is at work pumping water out of the ground up through those magnificent trunks and transpiring it through the leaves. A normal-sized karri tree transpires 150 000 litres of water per year and in the process produces about 300 kilograms of new wood. In a ten-acre-plot of good karri, there are about 1 000 trees. In one year, that section of forest pumps and transpires 150 million litres and grows about 300 tonnes of high quality karri timber.

Locals say that on a warm day, if you put your ear on the karri, you hear a faint hum of activity — and that is the only sound heard while the forest is at work.

Cavan Brown

With that deep hush subduing all
Our words and works that drown
The tender whisper of thy call,
As noiseless let they blessing fall,
As fell thy manna down.

Drop thy still dews of quietness,
Till all our strivings cease;
Take from our souls the strain and stress,
And let our ordered lives confess
The beauty of thy peace.

Breathe through the heats of our desire
Thy coolness and thy balm;
Let sense be dumb, let flesh retire;
Speak through the earthquake, wind and fire,
O still small voice of calm!

J.G. Whittier (1807–1892)

Lord:
My world is not a silent world.
I am woken by the noise of an alarm
And then the radio, the boiling kettle, electric razor,
Then the transport to work.
Work was once silent, but then someone discovered that
we are more efficient when we work to piped music —
and now even the phone system will not allow silence
while we wait.
For some reason, silence has been connected with emptiness.
And after midday the noise continues.
Homeward bound is still through the space invaded by
noise. The evening meal is against the background noise
of TV, CD and ABC–FM. Some are nice noises, some
grate, some dull and blunt my mind. My emotions are
dragged artificially along the programs filled with fictional
noise. And at the end of the day, I am left to wonder
what has the noise done for me.
But I keep my mind occupied avoiding silence and the
risk of depth. What drives me to remain in the atmos-
phere of noise? Was Pascal right in suggesting that all
our miseries stemmed from a single cause: our inability
to remain quietly in a room?
And I know, Lord, what I need.
I need times of detachment — not merely a sometimes
selfish, irresponsible 'get away from it all', but a 'getting
into' quietness and depth.
I need to know that, as you inhabit eternity, you also
inhabit silence. You are the God who is present and is
mediated in the eloquence of silence.
Forgive me when I come to you in silence and my com-
munication is twitchy. It's hard living at peace with
silence in a world whose heroes are upwardly mobile and
need telephones like the sick need drip feeds.

A Benediction
May silence become for you the well-spring of deep thoughts,
communicative prayer and a clearing house for sorting out what
is of eternity and what is only of time.

A silence most profound

There is a time for everything and a season for every activity under heaven: . . .a time to be silent and a time to speak.

Very early in the morning, while it was still dark, Jesus got up, left the house and went off to a solitary place, where he prayed.

But when you pray, go into your room, close the door and pray to your Father, who is unseen. Then your Father, who sees what is done in secret, will reward you.

. . .the Lord is in his holy temple; let all the earth be silent before him.

Be still, and know that I am God; I will be exalted among the nations, I will be exalted in the earth.

(Ecclesiastes 3: 1 and 7b; Mark 1: 35; Matthew 6: 6; Habakkuk 2: 20; Psalm 46: 10 — all NIV)

Come apart and rest awhile.

Perhaps our greatest need as Christians in this hyper-active world is for time to spend with God. Most Christians are agreed that some time needs to be given to prayer — but there remains a tension between time given to work and time spent in prayer. We must find time for prayer, and this is not always easy — it may even be stressful trying to fit it in.

Sometimes we come to prayer in a state of nervous fretfulness within an exhausted body. What happens to prayer under these conditions? We bring a shopping-list. Or we make a polite and hasty speech, or dutifully intone the liturgical readings of the day. Prayer becomes a chore, or at best a routine, and our daily lives reveal very little change.

What we need, then, is prayer that brings change, that refreshes us and brings new meaningfulness into our lives — prayer as Jesus practised it. When the disciples were beset by so many people that they could scarcely snatch a bite to eat, Jesus said to them: 'Come with me by yourselves to a quiet place and get some rest' (Mark 6: 31, NIV). The invitation still stands: to draw aside and rest awhile, to rest deeply in him.

Jesus found the need for that quiet time alone with God, even spending whole nights in prayer in the remote silence of the hills. The disciples would find him already absorbed in prayer when they went out early looking for him. He would sleep, but he would also seek God's face. In the stillness and the darkness, Jesus encountered his Father and found renewed energy to face the stresses of another day. And because he spent time with the Father in the stillness of the night, Jesus could also find him with ease in the busyness of the day.

Can we also enter into that prayer of deep self-giving to God? A time spent not in *doing* anything, but in simply *being* there with him. It's time well spent, like the time spent together by lovers, whose only need is to be in each other's company.

❧

O God, living Truth, unite me to yourself in everlasting love! Often I am wearied by all I read and hear. In you alone is all that I desire and long for. Therefore let all teachers keep silence, and let all creation be still before you; do you, O Lord, speak alone.

Thomas à Kempis, *The Imitation of Christ*

The great joy of the solitary life is not found simply in quiet in the beauty and peace of nature or in the song of birds or even in the peace of one's own heart. It resides in the awakening and the attuning of the inmost heart to the voice of God — to the inexplicable, quiet definite inner certitude of one's own call to obey him, to hear him, to worship him here, now, today in silence and alone, in the realisation that this is the whole reason for one's existence.

This listening and this obedience make one's existence fruitful and give fruitfulness to all one's other acts. It is the purification and ransom of one's own heart that has been long dead in sin. This is not simply a question of existing alone, but of doing with joy and understanding 'the work of the cell' which is done in silence, not according to one's own choice or to the pressure of necessity, but in obedience to God — that is to say, in obedience to the simple conditions imposed by what is here and now.

The voice of God is not clearly heard at every moment; and part of the 'work of the cell' is *attention*, so that one may not miss any sound of that voice. What this means, therefore, is not only attention to inner grace, but to external reality and to one's self as a completely integrated part of that reality. Hence, this implies also a forgetfulness of oneself as totally apart from outer objects, standing back from outer objects; it demands an integration of one's own life in the stream of natural and human and cultural life of the moment. When we understand how little we listen, how stubborn and gross our hearts are, we realise how important this inner work is. And we see how badly prepared we are to do it.

Thomas Merton, *A Vow to Conversation*

Silence. . .

It is bound to be in the purest part of the soul, in the noblest, in her ground, aye, in the very essence of the soul. That is mid-silence, for thereunto no creature did ever get, nor any image, nor has the soul there either activity or understanding, therefore she is not aware of any image either of herself or any creature.

Whatever the soul effects, she effects with her powers. When she understands, she understands with her intellect. When she remembers, she does so with her memory. When she loves, she does so with her will; she works, then, with her powers and not with her essence. Now every exterior act is linked with some means. The power of seeing is brought into play only through the eyes; elsewhere, she can neither do nor bestow such a thing as seeing.

And so with all the other senses; their operations are always effected through some means or other. But there is no activity in the essence of the soul; the faculties she works with emanate from the ground of the essence, but in her actual ground there is midstillness; here alone is rest and a habitation for this birth, this act wherein God the Father speaks his word, for it is intrinsically receptive of naught save the divine essence, without means.

Meister Eckhardt

In this temple of God, in this the divine dwelling place, God alone rejoices with the soul in the deepest silence. There is no reason for the intellect to stir or seek anything, for the Lord who created it wishes to give it repose here.

Teresa of Avila

> Be still
> Listen to the stones of the wall.
> Be silent, they try
> To speak your
> Name.
> Listen
> To the living walls.
> Who are you?
> Who
> Are you? Whose
> Silence are you?

Thomas Merton, 'In Silence'

. . . the most profound and necessary silence that allows us to live always in the presence of God and to surrender to his communication of himself to us in prompt obedience to his holy will is the harmony between our spirit and God's Spirit. It is here that heart speaks to heart in the language of self-surrendering love.

George A. Maloney, *Inscape*

Let us adore Jesus in our hearts, who spent thirty years out of thirty-three in silence; who began his public life by spending forty days in silence; who often retired alone to spend the night on a mountain in silence. He who spoke with authority now spends his earthly life in silence. Let us adore Jesus in the eucharistic silence.

Mother Teresa of Calcutta

Our whole life, however voiceless it may be — the life of Nazareth or the life of solitude in the desert, just as much as the public life — must preach the gospel by example. Our whole existence, our whole being, must cry the gospel from the rooftops. Our whole person must exude Jesus: all our acts and all our life must cry out that we belong to Jesus and be a portrait of gospel life. All our being must be a living preaching, a reflection of Jesus, a fragrance of Jesus, something that proclaims Jesus, that shows Jesus, that shines like an image of Jesus.

Brother Charles de Foucauld

What can I say to you, my God? I've said so much already. Now it's time to stop talking. And listen. Be here with you. Enjoy your presence. Breathe deeply. Sink deeper and deeper into you. Be enfolded in your embrace and be content. A child resting peacefully in my Father's arms.

A Benediction
May God, the living truth, unite you to himself in everlasting love. May you find in God all you desire and long for. And may you find that most profound and necessary silence that enables you to live always in the presence of God. Amen.

18

How to be a child of God

In days to come
the mountain of the Lord's house
shall be established as the highest of the
mountains,
and shall be raised up above the hills.
Peoples shall stream to it,
and many nations shall come and say:
'Come, let us go up to the mountain of the Lord,
to the house of the God of Jacob;
that he may teach us his ways and
that we may walk in his paths.'
For out of Zion shall go forth instruction,
and the word of the Lord from Jerusalem.
He shall judge between many peoples
and shall arbitrate between strong nations far away;
they shall beat their swords into ploughshares
and their spears into pruning hooks;
nation shall not lift up sword against nation,
neither shall they learn war any more;
but they shall all sit under their own vines
and under their own fig trees
and no-one shall make them afraid;
for the mouth of the Lord of hosts has spoken.

For he is our peace; in his flesh he has made both groups into one and has broken down the dividing wall, that is, the hostility between us. He has abolished the law with its commandments and ordinances, that he might create in himself one new humanity in place of the two, thus making peace, and might reconcile both groups to God in one body through the cross, thus putting to death that hostility through it. So he came and proclaimed peace to you who were far off and peace to those who were near; for through him, both of us have access in one Spirit to the Father.

Peace I leave with you; my peace I give to you.

Blessed are the peacemakers, for they will be called children of God.

(Micah 4: 1–4; Ephesians 2: 14–18; John 14: 27a; Matthew 5: 9 — all NRSV)

There once were two cats of Kilkenny,
Each thought there was one cat too many;
So they fought and they spat,
And they scratched and they bit,
Till, excepting their nails,
And the tips of their tails,
Instead of two cats there weren't any.

The world spends more on arms than it spends on anything else. Wars are as old as history. Only saints and simpletons believe wars in this kind of world will cease. Wars are the ultimate tragedy. Unlike natural disasters they are preventable. Wars mean horrifying injuries: burns, spinal injuries, blindness, loss of limbs. Families lose loved ones. People are wasted in the prime of life.

Views by Christians about war range across a wide spectrum: from fundamentalist preachers in America who bless military weapons, to conscientious pacifists who would not resist an aggressor to protect their own children. It's horrifying to hear sometimes of Christians who find war — or war movies — entertaining. In general, Christians have taken one of three stances on war and peace: pacifism (which probably originated with them), the 'just war', and the Crusade (inherited from the Roman world and the Old Testament).

One of our problems is harmonising the Old Testament with the New Testament. War is a dominant theme in the Old Testament. Yahweh, the God of the Hebrews, is a warrior-God, 'the Lord of Hosts'. He leads his people into battle — defeats the Egyptians, the Canaanites, the Philistines etc. David's military victories make him Israel's greatest hero.

But throughout the Old Testament there is also another view: the promise of 'shalom', peace (Numbers 6: 2; Judges 6: 24; Leviticus 26: 6; etc.). David is not allowed to build the Temple because he is a warrior and has shed blood. The prophets from the eighth century onwards stopped blessing Israel's war and said they deserved punishment instead (Amos 5: 18–20; Zechariah 8: 16ff.), turning their people's gaze towards a future Messianic era of universal peace (Isaiah 10: 12–15; Jeremiah 51; Ezekiel 38–39).

The idea of peace pervades the New Testament even more. Jesus is the Prince of Peace (Luke 1: 77–79, 2: 13–14, cf. Isaiah 9: 1–6). His is a kingdom of peace (Luke 4: 5–8; 19: 33ff.). He promises peace to his followers (John 14: 27; 20: 21) who, through his death, have peace with God (Romans 5: 1; 5: 10; 2 Corinthians 5: 17–19; Colossians 1: 21–22). Indeed, we must look at the Old Testament through the prism of the life and teaching of Jesus.

He taught that his followers must live in peace and be actively engaged in peacemaking — even loving their enemies (Matthew 5: 9, 39, 43–45). The apostles similarly urged the young churches to be communities of peace (Ephesians 4: 3; 1 Thessalonians 5: 13; Colossians 3: 15). The question, 'Whose side is God on in this war?', must always be answered, 'God is on the side of the suffering.'

Any theological understanding of war and peace must begin with the idea of humans — mothers and fathers, sons and daughters — being made in the image of God. What's the most important thing you can say about Saddam Hussein, Adolf Hitler, Pol Pot, Idi Amin? They are like God!

But they — and we all — are like the devil. We want our own way and not God's. We want our own way, even at the expense of others. This is called pride. God, according to James 4: 6, opposes the proud. It's pride that creates an 'us and them' mentality. It's pride that wants to make our nation 'the greatest'. It's pride that makes us want to be number one. A Danish scientist-poet expresses this in the following aphoristic advice:

The noble art of losing face
may one day save the human race
and turn into eternal merit
what weaker minds would call disgrace.

Nations are proud and go to war for all the same reasons individuals fight. And let us be realistic. Nations, like people, are selective about who they fight: they may intervene in a conflict when they shouldn't, or fail to intervene when they should (oil under the ground plays a vital part in the calculation).

What can we do to encourage peace? First, we must affirm that Christians are people of *hope*. Hope leads to action whereas despair leads to apathy. We must develop a vision of 'shalom community', where all are brothers and sisters rather than allies or enemies. We begin with prayer, using the spiritual resources available to us to fight this battle on the spiritual front. Let us then unite with other Christians around the world and with them speak out prophetically against militarism. Humans have been incredibly creative in other directions: we now need new ways of thinking about conflict.

Wars result from teaching children to hate, to fear. Hitler used fear of the Jews to power his juggernaut. (The Fuhrer once said: 'If the Jews didn't exist, we would have to invent them.').

You've got to be taught
to hate and to fear.
You've got to be taught
from year to year.
You've got to be taught
before it's too late.
Before you are six,
or seven or eight.

To hate all the people
Your relatives hate.

Thus wrote Richard Rogers in *South Pacific*.

Every Christian, pacifist or nonpacifist, should pray for peace, should strive for peace and in every way possible turn people's hearts from war to peace; every Christian should keenly anticipate that wonderful time when the Prince of Peace will return to this warring earth and set up a kingdom of peace and justice and love that will never end.

❧

To those who ask us where we have come from or who is our commander, we say that we have come in accordance with the counsels of Jesus to cut down our warlike and arrogant swords of dispute into ploughshares. . . For we can no longer take a sword against a nation, nor do we learn any more to make war, having become [children] of peace for the sake of Jesus, who is our commander.

Origen

Peace has come to mean the time when there aren't any wars or even when there aren't any major wars. Beggars can't be choosers; we'd most of us settle for that. But in Hebrew, 'peace', *shalom*, means 'fullness' — it means 'having everything you need to be wholly and happily yourself'.

One of the titles by which Jesus is known is 'Prince of Peace' and he used the word himself in what seems at first glance to be two radically contradictory utterances. On one occasion he said to the disciples, 'Do not think that I have come to bring peace, but a sword' (Matthew 10: 34). And later on, the last time they ate together, he said to them, 'Peace I leave with you; my peace I give to you' (John 14: 27).

The contradiction is resolved when you realise that, for Jesus, peace seems to have meant not the absence of struggle, but the presence of love.

Frederick Buechner, *Wishful Thinking*

In his epistle, James tells us that our wars and conflicts start out in our hearts, in our disordered motives (James 4: 1–3). And when one Orthodox monk was asked what a monk was, he said, 'A monk is someone who can weep for the whole world.'

John Garvey, *Modern Spirituality: An Anthology*

'Acquire inward peace,' said St Seraphim, 'and a multitude. . . around you will find their salvation.'

Kallistos Ware, 'The Spiritual Father in Orthodox Christianity'

More than half the world's scientists and engineers are working for the military.

David Suzuki, *Inventing the Future: Reflections on Science, Technology and Nature*

The greatest happiness is to scatter your enemy and drive him before you, to see his cities reduced to ashes, to see those who love him shrouded in tears, and to gather to your bosom his wives and daughters.

Genghis Khan

Because [nuclear weapons] are indiscriminate in their effects, destroying combatants and non-combatants alike, it seems clear to me that they are ethically indefensible and that every Christian, whatever he or she may think of the possibility of a 'just' use of conventional weapons, must be a nuclear pacifist.

John Stott

All of this means that for me and my one little life amid the principalities and powers of this day, I want to take this stance of love and humanness and attempt to hold to it against all comers. This will involve starting the battle with evil at the point where I am closest to it; namely, with the evil in my own life.

I have been much impressed lately by Jesus' words in the Sermon: 'Do not judge, so that you may not be judged. . . The measure you give will be the measure you get' (Matthew 7: 1–2). These words are utterly realistic, for whenever I conclude the problem of evil centres in you and moves towards you in attack, your reaction will always be defensive and you will proceed to counter-attack and give me back just what I am giving you. How much better it is to go to work on the beam in my own eye — that is, to begin struggling with evil as I find it manifesting itself in my life.

To this kind of struggle, others with motes in their eyes may come to say: 'Help me, you who obviously realise that you have a problem too. Let's help each other with our common problem of evil.' How much wiser a strategy this is than the self-righteous attack that seems to feel the trouble is all 'over there' and none 'in here'. . .

If we would struggle with the beams in our own eyes, the problem of motes in others might show astonishing improvement. . .

Such a stance of love involves trying to remain human no matter how inhuman the treatment becomes. Thus, I must attempt to keep on listening even when I am no longer listened to, to keep on being sensitive even when others are insensitive to me, to try, like [Jesus] did, 'when reviled, not to revile in return'.

Now to be sure, it may not work. In such a stance, I realise I could get run over by the Juggernaut and nothing at all would remain to show for so fragile an approach. But even at that, it would be going down at one's best and not at one's worst by trying to remain human and not get sucked into the swirl of inhumanity. If I have got to go down, that is the way I would most prefer to go. . .

And by God's help, this is what I most want to do. Will you join me? If there is any hope, this has to be the way!

John R. Claypool, 'Living by the Sword'

About five years ago I was reading a book about the war and someone who was in a concentration camp There was a part in it that was so horrible that I would not have been able to read it if I had known what was coming — and I was absolutely shaken by the cruelty of it. The awful thing was that I put the book down and I knew for the first time how it could have happened and I thought, 'It could have been me, committing those atrocities.'

I don't think I've ever been able to pray in the same way since. I can only pray now in penitence and in adoration because God is so tremendous when you set him against what you are.

Anonymous woman in a radio interview

Thank you, Lord, that you bring hope to this world,
which is otherwise hopelessly lost.
Lord, we praise you — we believe you are victorious!
Thank you for the opportunity to live in these times,
To serve you and witness to your kingdom in this
moment of history,
To find your presence in the heart of the ever-escalating
arms race,
To find you in the faces of the homeless and oppressed.
Lord, you are with us and we thank you.

Dawn Longenecker, Sojourners Peace Ministry

Lord, make me an instrument of your peace;
where there is hatred, let me sow love,
where there is injury, pardon,
where there is doubt, faith,
where there is despair, hope,
where there is sadness, joy.

O Divine Master,
Grant that I may not so much
seek to be consoled as to console,
to be understood as to understand,
to be loved as to love;
For it is in giving that we receive,
it is in pardoning that we are pardoned,
it is in dying that we are born
to eternal life.

St Francis of Assisi

Eternal God, our Father,
may your Spirit of peace speak to us
in such a way
that we live out our lives
with the conviction that
'all that is necessary
for the forces of evil
to win the world
is for good people
to do nothing'.
Lord, give us:
the serenity to accept
what cannot be changed;
the courage to change
what ought to be changed;
and the wisdom to distinguish
the one from the other.

War, Peace and the Bible

Jesus our inspiration, you come in the evening as our doors are
shut and bring peace.
Grant us sleep tonight, and courage tomorrow to go wherever
you lead. Amen.

A New Zealand Prayer Book

A Benediction
Go with understanding, have courage, always keep your in-
tegrity; encourage those who have no hope, support the weak,
confront the strong. Love and serve the Lord. And may the
grace, mercy and peace of God the Father, Son and Holy Spirit
go with you always. Amen.

God in the emptiness

In the beginning, God created the heavens and the earth. Now the earth was a formless void, there was darkness over the deep, and God's spirit hovered over the water.

Come, behold the works of the Lord;
see what desolations he has brought on the earth.
He makes wars cease to the ends of the earth;
he breaks the bow and shatters the spear;
he burns the shields with fire.
Be still, and know that I am God!
I am exalted among the nations,
I am exalted in the earth.

But the Lord says: 'Do not cling to the things of the past or dwell on what happened long ago. Watch for the new thing I am going to do. It is happening already — you can see it now! I will make a road through the wilderness and give you streams of water there.'

Thus says the Lord who made you, who formed you in the womb and will help you: . . .'I will pour water on the thirsty land, and streams on the dry land. I will pour out my spirit upon your descendants and my blessing on your offspring.'

Let the same mind be in you that was in Christ Jesus who, though he was in the form of God, did not regard equality with God as something to be exploited, but emptied himself, taking the form of a slave, being born in human likeness. And being found in human form, he humbled himself and became obedient to the point of death — even death on a cross.

For you know how generous our Lord Jesus Christ has been: he was rich, yet for your sake he became poor, so that through his poverty you might become rich.

At midday a darkness fell over the whole land, which lasted till three in the afternoon; and at three Jesus cried aloud, *Eli, Eli, lema sabachthani?*, which means, 'My God, my God, why hast thou forsaken me?'

The righteous one, my servant, shall make many righteous, and he shall bear their iniquities. Therefore I will allot him a portion with the great and he shall divide the spoil with the strong; because he poured out himself to death and was numbered with the transgressors; yet he bore the sin of man and made intercession for the transgressors.

Jesus said, 'Leave her alone. She bought it so that she might keep it for the day of my burial. You always have the poor with you, but you do not always have me.'

Jesus. . . began to speak, and taught them, saying: 'Blessed are the poor in spirit, for theirs is the kingdom of heaven.'

(Genesis 1: 1–2, JB; Psalm 46, 8–10, NRSV; Isaiah 43: 18–19, GNB; Isaiah 44: 2–3, NRSV; Philippians 2: 5–8, NRSV; 2 Corinthians 8: 9, NEB; Mark 15: 33–34, NEB; Isaiah 53: 11–12; John 12: 7–8; Matthew 5: 2–3 — all NRSV)

Jesus said, 'You always have the poor with you, but you do not always have me.'

What does Jesus mean by this reference to the poor? It sounds as if he is saying that it's all right to forget about the poor if you are doing something for Jesus. But that's the very opposite of all his other teachings and actions. All through the Gospels, Jesus shows a special concern for the poor and outcast — and he rejects any kind of devotion to God that neglects the needy and dispossessed.

Obviously Mary, the one who provoked Jesus to make this statement by anointing him with oil, had saved her money — perhaps these were her life's savings. She had been careful up to now, perhaps, but now is the time for action. She senses something about Jesus, that in fact his burial is not one day — a day in the future or a day in the past — but that every day Jesus is being buried and every day he is being cut down and put away and laid to rest by those who would rather him be out of their way. . .

The day of his burial is today. That's her point. And now is the very best time to pour out your love for him. The silent Mary speaks volumes with her love.

Jesus in these words addresses Judas and his concern for economics, for a rational allocation of resources. And Jesus addresses all those who are tired and weary from carrying heavy loads, including heavy loads of care. And this I think is what he says: Look to this woman, listen to the song of her love and learn from her.

Mary has decided to focus on the death of Jesus and if we will really do that and not flinch from what it means for our lives, we will find healing and new life.

The way of the cross transforms all the values and concerns of our lives. Judas, you see, wanted to avoid bankruptcy. He wanted to be able to cope. When someone came to the door, he wanted to be able to give them something. But the cross is about *having nothing left*. It is about being empty and being poured out into emptiness.

The way of the cross is about having nothing to give and nothing to say. In fact, it is about becoming poor: poor and contrite of spirit, broken with the broken, weeping with the weeping, defeated with all those who cannot defend themselves.

And, at this cross, we discover something else about the poor. We do not only have them with us always, but it can be a *blessing* that we have them with us. For Jesus is with them; in their faces we see our Lord; he comes to us among the least of his little ones; and, more than that, in giving, we find we receive grace and peace and joy we did not have.

That is Jesus' response to the economics of Judas and the weariness of the compassion-fatigued. He poured out himself, even as Mary poured out her love. For in this story it is Mary who is a parable of God's grace, poured out for the world. This is the image of God 'inside-out': not a deity centred within itself, but a personal God who centres upon others, who pours out the Spirit, giving life and healing and becoming empty with us and for us.

In Mary, as in Jesus, we see the God who becomes empty, poured out in suffering love. The cross is what God is like; and here we learn to find God in the emptiness. Indeed, it may be that this is how best we can know him: God in the emptiness, the sacred void.

❧❧

I have spoken of the stage of emptiness largely as if it were something that occurs solely within the minds and souls of the individuals present. Pseudocommunity, chaos and emptiness are not so much individual stages as group stages. The transformation of a group from a collection of individuals into genuine community requires little deaths in many of those individuals. But it is also a process of group death, group dying. . . When its death has been completed, open and empty, the group enters community. In this final stage, a soft quietness descends. It is a kind of peace. The room is bathed in peace.

M. Scott Peck, *The Different Drum: Community Making and Peace*

The God who lets us live in the world without the working hypothesis of God is the God before whom we stand continually. Before God and with God we live without God. God lets himself be pushed out of the world on to the cross. He is weak and powerless in the world, and that is precisely the way, the only way, in which he is with us and helps us. Matthew 8: 17 makes it quite clear that Christ helps us, not by virtue of his omnipotence, but by virtue of his weakness and suffering.

Dietrich Bonhoeffer, *Letters and Papers from Prison*

The question now demanding our response is much more radical: 'Who is God?'

The answer is, God is the God of Jesus Christ. That is, God is a God who saves us not through his domination, but through his suffering. Here we have Bonhoeffer's famous thesis of *God's weakness*. It will make its mark in theology after he is gone. It is of this God, and only of this God, that the Bible tells us. . .

But here we strike bottom, too. Here we are at the very heart of things. The cup of humanity's maturity must be drunk to the dregs. The correct response to modernity is not to place God beyond the limits of reason, or drag him into history from the outside, or domesticate him in 'religious sentiment,' or bottle him up in bourgeois mentality by making belief in him a human excellence. Nor again is it the answer to assert that to move away from him is the destruction of the root of all human culture. Nor, finally, is the answer to make of him the object of a free personal decision. God in Christ is a God suffering, and to share in his weakness is to believe in him. This is what it means to be a Christian.

Gustavo Gutierrez,
The Power of the Poor in History

When the crucified Jesus is called the 'image of the invisible God', the meaning is that *this* is God and God is like *this*.

God is not greater than he is in this humiliation. God is not more glorious than he is in this self-surrender. God is not more powerful than he is in this helplessness. God is not more divine than he is in this humanity. The nucleus of everything that Christian theology says about 'God' is to be found in this Christ event.

The Christ event on the cross is a God event. And, conversely, the God event takes place on the cross of the risen Christ. Here God has not just acted externally, in his unattainable glory and eternity. Here he has acted in himself and has gone on to suffer in himself. Here he himself is love with all his being. So the new christology which tries to think of the 'death of Jesus as the death of God' must take up the elements of truth which are to be found in kenoticism (the doctrine of God's emptying of himself).

Jürgen Moltmann, *The Crucified God*

The God who is silent and emptied, however, is not a God of remoteness and impotence. This God from the beginning is one who broods over his creation, bringing order out of chaos, new life out of the old, sustaining life, imparting grace and directing his purposes. . .

Australian theology needs a desert dawn. It needs to see that the image of the brooding, controlling, creating and caring Spirit has the potential to create fresh forms of thinking about God, fresh expressions of worship that arise from the green eucalypts and red ochres of the Australian soil, and fresh expressions of evangelism that touch the Australian soul. Fear of fresh forms is out of sync with a continent that is emotionally captured best in a desert dawn. . . The Creator Spirit continues to brood over creation, replacing old forms with new forms and creating life with the quality of freshness. When the forms of Israel became tired in the time of the prophets, the Spirit said through them:

See, I am doing a new thing!
Now it springs up; do you not perceive it?
I am making a way in the desert
And streams in the wasteland (Isaiah 43: 19).

Cavan Brown, Pilgrim through this Barren Land

The self-emptying of the Son also expresses the self-emptying of the Father. Christ is crucified 'in the weakness of God' (2 Corinthians 13: 4). In the forsakenness of the Son, the Father also forsakes himself. In the surrender of the Son, the Father also surrenders himself. But not in the same way. For Jesus suffers dying in forsakenness, but not death itself; for it is impossible to 'suffer' death, since suffering presupposes life. But the Father who abandons him and delivers him up suffers the death of the Son in the infinite grief of love.

Here the Father is not in confrontation with Jesus as 'dominating, almighty Father', or as a God who, feeling no pain himself, causes pain. For where the Son goes, the Father goes, too.

Jürgen Moltmann, The Way of Jesus Christ

Neither silence nor inarticulateness necessarily mean absence of spiritual depth. The lack of expression may be merely an absence of the skill or opportunity to name what is most meaningful; or, more simply, for whatever reason, having no desire to do so.

There are reasons in Australian history for both these possibilities: our antipodean isolation, the brutality of our historical origins as a 'cesspool. . . the dregs of the offscourings of all mankind' (Bishop Ullathorne), a general sense of something new struggling for expression in the harsh, raw world of Down Under. What Australians were about looked like 'nothing' compared to older habits of thought and expression. Australia had entered into a kind of cultural 'cloud of unknowing', its own *via negativa*, in which the lush ideologies and cultured thinking of the old countries had to be denied before the new reality could be expressed.

Yet something was going on, even if it never reached full philosophical expression or merited the attention of the theological traditions available to us: we were involved in something, a new way of being human, in the living and dying demanded in the conditions of 'Down Under'. . . There is something about us Australians that prefers to communicate in silences rather than in words. Perhaps we are defeated by it all, tongue-tied in the presence of ultimate things. Perhaps we feel safer with the great things left unsaid, meaning them only in silence: we, the inarticulate, offering our homage to the ineffable.

Ultimate truths are not to be captured in any expression. They are not the exclusive possession of anyone; nor are they to be taken merely on anyone's authority. For someone to really know these things is to keep a decent reserve, to hold what is sacred in silence.

I suppose it blends in with all the other silences about us — the haunting silence of the bush; the daunting silence of the desert; the surrounding silence of the sea; even the silence of our conversations when, as we talk of sport or work, or yarn over the fence in the front garden, we are quietly assessing whether someone is really a good bloke, or whether some woman is. . . well, what do we say when we admire women and never quite know how to express it?

Tony Kelly, *A New Imagining: Towards an Australian Spirituality*

But this land before all others is one where the claim of the creator Spirit to be present and active before anything that human life can conceive is to be tested in the desert experience. One enters the desert to find freedom and life. There the people found their identity and their dependence. Justice is given in the desert along with the demands that flow from those claims. In the desert is the cry of hope and the word of waiting. There the decisions for transformative action are wrestled through and owned.

In all this, the Spirit claims to be present as creative energy and energising life. When the desert is seen as arid with no life, the Spirit has not departed, but is blocked from vision. Where the struggle demands so much that there is no energy for living beyond the totally absorbing demands for survival, the Spirit is not engaged. But where the desert way opens the possibility for hope and vision, the Spirit who has been from the beginning can act to reveal the sacred places or envision the new future, when God will again be deliverer.

Naming the response to this type of experience is also part of recognising the new forms of living in the Spirit in the desert places.

The Desert is Alive

Christianity presents us with a man upon a cross, a man whose teaching still has the power to thrill, whatever we believe about him, a man who gave everything away in love for others, even life itself. And it points to this man in his death-agony and says that there, in utter complete self-giving, there alone is what satisfies totally.

Most of us have brief moments when we know with absolute certainty that so to give ourselves away in love is the full, perfect satisfaction for which we crave. But such moments do not stay. The Crucified soon passes in a cloud out of our sight. And we are left only half-believing, left to win the truth for ourselves, by trial and error, by false hopes and shattered illusions, and by joy unspeakable and full of glory.

H.A. Williams, *The True Wilderness*

So crush all knowledge and experience of all forms of created things, and of yourself above all. For it is on your own self-knowledge and experience that the knowledge and experience of everything else depend. Alongside this self-regard, everything else is quickly forgotten. For if you will take the trouble to test it, you will find that when all other things and activities have been forgotten (even your own), there still remains between you and God the stark awareness of your own existence. And this awareness, too, must go, before you experience contemplation in its perfection.

The Cloud of Unknowing

The future is somehow. . .
somewhere in the despised and neglected desert,
the belly of the country
not the coastal rind.
The secret is in the emptiness.
The message is the thing we have feared,
the thing we have avoided
that we have looked at and skirted.
The secret will transform us
and give us the heart to transform emptiness.
If we go there,
if we go there and listen
We will hear the voice of the eternal.
The eternal says that we are at the beginning of time.

David Ireland, *A Woman of the Future*

Holy God:
How different you are from all my imaginings!
How swiftly and simply you break down all my chosen
ideas of you, all my images and idols.

You leave me nowhere to hide.
You are so different — so holy, and yet closer to me than
breathing. You are with me.
All my spiritual riches are brought to nothing. Yet in my
poverty, there you are.
Help me to understand that you empty yourself for my
sake, you pour yourself out in love for me, as for all the
world:
all that I see and sense, all that meets me has its origin in you;
yours is the food, the friendship, the truth that nourishes
and guides me;
yours, too, is the challenge and struggle that goads me to
grow;
yours is the love that suffers for my healing.

O God of Jesus, self-emptying God: in the emptiness of my
place, my land, my experiences, so often I see nothing. I despair.
I turn to dust. This day and every day remake me with the
same hovering Spirit, the Spirit of hope in the desert, till I see
that all my emptiness is tinged with the splendour of your peace.
In the name of the Crucified One. Amen.

A Benediction
Go now, into the emptiness, without fear.
Share the poverty of all God's children, with courage and
with hope.
Trust in the creative, hovering Spirit,
set your sights on the Crucified One,
and the peace of God be with you, always. Amen.

Praise be!

Sing to the Lord, all the earth. Tell of his salvation from day to day. Declare his glory among the nations, his marvellous works among all the peoples. For great is the Lord and greatly to be praised; he is to be revered above all gods. For all the gods of the peoples are idols, but the Lord made the heavens. Honour and majesty are before him; strength and joy are in his place.

Great and amazing are your deeds, Lord God the Almighty! Just and true are your ways, king of the nations! Lord, who will not fear and glorify your name? For you alone are holy. All nations will come and worship before you, for your judgments have been revealed.

O come let us sing to the Lord; let us make a joyful noise to the rock of our salvation! Let us come into his presence with thanksgiving; let us make a joyful noise to him with songs of praise! For the Lord is a great king above all gods. In his hand are the depths of the earth; the heights of the mountains are his also. The sea is his, for he made it, and the dry land, which his hands have formed. O come let us worship and bow down, let us kneel before the Lord our Maker!

He [Christ] is the image of the invisible God, the firstborn of all creation; for in him all things in heaven and on earth were created, things visible and invisible, whether thrones or dominion or rulers or powers — all things have been created through him and for him.

But the hour is coming, and is now here, when the true worshippers will worship the Father in spirit and truth, for the Father seeks such as these to worship him.

God is spirit, and those who worship him must worship in spirit and truth.

Therefore God also highly exalted [Christ] and gave him the name that is above every name so that at the name of Jesus every knee should bend, in heaven and on earth and under the earth, and every tongue confess that Jesus Christ is Lord to the glory of God the Father.

He was revealed in flesh, vindicated in spirit, seen by angels, proclaimed among Gentiles, believed in throughout the world, taken up in glory.

He is the reflection of God's glory and the exact imprint of God's very being, and he sustains all things by his powerful word.

Jesus said to him, 'Away with you Satan! For it is written, "Worship the Lord your God and serve only him".'

My soul magnifies the Lord, and my spirit rejoices in God my Saviour.

Ascribe to the Lord, O heavenly beings, ascribe to the Lord glory and strength. Ascribe to the Lord the glory of his name, worship the Lord in holy splendour.

(1 Chronicles 16: 23–27; Revelation 15: 3–4; Psalm 95: 1–6; Colossians 1: 15–16; John 4: 23–24; Philippians 2: 9–11; 1 Timothy 3: 16; Hebrews 1: 3; Matthew 4: 10; Luke 1: 46–47; Psalm 29: 1–2 — all NRSV)

We humans give praise and honour to those people and things which we find especially pleasing and outstanding. We applaud outstanding achievement, we photograph beauty, we celebrate fine acting with Oscars and Emmys and Tonys and Logies. All of these are, in fact, ways in which we 'worship' others.

Certainly, then, when we look around at what God has done, we can hardly justify doing anything less than giving him the highest worship possible. For he has proven himself to be the best at everything! His creation is magnificent! All we have to do is look at one beautiful sunrise or sunset, ponder the majesty of a snow-capped mountain range, or consider the vastness of an ocean and we realise that no human could ever accomplish such a feat. Scientists could never have created an organism as wonderfully complex and ingeniously designed as the human body, for example.

These reasons alone are enough to bring many of us to a place where we worship God for who he is and what he has done. But beyond this, we can discover so much more for which we might worship him. We can turn to God for help and guidance and know that, because he is all-knowing, we will receive the best guidance possible. When troubled, we can seek his comfort and loving care and know that no-one will care more for us — after all, he did give his Son for us, that we might experience forgiveness and have life forever with him.

How do we worship him? We go to a church service and call it worship. But our worship of God is far more than a mere hour of singing songs of praise and listening to someone else pray and read the Bible and explain how to apply the Bible reading to life. Worship is to be an ongoing process. It is something we do all the time, not just an hour or two a week.

Worship means 'worthship', giving God praise for his worthiness. We can praise him in our everyday choice of words. We can praise him in our attitude toward life — no matter how routine or dull or boring particular tasks may be. We can praise him as we meet others — caring about their needs and placing them above our own.

Paul says that we are to present our bodies to God as a living sacrifice, holy and acceptable to him. That, says Paul, is our 'spiritual worship' (Romans 12: 1). In other words, all that we do and say and are can be worship of God — but it can just as easily show contempt for him and rejection of his love.

❦

Worship and prayer are not ways in which we express ourselves, but ways in which we hold up before the Father his beloved Son, take refuge in his atoning sacrifice and make that our only plea. . . In worship and prayer, Jesus

Christ acts in our place and on our behalf in both a representative and a substitutionary way so that what he does in our stead is nevertheless effected as our very own, issuing freely and spontaneously out of ourselves.

Thomas F. Torrance, *The Mediation of Christ*

If worship does not change us, it has not been worship. To stand before the holy one of eternity is to change. . . If worship does not propel us into greater obedience, it has not been worship. Just as worship begins in holy expectancy, it ends in holy obedience.

Richard J. Foster, *Celebration of Discipline*

Happy are the simple followers of Jesus Christ who have been overcome by his grace and are able to sing the praises of the all-sufficient grace of Christ with humbleness of heart. Happy are they who, knowing that grace, can live in the world without being of it; who, by following Jesus Christ, are so assured of their heavenly citizenship that they are truly free to live their lives in this world. Happy are they who know that discipleship simply means the life which springs from grace and that grace simply means discipleship. Happy are they who have become Christians in this sense of the word. For them, the word 'grace' has proved a fount of mercy.

Dietrich Bonhoeffer, *The Cost of Discipleship*

My whole body, soul and spirit become engaged in rehearsing the work of Christ which gives shape and form to my life. It is the source of my values, the energy that holds my family together and the purpose of my work. Worship connects me with the past, gives meaning in the present and inspires hope for the future as my soul and spirit become blended again into the drama of Christ's life, death and resurrection.

Robert E. Webber, *Worship is a Verb*

Jesus Christ in his own self-oblation to the Father is our worship and prayer in an acutely personalised form, so that it is only through him and in him that we may draw near to God with the hands of our faith filled with [nothing else].

Thomas F. Torrance, *The Mediation of Christ*

We must listen carefully to the scriptures as they are read and expounded, discipline our minds to concentrate on the words of the hymns we sing and the prayers we pray, and open them to receive the truth God wants to share with us. Even if we engage in periods of corporate silence such as are advocated by some traditions within the church or, going to the other extreme, [engage in] the kind of corporate 'singing in tongues' to be found in charismatic circles today, our minds are still not to be blank, but rather concentrated on the Lord we seek to adore.

Howard Belben, *Ministry in the Local Church*

In summarising what is required for the true knowledge of God, we have taught that we cannot conceive him in his greatness without being immediately confronted by his majesty and so compelled to worship him.

John Calvin, *Institutes of the Christian Religion*

Teach me that worship in spirit and truth is not of [humans] but only comes from thee; that it is not only a thing of times and seasons, but the outflowing of a life in thee. Teach me to draw near to God in prayer under the deep impression of my ignorance and my having nothing in myself to offer him and, at the same time, thou my Saviour, [may there be] the Spirit's breathing in my childlike stammerings.

Andrew Murray, *With Christ in the School of Prayer*

Wonderful God, Father of glory, my God and Father, accept the desire of your child who has seen that your glory alone is worth living for. O Lord, show me your glory. Let it overshadow me. Let it fill the temple of my heart. Let me dwell in it as revealed in Christ. And Father, I pray that you might fulfil in me your own good pleasure, that I should find glory in seeking your glory. Amen.

A Benediction

To him who is able to keep you from falling and to present you before his glorious presence without fault and with joy — to the only God our Saviour be glory, majesty, power and authority, through Jesus Christ our Lord, before all ages, now and forevermore! Amen.

Come let us worship

I will celebrate your love for ever, Lord,
age after age my words shall proclaim your faithfulness;
for I claim that love is built to last forever
and your faithfulness founded firmly in the heavens.
Some of the Pharisees in the crowd said to him,
'Teacher, order your disciples to stop.' He answered, 'I
tell you, if these were silent, the stones would shout out.'
Then I heard every creature in heaven and on earth
and under the earth and in the sea, and all that is in
them, singing:
'To the one seated on the throne and to the lamb
be blessing and honour and glory and might forever
and ever!'
And the four living creatures said, 'Amen!' And the
elders fell down and worshipped.

(Psalm 89: 1–2; Luke 19: 39–40, NRSV; Revelation 5: 13–14, NRSV)

Christian worship has a shape, a form — a shape and a
form that show movement. Worship is an art form and
an activity. Worship resumes and repeats the falling and
rising, the 'with-us' and 'unto-him'. Have you noted, for
example, the moving form of the Lord's Prayer?

It begins in heaven:

Our Father, who art in heaven,
Hallowed be Thy name

Then it moves earthward:

Thy kingdom come,
Thy will be done on earth

It stays with us:

Give us this day. . .
Forgive us. . .
Lead us not. . .
Then it returns:
For thine is the kingdom. . .
The Doxology is another example of the movement of worship: from him, to us, to him — the circuit of grace.
It begins with God:
Praise God
Then it moves earthward:
From whom all blessings flow,
It stays with us:
Praise him all creatures here below,
Then it returns:
Praise him above ye heavenly host,
It reaches its goal:
Praise Father, Son and Holy Ghost.
In Christian worship, we recapitulate the art of God, the movement of love, the circuit of grace which is the initiative of revelation and the response of faith. The two basic characteristic moments and movements of Christian worship are revelation and response — and in that order. Christian worship recapitulates and reflects the Christian gospel: the gospel of incarnation, the coming of God, the lodging of God in the human heart, the return of God to himself.

❦

How seldom one takes part in a church service which goes to the marrow and causes us to experience the spiritual power of God's word in a living congregation. When it does happen, it gives the most uplifting joy one can encounter. In fact, I still draw sustenance from the few times I have experienced it.

Helmut Thielicke, *African Diary*

Why do people come to church? he asked himself. To satisfy an old habit? To be entertained and instructed? To be edified? What makes people leave their work or their homes, the possibility of enjoying themselves in the open air, to go into a church building when the bells begin to ring? They expect something. They are looking for the presence of God.

But how are they to find God? How is he present? Certainly not as when the divine presence is sensed in the beauties of nature, of music and the arts, of personal relationships. If God is present in church, he must be present in the forms of praying and singing, of reading and hearing the Bible, of preaching. Preaching, above all, is the way in which God is brought to a particular congregation on a particular Sunday morning.

John Bowden, *Karl Bath*

To worship is to quicken the conscience by the holiness of God, to feed the mind with the truth of God, to purge the imagination by the beauty of God, to open the heart to the love of God, to devote the will to the purpose of God.

William Temple, *Readings in St John's Gospel*

Kierkegaard said that many people go to church as they would go to the theatre, expecting to hear a performance by the minister and to judge how well he does. But in reality, he declared, the roles are quite different. In church, it is the hearer who is on the stage, under the spotlight. The preacher is the prompter who is just off the scene, whispering the lines to the players. If they forget their parts, he is there to remind them. The hearer, out on the stage, is supposed to catch the prompter's lines and work them into their act. The audience, who is watching the players and judging how well they do their parts, is Almighty God.

George Sweazy, *Preaching the Good News*

All ministries and the ministry of all come together in divine service or worship. For all receive their call and promise from common hearing. All answer what is heard in common prayer. All join in festal praise of him who calls them. All bow in common repentance in confession of their continuing guilt. Through the gospel, all receive together remission from their guilt and bondage. All begin their way together in baptismal calling and all celebrate fellowship with their Lord and with one another at his table.

Strengthened by commissioning and promise, all are sent out together, with a parting blessing to tasks and burdens and joys and even loneliness and enforced inactivity (in age or sickness). The Christian life begins, continues and ends in worship.

Helmut Thielicke, *The Evangelical Faith*

Christian worship is above all a corporate act. We pray, 'Our Father'. As soon as we become Christians, there is a sense in which we cease to be individuals and we become members of a great community in Christ. I can lose my uncertainty in the certainty of the whole church, of the whole company of God's worshipping people. My faith may be puny and meagre and inadequate but, when I enter into the church, I enter into the tradition and a heritage which is far beyond anything I, as an individual, possess. I am no longer under the grim necessity of being unable to go beyond what I believe; I can remember what we believe and take comfort in that. I can even, in my belief, unite myself with the fellowship of all believers.

William Barclay

What we must see is [that] the real question in worship is not 'What will meet my need?' The real question is 'What kind of worship does God call for?' Real worship thus demands the discipline of submission. If worship does not change us, it has not been worship. To stand before the Holy One of eternity is to change. Worship begins with holy expectancy and propels us into greater obedience. Willard Sperry declared, 'Worship is a deliberate and disciplined adventure in reality.'

Who pastors the pastor? The organist, the choir and the congregational singing minister to me in a significant way. In the music of the church I am incorporated into the larger whole. Here my normal solo existence joins with the people of God; here I am strengthened by our common praise of God.

Kelvin Yelverton

Worship the Lord in the beauty of holiness,
Bow down before him, his glory proclaim;
Gold of obedience and incense of lowliness
Bring and adore him; the Lord is his name!

Low at his feet lay thy burden of carefulness,
High on his heart he will bear it for thee,
Comfort thy sorrows and answer thy prayerfulness,
Guiding thy steps as may best for thee be.

Fear not to enter his courts in the slenderness
Of thy poor wealth thou wouldst reckon as thine;
Truth in its beauty and love in its tenderness —
These are the offerings to lay on his shrine.

These, though we bring them in trembling and fear-fulness,
He will accept for the name that is dear;
Mornings of joy give for evenings of tearfulness,
Trust for our trembling and hope for our fear.

J.S.B. Monsell

Since I am coming to that holy room
Where with the choir of saints for evermore,
I shall be made thy music; as I come
I tune the instrument here at the door,
And what I must do then, think here before.

John Donne

Eternal God, we who meet in one church building in one town of one country, remember now the millions of people who today, in many towns, villages and cities, offer you worship. Our language is different, but our worship is one; different in nationality and race, our praise is united.
    Let all the world join its praise so that one great chorus of

adoration and love is offered up to you, our God and Father.
                                        Roy Chapman and Donald Hilton

A Benediction
Now, Lord, let your servant go in peace:
Your word has been fulfilled.
My eyes have seen the salvation
which you have prepared in the sight of every people;
a light to reveal you to the nations
and the glory of your people Israel.

                                        Luke 2: 29–32

22

Renewing the 'our' of prayer

Beware of practising your piety before others in order to be seen by them; for then you have no reward from *your Father* in heaven.

So whenever you give alms, do not sound a trumpet before you, as the hypocrites do in the synagogues and in the streets, so that they may be praised by others. Truly I tell you, they have received their reward. But when you give alms, do not let your left hand know what your right hand is doing, so that your alms may be done in secret; and *your Father* who sees in secret will reward you.

And whenever you pray, do not be like the hypocrites; for they love to stand and pray in the synagogues and at the street corners, so that they may be seen by others. Truly I tell you, they have received their reward. But whenever you pray, go into your room and shut the door and pray to *your Father* who is in secret; and *your Father* who sees in secret will reward you.

When you are praying, do not heap up empty phrases as the Gentiles do; for they think that they will be heard because of their many words. Do not be like them, for *your Father* knows what you need before you ask him.

Pray then in this way: Our Father in heaven hallowed by your name. . .

(Matthew 6: 1–9, NRSV, emphasis added)

When Jesus prays to his Father, he invites us to stand and pray with him, saying, 'Our Father' — that is, his Father and your Father. As our mediator and advocate, Jesus not only prays in company *with* us as we pray, but he also prays to the Father on *behalf* of us as we pray through him. This is the essence of what it means to pray 'in the name of Jesus'.

To pray in Jesus' name, therefore, is to take refuge in the prayer ministry of Christ our high priest. He constantly appears before the Father with a prayer on his lips and a burden on his heart for us. As our mediator, he doesn't merely stand between us and the Father, bridging the gap, as it were. Rather, as advocate and mediator, Christ bears us on his breast, presenting us personally to our heavenly Father. This is consistent with the Old Testament image, where the priest wore a breastpiece bearing the names of the Israelites upon his heart before the Lord continually (Exodus 28: 29–30).

This is why prayer in Jesus' name works. For all human prayer is grounded in Christ's personal relationship to the Father. Our prayers, which are offered in Jesus' name, are mingled with the prayers of Christ offered to the Father for us. This, and only this, makes our prayers efficacious. Our feeble prayers are charged, transformed and sanctified by the pure and perfect prayers of Jesus.

Christ's mediation in prayer, therefore, should be understood in this personal, relational sense. It is not merely Christ representing us to the Father on account of our unworthiness to approach him on our own terms. It goes far beyond this. Christ our mediator draws us with him into the Father's presence, where we can address *our* mutual Father directly, not in our name, but in Jesus' name (John 16: 16–28; Hebrews 4: 16).

Therefore, when I pray, 'Our Father. . .', to me that always means *Jesus'* Father and *my* Father. We address him together. This is the 'our' of prayer.

❦

The best prayer is not that which *feels* most, but that which *gives* most.

Fr Andrew SDC

Is prayer your steering wheel or your spare tyre?

Corrie Ten Boom

And all day, I sent prayer like incense up
To God the strong, God the beneficent,
God ever mindful in all strife and strait
Who, for our own good, makes the need extreme,
Till at the last he puts forth might and saves.

Robert Browning

When thou prayest, rather let thy heart be without words than thy words without heart.

John Bunyan

Prayer is the sum of our relationship with God. We are what we pray. The degree of our faith is the degree of our prayer. Our ability to love is our ability to pray.

Carlo Carretto

If you do not pray, everything can disappoint you by going wrong. If you do pray, everything can still go wrong, but not in a way that will disappoint you.

Hubert van Zeller, *Praying While You Work*

Christian prayer entails both external and internal relations. It is both an external act of communication and an inner act of communion (Nels Ferre). In the act of prayer, we are related to the God who stands outside and above us but who also, by his Spirit, dwells within us.

Donald G. Bloesch, *The Struggle of Prayer*

Accordingly, we worship with all our power the one God and his only Son, the Word and the image of God, by prayers and supplications; and we offer our petitions to the God of the universe through his only-begotten Son. To the Son we first present them, and beseech him, as 'the propitiation for our sins' and our high priest, to offer our desires, and sacrifices, and prayers to the Most High.

Origen, *Against Celsus*

So let us pray, most beloved brethren, as God the teacher has taught. It is a friendly and intimate prayer to beseech God with his own words, for the prayer of Christ to ascend to his ears. Let the Father acknowledge the words of his Son when we make prayer. Let him who dwells within our breast himself be also in our voice and, since we have him as the advocate for our sins before the Father, let us put forward the words of our advocate. For since he says: 'Whatsoever we shall ask the Father in his name, he will give us,' how much more effectively do we obtain what we seek in the name of Christ, if we ask with his own prayer?

Cyprian, *The Lord's Prayer*

Since we are not worthy to present ourselves to God and come into his sight, the heavenly Father himself, to free us at once from shame and fear which might well have thrown our hearts into despair, has given us his Son, Jesus Christ our Lord, to be our advocate [1 John 2: 1] and mediator with him [1 Timothy 2: 5], by whose guidance we may confidently come to him, and with such an inter-cessor, trusting nothing we ask in his name will be denied us, as nothing can be denied to him by the Father.

John Calvin, *Institutes of the Christian Religion*

Our Father in heaven, we offer this prayer in the name of your Son. As we approach you, not in our own name, but in Jesus' name, the throne of dread becomes a throne of grace. So we come boldly, laying our needs, fears and trials before you. Hear the prayer which your Son placed upon our lips. . . your kingdom come, your will be done. Provide our daily needs. Forgive us as we forgive others. Spare us from temptation and from the evil one. Amen.

A Benediction
May you ever be aware in prayer of the beloved Son who, in his perfected humanity, meets you where you are, praying with you as you pray to the Father with and through him. May the awesome divinity of this risen Christ also raise you up to share

in his own communion with the Father in the heavenly place. May your life and prayer become one with that of the divine/human Christ, as he brings you and your prayers, together with all that you are, into his eternal fellowship with the Father. Amen.

God, our portion

The Lord is my chosen portion and my cup; you hold my lot.

Whom have I in heaven but you? And earth has nothing I desire besides you. My flesh and my heart may fail, but God is the strength of my heart and my portion forever.

But to the tribe of Levi Moses gave no inheritance; the Lord God of Israel is their inheritance. . .

The Lord is my shepherd, I shall not want.

My expectation is from him.

Though the fig tree does not bud and there are no grapes on the vine, though the olive crops fail and the fields produce no food, though there are not sheep in the pen and no cattle in the stalls, yet I will rejoice in the Lord, I will be joyful in God my Saviour.

I have loved you with an everlasting love; I have drawn you with lovingkindness.

I will never leave you or forsake you.

Lo, I am with you always even to the end of the age.

He who did not spare his own Son but gave him up for us all, will he not give us all things with him?

Who shall separate us from the love of Christ?

I am my beloved's and my beloved is mine.

(Psalm 16: 5, NRSV; 73: 25–26, NIV; Joshua 13: 33, RSV; Psalm 23: 1; 62: 5 — both NKJV; Habakkuk 3: 17–18; Jeremiah 31: 3 — both NIV; Hebrews 13: 5, NRSV; Matthew 28: 20, NKJV; Romans 8: 32 and 35, RSV; Song of Solomon 2: 16, KJV)

The world today suffers from a malady of accruing. We

accrue academic qualifications, positions, possessions and so on. To some the ability to accrue is a measurement of success. The more our qualifications, the higher our positions, the bigger our houses and cars, the more successful we are. Underlying this accruing mentality is insecurity. Uncertain of who we are and why we are here, we hope to find ourselves in what we have. The world is divided between the haves and the have nots.

Nations want a bigger portion of world economy, of world power and control. Yet having more does not satisfy us, can never satisfy us. There is and always will be more to have. All is vanity and striving after the wind, says Ecclesiastes.

But Christians do not need to suffer from this malady. The Almighty God of the universe says, 'I am your portion, your inheritance.' Have you ever pondered what this means? Yes, it means you have him, even God himself. To have God is to have everything. Those who have God and everything else have no more than those who have God only; and those who have everything else and not God have nothing. If you truly have God, you need nothing else. When God gives himself to you, he gives you everything else that you ever need to live the most meaningful and fulfilled life.

The most contented and successful men and women of God know this truth well. George Mueller said: 'I was converted in November 1825, but I only came into full surrender of the heart four years later, in July 1829. The love of money was gone, the love of place was gone, the love of worldly pleasures and engagements was gone. God, God alone became my portion. I found my all in him; I wanted nothing else. And by the grace of God this has remained and has made me a happy man.'

God has given himself to you. He is your portion. He has found you, revealed himself to you. Seek him and in him find all your needs met. Trust God enough to know that that which he does not give you, you do not need. Do not join the world in its accruing malady. You do not need to. You know your identity. It has nothing to do with your position or your wealth. You have an infinitely better security, a superior inheritance to anything the world can offer you. God is your portion: take hold of him.

❧❦❧

If I am the Lord's, then the Lord is mine. If Christ owns me, I own him. And so faith must reach out and claim its full inheritance and begin to use its great resources. Moment by moment we may take him as our grace and strength, our faith and love, our victory and joy, our all in all.

A.B. Simpson, *Days of Heaven on Earth*

'The Lord is my shepherd' is on Sunday, is on Monday and is through every day of the week; is in January, is in December and every month of the year; it is at home and is in China; is in peace and is in war; in abundance and in poverty.

J. Hudson Taylor

We may have as much of God as we will. Christ puts the key of the treasure-chamber into our hand and bids us take all that we want. If someone is admitted into a bullion vault of a bank and comes out with one cent, whose fault is it that he or she is poor? Whose fault is it that Christian people generally have such scanty portions of the free riches of God?

Alexander McLaren

To have a portion, therefore, in God is to possess that which includes in itself all that is created. Surveying the wonders of creation. . . the Christian can say, 'Glorious those things be, [but] to me belongs that which is more glorious far. The streams are precious, but I have the fountain; the vesture is beautiful, but the weaver is mine, my own. God is my portion; the Lord is my inheritance.'

To me belongs all created and uncreated beauty, all that eyes have seen or imagination conceived; and, more than that, for 'eye has not seen, nor ear heard and has it entered into [our] hearts to conceive what God has prepared for those who love him'. All things and beings, all that life reveals or death conceives, everything with the boundless possibilities of creating wisdom and power is mine; for God, the Creator and foundation of all is mine!

G.B. Caird

All plenty which is not my God is poverty to me.

St Augustine

Those who live to satisfy their ambition have before them the labour of Sisyphus, who rolled uphill an ever-rebounding stone. Could we know the secret heartbreaks and weariness of the ambitious, we should need no Wolsley's voice crying, 'I charge thee, fling away ambition', but we should flee from it as from the most accursed bloodthirsty vampire.

Charles Haddon Spurgeon

He is a path, if any be misled;
    He is a robe, if any naked be;
If any chance to hunger, he is bread;
    If any be [in bondage], he is free;
    If any be weak, how strong is he!
To the dead, life he is; to the sick, health;
To the blind, sight; and to the needy, wealth;
A pleasure without loss, a treasure without stealth.

Giles Fletcher

The Lord who gives us in yourself all things,
we praise and thank you for the inheritance
that we have in you.
We ask you to open our eyes
to see the glorious resources
that you have made available to us
in yourself.
Yet, in seeing and knowing all the riches
that are ours in you,
we also pray that our delight and joy
may not be in them, but rather in you,
the giver.

*Grant us, Lord, the faith and trust that we need
to appropriate our portion, even the Almighty God himself.
In Jesus Christ our Lord.* Amen.

A Benediction
*May you dwell in the shelter of the Most High and rest in the
shadow of the Almighty. May you say of the Lord, 'He is my
refuge and my fortress, my God in whom I trust.'* Amen.

24

Seeing the unseen

You cannot see my face, for no-one may see me and live. . . you will see my back: but my face must not be seen.

No-one has ever seen God, but God the One and Only, who is at the Father's side, has made him known.

Anyone who has seen me has seen the Father.

Because you have seen me, you have believed; blessed are those who have not seen and yet have believed.

Though you have not seen him you love him; and even though you do not see him now, you believe in him and are filled with an inexpressible and glorious joy.

We live by faith, not by sight.

Now faith is being sure of what we hope for and certain of what we do not see.

And without faith it is impossible to please God, because anyone who comes to him must believe that he exists and that he rewards those who earnestly seek him.

Blessed are the pure in heart, for they will see God.

The throne of God and of the Lamb will be in the city, and his servants. . . will see his face.

(Exodus 33: 20–23; John 1: 18; 14: 9; 20: 29; 1 Peter 1: 8; 2 Corinthians 5: 7; Hebrews 11: 1; Matthew 5: 8; Revelation 22: 3–4 — all NIV)

Bob Evans, a devout and dedicated Baptist missionary who has worked in East Malaysia for the last few decades, was once asked by someone in the middle of his sermon: 'Pastor Evans, you have been serving with the Lord for such a long period of time. . . but have you ever seen God?' With a smile on his face, he answered, 'No'. His response was biblical.

'No-one has ever seen God. . .' says the scripture. Though spiritual people have been given a vision of God, what they saw was but a glimpse. When Moses earnestly pleaded for God to show him his 'glory', God conceded only by revealing his back! What the elders who accompanied Moses up on Mount Sinai beheld was just a distant glow of the glory of God. Isaiah, while worshipping in the t-emple, and Stephen, in the moment of his martyrdom, were privileged to see the Lord of lords, but only in a vision and not in a 'face-to-face' encounter.

Down through church history, God has remained hidden. No-one has been privileged to say, 'I have literally seen my Lord!' When you think of it, you are led to wonder and amazement.

A young man was asked by his father-in-law what his Christian vocation was. His reply: 'I'm serving a Master whom I have not seen and working for a King whom I have not met.' His father-in-law looked puzzled and said, 'I wouldn't do a thing like that!' We trust in a Saviour who is unseen, toil for a Master who has not shown his face, and are directed, sustained and protected by a Shepherd who is invisible! That's absurdity for a realist.

But believers may always look forward to the day when they will meet their Lord face-to-face. The word of the unfailing God promises that the servants of God will see him in his eternal city. Then, it will not be just a glimpse, not through a vision, not at a distance — and certainly not at his back! Instead, it will be a meeting of love, face-to-face.

All of God's glory and majesty will be revealed before their very eyes. They will behold the One who existed from the beginning, the One who formed the heaven and earth out of nothing, the One who has demonstrated his love to a world of sinners. . . yes, and Jesus Christ, with his nail-pierced hands and wounded side. What unceasing 'wonder, love and praise' believers will begin to experience on that day of reunion!

However, we must not anticipate seeing God with a physical face. Writing on the 'face of God', Augustine of Hippo wrote: 'Let no thought be entertained here of a bodily face. . . Scripture speaks of the face of God, the arm of God, the hands of God, the feet of God. . . but think not in all this of human members.'

Augustine was right. 'God is Spirit' and therefore does not have a bodily face. What we can say is that we are looking forward to the face of God's unsurpassed glory, uninhibited greatness and boundless grace.

The best is yet to come. Nevertheless, followers of Christ can experience the reality of their invisible God in their particular time and age. The footsteps of their God can be seen in manifold ways, but through the eyes of faith. Their answered prayers reveal the workings of their Master. The transformation of their lives tells of the dynamic power of their Saviour. The protection and sustenance which enfolds them manifests the presence of their Shepherd. Jesus Christ, the exact representation and radiance of God, is the person through whom earthly believers 'see' their loving, heavenly Father.

The vision of God is both for now and the future. This calls for unswerving faith in the Son of God, who will ultimately usher his people into the very presence of God in the appointed time. This creates in God's people a desire to live in purity, for only those who are pure in heart will see the Lord face-to-face.

❧

'Blessed are the pure in heart, for they shall see God.' This is the end of our love; an end whereby we are perfected and not consumed. For there is an end of food and an end of a garment; of food, when it is consumed by the eating; of a garment, when it is perfected in the weaving. Both the one and the other have an end; but the one is an end of consumption, the other of perfection.

Whatsoever we do now strive for or are in laudable sort eager for or blamelessly desire, when we come to the vision of God, we shall require no more. For what need he seek for, with whom God is present? Or what shall suffice the one whom God suffices not? We wish to see God, we seek, we kindle with desire to see him. Who does not?

Augustine of Hippo

In the first age, no-one could see God's face, for he was too holy for mere mortal to look at and live. But in the new age the situation is changed. Thus, in 2 Esdras 7: 98 it is stated that the seventh and highest reward for the righteous following the judgment will be the joy of beholding 'the face of him whom in their lifetime they served'. So in Revelation, the *summum bonum* is the beatific vision of God which his servants will experience.

Martin Rist

There is an eye that never sleeps
  Beneath the wing of night;
There is an ear that never shuts
  When sink the beams of light.
There is an arm that never tires
  When human strength gives way;
There is a love that never fails
  When earthly loves decay.
That eye unseen o'erwatcheth all;
  That arm upholds the sky;
That ear doth hear the sparrows call;
  That love is ever nigh.

James Cowden Wallace

The world says, 'Seeing is believing'. But the Bible reverses the order: First, we must believe; then we will see. . . In Psalm 27: 13, David says, 'I would have despaired unless I had believed that I would see the goodness of the Lord in the land of the living.'

Derek Prince, *Faith to Live By*

God is to be trusted for what he is and not for what he is not. We may confidently expect him to act according to his nature, but never contrary to it. To dream that God will do this and that because we wish that he would is not faith, but fanaticism. Faith can only stand upon truth. We may be sure that God will so act as to honour his own justice, mercy, wisdom, power — in a word, so as to be himself. Beyond all doubt, he will fulfil his promises and when faith grasps a promise, she is on sure ground.

Charles H. Spurgeon, *Devotions and Prayers*

When an Arab chief was asked how he knew God, he answered: 'How do I know when a camel has passed my tent? By the footprints.' But the answer does not satisfy our strange time. We do not see the footprints of God. We see only man's footprints in the mud and blood of war, but not God's footprints. As for a camel's footprints, they are no more than an item in zoology. . .

Yet the Arab was right in this: the only proof of God is in the sign of his presence. He is not proved by logic. . . He cannot be demonstrated by science. . . The footprints of God are still and always to be found along the way Christ walked.

George Arthur Buttrick

In Jesus Christ, there is no isolation of us from God or of God from us. . . Jesus Christ is in his one person as true God our loyal partner, and as true man, God's. He is the Lord humbled for communion with us and likewise the servant exalted to communion with God. He is the Word spoken from the loftiest, most luminous transcendence and likewise the Word heard in the deepest, darkest immanence. He is both, without their being confused, but also without their being divided; he is wholly the one and wholly the other. Thus. . . Jesus Christ is the mediator, the reconciler, between God and us. Thus he comes forward to us on behalf of God, calling for and awaking faith, love and hope, and to God on behalf of us, representing us, making satisfaction and interceding.

Karl Barth, *The Humility of God*

O God, thou hast said only the pure in heart shall see thee. Blind us to any other vision than the vision of thee. Make us think about the things which belong to thy kingdom and save us from waywardness of affection which leads to waywardness of life. For Jesus' sake. Amen.

Augustine of Hippo

My Lord and my God, Creator and life-giver, my soul leaps for joy as I think of the promise of seeing you in the city which is to come. My heart is thrilled over that day when I shall see you in the fullness of your glory, greatness and grace, and not be consumed. How my whole being will be overwhelmed by the praises of your people before your very throne. . . with the sweet and majestic choir of people and angels, extolling and blessing you 'who was, and is, and is to come'.

Keep me always in the love of Jesus, for he is my only hope of meeting you in confidence. Grant me strength to live in purity as it is only those whose heart is pure who can see your face on that day. When I am down in hardship and crisis, remind me of this glorious promise that I shall see you, that I may be lifted up once again in anticipation of that great day when we will forever be set free from the toil of this life. In Jesus' name. Amen.

A Benediction
May the one 'whom we have not seen but yet we love'
cause you to rejoice in the hope of seeing him;
May he who is 'the way to the Father'
keep you in an abiding relationship with him;
May he who is going to appear in glory
create in you a motivation to live purely;
May the one who 'will live with his people' in the Holy City
live in peace with you now and forevermore. Amen.

25

The dark speech of the Spirit

When there are prophets among you, I the Lord make myself known to them in visions; I speak to them in dreams. Not so with my servant Moses. . . with him I speak face to face — clearly, not in riddles (dark speech); and he beholds the form of the Lord.

But just when he had resolved to do this, an angel of the Lord appeared to him in a dream and said, 'Joseph, son of David, do not be afraid to take Mary as your wife. . .'

For God speaks in one way and in two, though people do not perceive it. In a dream, in a vision of the night, when deep sleep falls on mortals, while they slumber on their beds, then he opens their ears. . . to spare their souls from the pit, their lives from traversing the river.

While your majesty was sleeping, you dreamed about the future; and God, who reveals mysteries, showed you what is going to happen. Now, this mystery was revealed to me, not because I am wiser than anyone else, but so that your majesty may learn the meaning of your dreams and understand the thoughts that have come to you.

I will pour out my spirit on all flesh; your sons and your daughters shall prophesy, your old men shall dream dreams, and your young men shall see visions.

While Peter was still thinking about the vision, the Spirit said to him, 'Look, three men are searching for you. Now get up, go down and go with them without hesitation; I have sent them.'

(Numbers 12: 6–8; Matthew 1: 20; Job 33: 14–16 and 18 — all NRSV; Daniel 2: 29–30, GNB; Joel 2: 28; Acts 10: 19–20 — all NRSV)

Whether we remember them or not, it is now certain that virtually everyone experiences periods of regular dreaming several times a night. The rapid eye movements characteristic of this fourth and last stage of sleep are observable. The brain wave patterns of all four stages are measurable. Not only that, but dreaming is evidently necessary to preserve our sanity. People deprived of it become mentally disturbed.

Even if we can't consciously decipher the rich creative symbolism of our dream life, the process is working for our health and wholeness. We can, however, increasingly find dreams to be a source of up-to-date insight and inspiration as we bring them into our prayer life. They can often be personal messages from God, as the Bible has always claimed.

Dreams have been important milestones in the spiritual growth of many Christians but, generally speaking, Christendom has ignored the dream as a means of inspiration since the thirteenth century. Morton Kelsey maintains that 'until the year 1200, there were no Christian writers or philosophers who ignored or underestimated the importance of visions or dreams'. Tertullian (AD 160–230), for instance, claims that 'nearly everyone on earth knows that God reveals himself to people most often in dreams'.

The first Christian writers responsible for looking at dreams seriously again as a means of guidance were Morton Kelsey and John Sanford, both Anglican priests, who studied Jung's work on dreams. Kelsey writes of that time: 'As I began to take an interest in my dreams, I became aware for the first time in my life that God wanted to speak to me. . . I soon noticed that there was a wisdom greater than mine that spoke to me in my dreams and came to my aid.'

While attending a training workshop in spiritual direction, my husband had the following dream. A young boy had just managed to sign something significant like a bank withdrawal form, but under strong opposition. The police had been called to stop the boy from taking such a drastic step. There was only one familiar voice encouraging him in his decision which he knew was right. My husband then awoke feeling very confused and a bit apprehensive.

During his prayer time that night, he invited Jesus to go with him into the scene and to lay his hands on the boy's head and bless him. Immediately, as if a blind had sprung up, letting in the light of day, my husband knew the meaning of the dream. All the characters, including the shady ones, were parts of himself, and the struggle was actually a cosmic one of light and dark — between that part of himself that wanted to grow in relationship to Christ and those parts that wanted to resist. This dreamwork gave him a strong sense of divine assurance of the rightness of the investment of himself that he was making at the workshop.

I was finding it difficult to write the prayer for this chapter, so I gave up, asking God for his guidance as I went to sleep. In a dream, the Lord and all my friends and loved ones all over heaven were busy writing letters to me and giving them to the Lord to deliver. My heavenly mail arrived each night by dream. I received it but, as I turned away from opening the letters, I heard clearly, 'It is your decision.'

In my waking moments, as I held that dream before God, I knew I had been shown the value of dreamwork. It was my choice whether my heavenly correspondence was read and acted upon — or ignored.

❦

Dreams not only reveal the stresses of the day past; they also reveal the forgotten depths of the human being and even give intimations of a spiritual world that surrounds the human being as totally as the physical one. . . I would suggest again that this Dreamer within is none other than the Holy Spirit. He helps us see ourselves as we are and even gives us a picture of what we can become. If one would find this inner Dreamer who speaks in the perennial language of images, we can find few better ways than writing down our dreams and then meditating upon them and bringing them before the One who gave them to us.

Morton Kelsey, *Dreams: A Way to Listen to God*

We may be tempted to assume, from some biblical texts, that people of the Old and New Testaments did things because they were literally commanded so by their dreams; however, such an assumption may be unwarranted. For example, it may seem that Joseph's dream told him to marry Mary; upon closer reading, however, we see that the angel did not tell Joseph to marry Mary, but rather *not to be afraid* to marry Mary. Instead of commanding, the dream was, among other things, confronting Joseph with his attitudes and feelings towards Mary.

Perhaps the dreams and visions as originally experienced were indeed as clear and explicit as they are reported in the Gospel texts. More likely, however, the narrator is merely reporting *the meaning of the dream as its symbolic material came to be understood by the dreamer upon reflection. . .* Perhaps Joseph's dreams were filled with symbolic imagery as most of our dreams are and Joseph is merely sharing with us the results of his dreamwork through which he learned, for example, to flee to Egypt, return to Israel and settle in Nazareth again.

Savary, Berne and Williams, *Dreams and Spiritual Growth*

The dream shows the inner truth and the reality of the patient as it really is; not as I conjecture it to be and not as he or she would like it to be, but as it is. . . the dream is specifically the utterance of the unconscious mind.

Carl Jung

Jung also pointed out that dreams are not simply personal. He suggested the helpfulness of relating to the images and symbols in a dream as if they were other people. The unconscious has a life of its own, he said. It is not merely the receptacle of psychologically repressed material, but is a living, creative, germinal layer in each of us. For this reason, many dream characters may be viewed as parts of the dreamer and many of the dominant qualities of the dreamer may be personified as dream characters.

Savary, Berne and Williams, *Dreams and Spiritual Growth*

If we believe that interpreting dreams is not Christian, we ought to take a look at these historical facts and the great tradition of which they are a part. . . What brought an end to this tradition? In the thirteenth century, Thomas Aquinas tried to interpret the life of the church with the help of Aristotle's philosophy — the idea that the human being can experience only through sensory perception and reason. There was no place for dreams. It took about three or four centuries for this view to become totally accepted. As this happened, Christians ceased interpreting dreams. The intellectual tradition of Europe in the last four centuries has taught people to think in conceptual terms only.

Morton Kelsey, *Dreams: A Way to Listen to God*

The only way anyone should go into the unconscious is, first, to ask Jesus Christ for his power and direction and protection. . . During meditation, it is helpful to confront the other person or persons in your dream (almost always part of you) and enter into imaginative dialogue with 'them'. Then invite Christ into this three-way dialogue for his thoughts and directives.

Morton Kelsey

As soon as you finish writing your Dream Report, do the TTAQ technique. It is perhaps the most universally helpful short technique in dreamwork, and provides a good first step toward understanding your dream when you have very little time to devote to dreamwork. . .

1. TITLE. Give your dream a title. Let it come to you spontaneously, or ask yourself, What title does this dream want itself to have?
2. THEME. State the major theme or issues which

surface in the dream. If there are more than one,
note them in sequence.

3. AFFECT. What was the dominant feeling or emotional energy experienced during the dream? If
there was a sequence of feelings, state them in
sequence.

4. QUESTION. What question is the dream asking of
me? What is the dream trying to help me become
conscious of?

A dream is better viewed as a question rather than an
answer. If we begin to look in a dream for questions
rather than answers, we begin actively relating to the
dream. We open ourselves to new possibilities and meaning. We begin establishing a relationship between the
dream and our spiritual life.

There is a need for answers. We do not deny that. But
the deepest answers come not out of the dream, nor out
of our own ego consciousness, but out of the *active relationship* between ourselves and the Source of the dream. . .

With regard to dreams, and even life itself, perhaps it
is better not to seek for answers, but to focus instead on
our responses. . . Responses open us up to fuller possibilities, while answers tend to close us down to narrow
and absolute definitions of things. At times, of course, a
very specific answer is appropriate to a situation. . . In
general, thinking in terms of responses guards against
seeing symbolic dream material as literal messages or
commandments to do this or that, or as promises that a
specific thing will surely happen.

Savary, Berne and Williams, *Dreams and Spiritual Growth*

Furthermore, we agree with Jung's insistence that the
dreamer's life and milieu, work and relationships, past
history and memories, conscious associations and
psychological state must all be taken into account for
dreamwork to be valid and reliable. Under these conditions, who could be better qualified to acknowledge the
true meanings of a dream through personal dreamwork
than the dreamer himself or herself?

Savary, Berne and Williams, *Dreams and Spiritual Growth*

One thing we strongly emphasise is *not* simply to take the words, images or actions in a dream literally. For example, if in a dream your dream ego is changing jobs or leaving a marriage, don't assume the dream means that you must change (or are destined to change) your career or your marriage partner. Instead, we would ask you to do dreamwork with the symbol of 'your job' or 'your marriage'. You cannot *assume* to know what the dream means without doing some discerning dreamwork.

Dreams don't usually give literal commands to act; rather, dreams ask questions, reveal issues, suggest alternatives, open up new possibilities, invite responses.

Savary, Berne and Williams, *Dreams and Spiritual Growth*

Psychology teaches us that every man carries within his dominant masculine psyche some largely unconscious feminine traits — what Jung chooses to call 'the anima'— just as every woman possesses some masculine traits, 'the animus'. Thus a feminine figure in a man's dream may be trying to point him to 'anima' qualities of sensitivity, of the emotional life, of the willingness to love and be loved. . . When one dreams of a husband or wife, it may not necessarily refer to the mate; rather what one is 'married to' emotionally and spiritually. . .

Ninety-five per cent of dream material refers to the dreamer rather than to the one being dreamed about. . . In those rare instances when dreams do warn of a coming event, the purpose is never to frighten or discourage us. The creator's work through the unconscious, as elsewhere, is affirmative, directed towards a constructive end. Therefore, the dream warnings present possibilities we are meant to avoid, seldom actualities. . .

At first, we may be able to interpret only a fraction of the dream material that comes to us. But if we persist in taking our dreams into our prayer life and acting upon what we understand, we will experience an unfolding progression. In the years ahead, I believe there will be exciting experimentation on this subject among Christians. God will lead us through our dreams to all sorts of provocative discoveries about our hidden selves in his plan to re-fashion us into whole people.

Morton Kelsey

In the depths of my being, Lord, you are there, touching my spirit, night after night. I ask for your protection from any messages and nightmares that are not from you. I know that you give it, for I am yours. I trust you that all is well with my spirit. Lovingly, yet with truthful realism, you help me see myself as I really am, including the dross still clinging — long buried fears, griefs and hang-ups make their way up, in meal-sized portions, night after night. You challenge and provoke me until I face my deepest callings; inspire and tantalise with glimpses of what the future could hold. Shame, sorrow, passion, drudgery, confirmation, love — the messages roll in, made to order. Waiting with dated page, I ask you to speak to me again, tonight. . .

Lord, this dream I bring to you. Will you help me unravel the meaning hidden here? What are you hinting at, asking of me? What part of my outer life is this dream referring to? With which character or symbol should I dialogue? I watch you as you walk with me into the scene, approaching the most meaningful character within it. Show me the link between my present outer life and this inner one. I wait in the silence for your word. . .

A Benediction
Go forth into your life, knowing the Dreamer within is on your side. The battle is an inner one and it is the Lord's! As the inner battle is won, the outer one must surely follow. What is whispered in the dark may be shouted from the housetops, but do not fear. The burning action of the crucible is to clearly reveal the gold within, not the dross. Let God prevail! Amen.

Darkness is as light to you

(Psalm 139: 12)

I am hemmed in by darkness, and thick darkness covers my face.

My God, my God, why have you forsaken me? Why are you so far from saving me, so far from the words of my groaning? O God, I cry out to you by day, but you do not answer, by night, and find no rest.

From the sixth hour until the ninth hour darkness came over the land. About the ninth hour Jesus cried out in a loud voice, *Eloi, Eloi, lama sabachthani?* — which means, 'My God, my God, why have you forsaken me?'

'Come, follow me,' Jesus said. . .

We do not want you to be uninformed, brothers [and sisters], about the hardships we suffered in the province of Asia. We were under great pressure, far beyond our ability to endure, so that we despaired even of life.

Let us fix our eyes on Jesus, the author and perfecter of our faith, who for the joy set before him endured the cross, scorning its shame, and sat down at the right hand of the throne of God.

I will give you the treasures of darkness, riches stored in the secret places, so that you may know that I am the Lord, the God of Israel, who summons you by name.

If I say, 'Surely the darkness will hide me and the light become night around me,' even the darkness will not be dark to you; the night will shine like the day, for the darkness is as light to you.

(Job 23: 17, RSV; Psalm 22: 1–2, NIV/RSV; Matthew 27: 45–46; Matthew 4: 19; 2 Corinthians 1: 8; Hebrews 12: 2; Isaiah 45: 3; Psalm 139: 11–12 — all NIV)

Did Jesus give a cry of pain as the nerves in his wrist were shattered by the nail and Roman hammer? He said, 'Father, forgive them, for they do not know what they are doing.' His composure convicted the hardened centurion of his divinity. Who could drink pain like this, who could love his murderers like this, save a God of awesome, wondrous grace? We glimpse the very heart of God — the all-enduring, inexorable power of the divine heart of love — as we gaze in wonder at the spectacle of Golgotha.

Yet whilst his love enabled him to transcend the extremes of human pain and rejection, Jesus' separation from God taxed him to his very limit. In Gethsemane, his soul was overwhelmed with sorrow to the point of death; and what was this cup that nearly overwhelmed him? I believe it was the terror of the separation from God he would face at the point of death. So he cries out in forsaken anguish whilst the very heart of darkness descends upon him at death.

Jesus saw the heart of darkness.

Joseph Conrad and many other great thinkers have sketched profoundly the deep darkness that is despair, futility, brooding and pointless evil, and suffocating lostness. In Conrad's novel *Heart of Darkness*, Marlow describes his river steamer voyage into the Congo early last century to retrieve an ivory hunter called Kurtz. Kurtz has a peculiar charisma which he uses to exploit the natives. Kurtz dies, and Marlow nearly dies on the outward voyage. The Congo is the darkness — yet the voyage is also a psychological and mystical journey wherein Marlow sees a glimpse behind the veil of surface reality and peeps into the chasm of an immense and impenetrable darkness. In the excerpts below you can savour his imagery of despair.

Now recall Jesus as he is cut loose from the arms of true reality by the spectre's blade of death. He is received by the despair reserved for humanity that has chosen to reject the presence of God. He plunges headlong into this same darkness that Marlow glimpsed. And this despair is a reality — for it is part of the human condition.

We have the real choice to love God and enjoy him forever, or not to love God and know the perpetual torment of being made of indissoluble stuff in the grip of ceaseless futility and crushing, mindless darkness. And we are all born into the latter state. To redeem us from it, he must conquer it for us — he must be sacrificed to it and then in death strike the fatal blow to its heart. Do we understand what we have been redeemed from as well as Conrad, Nietzsche, Freud, Russell, Clarke, Hume or Hess understood the nature of godless reality? Maybe they understand better than we what Christ faced as he cried, 'My God, my God, why have you forsaken me?' Maybe we can learn from them here.

What of our knowledge of despair, what of our struggle against the dark reality? The soul's black night is a part of the Christian experience. It is a part of many secular thinkers' experience. It is a part of the human condition.

Kierkegaard goes so far as to say that our capacity to experience this despair is a great privilege and — to the extent that Christianity is a process of 'becoming' in the mortal medium — our metamorphosis is perfected in refinement through the process of despair and death, for this strengthens and perfects true faith.

A profound realisation comes to us through despair. It is the realisation that there is *no* meaning, *no* value, *no* worthwhile activity, *nothing* of any value within us or the material universe, *no* beauty, *no* love. . . *none* of these contain value in themselves. Meaning and value is above and beyond; it is in God alone. And we only find meaning and value through our relationship with God.

The realisation of our need for spiritual growth in the area of our total surrender to the demands of God's relationship with us only truly comes as we see the reality of despair more clearly. And then death to our futile life is the point where we are resurrected into the fullness of life with Christ. Despair and death is the medium of conversion and of spiritual growth in this life. 'For Christ's love compels us, because we are convinced that one died for all and therefore all died. And he died for all, that those who live should no longer live for themselves but for him who died for them and was raised again' (2 Corinthians 5: 14–15, NIV).

So why then do Christians who grapple with despair, theological discontent, turmoil in darkness and a sense of alienation from God so often feel ostracised from the church? Could it be that our established Christianity is a comfortable and in many ways shallow shelter from the darkness? I believe this may be so. But I think it is more an issue of a lack of conception of the importance of spiritual struggle for spiritual growth in a culture where material comfort is the milestone of success.

There is a 'Christian myth' which states that Christians who show doubt, taste despair, struggle in darkness or lose a sense of the presence of God are by definition failing Christians who are probably caught in some deep sin. The 'myth' is a lie.

It is all right to struggle in darkness. Job did, and God spoke to Job's theologically correct companions and said, 'You have not spoken of me what is right, as my servant Job has.' Jacob struggled with God and was blessed because of it.

The same God who gives us the treasures of darkness is also the God in whom there is no darkness. When we cannot see, we must pursue the light through the darkness in faith. Then, if we succeed, we can see — with faith — in the darkness, just as our Lord did even in the very heart of darkness.

We can be angry, but we must not sin. We can be perplexed, yet we must not discard the child's faith. We can lose the sense of the presence of God, yet we must worship him. We can see ourselves as hypocrites and yet we must not judge others.

Darkness is an opportunity for God to birth a jewel within us and that is a jewel forged in our own character by our struggle to follow Jesus.

Those are perfect in faith who can come to God in the utter dearth of their feelings and desires — without a glow or an aspiration, with the weight of low thoughts, failures, neglect and wandering forgetfulness — and say to him, 'Thou art my refuge.'

George MacDonald

In Kierkegaard's book, *Gospel of Sufferings*, he describes how suffering — not success — was the unique medium whereby Jesus demonstrated his divine worthiness. As Revelation claims, '. . .worthy is the Lamb who was slain'. And Christ's work of worth in us is given scope to the extent to which we follow him. But to follow through suffering is not a self-debasing road; rather it is one that gives us real life and worth — and, as Jesus himself went to the cross out of the motive of joy ('Jesus who for the joy set before him endured the cross, scorning its shame'), we can rejoice in what he is accomplishing even through darkness.

If Jesus faced the ultimate crisis of a sense of hopeless separation from God and yet endured, why should we expect never to be led through the trials of a sense of separation?

Paul Tyson

. . .I raised my head. The offing was bared by a black bank of clouds and the tranquil waterway leading to the uttermost ends of the earth flowed sombre under an overcast sky. It seemed to lead into the heart of an immense darkness.

. . .The sun sunk. . . stricken to death by the touch of that gloom brooding over a crowd of men.

Droll thing life is — that mysterious arrangement of merciless logic for a futile purpose.

. . .The silent wilderness surrounding this cleared speck on the earth struck me as something great and invincible, like evil or truth, waiting patiently for the passing away of this fantastic invasion.

. . .'The horror!' He was a remarkable man. After all, this was the expression of some sort of belief; it had candour, it had conviction, it had a vibrant note of revolt in its whisper, it had the appalling face of a glimpse of truth.

What was there after all? Joy, fear, sorrow, devotion, valour, rage — who can tell? — but truth — truth stripped of its cloak of time. . .

. . .Going up that river was like travelling back to the earliest beginnings of the world, when vegetation rioted on the earth and the big trees were kings. . . And this stillness of life did not in the least resemble a peace. It was the stillness of an implacable force brooding over an inscrutable intention. It looked at you with vengeful aspect.

. . .It was as though a veil had been rent. I saw on that ivory face the expression of sombre pride, of ruthless power, of craven terror — of an intense and hopeless despair. Did he live his life again in every detail of desire, of temptation, and surrender during that supreme moment of complete knowledge? He cried in a whisper at some image, at some vision — he cried out twice, a cry that was no more than a breath — 'The horror! The horror!'

. . . We penetrated deeper and deeper into the heart of darkness.

. . . I affirm that Kurtz was a remarkable man. He had something to say. He said it. Since I had peeped over the edge myself, I understand better the meaning of his stare that could not see the flame of a candle, but was wide enough to embrace the whole universe, piercing enough to penetrate all the hearts that beat in the darkness. He had summed up — he had judged. 'The Horror!'

. . .No eloquence could have been so withering to one's belief in mankind as his final burst of sincerity.

For a moment it seemed to me as if I also was buried in a vast grave oppressing my breast, the smell of the damp earth, the unseen presence of victorious corruption, the darkness of an impenetrable night.

. . .I seemed at once bound to have been transported into some lightless region of subtle horrors.

Joseph Conrad, Heart of Darkness

In Kierkegaard's work on despair, *The Sickness Unto Death*, he explains how the innate sense of futility and purpose-lessness spurs us on to seek meaning. We do not find it in ourselves, we do not find it in the material world — we can only find it through a relationship with God. Comfort is the enemy of despair and the enemy of spiritual life, for then the searching is not attended to because of the relentless demands of petty routine, or even — in temporal terms — grandiose routine. Discomfort is an essential part of spiritual development.

Paul Tyson

When the bold warrior presses forward nothing daunted and takes in his breast the arrows of the foe, thus protecting his young henchman who follows him, can we indeed say the youth is following him?. . . Nay, we cannot say so; the case must be altered. The bold warrior must withdraw, so that it may be seen now whether his henchmen will truly follow him, follow him in actual danger when all the shafts are aimed at his breast, or whether like a coward he will turn his back on danger and lose his courage because he has lost his man of courage. . .

To follow therefore means to go the way he went whom you are following. . .

For there is a time when Christ goes almost visibly by the child's side, when Christ goes on before the child, but then there is also a time when he is taken from the view of sensitive imagination, so that now the seriousness of decision may show whether the child, grown old, will follow him.

Kierkegaard, Gospel of Sufferings

> Love's as hard as nails,
> Love is nails:
> Blunt, thick, hammered through
> The medial nerves of One
> Who, having made us, knew
> The thing he had done;
> Seeing (with all that is)
> Our cross, and his.

C.S. Lewis, Poems

Jesus' eyes have pierced the very heart of darkness, for he has been to the very heart of darkness; the darkness of spiritual void, oppressive crushing evil and rampaging futility. For what else could his forsaken cry on the cross be? He who was God made totally powerless, separated from the Father and taken into the dark oblivion of death and triumphant purposeless evil. Despair crushing all, save the enduring jewel of his faith — without sight — in God.

To him, darkness is as light. Oh blessed Saviour! With this confidence we can walk on in any darkness we face, knowing it is less than he faced and is effortlessly penetrated by his eyes. And in the darkness he faced he saw the joy set before him, without any light, and God gave him a name above every other name because of the metal of his jewel created in the totality of that darkness. And we are called to follow him. And we are called to share in his glory by following him. For if we die with him, we shall also be raised with him.

How did he die? He grappled with darkness to the mortal end in his life and in his death. So do we follow him to his death? May Paul's desire be ours, too: I want to know Christ and the power of his resurrection and the fellowship of sharing in his sufferings, becoming like him in his death and so, somehow, to attain to the resurrection from the dead (Philippians 3: 10–11, NIV).

Paul Tyson

Gracious Lord, my God, darkness is as light to you, and so my hope in you is not shaken, no matter how much I am shaken by darkness. Because you have conquered, I do not fear the darkness. Thank you my Lord, my refuge.

And in the darkness you forge a treasure in my soul. So I thank you even for the darkness. Not because of what it is, but because of what you use it for.

Merciful Redeemer, grant me faith to grasp the courage you have seeded within me not to shrink from my high calling — to follow Jesus. Complete the work you have begun within me, as I hold onto you in faith, even in the weakness of my fear of the dark.

I love you, Lord, for you have conquered the darkness through the light of your love, even for me. Amen.

A Benediction
The Lord delights in you. May you rest secure in his love, protected by his power, surrounded by his grace, even in the clouds of thick darkness.

Theme: The gentle re-creation beyond darkness

'It was I who. . . wrapped it in darkness' (Job 38: 9)

Who are you to question my wisdom
  with your ignorant, empty words?
Stand up now like a man
  and answer the questions I ask you.
Were you there when I made the world?
If you know so much, tell me about it.
Who decided how large it would be?
Who stretched the measuring-line over it?
Do you know all the answers?
What holds up the pillars that support the earth?
Who laid the corner-stone of the world?
In the dawn of that day the stars sang together,
  and the heavenly beings shouted for joy.
Who closed the gates to hold back the sea
  when it burst from the womb of the earth?
It was I who covered the sea with clouds
  and wrapped it in darkness.
I marked a boundary for the sea
  and kept it behind bolted gates.
I told it, 'So far and no farther!
Here your powerful waves must stop.'
Job, have you ever in all your life
  commanded a day to dawn?

Do you know where the light comes from
  or what the source of darkness is?
Can you show them how far to go,
  or send them back again?
I am sure you can, because you're so old
  and were there when the world was made!

Job 38: 2–12, 19–21, GNB

27

Take my life and let it be consecrated

(Frances Ridley Havergal)

O Lord, my heart is not lifted up, my eyes are not raised too high; I do not occupy myself with things too great and too marvellous for me. But I have calmed and quieted my soul, like a weaned child with its mother; my soul within me is like a weaned child. O Israel, hope in the Lord from this time on and forevermore.

Consecrate yourselves, therefore, and be holy; for I am the Lord your God. Keep my statutes and observe them; I am the Lord; I sanctify you.

Peter said to him, 'Lord, why can I not follow you now? I will lay down my life for you.' Jesus answered, 'Will you lay down your life for me? Very truly, I tell you, before the cock crows, you will have denied me three times.'

When they had finished breakfast, Jesus said to Simon Peter, 'Simon son of John, do you love me more than these?' He said to him, 'Yes, Lord; you know that I love you.' Jesus said to him, 'Feed my lambs.' A second time he said to him, 'Simon son of John, do you love me?' He said to him, 'Yes, Lord; you know that I love you.' Jesus said to him, 'Tend my sheep.' He said to him the third time, 'Simon son of John, do you love me?' and he said to him, 'Lord, you know everything; you know that I love you.' Jesus said to him, 'Feed my sheep. . . Follow me.'

As for me, I would seek God, and to God I would commit my cause.

Who then will offer willingly, consecrating themselves today to the Lord?

Now if you are unwilling to serve the Lord, choose this day whom you will serve. . . but as for me and my household, we will serve the Lord.

You are indeed my rock and my fortress; for your name's sake lead me and guide me, take me out of the net that is hidden for me, for you are my refuge. Into your hand I commit my spirit; you have redeemed me, O Lord, faithful God.

(Psalm 131: 1–3; Leviticus 20: 7–8; John 13: 37–38; John 21: 15–19; Job 5: 8; 1 Chronicles 29: 5b; Joshua 24: 15; Psalm 31: 3–5 — all NRSV)

Read again, slowly and meditatively, Psalm 131: 1–3 above. Allow the words, the Word behind the words, to speak to your heart as well as your mind. Allow yourself to be drawn into that place of vulnerability, where the child within you is being called from total dependence to chosen inter-dependence. . .

The following reflection on Psalm 131 may help to draw you further into that place of powerful vulnerability:

The Trusting Place
My walk this day with Christ
Was as a breast-weaned child.
No hunger pains, no temper cries,
No fear-filled clutching wild.
Instead I found this trusting place
Where warm contentment glowed.
A hand stretched out, a bending face,
A mother's soft love showed.
My heart was quiet, my soul was stilled,
Here was a place of peace.
My walk through life, so ego-filled,
Turned round by the Prince of Peace.
An act of will was the starting place,
To choose to be that small.
Christ's liberating love, his freeing grace,
Makes any 'child' walk tall.

We speak of people being made to 'feel small', and so much of our language and actions put other people down, revealing perhaps more than we realise our own feelings of inadequacy or inner bruising. But the Psalm, and the meditation above, suggest a different and positive perspective: we can actually choose in humility and vulnerability to be 'small'.

However much it may seem to fly in the face of our need for personal gratification and our need to meet social expectations, here is the place of real strength: chosen commitment to the One who is all-powerful, all-loving, all-giving, yet the One who in the mystery of eternity is the crucified God — the God who became like us, so that we might become like him.

To walk in the way of the One who is the Way, the Truth and the Life is to seek to follow in the steps of the One who 'emptied himself, taking the form of a slave. . . [and] humbled himself and became obedient to the point of death. . .' (Philippians 2: 7–8, NRSV). The prayer of consecration, the ongoing, oft-renewed prayer of dedication to the way of Christian discipleship, starts not from our strengths and publicly-acknowledged gifts and graces, but from our own recognition of what God already knows and we so often deny: our weakness and impoverishment of spirit. Here is the only starting place for the prayer — and life — of consecration.

❧

Now we can understand why the New Testament always speaks of our becoming 'like Christ'. We have been transformed into the image of Christ, and are therefore destined to be like him. He is the only 'pattern' we must follow. And because he really lives his life in us, we, too, can 'walk even as he walked' (1 John 2: 6), and 'do as he has done' (John 13: 15), 'love as he has loved' (Ephesians 5: 2; John 13: 34; 15: 12), 'forgive as he forgave' (Colossians 3: 13), 'have this mind, which was also in Christ Jesus' (Philippians 2: 5), and therefore we are able to follow the example he has left us (1 Peter 2: 21) and lay down our lives for the brethren as he did (1 John 3: 16). . .

It is only because we are identified with him that we can become like him. By being transformed into his image, we are enabled to model our lives on his. By simply following him, we can perform deeds and live a life which is one with the life of Christ. We are now able to render spontaneous obedience to the word of God. . . The disciple looks solely at his other Master. . . and has been called to be the 'imitator of God'. . . (Ephesians 5: 1).

Dietrich Bonhoeffer, The Cost of Discipleship

The crisis of self-surrender has always been, and must always be, regarded as the vital turning point of the religious life.

William James, The Varieties of Religious Experience

I will ponder with great affection how much God our Lord has done for me, how much he has given me of what he possesses and, finally, how much — as far as he can — the same Lord desires to give himself to me. . . Then I will reflect upon myself and consider, according to all reason and justice, what I ought to offer [God] — that is, all I possess and myself with it.

Louis J. Puhl, The Spiritual Exercises of St Ignatius

The glorious offer of the New Testament is that of a transforming, communicable sense of the power and presence of God. . . Something happens in the human soul which is done by God; which [by ourselves we] cannot achieve, since even Paul, whose mood one would interpret with the active voice, always uses the passive voice when he is talking about it, and says he is changed, is conformed, is justified, is raised up, is born, and speaks of [us] passing from death to life, darkness to light. . . things we cannot do for ourselves.

The message of the New Testament is that the most important thing in the world is that we should get our relationship right with God and receive this transforming experience. No hereditary Christianity such as some of us here possess is a substitute for it. . . The point is not what God demands, but what Christ offers.

Leslie D. Weatherhead, Discipleship

Christian faith is the decision in which [men and women] have the freedom to be publicly responsible for their trust in God's Word and for their knowledge of the truth of Jesus Christ, in the language of the church, but also in worldly attitudes and, above all, in their corresponding actions and conduct.

Karl Barth, *Dogmatics in Outline*

It needs to be emphasised that there are not two forms of the Christian life: an ordinary life of just being a Christian, and an extraordinary life of discipleship. All Christians are called to be disciples. Those who have not heard the call to discipleship cannot have clearly heard the call to be Christians either. How could one be a Christian without actually following Christ? It is only in taking the first steps of discipleship that the about-turn of conversion becomes a reality. Levi had to actually get up from his customs desk and follow Jesus. We all must do likewise.

Gordon Dicker, *Faith with Understanding*

DO YOU LOVE ME?
A meditative response to John 21: 15–19

Do you love me?
I hear your question again, Lord.
Probing, sifting, encouraging. . .
Lifting my sights to what is possible,
raising my hopes of what can yet be,
Drawing me:
upward in praise and awe,
inward in love and contentment,
outward in compassion and mercy.
Like Peter, I resent your repetition and persistence,
resist your challenge to my comfort,
crave your acceptance and healing. . .
You know that I love you.
Feed my sheep!
I hear your instruction again, Lord.
Directing, specifying, encouraging. . .
calling me back to your first call,

holding me firmly yet lovingly,
pointing me, first to my family, such blessing
then to the neighbours around me,
and beyond to a suffering world.
Like Peter, I get on my high horse —
are these more 'shoulds' and 'oughts'? —
and then I see in your face the transforming
peace of real love. . .
You know that I love you.
Follow me!
I hear your imperious command, Lord.
Echoing, disturbing, direct. . .
Cutting across my distractions
Centring my thoughts and my feet:
Follow you? Seems hard and yet what I want.
Seems endless, yet you're at the end.
Sounds daunting, but you're the Enabler.
Looks lonely, but you're the Companion, I see.
Love you? Follow you? Serve you?
In obedience.
And gradually. . . in love.

Robin Pryor

Jesus, may all that is you flow into me.
May your body and blood be my food and drink.
May your passion and death be my strength and life.
Jesus, with you by my side enough has been given.
May the shelter I seek be the shadow of your cross.
Let me not run from the love you offer,
But hold me safe from the forces of evil.
On each of my dyings shed your light and your love.
Keep calling to me until that day comes,
When, with your saints, I may praise you forever.
    Amen.

David L. Fleming, *A Contemporary Reading of the Spiritual
Exercises [of St Ignatius]*

Take my life and let it be
consecrated, Lord, to thee.
Take my moments and my days,

let them flow in ceaseless praise.
Take my hands and let them move
at the impulse of thy love.
Take my feet and let them be
swift and beautiful for thee.
Take my voice, and let me sing
always, only, for my King.
Take my lips and let them be
filled with messages from thee.
Take my silver and my gold,
not a mite would I withhold.
Take my intellect, and use
every power as thou shalt choose.
Take my will and make it thine;
it shall be no longer mine.
Take my heart, it is thine own;
it shall be thy royal throne.
Take my love: my Lord, I pour
at thy feet its treasure-store.
Take myself and I will be
ever, only, all for thee.

Frances Ridley Havergal

Take, Lord, and receive all my liberty, my memory, my
understanding and my entire will — all that I have and call
my own. You have given it all to me. To you, Lord, I return
it. Everything is yours; do with it what you will. Give me
only your love and your grace. That is enough for me.

David L. Fleming, *A Contemporary Reading of the
Spiritual Exercises [of St Ignatius]*

Take us, O God, and remake us.
Give us boldness to enter through the veil
that is his flesh: knowing in fullness of faith
that our hearts are cleansed from an evil conscience:
so that we may consider one another,
and provoke one another to good works,
and open our minds and hearts
to the meaning and the cost of a changing day.

George F. MacLeod, *The Whole Earth Shall Cry Glory*

May every thought and action of the day
be unified and offered to your praise;
and while I sleep may my heart wake,
giving unto you my love
to glorify your name,
that all that is not wholly reconciled to you
may be resolved and simplified by love,
the love which is the knowledge of yourself.

Gilbert Shaw, *The Face of Love*

Lift up your heart to God with a meek stirring of love, seeking God himself and none of his created things. Think of nothing but God himself, so that nothing will work in your mind, or in your will, but only God himself. You must then do whatever will help you forget all the beings whom God has created and all their works. Your thoughts and your desires are not to be directed toward them nor to touch them in any way. . .

If you wish to stand and not fall, therefore, never slack in your purpose, but beat constantly with a sharp dart of longing love upon this cloud of unknowing which is between you and God. As you do this, do not think of anything under God, and do not let up no matter what happens. For this is the work that destroys the ground and root of sin.

The Cloud of Unknowing

Teach us, good Lord,
To serve you as you deserve:
to give, and not to count the cost;
to fight, and not to heed the wounds;
to toil, and not to seek for rest;
to labour, and not to ask for any reward,
except that of knowing that we do your holy will;
through Jesus Christ our Lord.
Amen.

Ignatius Loyola

Lord, what is the point of your presence
if our lives do not alter?
Change our lives; shatter

our complacency.
Make your word
flesh of our flesh,
blood of our blood,
and our life's purpose.
Take away that self-regard
which makes our consciences feel clear.
Press us uncomfortably.
For only thus
that other peace is made.
Your peace.

Helder Camara

If any want to become my followers, let them deny them-
selves and take up their cross daily and follow me.

Luke 9: 23, NRSV

Lord, this is a troublesome saying,
heavy and hard.
We jealously protect our gains,
always on guard.
The more we have, the more we crave
success self-made.
When you speak of losing all,
we are afraid.
Lord, this is an embarrassing saying
for folk like us.
Even over the smallest disciplines,
we make a great fuss.
We are not made of that stuff of heroes,
without complaints.
We are just your little people,
not noble saints.
Lord, this is a persistent saying,
giving no rest.
In mind and soul we know it is sane,
offering the best.
By gaining and grasping we know we lose
life's deeper scope.
The strange logic of your cross remains
life's only hope.

Lord, this is a saving saying,
divine outlay.
The path of the cross the only glory
all the way.
Willing, though fearful, help us to bear it,
not growing slack.
Laughing and crying, help us to follow,
not turning back.

Bruce D. Prewer, 'The Way of the Cross'

I am giving Thee worship with my whole life,
I am giving Thee assent with my whole power,
I am giving Thee praise with my whole tongue,
I am giving Thee honour with my whole utterance.
I am giving Thee reverence with my whole
understanding,
I am giving Thee offering with my whole thought,
I am giving Thee praise with my whole fervour,
I am giving Thee humility in the blood of the Lamb.
I am giving Thee love with my whole devotion,
I am giving Thee kneeling with my whole desire,
I am giving Thee love with my whole heart,
I am giving Thee affection with my whole sense;
I am giving Thee my existence with my whole mind,
I am giving Thee my soul, O God of all gods.

A Celtic prayer, in Esther de Waal, *A World Made Whole*

You are admitting us now into a wonderful communion,
the foretaste of that final feast.
Help us to put on the wedding garment of rejoicing
which is none of our fashioning,
but your gift to us alone.
By the glories of your creation,
which we did not devise;
by the assurance of your freeing us,
which we could not accomplish;
by the wind of your Spirit —
eddying down the centuries through these walls renewed
whispering through our recaptured oneness,

fanning our faith into flame —
help us to put on the wedding garment.
So shall we go out into the world,
new created, new redeemed and new enchained together:
to fight for your kingdom
in our fallen world.

George MacLeod, *The Whole Earth Shall Cry Glory*

I am no longer my own, but yours.
Put me to what you will,
rank me with whom you will;
put me to doing, put me to suffering;
let me be full, let me be empty;
let me have all things, let me have nothing;
I freely and wholeheartedly yield all things
to your pleasure and disposal.
And now, glorious and blessed God,
Father, Son and Holy Spirit,
you are mine and I am yours,
to the glory and praise of your name.
Amen.

The Covenant Prayer

A Benediction

May the yoke of the law of God be upon this shoulder,
the coming of the Holy Spirit on this head,
the sign of Christ on this forehead,
the hearing of the Holy Spirit in these ears,
the smelling of the Holy Spirit in this nose,
the vision that the people of heaven have in these eyes,
the speech of the people of heaven in this mouth,
the work of the church of God in these hands,
the good of God and of the neighbour in these feet.
May God dwell in this heart
and this person belonging entirely to God the Father.
Amen.

Blessing attributed to St Fursa

28

The hardest thing in the universe

Praise the Lord, O my soul; all my inmost being, praise his holy name. Praise the Lord, O my soul, and forget not all his benefits — who forgives all your sins and heals all your diseases, who redeems your life from the pit and crowns you with love and compassion, who satisfies your desires with good things so that your youth is renewed like the eagle's.

No, the Lord has told us what is good. What he requires of us is this: to do what is just, to show constant love and to live in humble fellowship with our God.

Forgive us the wrongs we have done, as we forgive the wrongs that others have done to us. Do not bring us to hard testing, but keep us safe from the evil one. If you forgive others the wrongs they have done to you, your Father in heaven will also forgive you. But if you do not forgive others, then your Father will not forgive the wrongs you have done.

Then Peter came and said to him, 'Lord, if another member of the church sins against me, how often should I forgive? As many as seven times?' Jesus said to him, 'Not seven times but, I tell you, seventy-seven times.'

Then his lord summoned him and said to him, 'You wicked slave! I forgave you all that debt because you pleaded with me. Should you not have had mercy on your fellow slave, as I had mercy on you?' And in anger his lord handed him over to be tortured until he would pay his entire debt. So my heavenly Father will also do to every one of you, if you do not forgive your brother or sister from your heart.

You have heard that it was said, 'An eye for an eye, and a tooth for a tooth.' But now I tell you: do not take revenge on someone who wrongs you. If anyone slaps you on the right cheek, turn the other also. And if someone takes you to court to sue you for your shirt, give your coat as well. And if one of the occupation troops forces you to carry his pack one kilometre, carry it two kilometres. Give to everyone who begs from you and do not refuse anyone who wants to borrow from you.

So when you are offering your gift at the altar, if you remember that your brother or sister has something against you, leave your gift there before the altar and go; first be reconciled to your brother or sister, and then come and offer your gift.

(Psalm 103: 1–5, NIV; Micah 6: 8, Matthew 6: 12–15 — both GNB; Matthew 18: 21–22 and 32–35, RSV; Matthew 5: 38–42, GNB; Matthew 5: 23–24, RSV)

Forgiveness is at the heart of effective living. It is not a theme which is limited in its importance to a religious context. If we desire to make and keep strong close friendships, then we need to be able to accept and express forgiveness. When we cannot do so, we live with guilt and grudges. These are possibly the deepest pains and the most venomous poisons in life.

The normal process is that we must experience forgiveness (grace) before we can express it. As with many other key capacities for living such as love and trust, although we have a deep need for them, we cannot fulfil that need ourselves. It is only as we live with love, trust and forgiveness that we will have the capacity to express these key qualities.

Except for the unchanging, unqualified, inexhaustible love of God, which is the basis of and motivation for his forgiveness, we will run dry — indeed, the world will run dry.

We must recognise our need and deliberately open ourselves to experience this grace of his love and forgiveness.

In order to be willing to do so, we must be humble enough to admit that we need help, that we have gone in unwise directions, that we have lived as if the world should revolve around us. We should also be willing to accept that we do not have the resources within ourselves to make things right, that we need grace instead of always trying to 'pay our own way' in life.

This is not an irresponsible attitude; it is an absolute need.

In order to be able to express forgiveness, we must give up our just right to 'get back' or give an 'eye for an eye and a tooth for a tooth', recognising that that will not heal the damaged relationship. We need to be able to admit humbly, when we are tempted through pride to condemn the action of another, that 'there but for the grace of God go I'.

The helping professions usually do not offer many clues to the helper about how to be a reconciler. This is because, at its heart, the capacity to forgive and the willingness to accept forgiveness are spiritual dynamics that come from God. We cannot muster those resources from within ourselves.

Forgiveness is the deepest and most desperate need in personal, family, community, national and international life today. Is it any wonder that the Author of life, the One who said he came to bring us life to the full, paid the price by giving up his own rights in the heavenly places and sacrificed himself in order that we can receive the grace of forgiveness? If we have experienced this, we will express it to others. This will change us so dramatically that we will be able to begin again — we will be 'born again'.

❧❦

True forgiveness is the hardest thing in the universe.

David Augsburger, *Seventy Times Seven*

One has to be a psychotherapist to know how rare the forgiveness of others is.

Paul Tournier, *Guilt and Grace*

Forgiveness is the dynamic of the doctrine of justification. Forgiveness establishes the relationship which justification declares and as such constitutes the pivotal focus of Christianity.

H.D. MacDonald, *Forgiveness and Atonement
Was, Became, Remains. . .*

Jesus' prayer was, 'Father, forgive them;
  they know not what they do.'
A prayer born in death, writhing with pain.
A prayer risking in faith, facing the sorrow.
A prayer living in hope, seeing the future.
My prayer was, 'God, how can I forgive them?
  They do know what they did.'
A prayer saying, 'It still hurts.'
A prayer wanting vengeance.
A prayer seeking direction.
My prayer became, 'God, help me forgive them;
  they know what they did.'
A prayer saying, 'They were wrong.'
A prayer wanting reconciliation.
A prayer seeking courage.
My prayer became, 'God forgive them;
  they know what they did.'
A prayer that wrestled with injustice.
A prayer that acknowledges weakness.
A prayer that found hope in God's love.
My prayer remains, 'God, forgive them;
  they know what they did.'
Because forgiving recreates life from death.
Because forgiving cleanses the healing wound.
Because forgiving builds the bridge of freedom.

A client, in Jared P. Pingleton,
The Role and Function of Forgiveness

There is steadily mounting evidence that nothing is more radically redemptive — so 'relaxing' — as having no secrets, at least no shameful ones, from anybody.

O. Hobart Mowrer, *Groups That Work*

It was at a church service in Munich that I saw him, the former SS man who had stood guard at the shower room door in the processing centre at Ravensbruck. He was the first of our actual gaolers that I had seen since that time. And suddenly it was all there — the roomful of mocking men, the heaps of clothing, Betsie's pain-blanched face.

He came up to me as the church was emptying, beaming and bowing. 'How grateful I am for your message, *Fraulein*,' he said. 'To think that, as you say, he has washed my sins away!'

His hand was thrust out to shake mine. And I, who had preached so often to the people in Bloemendaal the need to forgive, kept my hand at my side.

Even as the angry, vengeful thoughts boiled through me, I saw the sin of them. Jesus Christ had died for this man; was I going to ask for more? Lord Jesus, I prayed, forgive me and help me to forgive him.

I tried to smile, I struggled to raise my hand. I could not. I felt nothing, not the slightest spark of warmth or charity. And so again I breathed a silent prayer. Jesus, I cannot forgive him. Give me your forgiveness.

As I took his hand, the most incredible thing happened. From my shoulder along my arm and through my hand a current seemed to pass from me to him, while into my heart sprang a love for the stranger that almost overwhelmed me.

And so I discovered that it is not on our forgiveness any more than on our goodness that the world's healing hinges, but on his. When he tells us to love our enemies, he gives, along with the command, the love itself.

Corrie ten Boom, *The Hiding Place*

Father:
I confess that I find it so hard to let go of hurts. It doesn't seem fair that they should get away with it. Justice gives me the right and I look for the opportunity to get even — an eye for an eye and a tooth for a tooth. I try to justify my simmering resentment by remembering the injustices I have suffered. I secretly wish that something bad would happen to those whom

I see as the opposition.

In my better moments, I realise that the grudges I am holding are a poison within me. They are not doing me or anyone else any good. I pray you will give me the power to give up my right to 'get back'. Help me to see other people as you see them — through eyes of that understanding which leads to love and forgiveness.

May I experience the release of your forgiveness so refreshingly and deeply that in the light of that relief and release it will be a small thing for me to extend grace and forgiveness to others.

Lord, you know how deeply I need this work of your Spirit so that I may experience the fulfilling life your Son died to make possible.

Thank you. Amen.

A Benediction
Now to him who is able to do immeasurably more than all we can ask or conceive, by the power which is at work among us, to him be glory in the church and in Christ Jesus from generation to generation evermore! Amen.

Ephesians 3: 20–21

29

The Christian life wasn't meant to be easy

The salvation of the righteous is from the Lord; he is their refuge in the time of trouble.

As servants of God we have commended ourselves in every way: through great endurance, in afflictions, hardships, calamities. And not only that, but we also boast in our sufferings, knowing that suffering produces endurance. [He] consoles us in all our affliction, so that we may be able to console those who are in any affliction with the consolation with which we ourselves are consoled by God. We are afflicted in every way, but not crushed; perplexed, but not driven to despair. For this slight momentary affliction is preparing us for an eternal weight of glory beyond all measure. I am overjoyed in all our affliction. For this reason, brothers and sisters, during all our distress and persecution we have been encouraged about you through your faith.

In your distress. . . in time to come, you will return to the Lord your God and heed him. Trust in him at all times, O people; pour out your heart before him. God is a refuge for us.

But [Lord] you do see! Indeed you note trouble and grief, that you may take it into your hands; the helpless commit themselves to you; you have been the helper of the orphan. Be gracious to me, O Lord, for I am in distress. Answer me when I call, O God of my right! You gave me room when I was in distress. Be gracious to me and hear my prayer. Relieve the troubles of my heart and bring me out of my distress.

The Lord is a stronghold for the oppressed, a stronghold in times of trouble. For he will hide me in his shelter in the day of trouble; he will conceal me under the cover of his tent; he will set me high on a rock.

When you pass through the water, I will be with you; and through the rivers, they shall not overwhelm you; when you walk through fire, you shall not be burned, and the flame shall not consume you. Do not fear, for I am with you.

In my distress I called upon the Lord; to my God I cried for help. From his temple, he heard my voice and my cry to him reached his ears. When the righteous cry for help, the Lord hears and rescues them from all their troubles.

Cast your burden on the Lord and he will sustain you; he will never permit the righteous to be moved.

(Psalm 37: 39; 2 Corinthians 6: 4; Romans 5: 3; 2 Corinthians 1: 4; 4: 8; 4: 17; 7: 4; 1 Thessalonians 3: 7; Deuteronomy 4: 30; Psalm 62: 8; 10: 14; 31: 9; 4: 1; 25: 17; 9: 9; 27: 5; Isaiah 43: 2 and 5; Psalm 18: 6; 34: 17; 55: 22 — all NRSV)

The Roman proconsul ordered: 'Take the oath, and I shall release you. Curse Christ.'
Polycarp said: 'Eighty-six years I have served him, and he never did me any wrong. How can I blaspheme my King who saved me?'
And when he had said these things and many besides, he was inspired with courage and joy, and his face was full of grace, so that the proconsul was astonished. . .
And with his hands put behind him and tied, he looked up to heaven and said:

Lord God Almighty, Father of the beloved and blessed servant Jesus Christ. . . I bless you, because you have deemed me worthy of this day and hour, to take part in the number of martyrs. . . for resurrection to eternal life . . . May I be received as a rich and acceptable sacrifice. For this and everything I praise you, I bless you, I glorify

you, through Jesus Christ, your beloved servant, through
whom be glory to you with him and the Holy Spirit both
now and unto the ages to come. Amen.

And when he had concluded the Amen and finished
his prayer, the men lit the fire. . .

How does someone facing a painful death get to have
this sort of faith?

First, here's a truism so obvious that it is likely to be
ignored or even denied: all of life is trouble. We in the
West have been seduced into believing that, properly organised, we can buy our way out of trouble. The
advertisers promise a trouble-free existence if we purchase
their product. The insurers promise to cover any contin-
gency, for a fee. We have government social welfare
benefits on a scale unheard of in most of the world for
most of history. This is why, of course, the suicide rate
is climbing in affluent countries. We have been 'sold a
dummy', and life is too catastrophic to endure when
trouble comes.

On a visit to the US, the well-known German preacher
Helmut Thielicke was asked the most important question
facing Americans. He said Americans did not know how
to deal with suffering. He thought they did not expect
trouble to be part of life. 'Again and again, I have the
feeling that suffering is regarded as something which is
fundamentally inadmissible, disturbing, embarrassing and
not to be endured.'

We are taught by our sick culture to indulge continually
in what Albert Camus called 'nostalgia for other people's
lives'.

One of the few generalisations you can make about the
greatest men and women of the Bible is that they all got
into trouble. God must love his special people a lot to
trust them with problems! An interesting text in the
Psalms says, 'Before I was afflicted I went astray, but now
I keep your word' (119: 67). Jesus promised his followers
three things — constant trouble, constant joy and his constant presence. The early Christian missionaries had this

important piece of encouragement(!) for young converts: 'It is through many persecutions that we must enter the kingdom of God' (Acts 14: 22).

The New Testament word *thlipsis*, 'affliction', is used fifty-five times in the New Testament, referring to persecution, oppression, famine, judgment, or even the labour pains of childbirth. The early Christian leaders said trouble was not merely to be endured, but even welcomed!

Thus St Augustine thanks God, in the *Confessions*, for 'mercifully sprinkling my path with thorns'.

Malcolm Muggeridge saw life as 'a very bright light and a very deep darkness, an inconceivable hope and blackest despair, an overwhelming love and abysmal desolation'.

There are some things we come up against which we have to adjust to, because they will not adjust to us. Our handicap or problem can become the foundation for strength — and even happiness. What you do to life is much more important than what life does to you. The way out is always the way through, not around or away. The good news really does come by facing the bad news. It is possible 'to fail forward', and sad indeed is the person who does not know this and thus allows the experiences of life to be wasted on him or her.

A young lady was just eighteen when she contracted a dreadful illness. To save her life, the doctor said he must amputate her feet. This he did, but the disease spread further, so he took off her legs to the knees. Later he amputated her thighs. Then it broke out again in her hands and arms: first one arm, then the other were taken off, right up to the shoulders. She was left with only her trunk.

For fifteen years, she lay there. The walls of her room were covered with Bible texts, all of them affirming God's gifts of love and peace and power. That woman mediated such grace from her room that hundreds of people were converted to faith in Christ through her letters.

How did she write? A carpenter friend fitted an instrument to her shoulder into which a pen could be inserted. We write with fingers, hand and arm: she had to use her whole body, but her writing became as beautiful as copperplate. She eventually collected fifteen hundred letters telling of people blessed by her. When asked how she did it, she smiled and replied: 'Well, you know, Jesus said that those who believed in him, from within them would flow rivers of living water. I believed in him — that's all!'

Mozart died in abject poverty; Beethoven — of all people — started to go deaf at 28; Stevenson was writing novels while dying of consumption; Handel wrote *The Messiah* when he was broke; George Matheson, the Scottish preacher who wrote the great hymn 'O Love That Will Not Let Me Go', was blind; Lord Byron had a club foot; the philosopher Kant had an incurable disease; Wilberforce took opium for twenty years to deaden his pain; Helen Keller was blind and deaf. . .

So our prayer is not for easier lives, but to be stronger in faith, hope and love. It is noteworthy that trouble comes to those who don't deserve it — but so does love!

St Theresa had problems, and once complained: 'Lord, if this is the way you treat your friends, it's no wonder you have so few of them.' But why is there a 'St' before her name? Because through her trouble she came to believe that 'everything is grace'. 'In his will, our peace' — T.S. Eliot called this statement, from Dante, the profoundest line in all of human writing.

❧

Life is difficult.

This is a great truth, one of the greatest truths. It is a great truth because once we truly see this truth, we transcend it. Once we truly know that life is difficult — once we truly understand and accept it — then life is no longer difficult. Because once it is accepted, the fact that life is difficult no longer matters.

Most do not fully see this truth that life is difficult. Instead, they moan more or less incessantly, noisily or subtly about the enormity of their problems, their burdens and their difficulties as if life were generally easy, as if life should be easy. They voice their belief, noisily or subtly, that their difficulties represent a unique kind of affliction that should not be and that has somehow been especially visited upon them, or else upon their families, their tribe, their class, their nation, their race or even their species, and not upon others. . .

What makes life difficult is that the process of confronting and solving problems is a painful one. . . Since life poses an endless series of problems, life is always difficult and is full of pain as well as joy.

Yet it is in this whole process of meeting and solving problems that life has its meaning. . . Problems call forth our courage and our wisdom; indeed, they create our courage and our wisdom. It is only because of problems that we grow mentally and spiritually. When we desire to encourage the growth of the human spirit, we challenge and encourage the human capacity to solve problems, just as in school we deliberately set problems for our children to solve. It is through the pain of confronting and resolving problems that we learn. As Benjamin Franklin said, 'Those things that hurt, instruct.'

It is for this reason that wise people learn not to dread, but actually to welcome problems and actually to welcome the pain of problems.

M. Scott Peck, *The Road Less Travelled*

There is no misfortune from which some good may not be derived.

Spanish Proverb

I came across something that would be with me throughout my life. Oppositions break or solidify a person. I determined they would solidify me. I wouldn't bear things; I would use them. As a radiant woman said, 'My cheeks have been slapped so much they are quite rosy.'

I. Stanley Jones, *A Song of Ascents: A Spiritual Biography*

Hello trouble, (you. . .)
I've met with you before —
So now you're here again,
Bigger than ever, larger than life,

Ready to cause more and more strife
And break me if you can.
My hands are tied behind my back,
My legs they are in chains,
My health is not what it used to be,
I do have aches and pains,
My responsibilities loom large
And there are those who on me depend
Whom I wouldn't see hurt for the world —
So buzz off, trouble. But if you're going to stay:
My brow you may crease, my shoulders you may
bow,
My mind you may scar, my nerves you may break.
Mark you, I said *may*,
But mark also if you stay
I shall surely grow and grow,
And my spirit, my soul, you cannot touch,
For they belong to God and me —
And no matter what you do or say
They always will be free.

Ken Walsh, *Sometimes I Weep*

When I read of the barbarous ages of slaughter and
carnage and brutality through which my long line of ancestors threaded its fearsome way, it is perfectly
astounding to me that not one of them got stabbed or
clubbed or shot until they had duly taken their places in
that long genealogical list. When I think of the wars and
famines and pestilences through which those forebears of
mine came unscathed, I catch my breath.

F.W. Boreham, *The Tide Comes In*

I repeat, then: the secret of responding heroically to
trouble is not something highly complicated; it lies in one's
view of the relation of God to each and every event. If
we separate the two, and see God off somewhere else as
impotent and indifferent, this means we are left alone with
our troubles and are thus inadequate and ultimately
defeated.   But if we take the biblical stance toward life
and see him everywhere, in each event, either intentionally

or permissively but always creatively, then we can take heart and be assured that our trouble is not totally bad or beyond the possibility of working good.

Our challenge then, in trouble, is to remember who is also there and what this means, and to work at the job of increasing that awareness until it is perpetual.

John R. Claypool, *Learning to Use our Troubles*

The saints look at their lives, half full of joys and half full of sorrows as anyone's life is, and they see it as half full, while others see it as half empty. The saints are grateful for the full half. They 'count their blessings'. They know that their very existence is sheer gift, and so they know that great and joyful virtue of gratitude, so tragically neglected in our day. No-one can understand life without being grateful for it. No-one can wholly misunderstand life if they are grateful for it.

Peter Kreeft, 'Seven Lessons from the Saints About Suffering'

Lord,
we cannot always see
beyond
our pain and sorrow to the triumph of faith!
We think
we have cause to complain
when things go badly for us:
when friends let us down,
when neighbours hurt our feelings,
when sickness and death
deprive us of happiness.
Help us to see clearly
how much greater
is our cause for joy
and hope
through the love
you pour into our hearts;
help us to see that all these things
that hurt us
are the trials through which we triumph

through the power of him who loved us;
so that in good times and bad
our lives may honour you,
through Jesus Christ our Lord.

Alan Gaunt, *New Prayers for Worship*

God and Father of our Lord Jesus Christ, though your people walk in the valley of darkness, no evil should they fear, for they follow in faith the call of the Shepherd whom you have sent for their hope and strength.

Attune our minds to the sound of his voice, lead our steps in the path he has shown, that we may know the strength of his outstretched arm and enjoy the light of your presence for ever.

Daily Mass Book, Lent 1991–1992

God, grant us the serenity to accept the things we cannot change, the courage to change the things we can, and the wisdom to know the difference.

In everything we do, in our troubles, difficulties and hardships, we show whether we are God's servants. By purity, patience and kindness, by the Spirit and by our love, and by our message of truth, we show ourselves for what we are. We may seem poor, but we make many rich; we seem to have nothing, but we possess all that there is to have. . .

If Christ's name is flung in our teeth we should count ourselves happy, because that glorious spirit, the Spirit of God, is resting upon us.

If we suffer, let it not be for murder, theft or sorcery, nor for infringing on the rights of others; but if we suffer as Christians we should feel no disgrace, but confess that name to the honour of God.

It gives us a share in Christ's sufferings. That is cause for joy!

Giver of the present, hope for the future: save us from the time of trial. When prophets warn us of doom, of catastrophe and of suffering beyond belief, then, God, free us from our helplessness, and deliver us from evil. Save us from our arrogance and folly, for you are God who created the world; you have redeemed us and you are our salvation.

Almighty God, you see that we have no power of ourselves to help ourselves; keep us both outwardly in our bodies and inwardly in our souls, that we may be defended from all adversities which may happen to the body, and from all evil thoughts which may assault and hurt the soul.

God of opportunity and change, praise to you for giving us life at this critical time. As our horizons extend, keep us loyal to our past; as our dangers increase, help us to prepare the future; keep us trusting and hopeful, ready to recognise your kingdom as it comes. Amen.

A New Zealand Prayer Book

Allow the strength of God to sustain you,
The wisdom of God to instruct you,
The hand of God to protect you,
The shield of God to defend you,
The Spirit of God to lead you,
The Son of God to redeem you,
Until by the grace of God,
We see him face to face. Amen.

E. Lee Phillips, *Prayers for Worship*

A Benediction

Rejoice in hope, be patient in suffering, persevere in prayer (Romans 12: 12). Blessed is anyone who endures temptation. Such a one has stood the test and will receive the crown of life that the Lord has promised to those who love him. And after you have suffered for a little while, the God of all grace, who has called you to his eternal glory in Christ, will himself restore, support, strengthen and establish you (James 1: 12; 1 Peter 5: 10). The Lord answer you in the day of trouble! The name of the God of Jacob protect you! (Psalm 20: 1).

Death and life are in the power of the tongue. Be quick
to listen, slow to speak, slow to anger.

The mouth of the righteous brings forth wisdom, but
the perverse tongue will be cut off. The great dragon. . .
that ancient serpent, who is called the Devil and Satan. . .
the accuser of our comrades. . . who accuses them day
and night. You are plotting destruction. Your tongue
is like a sharp razor, you worker of treachery. They all
deceive their neighbours and no-one speaks the truth;
they have taught their tongues to speak lies; they commit
iniquity and are too weary to repent. Oppression upon
oppression, deceit upon deceit! They refuse to know
me, says the Lord.

I am the scorn of all my adversaries, a horror to my
neighbours, an object of dread to my acquaintances;
those who see me in the street flee from me. I have
passed out of mind like one who is dead; I have become
like a broken vessel. For I hear the whispering of many
— terror all around! — as they scheme together against
me, as they plot to take my life. Who whet their tongues
like swords, who aim bitter words like arrows. I said,
'I will guard my ways that I may not sin with my
tongue; I will keep a muzzle on my mouth as long as
the wicked are in my presence.'

If any think they are religious, and do not bridle their
tongues but deceive their hearts, their religion is worthless . . .the tongue is a small member, yet it boasts of
great exploits. How great a forest is set ablaze by a
small fire! And the tongue is a fire. The tongue is
placed among our members as a world of iniquity; it

stains the whole body, sets on fire the cycle of nature and is itself set on fire by hell.

Rash words are like sword thrusts, but the tongue of the wise brings healing. To watch over mouth and tongue is to keep out of trouble. The mouths of the righteous utter wisdom and their tongues speak justice.

Let no evil talk come out of your mouths, but only what is useful for building up, as there is need, so that your words may give grace to those who hear.

Let us therefore no longer pass judgment on one another, but resolve instead never to put a stumbling block or hindrance in the way of another. Let your speech always be gracious, seasoned with salt, so that you may know how you ought to answer everyone.

Let no-one despise your youth, but set the believers an example in speech and conduct, in love, in faith, in purity.

(Proverbs 18: 21; James 1: 19; Proverbs 10: 31; Psalm 52: 2; Jeremiah 9: 5–6; Psalm 31: 11–13; 64: 3; 39: 1; James 1: 26; 3: 5–6; Proverbs 21: 23; Ephesians 4: 29; Romans 14: 13; Colossians 4: 6; 1 Timothy 4: 12 — all NRSV)

'Stop doing the devil's work!' she heard in her dream. Waking, she wondered why the Lord was bringing that message from her unconscious. She asked in her prayer, 'How am I doing the devil's work?' And then the preacher's text from last Sunday's sermon came to her mind: 'The devil is the accuser of our brothers and sisters' (Revelation 12: 10).

Over the next few days, she knew what she had to do. One evening after dinner, she asked her husband and family to gather in the living room. Briefly she shared what God had shown her, recalling people they'd heard her criticise. 'I have been doing the devil's work for him,' she confessed. 'That was sinful. You know the scripture that tells us to get rid of the pole in our eyes before we take out the splinter in another's.'

They nodded solemnly. 'Well, that's what I was doing.

God doesn't have to consult me about the way others lead their lives. God may have purposes and plans I don't understand. I grieved him when I was critical and judged by *my* standards. Only God has the right to judge. That doesn't mean we don't need correcting from time to time, but Matthew 18 tells us how we should handle it. We need to go directly to the one involved, without collecting opinions and gossip along the way.' Later she said, 'As I finished our conference, I sensed a sweet release. Now when the temptation to criticise comes back, I know it's time to re-examine my heart and mouth.'

As prayer is to God, so criticism is to Satan. The Bible severely condemns the type of criticism known as 'judging'. Christ has commanded us not to do it (Matthew 7: 1–2). It's inexcusable because we're *all* sinners (Romans 2: 1). Judging is not our prerogative (Romans 14: 10), but God's alone (James 4: 12). We are not acquainted with all the facts (1 Corinthians 4: 5). Judging puts a stumbling block in another's way (Romans 14: 13).

Occasionally, constructive criticism of another is legitimate, but only when it is made to the person concerned (Matthew 18: 15–17), or for a defence of the faith — but not just our version of the faith! (Galatians 2: 11–14), or when it is made on the basis of scripture for another's salvation (Proverbs 24: 25). When another sins against you, you are to go to that person and be ready to forgive them (Luke 17: 3–4).

We may rebuke another only when it is wise, true and needful (Psalm 141: 5; Proverbs 25: 12); when it is given by parents to children, or by God to his children (Proverbs 15: 5; Hebrews 12: 5–6); when it is for the receiver's advancement in a life of love and holiness (Proverbs 10: 17); when the person rebuked is harming the life of the church, by being openly immoral, heretical, idle or factious (1 Corinthians 5: 1–5, 9–13; 3 John 9–10; 1 John 4: 1; 1 Thessalonians 5: 14; 2 Thessalonians 3: 14–15). *It is our duty to offer this sort of 'reproof'.*

Your words will echo throughout the cosmos forever! Scientists tell us it is feasible that instruments will one day pick up any sounds from any source at any time in the past. Actually, Jesus the judge of all of us will switch on such a 'machine': 'Whatever you have said in the dark will be heard in the light, and whatever you have whispered behind closed doors will be proclaimed from the housetops!' (Luke 12: 3).

Here is a pot-pourri of wisdom about the right use of our tongues:

* Don't say everything you think. It may not be helpful, healing or edifying.
* The old tests: 'Is it true, is it loving, is it necessary?'
* Most of us would rather be ruined by praise than saved by criticism.
* Changing one thing for the better is worth more than proving a thousand things wrong.
* Blowing out others' candles won't make yours shine more brightly. But as you use yours to light theirs, you'll have more light!
* The ratio of prayer to criticism should be about 100 to 1!

Your life is the sum total of all the words you have spoken and which have been spoken to you. 'To speak ill of others is a dishonest way of praising ourselves,' declared Will Durant. Unless we can help someone overcome their faults, there's no value in pointing them out.

A sharp tongue is the only edged tool that grows keener with use! Trouble is, the person with a sharp tongue is usually lonely: we tend to avoid such people because they seem to live in an atmosphere of gloomy depression and discouragement which is quickly transferred to others. The world has too many discouragers!

Language is the dress of thought. Those who empty buckets of cold water over the hopes and aspirations of others are revealing their own frustration, poor self-image or anger. To discourage others is an easy way out and, in fact, it's dishonest to be critical of others without offering a better way.

An American preacher of a previous generation, Clovis

G. Chappell, once said: 'No-one has a right so to preach as to send their hearers away on flat tyres. Every discouraging sermon is a wicked sermon. . . A discouraged person is not an asset, but a liability.'

The influential author Dale Carnegie goes to the heart of the issue: 'If you want to change people without giving offence or arousing resentment, use encouragement. Make the fault you want to correct seem easy to do. . . If you and I will inspire the people with whom we come in contact to a realisation of the hidden treasures they possess, we can do far more than change people. We can literally transform them.'

Accentuating the negative is self-defeating because it makes change almost impossible. Such an approach only serves to emphasise limitations and it never stimulates personal growth. To stress the positive and the possible is to extend life's horizons.

Paul's timely advice is: 'Let us therefore stop turning critical eyes on one another. If we must be critical, let us be critical of our own conduct and see that we do nothing to make another stumble or fall' (Romans 14: 13, J.B. Phillips). It would be far more profitable to be constructively critical of ourselves than to be destructively critical of others.

'The measure you give,' said Jesus, 'will be the measure you get.' In Martin Thornton's novel, *Not as a Stranger*, young Dr Marsh goes to the president of the District Medical Association to accuse an older colleague of malpractice. The president listens to him patiently, then asks him to reconsider his charges and says: 'I am going to suggest this to you — that if you persist in bringing formal charges, then be sure of one thing. Don't ever, as long as you live, make a single mistake.' When you criticise others, you invite the world to do the same to you.

Encouragement creates openness and flexibility. Carping criticism develops a closed mind and a narrow outlook. Criticism which results in discouraging others so that they don't have the heart to try again is almost criminal. To undermine another person's self-confidence and self-respect is contrary to the will of God.

Arthur James Balfour provided us with a helpful insight when he wrote: 'The best thing to give your enemy is forgiveness; to an opponent, tolerance; to a friend, your heart; to your child, a good example; to your father, deference; to your mother, conduct that will make her proud of you; to yourself, respect; and to everyone, charity.'

Admittedly, that is an idealistic picture. But is it beyond us? And aren't the rewards, personal and social, worth the effort? The gloomy alternative leaves us with little option.

We need many more encouragers in our world. There already exist more than enough discouragers. It is easy to shoot a skylark, but it is not so easy to produce its song. (Dame Nellie Melba is reported to have said: 'You won't be famous till people start saying the worst they can of you. Don't worry — it's a good sign!')

We have enough faults of our own to answer to God for and to correct without wasting energy judging others. A dear old saint once scribbled this note for our church bulletin:

Boys flying kites haul in their white winged birds.
You can't do that when you are flying words.
Thoughts unexpressed can sometimes fall back dead,
But God himself can't kill them when they're said!

❧

Keep your mouth shut and you'll never bite off more than you can chew (W.G.P.). To keep your secret is wisdom, but to expect others to keep it is folly (Oliver Wendell Holmes). Do you wish others to speak well of you? Then never speak well of yourself (Blaise Pascal). Admonish your friends privately, but praise them openly (Syrus). If your lips would keep from slips, five things observe with care: to whom you speak; of whom you speak; and how, and when, and where (William Norris).

I have often regretted my speech, never my silence (Publius). Never complain. Never explain (Disraeli).

Blessed is the one who, having nothing to say, abstains from giving in words evidence of the fact (George Eliot). One can only face in others what one can face in oneself (James Baldwin). Tact is the ability to describe others as they see themselves (Abraham Lincoln). By examining the tongue, doctors find out the diseases of the body; and philosophers the diseases of mind and heart (Justin, AD 150). Three may keep a secret, if two of them are dead. Better to remain silent and be thought a fool than to speak out and remove all doubt. Forget others' faults by remembering your own. Tell not all you know, all you have, or all you can do (Torriano). In one's mouth a hatchet grows, with which fools cut themselves, when they utter evil words (Buddha). Drawing on my fine command of language, I said nothing. A man can't argue with the woman he loves.

Desk calendar quotes

Genuine dialogue is non-exploitive; it is a great resource in relationships, leading to reciprocal giving and mutual benefit. . . In this type of meeting, presence, directness and immediacy characterise the moment in which two people genuinely care about each other's side of the dialogue.

Leslie D. Greenberg and Susan M. Jonson,
Emotionally Focused Therapy for Couples

No-one who attended Marietta Tree's eclectically cast dinner parties ever forgot its hostess. . . She would prod guests to engage in what she called 'gencon' — general conversation. You'd be allowed to talk to your table partner on each side for just a few courses. Then she'd announce, 'Let's have gencon', and we'd all talk about a problem of the day.

Chitchat has its place. It humanises. It allows for what Tillich called 'holy waste' in the form of conversation. It makes room for the 'I-Thou'. . . Chitchat, however, left to itself, victimises and abuses. Think of the dinners with what the author of the Timothy letters called 'empty and irreligious chatter'. Think of the dinners we ruined with such chatter. And think of the guilt we had to fight off

during the drive home. Recall the boredom and forget-
tability of most party chitchat.

The weather? All talk about weather, except in the case
of cyclones, is mind-numbing. All talk of temperature,
unless you are in an igloo or sweat lodge, is distracting
and banal. All talk in my city — maybe not yours —
about local baseball teams is appropriate only for
masochists. Some talk about offspring and their offspring
— yours, not mine — can go on too long.

Martin Marty

Conversation. . . is a game where we learn to give in to
the movement required by questions worth exploring. . .
A conversation. . . is not a confrontation. It is not a debate.
It is not an exam. It is questioning itself. It is a willingness to follow the question wherever it may go. . . [The
rules of conversation] are merely variations of the transcen-
dental imperatives elegantly articulated by Bernard
Lonergan: 'Be attentive, be intelligent, be responsible, be
loving and, if necessary, change.'

David Tracy

I still have a bookmark with the old Sioux Indian prayer
on it: 'Oh Great Spirit, grant me the wisdom to walk in
another's moccasins before I criticise or pass judgment.'

Dennis Waitley, *Seeds of Greatness*

When you reprimand someone or express your unhappi-
ness, try to do so after the urge to fight or become upset
has subsided. The best way to get your feelings across is
when you can speak in a normal voice, without all of the
warlike body language. When you are upset, try a substitute physical exercise such as running, [or] tennis in
which there is impact involved to release the pent-up
adrenalin in your system. Do speak your mind, but
criticise the behaviour without attacking the other person.
There is no such thing as winning an argument. There is
only winning an agreement.

It's about time we did far more about the 'tongue
pollution' in our societies. Dirty tongues are dangerous.

We need a 'tongue clean-up campaign'.

Why do people gossip? There are four main reasons. Some gossip because they lack healthy God-pleasing self-confidence and self-respect. Somehow or other they believe that rubbing some of the glitter off the other guy's crown, their own won't look so tarnished. By cutting others down, they think they will stand taller. Others gossip because they are pretty empty-headed. . .

Gossiping doesn't take any brain-power. Charles Allen said: 'Those of great minds discuss ideas. People of mediocre minds discuss events. But those with small minds discuss other people.' Still others gossip because they've got nothing better to do. . . The apostle Paul spoke out against those types of people: 'Not only do they become idlers, but also gossips and busybodies, saying things they ought not to,' and told them to occupy themselves in something. The fourth reason. . . is simply that people are in the habit of gossiping, and so they gossip. . . If you don't believe it, just look over your last month's conversations. . . did you talk about ideas and ideals and events, or was it people?

Robert Winderlich, *Tame that Tongue*

As soon as we moved out of the church into the bright light of day, the never-ending war of humanity broke out again.

Those who were of 'riper years', as the Prayer Book puts it in one of its many glosses on what we do not like to see, as it were, face to face, were displaying their talent for insinuation. 'I'm surprised that. . . feels qualified to take Communion. Mind you, I'm sure everything's all right and I don't wish to imply anything about her. But it does make you wonder, doesn't it? I mean, I wonder where she got to after the dance in the Memorial Hall?'

I used to move around from group to group, standing always a pace or two apart, listening to what they had to say, and puzzled why, after they had destroyed someone's character and reputation, they would then shake hands so warmly and look at each other with such eyes of trust and love, having just made it clear, or so it seemed to me, that they trusted nobody.

Manning Clark, *The Puzzles of Childhood*

I have never understood why in denominational colleges and schools men and women who go down on their knees each Sunday, and hear the chaplain exhort all those who are 'in love and charity with their neighbour' and intend to lead a new life following the commandments of God, should spend the other six days of the week practising the art of the character assassin.

As a vicarage child. . . such behaviour had been one of the puzzles of my childhood. . . I was both the observer and the victim of such attacks. In time, I would learn that the only response to a character sketch is to get on with one's work and not to consume one's energies conceiving wounding replies. But then, alas, mockery was the one weapon in my armoury, the one weapon with which to soothe my wounds. It did not occur to me that by indulging in such satisfactions I might be hurting other people. There would be many years of remorse and regret for having been both a corrupter and one of the corrupted.

Manning Clark, *The Quest for Grace*

'I judge no-one. . . but if I judge'. . . The gentle and gracious souls who would never dream of criticising us are the very people whose silent and unconscious condemnation is the most devastating. A straight stick, lying beside a crooked one, does not judge its twisted neighbour, yet its very straightness is the crooked stick's most terrible exposure.

It seems to vindicate the contention of Francis of Assisi, who held that those who live a beautiful Christian life have no need to resort to words in order to rebuke the iniquities that disfigure the Church and the world.

F.W. Boreham, *The Tide Comes In*

Psychologists have spent years studying the effects of destructive remarks on the psyche. According to one of them, Dr. Honor Whitney: 'A constant stream of negatives, sarcasm, doubts and putdowns cuts emotional scars even in the sturdiest ego. Ultimately, negative statements seriously undermine the way people feel about themselves. The self-image, the inner sense of value as an individual, is weakened. . .'

Try constructive criticism. . . This five-point guide may help. (1) What do I want to change? (2) Can the behaviour be changed? (3) What do I want my criticism to accomplish for me/us? (4) Am I expressing empathy with the person I am criticising? (5) Is the criticism being offered in an appropriate environment?

Victoria Barclay, 'Can You Take as Good as You Give?'

My writings and teachings are frequently scrutinised in the Christian media. Rarely a week goes by that I don't receive an article or book in which I am critiqued. . . In a few instances, serious accusations are levelled against me. . .

I do not respond, for two reasons: Matthew 18: 15–17, Galatians 6: 1, and 1 Timothy 5: 1 provide clear teaching about how to relate to [those] we suspect of wrongdoing. . . The proper procedure is that the concern should first be voiced directly to the person we suspect of wrongdoing. This can be done in person or through a letter. . . The primary reason: we may be wrong; he or she might not be guilty!

[Second] in 1977 the Lord told me [through] a woman prophesying to me about a future worldwide ministry: 'Your brother and sister are never your enemies. . . even when they act like it. Learn to turn the other cheek.' It is difficult not to defend myself, because it gives occasion for misunderstanding and further attack. I suppose anxiety about being misunderstood has been an overriding fear all my life. And the Lord, knowing this, simply eliminated for me what could easily become a sinful response.

John Wimber

Lord, why do I look at the speck in someone else's eye, but ignore the log in my own? Help me not to judge others, not only to avoid condemnation myself, but out of obedience to your word and love for others. May I easily forgive, not only to be forgiven by you, Lord, but, again, out of motives of obedience and love. Help me to give encouragement generously, to find matters for thanksgiving easily, and be slow to speak and quick to listen.

Help me, Lord, as I commit myself to this covenant towards obedience in my speech:

BECAUSE
* God alone is our law-giver and judge, but Satan is the accuser of our brothers and sisters;
* We will give an account to God for every word we speak;
* Death and life are in the power of the tongue;
* The tongue is like a fire and can get out of control;
* We are commanded to say what is helpful, not harmful, and never pass judgment on others.

WITH GOD'S HELP
* I will guard my ways so that I will not sin with my tongue;
* I will be quick to listen, slow to speak, slow to anger, and be patient and kind with everyone;
* I will not judge another brother or sister because my Lord has commanded me not to do it;
* I will remember we're all sinners anyway; that judging is not our prerogative, but God's; that I don't know all the facts, and judging puts a stumbling-block in the other's way.

RATHER
* I will speak only to the person concerned if there is something between us that needs sorting out;
* I will go to the person who I feel has sinned against me and be ready to forgive them;
* I will pray very hard and with humble love, before rebuking troublemakers or those who commit sins of immorality, heresy or idleness.

A Benediction

Work hard to live in peace with others, to be kind to others, and to encourage others; to be joyful always, pray continually, give thanks in all circumstances and avoid every kind of evil. And the Lord bless you abundantly as you bless others with your words! Amen.

31

The gentle darkness of sickness

'Teacher, whose sin caused him to be born blind? Was it his own or his parents' sin?' Jesus answered, 'His blindness has nothing to do with his sins or his parents' sins. He is blind so that God's power might be seen at work in him. As long as it is day, we must do the work of him who sent me; night is coming when no-one can work. While I am in the world, I am the light of the world.'

I will take away sickness from among you, and none will miscarry or be barren in your land. I will give you a full lifespan.

What is sown is perishable, what is raised is imperishable. It is sown in dishonour, it is raised in glory. It is sown in weakness, it is raised in power. It is sown a physical body, it is raised a spiritual body. What I am saying, brothers and sisters, is this: flesh and blood cannot inherit the kingdom of God, nor does the perishable inherit the imperishable. Listen, I will tell you a mystery! We will not all die, but we will all be changed, in a moment, in the twinkling of an eye, at the last trumpet. For the trumpet will sound, and the dead will be raised imperishable, and we will be changed. For this perishable body must put on imperishability, and this mortal body must put on immortality.

Whoever, therefore, eats the bread or drinks the cup of the Lord in an unworthy manner will be answerable for the body and blood of the Lord. Examine yourselves, and only then eat of the bread and drink of the cup. For all who eat and drink without discerning the body, eat and drink judgment against themselves. For this reason many of you are weak and ill, and some of you have died.

The sisters sent Jesus a message: 'Lord, your dear friend is sick.' When Jesus heard it, he said, 'The final result of this sickness will not be the death of Lazarus; this has happened in order to bring glory to God and it will be the means by which the Son of God will receive glory.'

When the sun was setting, the people brought to Jesus all who had various kinds of sickness and, laying his hands on each one, he healed them.

Because he himself suffered when he was tempted, he is able to help those who are being tempted. For we do not have a high priest who is unable to sympathise with our weaknesses, but we have one who has been tempted in every way, just as we are — yet was without sin.

For as in Adam all die, so in Christ all will be made alive.

(John 9: 2b–5, GNB; Exodus 23: 25b–26, NIV; 1 Corinthians 15: 42b–44a and 50–53; 11: 27–30 — both NRSV; John 11: 3–4, GNB; Luke 4: 40, NIV; Hebrews 2: 18; 4: 15 — both NIV; 1 Corinthians 15: 22, NIV)

Sickness comes to us for reasons even devoted, faith-filled Christians find hard to accept. Who has sinned: we or our parents? Does the Lord allow sickness as one of the trials by which Satan tests our love of Christ, or do we bring these ailments upon ourselves? Why is it that when we pray hard and long for a healing, it is sometimes withheld?

Perhaps it is important that we address the last dilemma. The finest healing which can occur is the translation of the frail, imperfect physical body in which we traverse this world into that perfect and eternal spiritual body which is ours when we go to be with our Master, and this can only happen through what Satan has deceived us into calling 'death'. We really need another term for the final failing of the clay of our earthbound existence. Perhaps when we pray for the healing of a loved one, and that loved one then goes on ahead of us, our prayer has been answered. . . perfectly. Thus we should sometimes rejoice rather than grieve for our loss, but who among us is Christlike enough to achieve that degree of selflessness?

Perhaps God will be glorified by the cure of the illness with which Satan has tried to crush us or those whom we love. In this case, earnest prayer will bring about the healing which we long for and, in such cases, nothing is more beautiful than to watch a miracle take place. I say 'miracle' but, while to us a healing may be miraculous, it is in the spiritual realm merely the obvious and run-of-the-mill way of doing things. Why is it that we are always so amazed when our omnipotent God quietly displays a tiny fragment of the power which we ascribe to him? Christians should expect miracles; they are the very trade mark of the Father, Son and Holy Spirit.

There are many cases in which we actually encourage sickness and neuroses. We open ourselves to spirits of ill-health by actively courting them. Even as children, we start along this wide, well-used road. Haven't we all said, 'I can't go to school/work today; I don't feel well'? Or perhaps, 'Not now, dear; I have a headache'! And the father of lies loves to hear us, quickly sneaking in a little demon through the doorway of our dishonesty to grow within us, until we are trading lies for sympathy, deceit for extra attention from those who love us.

If we indulge in them, feeding them on our own selfishness, such malaises will grow until they take us to our graves. The love of others will be sickened until that love turns, via the path of fatigue, to resentment and bitterness to end in a miasma of something so close to hatred that Satan can laugh at what he has wrought.

We must turn to Christ in our sicknesses, whether mild flu or terminal cancer, for God is the only one who really knows what is best for us. Christians must also beware of confusing what they want with what they need. Often what we want is the very thing we should not have.

If we pray in sincere humility and with trust, we know that God will do what is best for us. The difficult part is to accept that what happens is best for us, even though we may see it as a terrible tragedy.

When I watched someone whom I loved — the person I loved most in all the world — dying slowly and in agony, I could not understand what was happening or why. Now I know that the experiences she went through and the pain she learnt to bear brought her to the arms of Jesus before she died. Perhaps the agonies were instrumental in saving her life and I will see her again amidst the saints.

In the darkness of sickness, we learn that we are not in control; we learn patience, acceptance, charity. We can learn so much from sickness if we are prepared to try. Let us pray that we have the wisdom to turn to Christ whenever we are ill, waiting to see what lessons our Father has for us.

For those of us who remain healthy, illness in others is, like famine, a wonderful opportunity for us — an opportunity to live the Jesus we profess.

❧

Among Christians, there is as much confusion about health and sickness as there is about wealth or poverty. If you're always well and healthy, you 'must have done something good'. And if you're stricken with any serious illness, God is furious with you and you are being punished.

This confusion is topped only by the mixed feelings about God's healing. If you pray and do get healed, you must be very spiritual (or somebody is sure to tell you it would have happened anyway, whether you prayed or not). And if you don't get healed, you either didn't have enough faith or you still have secret sins in your life. In all this theorising, we leave out one great overwhelming fact — *the sovereignty of God*.

Ethel Barrett, *Will the Real Phony Please Stand Up?*

But not long after my accident, I underwent several weeks of operations in that very hospital. When God moved *me* a few notches up the scale of suffering — ah, then it was a different story. *Now* the sterile and lonely institutional atmosphere became more than just something I'd seen on a TV medical show. A whole new world had opened up and become real to me — and an unpleasant world at that.

I was eventually to come to the conclusion that *one of God's purposes in increasing our trials is to sensitise us to people we would never have been able to relate to otherwise.*

Joni Eareckson Tada, *A Step Further*

If anything, AIDS can be seen as the modern-day equivalent to the disease of leprosy as described in the Bible. In New Testament days, people who had leprosy were viewed very much the same way that modern-day religious people view AIDS victims. Those with leprosy were seen as having their disease because of some special sin they or their fathers had committed. People kept their distance from leprosy victims, believing that even to have the shadows of lepers fall upon them would render them mysteriously contaminated by evil.

Certainly, no-one would touch a leper. Lepers had to carry a bell when they walked about and constantly ring it while calling out 'Unclean! Unclean!'

All that has been said about lepers can also be said about AIDS victims. They, too, are believed to be spiritually unclean in a way that the rest of us are not. They, too, are 'untouchables' who, in some cases, are rejected by even the doctors and nurses who are assigned to care for them. They, like their leper counterparts in the ancient world, are viewed as especially despicable and deserving of being run out of decent society.

Two thousand years ago, when Jesus was physically present among us, he reached out to lepers. He touched the untouchables. He showed special compassion towards those who had been treated in such a cruel manner by the people around them. His willingness to lovingly lay hands on those whom society deemed unclean should set an example for all of us who sing 'I would be like Jesus'.

Tony Campolo, *20 Hot Potatoes Christians are Afraid to Touch*

To understand what it cost the Saviour to be our Healer, we need to walk with him through his passion and suffering, as shown in the Gospels and in the Book of Isaiah.

Come with me now into the Garden of Gethsemane. Discover what it cost our Saviour to be Emmanuel, God with us. Listen to his prayers. Can you hear them, as if for the first time? He began to be sorrowful and very heavy. Then saith he unto them, 'My soul is exceeding sorrowful even unto death' (Matthew 26: 37–38, KJV).

Wait a minute, Jesus. What did you say? 'My soul is exceeding *sorrowful, even unto death*'? Do you mean to say that you experienced such feelings, such emotions and pain in that wretched hour that you even wanted to die? Do you mean to say, Lord, you understand when I am so depressed that I no longer want to live?

David Seamands, *Healing for Damaged Emotions*

February her mood changed; she fell into a pit of despair. She wasn't getting well, the radiation treatment seemed to have no effect, and her pain never took flight. She was showing neither signs of recovery, nor imminent death. Her despair was poured out in a letter to her confidants in America:

> I am in rather a bad state of mind as yet — they promised me definitely that the X-rays would work; I'd pinned all my hopes to having a year or so of happiness with Jack at least — and, indeed, it seems I shall lie about the hospital with my broken femur waiting for death, unable to make my last shreds of life useful or bearable.

Joy went on to say, 'I am trying very hard to hold onto my faith, but I find it difficult; there seems such a gratuitous and merciless cruelty in this.' She despairingly said, 'I hope all we have believed is true. I dare not now hope for anything in *this* world.'

Joy was not totally devastated, despite these cries from a disciple who was asking God, 'Why?' A ray of optimism came at the end of the letter: 'I fear all this will be horribly depressing for you; I shall go on praying for the grace to endure whatever I must endure and perhaps I'll be more cheerful next time I write.'

Joy had rallied by the time she wrote to her friends a week later. She told the Walshes:

> Everything looks much brighter than it did before. For one thing, my prayer for grace has been answered. I feel now that I can bear, not too unhappily, whatever is to come, and the problem of pain just doesn't loom so large — I'm not at all sure I didn't deserve it after all, and I'm pretty sure that in some way I need it. . . Jack pointed out to me that we were wrong in trying to accept utter hopelessness; *uncertainty* is what God has given us for a cross.
>
> Lyle Dorsett, *And God Came In*

Give us in our sickness, Lord, gratitude for the well-being we have lost;

Show us in our illness the beauty of health that we may praise you for it.

Empower us with your strength to fight the temptation which the evil one brings upon us and teach us always to turn to you.

When we feel deserted, Lord, remind us of your love and remind us also that you have suffered all that we suffer, that you share all our pain.

Give us, Lord, the strength we need to be brave and constant in our love for you as you have always been in your love for us.

When we must bear our cross, Lord, give us the ability to do it with grace.

In our sickness, Lord, give us faith, hope and love.

We pray this in the power of Jesus whose agony was freely given, and whose resurrection in perfection gives us the right to use his holy name. Amen.

A Benediction

May the Lord keep us in faith and joy whether in health or in sickness.

May he bring us humility and gratitude in well-being, and

patience and courage in illness.

May we all be given the wisdom to enable us to see and recognise the opportunities which abound in both conditions, the determination to grasp them and the fortitude to see them through.

May we, when the time comes for us to depart, have the joy of the Holy Spirit that we may go gladly and in peace, grieving only for the sadness of those we leave behind.

May God guide us and guard us all the days of our lives, taking us unto himself when all our earthly tasks are done.

Amen.

First of all

Thus says the Lord, the King of Israel, and his Redeemer, the Lord of hosts: I am the first and I am the last; besides me there is no god.

When I saw him, I fell at his feet as though dead. But he placed his right hand on me, saying, 'Do not be afraid; I am the first and the last, and the living one. I was dead and, see, I am alive forever and ever; and I have the keys of Death and of Hades.

And to the angel of the church in Smyrna write: These are the words of the first and the last, who was dead and came to life.

Elijah said to her, 'Do not be afraid; go and do as you have said; but first make me a little cake of it and bring it to me, and afterwards make something for yourself and your son.'

Another of his disciples said to him, 'Lord, first let me go and bury my father.'

Leave your gift there before the altar and go; first be reconciled to your brother or sister, and then come and offer your gift.

He sat down, called the twelve and said to them, 'Whoever wants to be first must be last of all and servant of all.'

When they kept on questioning him, he straightened up and said to them, 'Let anyone among you who is without sin be the first to throw a stone at her.'

'Honour your father and mother' — this is the first commandment with a promise.

If a widow has children or grandchildren, they should first learn their religious duty to their own family and make some repayment to their parents; for this is pleasing in God's sight.

But strive first for the kingdom of God and his righteousness, and all these things will be given to you as well.

But first he must endure much suffering and be rejected by this generation.

They gave themselves first to the Lord and, by the will of God, to us. . .

We love because he first loved us.

But I have this against you, that you have abandoned the love you had at first.

This is the greatest and first commandment.

For if the eagerness is there, the gift is acceptable according to what one has — not according to what one does not have.

But the wisdom from above is first pure, then peaceable, gentle, willing to yield, full of mercy and good fruits, without a trace of partiality or hypocrisy.

But many who are first will be last and the last will be first.

When evening came, the owner of the vineyard said to his manager, 'Call the labourers and give them their pay, beginning with the last and then going to the first.'

Or how can one enter a strong man's house and plunder his property, without first tying up the strong man? Then indeed the house can be plundered.

You blind Pharisee! First clean the inside of the cup, so that the outside also may become clean.

For which of you, intending to build a tower, does not first sit down and estimate the cost, to see whether he has enough to complete it? Or what king, going out to wage war against another king, will not sit down first and consider whether he is able with ten thousand to oppose the one who comes against him with twenty thousand?

(Isaiah 44: 6; Revelation 1: 17–18; 2: 8; 1: 11; 1 Kings 17: 13; Matthew 8: 21; Luke 9: 59; Matthew 5: 24; Mark 9: 35; John 8: 7;

Ephesians 6: 2; 1 Timothy 5: 4; Matthew 6: 33; Luke 17: 25; 2 Corinthians 8: 5; 1 John 4: 19; Revelation 2: 4; Matthew 22: 38; 2 Corinthians 8: 12; James 3: 17; Matthew 19: 30; 20: 8; 12: 29; 23: 26; Luke 14: 28 and 31 — all NRSV)

'First things first,' we say. Sure, but what are the first things for a Christian? Amos' famous words thunder down the centuries: 'Let justice roll down like waters and righteousness like an ever-flowing stream.' Without question, justice and righteousness are twin cornerstones undergirding all our Christianity, but what do the scriptures suggest when the word 'first' is considered? In our determination of priorities, this word and its biblical use are key.

Our God is the prime cause in the universe, but the use of the word 'first' in this context is rare in the Bible. The New Testament's use of 'first' for the Christian often concerns human relationships: reconciliation, forgiveness, integrity and obedience.

The key 'firsts', however, relate to our relationship to the King and his love for us. We are bidden to seek first Christ's kingdom and to give ourselves to him, recognising that to love God (and to accept the suffering that may come with it) is our chief end and purpose.

Other instances of using 'first' reflect the immediacy of what it means to put Christ and his teaching first.

'First' is sometimes used in the sense of foremost, commencement, beginning or prior, such as 'In Antioch, the disciples were for the first time called Christians' (Acts 11: 26), but this use is relatively rare, perhaps once in every fifty times. By far the majority (one-third in the Old Testament and two-thirds in the New) use the word in the sense of the first of two or three or more — they simply indicate the order.

It is in relationship to *time*, however, that the Old Testament scores heavily — altogether a third of the references are to the first day, the first month, the first year (including the first year of someone's reign). In the New Testament, only one-tenth of the uses of 'first' occur in this way, reflecting the rigidity of the legal system of the Old Testament ('on the first day do this') and its change to the prioritisation of relationships in the New with the formal code emphasised far less.

The especial use of 'first' for priorities is thus underlined. Scripture does not give us five things to do and tell us in which order to do them — it points out the one thing we should do first. That priority is primarily seen in terms of our relationship under the new covenant — in a twin fashion — to God and to others. The truth of the first commandment, to love God, and the second, to love our neighbours, is given not only in formal terms by Jesus, but reflected throughout by the use of the word 'first'.

God is. . . what? Love. The doctrine of the Trinity, wrote Karl Fahner, is the doctrine of the altruism of God. Augustine described the 'threeness' of God as that of lover, beloved and love. In the act of creating humans, this loving God created a restlessness for himself in the hearts of those creatures. And whenever we love other human beings, we are indeed loving God.

When we love, we are engaging in a human activity that is essentially non-terrestrial, said Augustine: when we love, we look beyond this changing world to the unchanging God, seeing others as created in his image. Love, he says, 'prevents us from being content with the world's darkness which through habit has become pleasant'. 'The whole life of the good Christian is a holy longing' to be loved and to love.

Let our final word come from Julian of Norwich: 'In his love [the Lord] clothes us, enfolds and embraces us; that tender love completely surrounds us, never to leave us. . . You would know our Lord's meaning in this thing? Know it well. Love was his meaning. Who showed it to you? Love. What did he show you? Love. Why did he show it? For love. Hold on to this and you will know and understand love more and more. But you will not know or learn anything else — ever!'

Because God knows the number of our days and their purpose, he wants to direct us so that we can come to old age without regret. He wants us to come to the day of our death knowing that we have done the work God gave us to do, enabling us to say, as Jesus did, 'It is finished.'

Janice Wise, 'Needed: Grace for Growing Old'

There is a sense of journey into the unknown and an openness to the opportunities that beckon, but which normally cannot be anticipated. Thus it implies a process of ongoing assessment about your talents and gifts, strengths and weaknesses, commitments and constraints — and about the opportunities or calls on one's time, talents and energy which emerge in the normal course of events.

Anonymous

When the American baseball favourite, Yogi Berra, was asked to speak at a special father-and-son banquet, he gladly signed bats and balls given to him by the youngsters present until he noticed a group of lads who had no gifts. Inquiring, he found they were from the local orphanage and left the head table to talk with them and sign their programs. When asked to return to speak, he said, 'Go on with the program. I am busy talking to my friends.'

'Little Things Mean a Lot'

Focus on minimising or eliminating the many activities in your day that take up so much of your time, yet produce such a small part of your overall result. If you think you don't have enough time to spend with your family, begin to eliminate the activities each week that contribute little to your productivity. You can find time for your family and still get all the important things done as well.

Myron Rush, *Burnout*

I learned not to let the urgent get in the way of the important. The urgent is the paperwork on my desk, my appointments, my daily routine, some of my coaching responsibilities. The important is my faith, my family, my friends and my relationships with my players. I'm still learning, but with time I am getting my priorities in the right order.

Kay You, Sports Coach, 'I Reached a Dream'

You don't have to be in business to be over-committed. Women with small children know what it means to do ten thousand revolutions per minute, the speed of a racing motor engine. Pastors, elders, church members operate at the same relentless pace as everyone else. Never a dull moment — never a reflective moment, either.

Authentic Christianity is not simply humanitarian service to the less fortunate. It is a supernatural walk with a living, dynamic, communicating God. Authentic Christians are persons who stand apart from others, even other Christians, as though listening to a different drummer. Authentic Christians are full of surprises. That's because authentic Christians have strong relationships with the Lord, relationships that are renewed every day.

Embarrassingly few Christians ever reach this level of authenticity; most Christians are just too busy. A key ingredient in authentic Christianity is time. Not left-over time, throw-away time, but quality time. Time for contemplation, meditation and reflection. Unhurried, uninterrupted time.

Bill Hybels, Too Busy Not to Pray

Carpe diem, 'Seize the day'!

Horace

For the want of a nail the shoe was lost,
For the want of a shoe the horse was lost,
For the want of a horse the rider was lost,
For the want of a rider the message was lost,
For the want of a message the battle was lost,
For the want of a battle the war was lost.

Unknown eighteenth-century author

I said to the man who stood at the gate of the year, 'Give me a light that I may tread safely into the unknown.' And he replied, 'Go out into the darkness and put your hand into the hand of God. That shall be to you better than light and safer than a known way.'

From King George VI's Christmas message

O Lord, forgive what we have been.
Amend what we are.
Direct what we should be, that we may delight
in your will and walk in your ways

International Evangelical Lutheran Church

God the Sender, send us,
God the Sent, come with us,
God the Strengthener of those who go, empower us
  that we may go with you
  and find those who will call you
Father, Son and Holy Spirit

Ascension Day prayer of the Church in Wales

O, Lord, I do not pray for tasks equal to my strengths: I ask for strength equal to my tasks.

Phillips Brooks

Lord, let me not live to be useless.

John Wesley

O, Lord, help us to put first things first and second things second. Encourage us in our duties, enthuse us for our vision and so energise us that we may serve both you and others with your patience, perseverance and protection — by the power of your Holy Spirit, for the extension of the kingdom of God and the glory of the name of Jesus Christ.

A Benediction
May God bless you, direct you and keep you true to your calling, strong in your dedication, loyal to your vision, clear in your priorities and wise in the fulfilment of the same, through our Saviour, Jesus Christ our Lord. Amen.

 33

Living the life: spreading the word

You are the salt of the earth; but if salt has lost its taste, how can its saltiness be restored? It is no longer good for anything, but is thrown out and trampled underfoot. You are the light of the world. A city built on a hill cannot be hid. No-one after lighting a lamp puts it under the bushel basket, but on the lampstand and it gives light to all in the house. In the same way, let your light shine before others, so that they may see your good works and give glory to your Father in heaven.

Do everything without complaining or arguing, so that you may be innocent and pure as God's perfect children, who live in a world of corrupt and sinful people. You must shine among them like stars lighting up the sky, as you offer them the message of life.

You have heard of this hope before in the word of truth, the gospel that has come to you. Just as it is bearing fruit and growing in the whole world, so it has been bearing fruit among yourselves from the day you heard it and truly comprehended the grace of God.

Live good lives among the pagans that, though they accuse you of doing wrong, they may see your good deeds and glorify God on the day he visits us.

This is what is written: the Messiah must suffer and must rise from death three days later, and in his name the message about repentance and the forgiveness of sins must be preached to all nations, beginning in Jerusalem.

But when the Holy Spirit comes upon you, you will

be filled with power, and you will be witnesses for me in Jerusalem, in all Judaea and Samaria and to the ends of the earth.

Therefore, knowing the fear of the Lord, we try to persuade others. . . For the love of Christ urges us on, because we are convinced that one has died for all; therefore all have died. And he died for all, so that those who live might live no longer for themselves, but for him who died and was raised for them. . . So if anyone is in Christ, there is a new creation: everything old has passed away; see, everything has become new! All this is from God, who reconciled us to himself through Christ and has given us the ministry of reconciliation; that is, in Christ God was reconciling the world to himself, not counting their trespasses against them, and entrusting the message of reconciliation to us. So we are ambassadors for Christ, since God is making his appeal through us; we entreat you on behalf of Christ, be reconciled to God.

And you became imitators of us and of the Lord, for in spite of persecution you received the word with joy inspired by the Holy Spirit, so that you became an example to all the believers in Macedonia and Achaia. For the word of the Lord has sounded forth from you not only in Macedonia and Achaia, but in every place your faith in God has become known, so that we have no need to speak about it.

(Matthew 5: 13–16, NRSV; Philippians 2: 14–16, GNB; Colossians 1: 5–6, NRSV; 1 Peter 2: 12, NIV; Acts 1: 8, GNB; 2 Corinthians 5: 11–20 NRSV; 1 Thessalonians 1: 6–9, NRSV)

Our scripture selection draws together a number of vital strands, all of which must be held together firmly if we are to communicate effectively and authentically the good news of new life in Jesus Christ in today's society. Our life must measure up to the message that we share, for that message is about restored relationships and transformed lives.

When we demonstrate that we cannot get on with people; that our word cannot be trusted; that we are too wrapped up in our own selfish interests to notice the signals people send indicating their need of attention and help; that our moral and ethical standards are indistinguishable from broader society — then we are revealing that our relationship with God has become distant or interrupted.

Does that mean I have to pass an advanced spiritual aptitude and achievement test before I can ever fulfil the role of a witness to the truth of the gospel? No, it simply means that I have to be honest with myself, concerned to become more Christ-like and open. Try the following 'openness test': when I confess my inconsistencies and shortcomings to God, am I offended when others make the same observations about me?

The world is not looking for perfection from those who bear Christ's name — but it is looking for reality. Does the kind of life I am living require a supernatural explanation? Is there evidence of divine intervention and redirection? Am I unmistakably part of God's 'new creation' described by Paul in 2 Corinthians 5: 17? If so, then I am in business, I don't need to be a walking religious encyclopedia, or an aura-enveloped super-saint. As the Indian evangelist, D.T. Niles so aptly described the role of the witness: 'I am one beggar telling another beggar where to buy bread.' But it helps in the telling if I have bread in hand and show some evidence of being nourished by it.

Notice that Jesus commissioned his disciples to spread the word and share the life. A disciple is not a finished product, but a learner with a great deal more yet to learn. For discipleship is a lifelong process. There is no graduation from the school of discipleship this side of heaven. This means that we do not go to others with a total grasp of the implications of the message; neither do our lives model it in every aspect. In our 'modelling' of the message, we have to recognise that a 'model' is often a very small and rough-hewn version of the real thing.

Sharing the good news is not an exclusively one-way

communication. The Lord may want to address our inconsistencies and challenge our shallow thinking and rhetorical sleight of hand through the responses of those with whom we seek to share the message. Not infrequently, evangelists discover that they have been evangelised in the process. For God has had significant things to say to them through the protesting unbeliever or seeking individual.

When Peter with his Jewish racial prejudice had to be divinely coerced into entering the home of the non-Jewish officer in the Roman army, who was converted? Cornelius began a new life in Christ, but Peter had his attitudes radically changed. There could be no restrictive practices in the spreading of the gospel. It was for the Gentiles as well as the Jews. Our witness to the gospel is limited by how much we know and how much people are able to hear. Keeping in touch with God entails keeping in touch with his world, especially that part which swirls around us during our daily living.

Another significant aspect of the witness of the early Christians is its corporate aspect. It takes a community to communicate. Witness needs to be a choral statement of the church. This was easier in some ways in New Testament times because of the way that society was then organised. In pre-industrial cities and towns, most people lived out their lives within one face-to-face community. Before the Industrial Revolution, people worked out of their homes or with their neighbours in nearby fields. This meant that the fellowship of believers was in constant contact with one another and an integral part of a wider community. They lived in a goldfish bowl, with the outside world observing their manner of life and overhearing their discussion of the message which was shaping their lives. They had to be 'for real'. No wonder that the letters of the New Testament devote so much attention to the practical aspects of living their Christian life.

We live in a more mobile age and our lives are more fragmented. We live in one place, work in another and our social life takes us to many other places. Husband, wife and other family members each head off in different directions every working day.

If the gospel is to be effectively communicated in our day, we need supportive structures for believers in these various social spheres. The congregation gathered for Sunday worship and fellowship must be viewed as a federation of witnessing teams, brought together to be motivated and equipped for their witness in the front lines during the rest of the week.

❧

Very many of the disciples of that age, whose hearts had been ravished by the divine word with a burning love of Christianity, first fulfilled the command of the Saviour and divided their goods among the needy. Then they set out on long journeys, doing the work of evangelists, eagerly striving to preach Christ to those who had never heard the word of faith and to deliver to them the holy Gospels. In foreign lands, they simply laid the foundations of the faith. That done, they appointed others as shepherds, entrusting them with the care of the new growth, while they themselves proceeded with the grace and cooperation of God to other countries and other places.

Eusebius

Evangelism may be defined as that dimension and activity of the church's mission which seeks to offer every person, everywhere, a valid opportunity to be directly challenged by the gospel of explicit faith in Jesus Christ, with a view to embracing him as Saviour, becoming a living member of his community, and being enlisted in his service of reconciliation, peace and justice on earth.

David Bosch, Theological Currents and
Cross-currents Today

Like Christ during the time of his preaching, like the Twelve on the morning of Pentecost, the Church, too, sees before her an immense multitude of people who need the gospel and have a right to it. God 'wants everyone to be saved and reach full knowledge of the truth'.

Pope Paul VI

The mission of the church in the pages of the New Testament is more like the fallout from a vast explosion, a radioactive fallout which is not lethal but life-giving.

Lesslie Newbigin, *The Gospel in a Pluralistic Society*

The gospel is constituted by the mighty acts of God in history for the liberation of the cosmos. It is not a set of rickety arguments about the divine order; it is not the expression of some sublime, religious experience brought mysteriously to verbal form; it is not a romantic report about awareness of God in nature; it is not speculative, philosophical theory about the nature of ultimate reality; it is not a set of pious or moral maxims designed to straighten out the world; it is not a legalistic lament about the meanness of human nature; it is not a sentimental journey down memory lane into ancient history.

It is the unique narrative of what God has done to inaugurate his kingdom in Jesus of Nazareth, crucified outside Jerusalem, raised from the dead, seated at the right hand of God, and now reigning eternally with the Father, through the activity of the Holy Spirit, in the church and in the world. Where this is not announced, it will not be known.

William Abraham, *The Logic of Evangelism*

There is more involved in witness to Christ than throwing pre-arranged clumps of texts at unbelieving heads; the meaning and application of the gospel must be explained to men and women in terms of their actual situation. This requires hard thinking.

J.I. Packer, *Fundamentalism and the Word of God*

Evangelism is everything we do to make faith in Christ an option.

Myron Augsburger

What do I want to say with my life about evangelism? That life is short, eternity is long. Jesus can make a difference in it all and I'm responsible for getting that message to others.

Calvin Ratz

In the parish setting, evangelism is not a matter of occasional special efforts, but a permanent element in all church activities, and that for which the whole worshipping community recognises that it is being trained.

Tom Allan, *The Face of My Parish*

Evangelism was rooted in the corporate experience of the rule of God that provided not only the psychological strength and support that was clearly needed in a hostile environment, but that also signified the active presence of God in their midst.

William Abraham, *The Logic of Evangelism*

Who is more naive? The liberal leader of what we now call 'the social gospel' with their passionate concern for a broken world and their never-ending optimism of how we may rectify it? Or the evangelical who has given up on the world's headaches in favour of a stripped-down form of evangelism reduced to four spiritual laws? Or the evangelical social activist who does not see intercessory prayer as the first and constant component of our 'social evangelism'?

Harvey Con, *Doing Justice and Preaching Grace*

It is a frustrating experience trying to get half-full Christians to overflow.

Anonymous

You servants of God,
your Master proclaim,
and publish abroad
his wonderful name;
the name all-victorious of Jesus extol;
his kingdom is glorious and rules over all.

Charles Wesley

I pray thee, make my way prosperous, not that I achieve high station, but that my life might be an exhibit to the value of knowing God.

Jim Elliott

Make me a channel of your peace.
Where there is hatred, let me bring your love.
Where there is injury, your pardon, Lord;
And where there's doubt, true faith in you.

Oh Master, grant that I may never seek
So much to be consoled as to console;
To be understood as to understand;
To be loved, as to love with all my soul.

Make me a channel of your peace.
Where there's despair in life, let me bring hope.
Where there is darkness, only light;
And where there's sadness, ever joy.

Make me a channel of your peace.
It is in pardoning that we are pardoned,
In giving to all that we receive,
And in dying that we are born to eternal life.

St Francis

Eternal God, you who have formed the universe and breathed
life into humankind; call out from your church men and women
to serve you in the world. Equip them with the gifts of your
Holy Spirit and entrust to them the great task of bringing new
life to the deadness which surrounds us, that there may be a
new creation in the hearts of all who turn to your Son in
repentance and faith. It is in his name, O God, that we bring
our prayer. Amen.

Michale Saward, *Prayers for Today's Church*

What are we for, Creator infinite, if not to show your likeness
to people, introducing godliness into humankind, life into death:
may we not hide you by our ways, nor cover your reality with
our fears. May hungry hearts which long for purpose find their
joy because you meet people not in the past alone, but in their
present deeds for which you did atone. Save, Lord! Then,
Bringer back from death, we salute you till you come. Amen.

Alan Goodson, *Prayers for Today's Church*

A Benediction

May our merciful God, who has made us all and hates nothing he has made; who does not desire the death of any sinner, but rather that they should be converted and live — have mercy on you. May he remove any ignorance, hardness of heart, or contempt for his word. And may he 'fetch you home' to his fold, so that you may be part of his flock forever.

To the glory of Jesus Christ our Lord, who lives and reigns with the Father and the Holy Spirit, one God, for ever.

Amen.

34

Teamship scores

There is one body and one Spirit, just as you were called in one hope of your calling; one Lord, one faith, one baptism; one God and Father of all, who is above all, and through all, and in you all. But to each one of us grace was given according to the measure of Christ's gift.

Then the eleven disciples went away into Galilee, to the mountain which Jesus had appointed for them. And when they saw him, they worshipped him; but some doubted. Then Jesus came and spoke to them saying, 'All authority has been given to me in heaven and on earth. Go therefore and make disciples of all the nations, baptising them in the name of the Father and of the Son and of the Holy Spirit, teaching them to observe all things that I have commanded you; and lo, I am with you always, even to the end of the age. Amen.'

And they continued steadfastly in the apostles' doctrine and fellowship, in the breaking of bread, and in prayers. Then fear came upon every soul, and many wonders and signs were done through the apostles. Now all who believed were together, and had all things in common, and sold their possessions and goods, and divided them among all, as anyone had need. So continuing daily with one accord in the temple and breaking bread from house to house, they ate their food with gladness and simplicity of heart, praising God and having favour with all the people. And the Lord added to the church daily those who were being saved.

Now you are the body of Christ, and members individually. And God has appointed these in the church:

first apostles, second prophets, third teachers, after that miracles, then gifts of healings, helps, administrations, varieties of tongues. Are all apostles? Are all prophets? Are all teachers? Are all workers of miracles? Do all have gifts of healings? Do all speak with tongues? Do all interpret? But earnestly desire the best gifts. And yet I show you a more excellent way.

Love suffers long and is kind; love does not envy; love does not parade itself, is not puffed up; does not behave rudely, does not seek its own, is not provoked, thinks no evil; does not rejoice in iniquity, but rejoices in the truth; bears all things, believes all things, hopes all things, endures all things. Love never fails. But whether there are prophecies, they will fail; whether there are tongues, they will cease; whether there is knowledge, it will vanish away. For we know in part and we prophesy in part. But when that which is perfect has come, then that which is in part will be done away. When I was a child, I spoke as a child, I understood as a child, I thought as a child; but when I became adult, I put away childish things. For now we see in a mirror, dimly, but then face to face. Now I know in part, but then I shall know just as I also am known.

And now abide faith, hope, love, these three; but the greatest of these is love.

(Ephesians 4: 4–7; Matthew 28: 16–20; Acts 2: 42–47; 1 Corinthians 12: 27–31; 13: 4–12 — all NKJV)

Partners perform better by accepting, not erasing their differences. While God does not need our help in doing his will and carrying out his work, he has nevertheless chosen us to work with others to achieve his plan and purpose. Working with others requires partnership — teamship if you like.

Teamship is what Jesus practised. In practising leadership, we serve him. As Peter Taylor Forsyth put it, 'A freelance is a futility.' We are called to be followers together — team-mates or team-makers for Christ as we have fellowship together. Such a bonding will gain its clues not from the world, but from Christ himself.

In his book, *Dropping Your Guard*, Charles Swindoll tells of an unusual case before the courts in Massachusetts in the 1920s. A man had been strolling along a pier when he tripped on a rope and fell into cold, deep waters. He surfaced spluttering, screamed for help, then sank under the surface. He could neither swim, nor stay afloat. Friends heard his faint cries from a distance, but were too far away to rescue him. Yet close to the drowning man only a few metres away was a young man sunbathing in a deckchair. Not only did he hear the drowning man yell, 'Help, I can't swim': he was also an excellent swimmer. The tragedy is he did nothing except turn his head indifferently as the man sank and drowned.

The family of the victim were so upset by such indifference they sued the sunbather — but lost the case. Reluctantly the court ruled the man in the deckchair had no legal responsibility whatever to try and save the drowning man.

While this is an extreme example, it is symptomatic of our current failure to work together. Harry Blamires says that our century has produced generations of men and women who are too small-minded to be aware of their own small-mindedness. . . many pull down the shutters on anything that goes beyond their immediate needs. The press and television are influences of this kind. They pin our attention feverishly on getting and spending to satisfy our individual needs.

Only as we become involved in working together and serving each other can we advance the cause of Christ. This does not mean failing to acknowledge our differences. Partners perform far, far better when they accept their differences rather than spend their time attempting to erase them.

❧❧

Teamwork is a plural process. It cannot be done by one person. When people come together to form groups, each member brings a personal set of knowledge, skills, values and motivations. How these interact to form a collectivity can be positive or negative.

In some cases, members neutralise each other to produce ineffectiveness or inaction. The whole becomes less than the sum of its parts. In other cases, they can be partly or wholly additive. There is yet another possibility: the interaction can stimulate a transcendent state that exceeds the contribution of any member or the sum of all the members. When that happens, the team has achieved synergy. The whole is greater than the sum of its parts. The team result has exceeded the sum of individual contribution; that's the meaning of excellence in teamwork when teamwork becomes spectacular.

Robert R. Blake, Jane Srygley Mouten, Robert L. Allen,
Spectacular Teamwork

Was it empty rhetoric when David Livingstone said it was not just himself who went tramping through darkest Africa: it was David Livingstone and Jesus Christ together? Was it fever or delirium when Samuel Rutherford wrote to a friend from prison: 'Jesus Christ came into my cell last night and every stone flashed like a ruby'? Was it credulity or distortion of fact that made a great scholar of this generation say, after visiting a friend in the Christian ministry who had worked himself almost to death in a Midland slum, that in that poor room he encountered Christ: there was his friend living in that hell and there was Christ beside him?

James S. Stewart, *A Faith To Proclaim*

History and folklore are full of examples of successful teams/groups of men and women who, against seemingly impossible odds, won the day. Jason and the Argonauts faced a hazardous sea voyage with several monsters thrown in for good measure. Horatio held the bridge with his two companions against uncountable odds. Sir Edmund Hillary and Sherpa Tensing combined in a team of two to conquer the last few hundred feet of Mount Everest. A team of highly trained military personnel broke the Iranian Embassy siege in London while the world looked on. And every moment of every day, successful teams carry air passengers around the world.

Not all teams are successful. Captain Scott's ill-fated Antarctic expedition, although in many ways an example of outstanding team spirit, was a failure in terms of the task. The American space program has provided the world with outstanding success and failure, while the world of sport has endless examples of surprising team performances — both good and bad.

David Cormack, *Team Spirit*

Dr Meredith Belbin studied successful teams in Britain during the late 1960s and early 1970s. He wished to identify why some teams of very able people could perform badly, while teams of quite unremarkable individuals could do well. His research showed that successful teams did not have to be made up of the best individuals around. I find this encouraging because what Belbin is saying is that whoever you are, whatever your skills, you can be part of a successful team if you and the other members make the right contributions to the working of the group.

David Cormack, *Team Spirit*

The six most important words:
'I ADMIT I MADE A MISTAKE.'
The five most important words:
'YOU DID A GOOD JOB.'
The four most important words:
'WHAT IS YOUR OPINION?'
The three most important words:
'IF YOU PLEASE.'
The two most important words:
'THANK YOU.'
The one most important word:
'WE.'
The least important word:
'I.'

Anonymous

Team Spirit

Though I understand all the words used in team
  building,
And though I can appreciate different cultures,
If I do not know the meaning of team spirit,
My words are hollow and carry no weight.
And though I am a visionary and can set objectives,
Solve problems and analyse situations;
And though I believe in myself and can achieve
  great things,
If I am not motivated by team spirit, my actions will
  come to nothing.
And though I spend all my time and resources on
  behalf of the group
And burn myself out in the course of my effort,
If I do these things outside all the spirit of the team,
  no-one benefits.

Team spirit is characterised by patience, acceptance
  and humility;
It is not associated with force, imposition,
  provocation or treachery.
Team spirit is concerned with true facts and feelings.
Its concern with the truth enables the team to cope
  with difficulties
And to maintain the team vision in the face of the
  strongest opposition.

Team spirit will see the team through every setback.
The team may fail to meet its objectives,
Communication may break down,
And the team may fail to practise its skills and gifts.
All this might happen, for no team is perfect,
And like children with so much still to learn, we all
  struggle for understanding.
But with team spirit we can learn to grow together,
And as we learn we can put behind us the immature
  behaviour.
At the moment our vision of what our team might
  be is unclear,

But as we move forward together, the possibilities
will open before us.
A team depends on commitment, motivation and
team spirit.
No team can survive without these three, but team
spirit is the ultimate objective.

Based on the writings of St Paul.
For 'team spirit' also read 'love'.
David Cormack, *Team Spirit*

---

*Lord, I'm aware that all too often I have grumbled and com-
plained about my co-workers, forgetting that they are also your
co-workers. I have failed to see them as your servants, as
partners in the work of the kingdom. I have been far too slow
to accept the differences in opinion, far too quick to try to erase
the differences. Forgive me, Father, and please help me to be a
better partner. Help me to grow in grace and in the knowledge
of my Lord and Saviour to the extent that I become far more
concerned about how I perform, about how I partner others than
how others partner me. Make me I pray a far better teammate
so that your kingdom will advance and others be able to say
with truth, 'See how these Christians love each other.'*

*Father in heaven, so much of my life is lived below its potential.
The brainpower I bring to bear on life is so much like the iceberg
tip, I'm ashamed. You have created me in your image and while
the image has been defaced, you have nevertheless told me in your
word: 'The One who is in you is greater than the one who is in
the world.' Please help me to apply my active mind to all that
enters it throughout the day. Increase my 'kingdom' input so that
I might truly live as risen with Christ.*

David Cormack, *Team Spirit*

A Benediction
*May you enrich the lives of others as Christ has enriched yours
and, as a co-redeemer with Christ in a lost world, may your
teamwork with him result in blessing many. For his glory
alone!*
Amen.

35

His banner over us is: Mine!

God saw all that he had made, and it was very good.

You are a holy people to the Lord your God. [He] has chosen you. . . to be his people, his treasured possession.

Fear not, for I have redeemed you; I have summoned you by name; you are mine. I will remember my covenant between me and you. . .

'They will be mine,' says the Lord Almighty.

'You are Peter, and on this rock I will build my church, and the gates of Hades will not overcome it.'

Be shepherds of the church of God, which he bought with his own blood.

To the church of God in Corinth, to those sanctified in Christ Jesus and called to be holy. . . do you despise the church of God? Excel in the gifts that build up the church.

God placed all things under [Christ's] feet and appointed him to be head over everything for the church, which is his body, the fullness of him who fills everything in every way. . . Christ is the head of the church, his body, of which he is the Saviour.

To the angel of the church in Philadelphia write: These are the words of him who is holy and true, who holds the key of David. What he opens no-one can shut; what he shuts no-one can open.

(Genesis 1: 31; Deuteronomy 7: 6; Isaiah 43: 1; Genesis 9: 15; Malachi 3: 17; Matthew 16: 18; Acts 20: 28b; 1 Corinthians 1: 2; 11: 22; 14: 12; Ephesians 1: 22–23; 5: 23; Revelation 3: 7 — all NIV)

At the Separatist, Expansionist Church of St Martin they were desperately interested in church growth. The problem was that there were two factions who decided to run a competition for twelve months to see who could gain more members and make them most sincere.

The first, the Additional Multiplication Society, set about its task. 'Statistics!' cried their leaders. 'Amen, statistics!' they sang to drum and synthesiser. So on the left all the banners were replaced with thermometer charts that measured the numbers coming in, the conversions and the monies collected for this fund and that. The group was carefully organised so that the youth were involved colouring each new increase, and the few elderly people handed out pamphlets carefully cataloguing another computer review of progress. Calculators replaced catechisms as they toiled to measure and report on growth by any means.

On the other side, the Alert Persons for Pure Doctrine Faction sat staidly and quietly, ignoring the noise and hullabaloo of their competitors. 'Purity, Holiness, Doctrine,' chanted the leaders, and their followers chorused, 'This is most certainly true.' It was all done in cautious and sombre tones that had withstood well the test of time and the Doctrine Preservation Committee. Both groups had one thing in common — they did not mention 'trust in God' for twelve months so that no-one could accuse the other of having an unfair advantage.

One day, an old lady turned up for worship and she was immediately set upon by the enthusiastic progressives who quickly added another number to their growth chart. She duly received her pledge card to complete and return next Sunday and reminder notices were prepared in case she didn't. But she seemed uneasy and, halfway through worship, she rose and moved to the right where, after carefully looking her over, an elder was appointed by a duly elected committee to approach her. She was taken to the interrogation room to make sure she believed everything in truth and purity.

But still she seemed uneasy and, as one faction was busy with erasers grumbling at the inconvenience she had caused and the smudges that now spoilt their charts, the others huddled together expressing their dismay because she wasn't sure if there were seven or eight petitions to the Lord's Prayer and whether Hezekiah was an Old or a New Testament book.

In the meantime, she sat in the aisle, took out her Bible (of all things!) and laid out a banner — IT IS GOD'S CHURCH — HE WILL MAKE IT GROW.

That, too, was the banner Jesus was hanging out as he told the parables of the seeds (Mark 4: 26-32). One parable portrays the seed that is planted, growing whether or not the farmer is awake or asleep. The other points to the tiny mustard seed, the smallest known seed in those days, which grew to a bush several metres high, indicating a place where people would come to find their security in God.

These stories aren't so much harsh criticisms as gentle reminders to us of the dangers when programs and uncaring desire for purity of doctrine blind us to the fact that God is at work. It is *his* word, *his* inspiration, *his* love, *his* forgiveness, *his* Son, *his* Holy Spirit and *his* church.

It is not that Jesus is opposed to programs or purity of doctrine or sees them as wrong. But when they become a passion and a fashion which exclude compassion for the lost and troubled, and when they cause us to close our eyes to God, his nature and power, then they are, in fact, evil.

A man once addressed an established, traditional-style congregation. He was an ex-street kid and gang leader who had been converted by the love of a young man he had beaten up several times. Yet this Christian had just kept coming back to his attacker with the love of Jesus. As the speaker addressed the congregation, he was decked out in Bikie gear, head nearly shaven, with prominent earrings and tattoos. His presence and his words challenged the church with the fact that, at times, we get too comfortable in the way we believe things must be done, that we forget the gospel and the people for whom it is intended.

We are often tempted to exclude those from our four walls with whom God has not yet finished. In so doing, we lose the simple joy of knowing Christ and his salvation and seeing him at work in the lives of others as he causes his church to grow. He reminded that church (who should have needed no reminding) that the gospel is the power of God that brings salvation.

We are called to trust in God. That trust is not so easy because we have either convinced ourselves God can't do it without our help, or we have taken him for granted. How many of us during this past week actually asked God to guide our day, strengthen our faith, and give us a chance to know him better? Or have we simply assumed he will work automatically — after all, we're a pretty likable bunch!

Really, that old lady should have had people joining her rather than closing her out. She didn't have it all together and she won't be recorded in history as some great saint of the church. She simply trusted God.

We are asked to approach the church as people touched by Jesus on the cross where we see God deeply, even desperately, concerned for us. But that can only come as we gather together at church like bees around a honey pot — showing that there is nowhere else we would rather be for our security and happiness in Christ than with these people. Every act needs to be a signboard which proclaims 'God's church — he is at work.' His banner over us is: Mine!

❧❦❧

What Luke reports in Acts 2 and 4 has been heard ever and again since the early days of the church as a call to repentance. 'They devoted themselves to the apostles' teaching and fellowship, to the breaking of bread and the prayers.' And we? 'All who believed were together and had things in common.' And we? '. . .continuing daily with one accord. . .' [KJV]. And we? '. . .with glad and generous hearts, praising God. . .' And we? Such questioning has ever and again been prompted by the account of the first congregation, and so it must be.   Here a mirror is held up to the church at all times, a call to repentance.

Hermann Sasse, We Confess The Church

One of the most exciting aspects of our age is the new ecumenical spirit.   Christians seem to have discovered their sense of belonging together: their unity in Christ. We are learning to think of other Christians as brothers rather than as enemies or heretics.   But in this wonderful new mood we should remember the source of our unity as Christians is not our good feeling for one another or even brilliant plans for a great and all-inclusive church; we are joined only in the gospel of Christ.

George W. Forell, The Augsburg Confession:
A Contemporary Commentary

'I can't build this church,' he declared.   'I haven't the foggiest idea how to do it.   But the Lord knows how, and he will do it if we just submit ourselves to him.   He is perfectly capable of building his own church.'

Bob Slosser, Miracle in Darien

Thy hand, O God, has guided
Thy flock, from age to age;
Thy wondrous tale is written,
Full clear, on every page;
Our fathers owned thy goodness.
And we their deeds record;
And both of this bear witness:
'One Church, one faith, one Lord.'

Edward Hayes Plumptre

I believe that on earth there is a holy little group or community made up entirely of saints under one head, Christ.   It has been called by the Holy Spirit; it has one faith, mind and understanding; it has different kinds of gifts, but lives together in love and harmony; it has no sects or divisions.   I'm part of this little group, too, and a member of it.   As a full partner, I share all the good things it has.   The Holy Spirit brought me there; and I became part of this body because I heard God's word, and still hear it — which is the first step in getting into this community.

Martin Luther, *Luther's Large Catechism*

It will be bad news if the court should emasculate the church by holding that it can't enforce biblical standards on its members; but it will be even worse news if it turns out that by ignoring our biblical responsibilities we have done it to ourselves.

Charles Colson, *Who Speaks for God?*

To me as a humanist, the most admirable aspect of Christian theology is its plea for universal love. How tragic that Christianity persistently ignores its Messiah's most intelligent commandment.

Phillip Adams, in John Smith, *Advance Australia Where?*

You work so hard at it. Just remember that the rose never invites anyone to smell it. If it is fragrant, people will walk across the garden and endure the thorns to smell it.

Mahatma Gandhi

We have got very set in our ways — and they are not always God's ways. But if the church is to move out in evangelism, it really has to flow with love. . . And Jesus needs to be kept at No. 1.

Michael Green, *Evangelism Through the Local Church*

Thank God, a seven-year-old child knows what the church is, namely, holy believers and sheep who hear the voice of their Shepherd.

Martin Luther, *Smalcald Articles*

[The churches] speak a language different to the world around them. They do not want to be museums. They want to invite us to be silent, to sit or kneel, to listen attentively and to rest with our whole being.

Henri Nouwen, *Clowning in Rome*

If the Lord is to be Lord, worship must have priority in our lives.

Richard Foster, Celebration of Discipline

May we be one -
Jesus' truth to bind us.
With his body he unites us all;
dying our death, he restores our life;
living with us now, he makes us one.

Robin Mann

The church seems impotent before the ecological crisis, for example, or in the face of mindless technology or the worldwide web of political power and intrigue. But the weapons of our warfare are spiritual, not carnal. Using the world's weapons, the church does not stand a chance. But when the church uses God's weapons (Ephesians 6: 14-17), it is the world which becomes weak.

Howard Snyder, New Wineskins

My conviction is that God wants his church, the body of Christ, healthy, and if it is healthy it will grow.

Peter Wagner, Your Church Can Be Healthy

One in the faith that unites us,
one in the Lord who has saved us,
one in the hope of life with Jesus our king,
one family, together we stay evermore.

Geoff Strelan

Since the beginning of time, O Lord, you have spoken to humanity. Even though people have sought to silence your voice, you have pierced the veil of silence with your powerful Word. Through Moses and the prophets you made your will known among us. When your messages were ignored, you miraculously embodied your Word in the person of Jesus Christ. Again some tried to still your voice by nailing your Word to a cross, but you could not be silenced. You raised your 'Word made flesh' from the dead so that many have heard the message.

We thank you, Lord, that we have heard the message through Christ.

Many have been the heroes and saints who have, at great personal sacrifice, handed the Gospel on to us today. Many have sacrificed their lives in the defence of your truth and the gospel. In spite of their efforts, however, human barriers have often curtailed the free distribution, teaching and preaching of your Word. Many times your Word has been buried under the rubble of man-made laws and traditons. But you have always brought forth one of your chosen servants to restore your Word. For giving us such people to lead us out of spiritual darkness into the marvellous light of the gospel, we give you thanks.

Help us, O Lord, to treasure your Word, and guard it with a due sense of appreciation for those who have made its presence in our midst possible. Help us to read, hear, and inwardly digest it so that we may grow in the knowledge of our Lord Jesus Christ, in whose name we pray. Amen.

Theodore P. Bornhoeft, *Prayers Responsively*

A Benediction

Go out into the world in peace; have courage; hold on to what is good; return no-one evil for evil; strengthen the faint-hearted; support the weak; help the suffering; honour all people; love the unloved; serve the Lord, rejoicing in the power of the Holy Spirit. And may the Almighty and merciful God, Father, Son and Holy Spirit, bless and keep us. Amen.

WEEK

36

Out of darkness into marvellous light

Moses drew near to the thick darkness where God was.

The true light, which enlightens everyone, was coming into the world. . . The light shines in the darkness, and the darkness did not overcome it.

God is light, and in him is no darkness at all. . . If we walk in the light as he is in the light, we have fellowship with one another. . .

I called to the Lord out of my distress and he answered me. . . You cast me into the deep, into the heart of the seas, and the flood surrounded me; all your waves and your billows passed over me. . . As my life was ebbing away I remembered the Lord; and my prayer came to you. . . But I with the voice of thanksgiving will sacrifice to you. . . Deliverance belongs to the Lord!

You are a chosen race. . . in order that you may proclaim the mighty acts of him who called you out of darkness into his marvellous light.

(Exodus 20: 21; John 1: 9 and 5; 1 John 1: 5–7; Jonah 2: 3–9; 2 Peter 2: 9 — all NRSV)

To be 'in the dark' is to be ignorant, alone, perhaps frightened. Black comedy or dark comedy presents a sombre or despairing view of the world. In our worst dreams we fall into a black, bottomless abyss.

The greatest and best Christians have experienced the utter solitude and horror of the 'dark night'. Moses' ascent of Mount Sinai (Exodus 19 and 20) to meet God in a cloud of darkness is a telling image of the authentic life of faith. Gregory of Nyssa was the first to combine this 'cloud' with the 'night' of the Song of Solomon to describe the darkness in which lovers meet.

We encounter our God in the darkness which is beyond all our knowing, our willing, our theologising, our natural striving or our desire. Like the seed in the ground, we are helpless there, waiting for the nurturing life of God to quicken or resurrect us from our 'dying', to bring life out of death. Gradually, we encounter 'luminous darkness'; we are freed from earthly attachments; God's grace shows up our created concerns and lesser loves for what they are.

The great Spanish mystic, St John of the Cross, is the classical exponent of the 'dark night'. He writes of two nights — of sense and spirit. The beginner in the spiritual life anticipates many 'consolations', but ultimately there is an experience of silent helplessness in the darkness. Many 'sensual' temptations erupt there. After a period of calm, there may follow the even more terrible experience of 'the dark night of the spirit'. Sense and spirit must be purified from injuries caused by sin if the soul is to be united to God in love.

St Teresa of Lisieux writes in her autobiography of the absolute and unrelenting darkness which oppressed her during the last eighteen months of her life. . .

The English spiritual classic, *The Cloud of Unknowing*, is also built on this idea. If one is to enjoy union with God, purification from all attachments to 'creatures' is necessary. Such 'purgatorial' suffering accompanies an intense love of God. Violent temptations are not overcome by active efforts to suppress them, but in passive, tranquil trust in God, in the abandonment of oneself to the loving therapy of God. By God's grace, the unity lost by Adam may be recovered. The cloud of unknowing is 'dark wisdom', grounded on faith and produced by love.

William Cowper, the English hymnwriter, wrote some memorable poetry about the pain of spiritual darkness. 'Sometimes,' he notes in one of his best-known hymns, 'a light surprises' — sometimes, not very often maybe. There are intimations of consolation, now and then. 'Where is the blessedness I knew/When first I saw the Lord?' he asks in another hymn. 'What peaceful hours I once enjoyed!/How sweet their memory still!/But they have left an aching void/The world can never fill.' The Calvinistic preachers had promised him a better Christian life than this. Suffering long bouts of suicidal depression, he tried insanely to kill himself every few years.

Cowper could not fully understand the ways of God and wrote so. 'God moves in a mysterious way,/His wonders to perform.' Such 'wonders' include calamities we call 'acts of God' — like the sinking of the warship 'The Royal George', not in high seas or in war, but when tied up by the harbour wall. With its complement of 'twice four hundred men' going down with it, it took real faith and courage to 'Judge not the Lord by feeble sense,/But trust him for his grace;/Behind a frowning providence/He hides a smiling face.'

R.S. Thomas, another English poet of 'the darkness of faith', describes (in 'The Porch') a man. . .

> driven
> to his knees and for no reason
> he knew. . .
> he had no power to pray. . .
> he looked out on a universe
> that was without knowledge
> of him and kept his place
> there for an hour on that lean
> threshold, neither outside nor in.

Then there's Geoffrey Hill:

> At this dark solstice filled with frost and fire,
> your passion's ancient wounds must bleed anew. . .

Drawn into the dark night, we can experience it as a night of transfiguration, as St John of the Cross did:

O guiding night!
O night more lovely than the dawn!
O night that has united
The Lover with his beloved,
Transforming the beloved in her Lover.

Remember, as Hemingway put it, we 'are *made strong* at the broken places'. Our Lord does not leave us orphans; he always comes to us. The heaviness experienced in the night gives way to joy in the morning (Psalm 30: 5). Hang in there: he is not finished with you yet! The darkest hour comes before the dawn.

❧

I said to my soul, be still, and wait without hope
For hope would be hope for the wrong thing; wait without love
For love would be love of the wrong thing; there is yet faith
But the faith and the love and the hope are all in the waiting
Wait without thought, for you are not ready for thought:
So the darkness shall be the light, and the stillness the dancing.

T. S. Eliot, *East Coker III*

Into my heart's night
Along a narrow way
I groped; and lo! the light,
An infinite land of day.

Rumi

Agony is the final test. When all hopes are dashed and all conceit is shattered, we begin to miss what we have long spurned. In darkness, God becomes near and clear (Isaiah 8: 21–9: 2). . . When all pretensions are abandoned, one begins to feel the burden of guilt. It is easier to return from an extreme distance than from the complacency of a good conscience, from spurious proximity.

Abraham Heschel, *The Prophets*

Writing cheerful graffiti on the rocks in the valley of deep shadows is no substitute for companionship with the person who must walk in the darkness. John Updike describes his famous everyman, Rabbit Angstrom, thus:

> Harry has no taste for the dark, tangled, visceral aspect of Christianity, the *going through* quality of it, the passage *into* death and suffering that redeems and inverts these things, like an umbrella blowing inside out. He lacks the mindful will to walk the straight line of a paradox. His eyes turn toward the light, however it glances into his retina.

The gospel that boldly sets the cross of Christ at the centre of its message also courageously accepts the cross of discipleship as part of its daily routines. Difficulties and suffering are not problems for which the gospel provides an escape, but part of a reality which the Christian experiences and in which Christians share a faith by encouraging one another in hope.

Eugene Peterson, *Five Smooth Stones for Pastoral Work*

I am convinced that we should solve many things if we all went out into the streets and uncovered our griefs, which perhaps would prove to be but one sole common grief, and be joined together in weeping them. . . A *miserere* sung in common by a multitude tormented by destiny has much value as a philosophy. It is not enough to cure the plague; we must learn to weep for it. . . Perhaps that is the supreme wisdom.

Miguel Unamuno

Here is the essence of mercy at its very best: it is not discounting the importance of imperfection and letting someone off from the consequences of what they have done. It takes evil seriously, but not ultimately. It dares to see a future beyond the event of imperfection and suggests that something positive can be made of what is left. Forgiveness is into *salvaging* rather than *scrapping*, and believes that one can yet become something other than he or she has been in the past. It is a way of dealing with evil that is at once utterly serious and yet genuinely hopeful, a way of facing up to reality without giving up on it, and the good news of the biblical religion is that Almighty God has chosen to deal with the imperfect this way.

In the face of human sin and faithlessness and our default on the promises of life, he neither discounts the importance of our failure, nor has he set out to destroy us — on the contrary, God moves to forgive. In the last analysis, it is not the will of the Father that any should perish. Therefore, he enters every situation of evil just as long ago he entered the nothingness and attempts to do there what he did back in the beginning: namely, bring forth light out of the darkness and shape and form out of chaos.

John Claypool, 'Forgive Us Our Trespasses'

In the ancient tradition of the church, excommunication was always conceived of as a step toward forgiveness and reconciliation. . . Such forgiveness is always experienced as a risk. You let go of the ordinary controls. You have to go beyond the limits of calculation: you are confronted with the question of what the ultimate reality is really like. . .

When we forgive, we adore, invoke, surrender to God as Universal Mercy. . . Faith is never merely a reaction to evil. It is an encounter with the only kind of love that can redeem us. It is not the problem of evil that is first (and last), but the mystery of love and goodness. . .

[Otherwise] we will only see evil around us. We become locked in a depressive despair, lost in a diseased cosmos. The sun will keep on going down on a million frustrations and an ever-growing anger. More and more enemies will be invented. They will increasingly occupy our minds and populate the space in which we live.

If, however, forgiveness is possible, the sun will go down on the necessary conflicts of each new day. But the night will be a time of rest and celebration, and of waiting for the dawn rather than a dread of it. In that darkness, there are intimations of an always greater mystery already at work, a universal compassion, a patience with the strange history of our freedom, a final forgiveness offered to each and all of us.

Tony Kelly, 'Free to Forgive'

There is never a moment when God does not come forward in the guise of some suffering or some duty, and all that takes place within us, around us and through us both includes and hides his activity. Yet, because it is invisible, we are always taken by surprise and do not recognise his operation until it has passed by us. If we could lift the veil and if we watched with vigilant attention, God would endlessly reveal himself to us and we should see and rejoice in his active presence in all that befalls us. At every event we should exclaim: 'It is the Lord!' (John 21: 17). Nothing could happen to us without our accepting it as a gift from God.

Jean-Pierre de Caussade, *Abandonment to Divine Providence*

And the evening and the morning were the first day (Genesis 1: 5). The evening was 'darkness' and the morning was 'light', and yet the two together are called by the name that is given to the light alone! In every believer, there is darkness and light and yet a believer is not a sinner because of indwelling sin, but is a saint because of the possession of some degree of holiness. This will be a most comforting thought to those who ask, 'Can I be a child of God while there is so much darkness in me?' Yes, for you, like the day, take not your name from the evening, but from the morning; and you are spoken of in the word of God as if you were even now perfectly holy.

If his dark nights are as bright as the world's days, what shall his days be? If I can praise the Lord in the fires, how will I extol him before the eternal throne! If evil be good to me now, what will the overflowing goodness of God be to me then? Wait, O soul, and let patience have her perfect work.

C.H. Spurgeon

And yet nothingness is the best condition for God's creativity; emptiness, the necessary prerequisite to be filled with God's grace; barrenness, the fertile ground for God's power to be fruitful. Creation is making something out of nothing. Therefore, the more we are and become nothing, the more can God make something out of us. Our nothingness leaves God completely free to make and mould us. Being something, even though it be just a 'little something', can offer some resistance to the divine Artisan. . .

But when we really are nothing, then God meets with no resistance whatever. He can do with us as he wills. He can handle us more easily. God works best when we are nothing! That is why it is so necessary to die spiritually. Death is the ultimate holocaust when all is consumed and everything annihilated. Death is the final surrender when we commend ourselves with supreme confidence into the Father's hands. 'It is a terrifying thing to fall into the hands of the living God!' (Hebrews 10: 31). But those hands, I have come to know, are the safest and strongest because they are the hands of an all-powerful and all-loving Father!

Alex Rebello, *Broken Stillness*

Where is God in the silence and darkness, in the laboured beatings of the heart? Where is the *idea* of God in this uttermost emptiness? Perhaps, after all, the ultimate truth is not light and goodness but darkness and horror! Surely this terrible happening, this extreme anguish of the poor naked human spirit, is proof that there is no God at all or that if there is he is without care of me? [This] is a note struck again and again in the Old Testament. But always the Lord comes to save, and is. . . by this extremity, defined in the fullness of his saviourhood. Jesus comes as the one who saves, the God who saves. Yet he is also Jonas and he enters into the darkness of Gethsemane and the darkness of the tomb.

Noel Dermot O'Donoghue, 'The Jonas Experience'

John of the Cross divides the night into three parts. There

is the growing obscurity of the 'night of sense', in which the self concentrates its desire on God alone rather than any external ends. But the darkest part of the night is the 'night of spirit' (usually called the Dark Night of the Soul) in which the self is stripped even of any remaining spiritual gratification and of every consoling image of itself. Only beyond this does the dawn of illumination break into final union [with God]. . .

Both 'nights' have active and passive aspects (struggle and receptivity together). John can use the language of 'annihilation' to describe what is happening in the night of the spirit yet. . . he consistently presupposes throughout the reality of a freely consenting will. . . John sees [however] the 'night' forced on us, not by a spiritual master. . . but simply by a combination of outer circumstances, an inner honesty about the necessary formlessness of our experience of God and a consequent suspicion of intellectual or spiritual satisfaction, of ideas or feelings suggesting achievement and finality.

[A] sense of dereliction is involved in the night of spirit (John refers here to Jesus' cry from the cross). . .

Rowan Williams, 'Dark Night, Darkness'

The darkness reveals what is wrong; the Spirit descending into 'the mud of our desires. . .' The darkness is the unknown attempting to break through and teach us. . . The harsh paradox is that we must often journey to the heart of darkness to find the heart of salvation in Christ's gift of an eternal Yes. . . There is no dark night without a deep objective sense of sin. . . It is a strange and severe mercy that calls us to live without the props of 'consolations'. . . If we are to be truly healed. . . touched and transfigured by this 'fearful symmetry' of grace operating through the depths of loving contemplation of God, then we must be ready to enter the alternating currents of hurt and healing, consolation and desolation, darkness and light, finding God in all things. . .

For he is Lord, Lord of light and darkness, and he does not play games. . . God's wounds are for our healing. . . In my own experience. . . I felt I wanted to say, 'Thank

you for your wounds', and he said 'Thank you for yours'. . .
The love of God is our only healing, and it is for that
glorious and terrible vocation that we are born and born
again.

Philip Seddon, Darkness

This darkness which is between you and your God, I do
not call a cloud of the air, but a cloud of unknowing. . .
Reconcile yourself to wait in this darkness as long as is
necessary, but still go on longing after him whom you
love. For if you are to feel him in this life, it must always
be in this cloud in this darkness.

And, therefore, you are to strike the thick cloud of
unknowing with the longing darts of love and never to
retreat, no matter what comes to pass.

The Cloud of Unknowing

I said to the man who stood at the gate of the year: 'Give
me a light that I may tread safely into the unknown.' And
he replied: 'Go out into the darkness and put your hand
into the hand of God. That shall be to you better than
light and safer than a known way.'

King George VI's Christmas address

---

*Lord I am alone, desolate. What have I done to deserve all
this? Was there some extraordinary wickedness I committed to
have you punish me in this way? Why are you absent when
I need you most? Why when I pray do the heavens seem as
brass? Why am I so trapped in the prison of my own dark
moods? I feel as if I am dying: indeed sometimes I'd rather
be dead. Lord, in my confusion, reveal yourself; in my helplessness, give me strength; in my despair, hear my prayer. . .*

*My son, my daughter, you are not alone. The dark night is
never an accident or misfortune. All true saints have had their
spirits perfected and transfigured in the darkness. It's the only
way my children can be stripped of all their comfortable illusions
and false securities. The obstacle to union with myself is
anything you worship which is not God — work, success,
ambitions, even your own past experience or present piety. It's*

the process of emptying in order to be filled, of purging in order to be cleansed, of removing all other props so that you can trust me alone. It's in the darkness of the night that the reality of my brightness will be apparent. The turmoil will give way to serenity; you will have a peace no suffering can disturb. . .

Lord, I surrender. Forgive me for wanting passionately to be in control. I now see that in my own will, my intentions and my activities I have denied you. Help me not to resist your action in me: you must love me greatly to trust me with all this. I submit to your loving providence, knowing that through this dark night eternal changes are being wrought within me, that eternal life will ensue from this dying. . .

A Benediction
Be still; the Lord is on your side. Bear patiently the cross of dark pain. Leave it to your God to order and provide: in every change he is faithful. Be still; your best, your heavenly Friend will lead you through the pain to healing, through darkness into his marvellous light. May this experience of darkness enable you to see him more clearly, love him more dearly and become more truly human — like Jesus. Amen.

37

Give me glue in my veins

The fruit of the Spirit is. . . faithfulness.

So let us not grow weary in doing what is right, for we will reap at harvest-time if we do not give up.

Let us run with perseverance the race that is set before us. . . let us go on toward perfection.

We want each one of you to show diligence so as to realise the full assurance of hope to the very end, so that you may not become sluggish, but imitators of those who through faith and patience inherit the promises.

No-one who puts a hand to the plough and looks back is fit for the kingdom of God.

Your steadfast love, O Lord, extends to the heavens, your faithfulness to the clouds.

He gives power to the faint,
and strengthens the powerless.
Even youths will faint and be weary,
and the young will fall exhausted:
but those who wait for the Lord shall renew their strength,
they shall mount up on wings like eagles,
they shall run and not be weary,
they shall walk and not faint.

My brothers and sisters, whenever you face trials of any kind, consider it nothing but joy, because you know that the testing of your faith produces endurance; and let endurance have its full effect, so that you may be mature and complete, lacking in nothing.

We. . . boast in our sufferings, knowing that suffering produces endurance, and endurance produces character, and character produces hope, and hope does not disappoint us, because God's love has been poured into our hearts through the Holy Spirit that has been given to us.

May the Lord direct your hearts. . . to the steadfastness of Christ.

If we endure, we will also reign with him. . .

I have fought the good fight, I have finished the race, I have kept the faith. From now on there is reserved for me the crown of righteousness, which the Lord the righteous judge will give me on that day. . .

(Galatians 5: 22; 6: 9; Hebrews 12: 1 and 61; 6: 11–12; Luke 6: 62; Psalm 36: 5; Isaiah 40: 29–31; James 1: 2–4; Romans 5: 3–5; 2 Thessalonians 3: 5; 2 Timothy 2: 12; 4: 7-8 — all NRSV)

An American mountaineer described the last moments of his ascent of Mount Everest. His entire body screamed for relief, but his mind was locked like radar on that point in space where the snowy cornice of the summit peak jutted into a blue-black sky. Indomitable perseverance underlies every great human achievement.

To a young church almost rent apart by dissension and the cross-currents of bitter theological controversy, Paul, himself the survivor of incredible hardships, dictated these words: 'The fruit of the Spirit is. . . faithfulness' (Galatians 5: 22). The message sent to those beleaguered Galatian converts is a timeless one, sorely needed by every generation of Christians since.

Closely related to faithfulness are two other words popular with New Testament writers and usually translated as *patience* and *steadfastness*. Together, they remind us of a quality essential to our Christian life. The English words which describe it best are old-fashioned ones: fidelity, longsuffering, fortitude and trustworthiness.

Today, we talk about 'stickability' or 'sheer guts': 'When the going gets tough the tough get going!' To borrow Elizabeth Goudge's metaphor, one of God's greatest gifts to us as his children is to put 'glue in our veins' — the 'glue' that enables us to adhere undaunted to our Christian principles, to pass through the stormy seasons of life and to remain faithful to our God and patient and reliable in all our relationships in the home, the church and the business world.

We face the pain and uncertainty of everyday life and the constant failure of others to meet our expectations. Moreover, we are, as C.S. Lewis reminds us, soldiers in 'enemy occupied territory', battling satanic powers which are frequently unidentifiable. We need that 'glue' to face the challenge of the impossible. God has chosen to entrust his work in this world to flawed human instruments, such as we know ourselves to be. We are so prone to fall before temptation. Even at our best, our judgments are warped by the prejudices and assumptions of our own particular age and culture. God, who in his sovereignty allows us freedom of choice, lets us make mistakes. We flounder and sometimes fail, miserably. Yet we must go on.

There is a practical, down-to-earth quality in this aspect of the fruit of the Spirit; it calls for dogged determination. Yet if it has within it a hint of the humdrum, it is also a reflection of the character of our covenantal God who has taken the initiative and kept faith with succeeding generations of his faulty, often faithless people. Nor is it a dour, negative concept. There is a warmth and challenge in it that prevents us not merely from outright quitting, but from treating life as a meaningless, joyless treadmill. It will encourage us neither to cling obstinately to a false course of action, nor to rely too much on external stimulation. Thus the New Testament writers constantly link our faithfulness with our growth to maturity and the glory of the goal of our Christian life.

Christians living in an earlier age, before 'happiness' was consistently set before Western society as the chief objective of humanity and easy choices therefore became acceptable, understood well just what such 'glue in our veins' can involve. Think of John Bunyan's famous pilgrim. He did not expect an easy journey. He wallowed in the mire of the Slough of Despond, he was all but vanquished by Apollyon in the Valley of Humiliation, and he felt distraught by demonic voices in the Valley of the Shadow of Death. He led his younger companion astray and was trapped in Doubting Castle by Giant Despair. Yet each time he picked himself up or retraced his steps and continued on along the road that led to the Celestial City, rejoicing in the companionship of other pilgrims and the sustaining reality of God's promises and provision. Finally, as the gates of the city opened to receive the transfigured pilgrims, all its bells rang out for joy.

We, too, can go on. The mountaineer standing on the summit of Everest knew what the reward of his effort would be. When we have struggled up the last defile, we know only that our compensation will be far beyond our present capacity to comprehend.

❧❧

Behind him lay the grey Azores,
Behind the gates of Hercules;
Before him not the ghost of shores,
Before him only shoreless seas.
Brave Admiral, say but one good word;
What shall we do when hope is gone?
The words leapt like a leaping sword:
'Sail on! sail on! sail on! and on!'

Joaquin Miller, *Columbus*

If you can force your heart and nerve and sinew
To serve your turn long after they are gone. . .
And so hold on when there is nothing in you,
Except the will which says to them: 'Hold on!'

Rudyard Kipling, *If*

Being. . . who?
One who never turned his back but marched breast
   forward,
Never doubted clouds would break,
Never dreamed, though right were worsted, wrong
   would triumph,
Held we fall to rise, are baffled to fight better,
Sleep to wake.

Robert Browning, *Epilogue*

To love God subtly alters a human being. If the simile is not too homely, lovers of God have glue in their veins. . . Christians should be judged, I think, by their stickableness, since by that alone can God get anything done in this world.

Elizabeth Goudge, *The Joy of the Snow*

[Faithfulness] describes the person on whose faithful service we can rely, on whose loyalty we may depend, whose word we can unreservedly accept. It describes the one in whom there is the unswerving and inflexible fidelity of Jesus Christ, and the utter dependability of God.

J.M.G. Barclay, *Flesh*

Now, at the end of this valley was another, called the Valley of the Shadow of Death, and Christian must needs go through it, because the way to the Celestial City lay through the midst of it. . . the pathway was here so dark, that oft-times, when he lift up his foot to set forward, he knew not where or upon what he should set it next. . .

Sometimes he had half a thought to go back; then again he thought he might be halfway through the valley; he remembered also how he had vanquished many a danger. . . so he resolved to go on. Yet the fiends seemed to come nearer and nearer; but when they were come even almost at him, he cried out with a most vehement voice, 'I will walk in the strength of the Lord!' So they gave back and came no further. . . and by and by the day broke; then said Christian, [God] hath turned 'the shadow of death into the morning' (Amos 5: 8).

John Bunyan, *Pilgrim's Progress*

Not a word of attraction can I write to [a prospective recruit]. It will be desperately hard work; iron would snap under the strain of it. I ask for steel, that quality which is at the back of all going on, patience which cannot be tired out, and love that loves in very deed, unto death:

Make us thy labourers,
Let us not dream of ever looking back,

Let not our knees be feeble, hands be slack,
O make us strong to labour, strong to bear,
From the rising of the morning till the stars appear.
Make us thy warriors,
On whom thou canst depend to stand the brunt
Of any perilous charge on any front,
Give to us skill to handle sword and spear
From the rising of the morning till the stars appear.

Amy Carmichael

One of my regular correspondents is a ninety-three-year-old man in an old folks' home. His name is Mr Secrest. I love reading his letters, because they are so full of a very active patient endurance, with a real measure of joy. His wife died in that same home some years ago. He has recently had an operation and must walk with a cane when he goes outdoors.

But what fills his letters? He counts the cloudy days, the sunny days and the cloudless days, and once gave me a list for the 'last five years'. Another time he told me he had just taken his 3,437th walk since he came into the home. . . He reads every afternoon to a blind woman and also to another person who cannot read. Mr Secrest is very concerned that so many people in the home are wasting their days — doing nothing, talking about nothing, not even caring to come to Bible classes. His patience is not just a matter of 'waiting to die', but of using the time as thoroughly as will all who believe that they are where the Lord wants them to be — for a reason, for a purpose, *right now*.

The 'patience' in the word of God is nothing like the passiveness of a grazing cow waiting to be hit by lightning or a falling tree — or simply waiting for the evening to come without making a fuss! The patience that God unfolds to us, in passages covering tribulation and difficulties, is an active, purposeful flowing of prayer and action that affects ourselves and other people and makes up part of the important victory that matters to God.

This patient endurance is acceptable to God, commendable to God, because in some tiny way we are following

the example which Christ gave us when he told us that
we were to follow in his steps.

Edith Schaeffer, *Affliction*

My heart goes out to all those for whom 'being a Christian'
has been like a marathon walk through ankle-deep mud.
Some drop out, some keep going, all wonder what on
earth it's all about. Why so many peaks and troughs?
Why so little peace? Why do some Christians seem to
have 'got it', whatever *it* is?

I've got no smart answers. I'm still trudging along
myself most of the time, but I am excited by three things.
One is the person of Jesus, one is the fact that God likes
me and wants me in his family, and the other is his
assurance that nothing is ever wasted. To all my fellow-
stragglers and Christian delinquents I say, with tears in
my eyes as I write, God bless you in whatever way you
need. Be wary about those once-for-all solutions, but hang
on — he'll rescue you.

Adrian Plass, *The Growing Up Pains of Adrian Plass*

If I find him, if I follow.
    What his guerdon here?
Many a sorrow, many a labour,
    Many a tear.
Finding, following, keeping, struggling —
    Is he sure to bless?
Saints, apostles, prophets, martyrs
    Answer, Yes!

Jason Mason Neale,
based on Stephen the Sabaite (eighth century)

Lord, give me glue in my veins.
I want to show my gratitude for your love and faithfulness
by my faithfulness to you and to all those I meet. Help me to
be faithful in the small duties of daily life and in everything
and at all times to seek first the kingdom of God, that my life
may conform to your perfect plan and, whatever the cost, that
I may glorify your name by accomplishing the work you have

given me to do.

Enable me to be totally reliable: loyal to my family and my friends, faithful in keeping my appointments, true to my word.

When I am discouraged or perplexed by conflicting ideologies and frustrated by the pressures of life, when my friends have disappointed me, when I am tired and sick, give to me then the energy, strength and determination to continue. When I fail, give me the humility to confess my mistakes and lift me up and set me once again on the right path.

Above all, teach me the lesson of joyful endurance, and give me the faith to believe that the whole of life, including doubt, failure and trial, is part of your plan to bring me to maturity. Grant to me a sure and certain hope in our ultimate destiny as the children of God.

Lord, covenantal God whose faithfulness extends to all generations, I want to thank you for your astounding patience, for your abundant provision for rest and refreshment along the way, and the blazing certainty of the glorious hope of eternal life at the end of the journey. Because you are faithful, I know that you require me, as your child, to be faithful.

Lord Jesus, thank you that, for the sake of the joy that was set before you, you endured the cross and made light of its shame. May I, too, be faithful unto death that I may receive a crown of life.

Holy Spirit, thank you again for your gift of faithfulness. . . and for the joy that is so often greatest in the path of obedience and suffering — and apparent drudgery!

A Benediction

Oh, grant unto our souls,
Light that groweth not pale with day's
   decrease,
Love that never can fail till life shall cease;
Joy no trial shall mar,
Hope that shineth afar,
Faith serene as a star —
   and Christ's own peace.

Colin Sterne, *Christ's Own Peace*

38

I have a dream

(Martin Luther King)

Take delight in the Lord, and he will give you the desires of your heart.

I appointed you to go and bear fruit, fruit that will last, so that the Father will give you whatever you ask him in my name.

I am with you, says the Lord. And the Lord stirred up the spirit of Zerubbabel son of Shealtiel, governor of Judah, and the spirit of Joshua son of Jehozadak, the high priest, and the spirit of all the remnant of the people; and they came and worked on the house of the Lord of hosts, their God. . . Take courage, all you people of the land, says the Lord; work, for I am with you, says the Lord of hosts. . . My spirit abides among you; do not fear.

You open your hand, satisfying the desire of every living thing.

The desire of the righteous ends only in good.

Very truly, I tell you, if you ask anything of the Father in my name, he will give it to you. Until now you have not asked for anything in my name. Ask and you will receive, so that your joy may be complete.

All things can be done for the one who believes.

For nothing will be impossible with God.

The angel who talked with me came again, and wakened me, as one is wakened from sleep. He said to me, 'What do you see?. . . This is the word of the Lord to Zerubbabel: "Not by might, nor by power, but by my spirit," says the Lord of hosts. "What are you,

O great mountain? Before Zerubbabel you shall become a plain."'

For truly I tell you, if you have faith the size of a mustard seed, you will say to this mountain, 'Move from here to there,' and it will move; and nothing will be impossible for you.

I can do all things through him who strengthens me.

(Psalm 37: 4; John 15: 16b; Haggai 1: 13b and 14; 2: 4b and 5; Psalm 145: 16; Proverbs 11: 23; John 16: 23b–24; Mark 9: 23b; Luke 1: 37; Zechariah 4: 1, 2a, 6 and 7a; Matthew 17: 20b; Philippians 4: 13 — all NRSV)

Gaze at the sky for fifteen minutes every morning and stretch your mind to take in the vastness of God. Breathe deeply of his fragrance and beauty and feel his love flowing around and in you, like the air. After three months, says Glenn Clark in *Windows of Heaven*, you should find yourself living in a new and heavenly world. Not that the universe has changed, but our receptors have been subjected to a spring-clean.

The sky was also very important to Corrie ten Boom in the hell of the concentration camps. Such a sustaining symbol of God's presence fortified her faith in the fact that God still held their shattered dreams in his loving hands.

The immensity of God's power and love is only hinted at by the distance of the sun, let alone those stars from distant galaxies, the light from some of which takes thousands of years to reach us. Similarly, the size of God's plans and dreams for us can be immeasurably larger than we think. We do not need to keep our prayers and dreams confined to our own backyard. Again and again in scripture, we are encouraged to be stout-hearted adventurers in prayer. 'The sky's the limit' in what we can ask for, says Jesus — if we can come to the place of truly believing that God is wanting us to set out on an exciting faith journey. Unfortunately, our dreams are often so small.

In contrast, Martin Luther King's dream cost him all he had and certainly didn't fulfil his family's short-term goals.

But as the years pass and the inspiration of his life continues through the generations of both black and white Americans in their struggle for equality, many are thankful that he followed his dream into the uncharted, dangerous regions of racial hatred and prejudice.

God invites, even yearns for us to be bold in our prayers. Perhaps our greatest dreams have yet to be conceived, let alone given birth. To find time to sit and daydream, letting our sanctified imaginations roam where they will, free from too great a tether to 'commonsense' and 'reason', seems to be God's invitation to us again and again in the scriptures. All things are possible with God on our side. If we can start to dream the big ones, beyond our own selfish little prayers, we too can be more used of God than we ever could have imagined.

The as-yet-unfulfilled longings and deepest desires of my heart sometimes surface in those first waking moments — my dreaming time when, still fresh from sleep's roamings, in the place of communion between earth and heaven, I can listen to God best, free from the day's distractions. And I can water those dreams with believing faith before 'commonsense' takes over. I used to feel guilty at such times that I wasn't getting up for a time with God, until I realised that I was doing just that. For isn't it the deep desires of our hearts, rather than the words we say, that are our most real prayers — wherever we are when we dream them?

Every act, both good and bad, starts with an idea, a picture in the mind. Dreaming prayers are only the start, but without them, no goal is born. It takes successive steps, working with God, to make our dreams come true.

In his workbook on prayer, *I Will Lift Up Mine Eyes*, Glenn Clark suggests we should hone the deepest desires of our hearts, once we have written them down, by putting them through the biblical tests in Philippians 4: 8. 'Whatever is true (to our personality, not an imitation of someone else's dream), whatever is honourable, whatever is just (fair to others), whatever is pure, whatever is pleasing, whatever is commendable, if there is any excellence and if there is anything worthy of praise, think about these things.' This weeding out of any dreams that are selfish, proud, revengeful, greedy and so on helps us to find our highest goals — those God-given dreams that are meant for us, however unattainable they may seem. It is by God's spirit alone, not our own efforts, that these highest goals could possibly be attained.

Many authors, therefore, emphasise the necessity of giving these dreams back to God in surrender, trusting him to bring them into being in his own way and time. This 'forgetting them' step, following the 'believing faith' step, is not negative or backward, but a time of positive, patient waiting. Sometimes this waiting period shows up the smallness of a dream compared with a larger vision that has come to us, so that we become content to let the smaller one die. But let us not be deterred by the possibility of the death of one of our dreams! Eternity is before us, as is the possibility of resurrection, in the fields where the locusts have been.

But what is so amazing is the way that often our sincerest dreams, when given back to God and forgotten about, come true as the years go by. Catherine Marshall's experience (*Adventures in Prayer*) paralleled my own, when she discovered later that all her recorded dreams for her son had come true. Ten years after I recorded my dreamings (which I had written down when I was twenty-two), I re-read them and was amazed, even awestruck, to find how virtually all of them had come into tangible reality. For me, this statement came true: *Our dreams are our greatest reality.*

So what is planted by faith as dream seeds in the fertile ground of God's love is no less real than the practical fruit of our dreaming, enjoyed later on. The seeds and the fruit are one and the same. Our deepest unselfish desires are as real as the practical fulfilment of them. So my gratitude to God, though ten years late, was immense. It proved to me, as nothing else did, that God was not only alive, but intimately involved in my life for good. God loved me!

When I haven't had enough silent time to remain close to God and a temptation to doubt this returns, I now see that this is the most important moment to dream imaginatively of Jesus' tender look of love and understanding for me alone, as his promises declare. We can imagine there are shut doors with God when there are none. Why not take him at his word and imagine open ones? Our imagination, expressing trust in God rather than doubt, is part of the victorious process that helps our dreams come true.

Journalling our dreams and working with them in prayer does another thing, besides being a record to look back on with thanksgiving. It motivates us and energises us to go for it! As we come to believe in the generosity and provision of God for us personally, we can trust that those deepest purified desires of our heart are in God's plan for us, because he has placed them within us.

And if God is for us, who can be against us? Nothing and nobody need stop our dreams from being fulfilled when all the power of heaven is behind us. Negative feelings of inadequacy, insurmountable problems — not the least among them being oneself — are all swallowed up in the incredible, positive vision of 'self', enabling God to fulfil his purposes in and for and through us. For God it is who does the work — even the work of planting our highest goals within us for us to find. Let us dig deep within and find them. And when faith rises, mountains beware!

⚜

What were the greatest dreams ever dreamed in the history of humankind? Two there are that stand out as eagles among birdlings. Let us consider these two.

Our Bible is divided into two Testaments, and each Testament centres around a dream. The dream of the Old Testament is of a redeemer that is to come some day and save Israel and the entire world from the suffering and sin in which it is submerged. . . And out of that dream, dreamed by an entire nation for thousands of years, there at last emerged the fulfilment of the dream. . . Jesus of Nazareth. Jesus was the greatest Dream ever dreamed by humankind. . .

Then after Jesus came, he too dreamed a dream. He dreamed a dream that filled the entire New Testament, even as the dream of his coming had filled the Old Testament. Let us pause before this thought. Jesus, the greatest incarnation of a dream of all the ages, himself dreamed another dream! A dream within a dream!. . . And what was the dream that Jesus dreamed? *Jesus dreamed of the kingdom of God coming into fulfilment on earth.*

He began his Sermon on the Mount with the statement, 'Blessed are the poor in spirit, for of such is the *kingdom of heaven.*' The climax of the Sermon on the Mount was, 'Seek first the kingdom of God and his righteousness and all these things shall be added unto you.' The centre of the Lord's Prayer contains the words, 'Your kingdom come, on earth as in heaven.'

Let us all unite together in dreaming this great dream with Jesus.

Glenn Clark, The Soul's Sincere Desire

I say to you today, even though we face the difficulties of today and tomorrow, I still have a dream. It is a dream deeply rooted in the American Dream.

I have a dream that one day this nation will rise up, and live out the true meaning of its creed: 'We hold these truths to be self-evident, that all are created equal'. . .

I have a dream that my four little children will one day live in a nation where they will not be judged by the colour of their skin, but by the content of their character.

I have a dream that one day every valley shall be exalted, every hill and mountain shall be made low. The rough places will be made plain, and the crooked places will be made straight. . .

With this faith we will be able to hew out of the mountain of despair a stone of hope. With this faith we will be able to work together, to pray together, to struggle together, to go to jail together, to stand up for freedom together, knowing we will be free one day.

Martin Luther King, I Have A Dream

And as for the danger that our dreams may spring from our selfish human will rather than God's will, there are tests for this. Only when a dream has passed such a series of tests — so that we are certain that our heart's desire is also God's dream *before* we pray — can we pray the Dreaming Prayer with faith and thus with power. . . For example, ask yourself questions like these:

* Will my dream fulfil the talents, the temperament and emotional needs which God has planted in my being?
* Does my dream involve taking anything or any person belonging to someone else?
* Am I willing to make all my relationships with other people right?
* Do I want this dream with my whole heart?
* Am I willing to wait patiently for God's timing?
* Am I dreaming big? The bigger the dream and the more persons who will benefit, the more likely it is to stem from the infinite designs of God.

If your heart's desire can pass a series of tests like this, then you are ready for the final necessary step in the Dreaming Prayer! Hand your dream over to God and then leave it in his keeping. There seem to be periods when the dream is like a seed that must be planted in the dark earth and left there to germinate. . .

But in the meantime, long before we see the fruition of our hopes, in fact the very moment a God-given dream is planted in our hearts, a strange happiness flows into us. I have come to think that at that moment, all the resources of the universe are released to help us. Our praying is then at one with the will of God, a channel for the Creator's always joyous, triumphant purposes for us and our world. . . God does have his 'fullness of time' for the answer to each prayer. It follows then that he alone knows the magnitude of the changes that have to be wrought in us before we can receive our hearts' desires. . . Thus the Lord seems constantly to use waiting as a tool for bringing us the very best of his gifts.

Catherine Marshall, Adventures in Prayer

The spiritual dimension of human development has four related capacities: (a) the capacity to have and to respond to dreams, visions, ideals, spiritual teachings, goals and theories; (b) the capacity to accept these as a reflection of our unknown or unrealised potential; (c) the capacity to express these in speech, art or dance; (d) the capacity to use these symbolic expressions for action, directed at making the possible a reality. . .

All the Aboriginal ceremonies and sacred sites are based on our Dreaming. In our Dreaming, God the Creator gave to us everything that is here now: the birds, the trees, the rivers, the lakes, the food, the caves, the mountains, the morning, the day and night. Then God created man and woman, and with that creation God came to walk this land with our people, to lay down the law between God and the people, thus teaching us the worth and value of this law of God's creation.

Anne Pattel-Gray, Through Aboriginal Eyes

To me as a tribal Aboriginal, dreaming is more than just an ordinary dream which one would dream at night or day. To us, dreaming is reality, because it takes in all the Aboriginal spirituality. When the religious tribal elder says, 'This mountain is my dreaming' or 'That land is my dreaming', he is really saying to us that this mountain or that land holds very sacred knowledge, wisdom and moral teaching, passed on to us by the spirit of the Creator, who has created for us the holy sacred sites and the sacred mountains which exist today. . .

The Aboriginal Christians are convinced and believe that the God of the Bible was with us and our people in the Dreamtime. He was very active in our history. He has come to us in many different ways and many different forms to reveal his presence. . . If this God of the Bible was active in Hebrew history in both the Old and New Testament, then he was also active in

Aboriginal history and dreaming. . . We are prepared to throw away any wrong interpretation of the creator spirit which the Holy Spirit now reveals to us. . .

Early immigrants from Europe should have pride in their own dreaming and spirituality. When we have this pride in our particular heritage, we can be more open to one another. . .

In Aboriginal culture, when persons approach a sacred site, a sacred object or a totem, it is as if they are approaching the tablets of stone Moses brought down from the mountain. In special places in Australia, a kind of law from long ago is thought to be retained.

Djiniyini Gondarra, *Father, You Gave us the Dreaming*

If faith thus depends on hope for its life, then the sin of unbelief is manifestly grounded in hopelessness. To be sure, it is usually said that sin in its original form is our wanting to be as God. But that is only the one side of sin. The other side of such pride is hopelessness, resignation, inertia and melancholy. From this arise the *tristesse* and frustration which fill all living things with the seeds of a sweet decay. Among the sinners whose future is eternal death in Revelation 21: 8, the 'fearful' are mentioned before unbelievers, idolators, murderers and the rest. . . Temptation then consists not so much in the titanic desire to be as God, but in weakness, timidity, weariness, not wanting to be what God requires of us.

God has exalted us and given us the prospect of a life that is wide and free, but we hang back and let ourselves down. God promises a new creation of all things in righteousness and peace, but we act as if everything were as before and remained as before. God honours us with his promises, but we do not believe ourselves capable of what is required of us. That is the sin which most profoundly threatens the believer. It is not the evil we do but the good we do not do, not our misdeeds but omissions that accuse us. . . These so-called sins of omission all have their ground in hopelessness and weakness of faith. 'It is not so much sin that plunges us into disaster, rather despair,' said Chrysostom.

Jürgen Moltmann, *The Theology of Hope*

THE EIGHT STEPS OF MOUNTAIN-MOVING FAITH

STEP 1: DREAMING. . . When God made you, he gave you what was given to no other living organism in the universe — the immeasurable power to visualise great dreams!. . . The daring power of human imagination is exciting proof that you are made in the image of God. . . Faith begins with an act of imagining. If you don't have a dream, how can dreams come true? Begin now by using this God power within yourself to paint a picture of what you would like to accomplish. . .

STEP 2: DESIRING. . . More faith is shattered by lack of desire than by real doubt. . . Faith is wanting something with all your heart. . . After you know what you want, you must censure these desires.

STEP 3: DARING. . . to risk failure. Even indecision is a decision. And even if you decide to do nothing, you run the risk of failing to attempt what might have become a marvellous miracle. . . Obviously, our goals must be realistic, but high enough so that success can be termed a miracle. Not a few people claim to be a success because they've reached every goal in life. The truth is they are really failures because their goals were deceptively low. . .

STEP 4: BEGINNING. . . Act as if nothing is going to stop the dream from succeeding. God seldom performs a miracle until we try.

STEP 5: EXPECTING. . . When you expect success, then you hold nothing back, but sink your last dime, spend your second-wind energy and gamble your priceless reputation, confident that you'll make it. . . Attempt great things for God and expect great things from God. . . *This does not mean that we will always reach our goals. . . Even if the maximum goal is not attained, the realised achievement will represent the ultimate of our abilities.*

STEP 6: AFFIRMING. . . Was St Paul modest when he said, 'I can do all things through Christ who strengthens me'? Was he exaggerating a bit? Or was this an extreme exercise of mountain-moving faith talking?. . . Affirm success and you will visualise yourself winning. When you imagine yourself winning then that mysterious force of enthusiasm suddenly surges through your being.

STEP 7: WAITING. . . How often I have been asked by discouraged people, 'Reverend, I have prayed, but it doesn't seem to work for me'. . . In almost every instance, I have to advise them that there is one vital ingredient missing in their faith. And that dynamic ingredient is patience.

STEP 8: ACCEPTING (sometimes referred to as SUR-RENDERING). . . 'Thy will be done' towers above all human utterances as the supreme statement of faith on the deepest level!. . . If your mountain will not move, surrender it to God. He will either move it or show you how you can turn it into a mine or a monument. . . Most people who succeed in the face of seem-ingly impossible conditions are people who simply don't know how to quit. When unex-pected damage wreaks havoc with your dreams, then what? Never dwell on what you have lost. If you do, you will be discouraged and defeated. Look not at what you have lost, but at what you have left. . . 'I was never happier before polio than I am today. I never really started to live until I got into the iron lung. I learned to think differently,' he told me as we visited. Of course, he's a possibility thinker. I have never met a happier man in my life.

Robert H. Schuller, *Move Ahead With Possibility Thinking*

Dream large, my soul, dream large,
God thinks his thoughts through thee,
If thou canst dream freedom for all,
Mankind shall yet be free.
Dream large, my soul, dream large,
God wills for all his peace.
If thou canst dream true brotherhood,
Someday all war shall cease.

Myrtle Williamson, *CFO Sings*

Father, once — it seems long ago now — I had such big dreams, so much anticipation of the future. Now no shimmering horizon beckons me; my days are lack-lustre. I see so little of lasting value in the daily round. Where is your plan for my life, Father?

You have told us that without vision, we perish. So, Father in heaven, knowing that I can ask in confidence for your expressed will, I ask you to deposit in my mind and heart the particular dream, the special vision you have for my life.

And along with the dream, will you give me whatever graces, patience and stamina it takes to see the dream through to fruition? I sense that this may involve adventures I have not bargained for. But I want to trust you enough to follow even if you lead along new paths. I admit to liking some of my ruts. But I know that habit-patterns that seem like cosy nests from the inside, from your vantage point may be prison cells.

Lord, if you have to break down any prisons of mine before I can see the stars and catch the vision, then Lord, begin the process now. In joyous expectation. Amen.

Catherine Marshall, *Adventures in Prayer*

A Benediction

Look up and see the immense possibilities there are for God to work through you. Take heart. If Jesus dreamed of the Father's kingdom on earth as it is in heaven, it will surely come to pass. Go forth then with confidence in the unlimited resources and generosity of God to help you turn those dreams into practical reality. Amen.

Theme: The gentle empowering through darkness

'God. . . gave me light as I walked through the darkness'
(Job 29: 3)

If only my life could once again
    be as it was when God watched over me.
God was always with me then and
    gave me light as I walked through the darkness.
Those were the days when I was prosperous,
    and the friendship of God protected my home.
Almighty God was with me then,
    and I was surrounded by all my children.
My cows and goats gave plenty of milk,
    and my olive-trees grew in the rockiest soil.
Whenever the city elders met
    and I took my place among them,
        young men stepped aside as soon as they saw me
        and old men stood up to show me respect.
The leaders of the people would stop talking;
    even the most important men kept silent.

Everyone who saw me or heard of me had good
    things to say about what I had done.
When the poor cried out, I helped them;
    I gave help to orphans who had nowhere to turn.
Men who were in deepest misery praised me
    and I helped widows find security.
I have always acted justly and fairly.
I was eyes for the blind
    and feet for the lame.
I was like a father to the poor
    and took the side of strangers in trouble.
I destroyed the power of cruel men
    and rescued their victims.

Job 29: 2–17, GNB

39

I trace the rainbow through the rain

I create both light and darkness; I bring both blessing and disaster.

Dear friends, do not be surprised at the painful trial you are suffering, as though something strange were happening to you. These have come so that your faith — of greater worth than gold, which perishes even though refined by fire — may be proved genuine.

For our light and momentary troubles are achieving for us an eternal glory.

We must go through many hardships to enter the kingdom of God.

Jesus said to them, 'Can you drink the cup of suffering that I must drink?'. . . 'We can,' they answered.

For you have been given the privilege of serving Christ, not only by believing in him, but also by suffering for him.

I consider that what we suffer at this present time cannot be compared at all with the glory that is going to be revealed in us.

You can be sure that the more we undergo sufferings for Christ, the more he will shower us with his comfort and encouragement.

We also rejoice in our sufferings, because we know that suffering produces perseverance; perseverance, character and character, hope.

Do not regard lightly the discipline of the Lord, nor lose courage when you are punished by him. For the Lord disciplines him whom he loves and chastises every [child] whom he receives.

You have put us to the test, God; as silver is purified by fire so you have tested us.

If we are his children, we share his treasures and all that Christ claims as his will belong to all of us as well! Yes, if we share in his sufferings, we shall certainly share in his glory.

He will wipe every tear from their eyes. There will be no more death or mourning or crying or pain.

(Isaiah 45: 7, GNB; 1 Peter 4: 12; 1 Peter 1: 7; 2 Corinthians 4: 17; Acts 14: 22b — all NIV; Mark 10: 38-39; Philippians 1: 29; Romans 8: 18 — all GNB; 2 Corinthians 1: 5, LB; Romans 5: 3, NIV; Hebrews 12: 5b-6, RSV; Psalm 66: 10, GNB; Romans 8: 17, JB; Revelation 21: 4, GNB)

It is not uncommon today to hear people talk about 'downsides' and 'upsides' — meaning the disadvantages or advantages of a situation. Too often, our theology focuses only on the upside of the Christian life: the blessings, presence, providence and protection of God; Christ's love for us; the rewards of our ultimate destiny; and so much more. We forget, tend to ignore or deliberately repress the biblical theme of the suffering of the people of God.

This is despite the words of our Master to his followers: 'Here on earth you will have many trials and sorrows' (John 16: 33).

We avoid pain like the plague, resenting even minor discomfort and inconvenience. Sometimes, we even cast sideways glances at those saints who are suffering and wonder pharisaically what they have done to earn God's wrath and judgment (see John 9: 1-3).

The reality is that God is in all of life (Acts 17: 28), even — or some would say especially — in our pain. If we flee from suffering, deny it or indulge ourselves with a painless theology, we may end up bypassing enriching and significant learning experiences. Part of our fallenness is the inevitability of suffering. We do ourselves a disservice and God an injustice, if we fail to appreciate that as we walk through the valley of shadows, he is with us.

Often, as we are buffeted by the storms of life, a rainbow will appear. The rainbow proves that the Son is there: unseen, perhaps unfelt, even unsought, but breaking through the clouds and circumstances with a glorious display of his beauty and presence.

Selwyn Hughes has wisely said, 'A mentally and spiritually healthy person is someone who is willing to face and feel sorrow, and recognise that it can be made to deepen one's life — not devastate it.'

As we experience the downside of our humanness and our faith walk, it is worth reminding ourselves that our suffering is momentary, is temporary; that it is worth facing the darkness and pain, tracing the hand of the One who is with us, who is committed to the best for us, who is developing within us character and maturity, who is leading us to wholeness and consummation with his Son who suffered so that we could be glorified.

❦

O joy that seekest me through pain,
I cannot close my heart to thee:
I trace the rainbow through the rain
and feel the promise is not vain,
that morn shall tearless be.

George Matheson

Just realise, I am sixty-nine and I have never seen a person die. I have never even been in the same house while a person died. How about birth? An obstetrician invited me to see my first birth only last year. Just think, these are the greatest events of life and they have been taken out of our experience. We somehow hope to live full emotional lives when we have carefully expunged the sources of the deepest human emotions. When you have no experience of pain, it is rather hard to experience joy.

George Wald

Stifter once said, 'Pain is a holy angel, who shows treasures to us which otherwise remain forever hidden; through him we have become greater than through all joys of the world.' It must be so and I tell this to myself in my present position over and over again — the pain of longing which often can be felt even physically must be there, and we shall not and need not talk it away.

Dietrich Bonhoeffer

There is none in this world, even though a king or pope, without some tribulation or perplexity. Who is [the one] who has the better lot? Assuredly [the one] who is able to suffer something for God.

Thomas à Kempis, *Of the Imitation of Christ*

Stars may be seen from the bottom of a deep well when they cannot be discerned from the top of a mountain: so are many things learned in adversity which the prosperous dream not of. We need affliction as the trees need winter, that we may collect sap and nourishment for future blossoms and fruit. Sorrow is as necessary for the soul as medicine is to the body.

C.H. Spurgeon

And a woman spoke, saying, Tell us of Pain.
And he said:
Your pain is the breaking of the shell that encloses your understanding.
Even as the stone of fruit must break, that its heart may stand in the sun, so must you know pain.
And could you keep your heart in wonder at the daily miracles of your life, your pain would not seem less wondrous than your joy;
And you would accept the seasons of your heart, even as you have always accepted the seasons that pass over your fields.
And you would watch with serenity through the winters of your grief.
Much of your pain is self-chosen.
It is the bitter potion by which the physician within you heals your sick self.
Therefore, trust the physician and drink his remedy in

silence and tranquillity:
For his hand, though heavy and hard, is guided by the tender hand of the Unseen.
And the cup he brings, though it burns your lips, has been fashioned of the clay which the Potter has moistened with his own sacred tears.

Kahlil Gibran, *The Prophet*

I have never read a poem extolling the virtues of pain, nor seen a statue erected in its honour, nor heard a hymn dedicated to it. . . We seem to reserve our shiniest merit badges for those who have been healed, featuring them in magazine articles and TV specials, with the frequent side-effect of causing unhealed ones to feel as though God has passed them by. We make faith not an attitude of trust in something unseen, but a route to get something *seen* — something magical and stupendous, like a miracle or supernatural gift. Faith includes the supernatural, but it also includes daily, dependent trust in spite of results.

Philip Yancey, *Where Is God When It Hurts?*

My life is but a weaving between my Lord and me;
I cannot choose the colours —
he worketh steadily.
Of times,
he weaveth sorrow and I, in foolish pride,
forget he sees the upper and I,
the underside.
Not till the loom is silent, and the shuttles cease to fly,
shall God
unroll the canvas and explain the reason why.
The dark threads
are as needful in the Weaver's skilful hand,
as the threads of gold and silver
in the pattern he has planned.

Anonymous

I. . . believe that for all of us, at our different stages and in our different states, it is possible between and around and through the trials and tribulations that beset us to taste the joy of heaven. . .

Adrian Plass, *View from a Bouncy Castle*

It was only when I lay there on rotting prison straw that I sensed within myself the first stirrings of good. Gradually, it was disclosed to me that the line separating good and evil passes, not through states, nor between classes, nor between political parties either, but right through every human heart and through all human hearts. So, bless you, prison, for having been in my life.

Alexander Solzhenitsyn, *The Gulag Archipelago*

'Do not go gentle into that good night.' So wrote Dylan Thomas, the Welsh poet. 'Rage,' he said, 'rage against the dying of the light.' The trouble is that we live in an age in which people have increasingly justified going quite gently and quite passively into more than the good night of death. We have gone a long way in rationalising our way out of ever having to face and work through pain, anxiety or even an occasional sleepless night. Better by far to take the appropriate pill that puts pain and bad moods behind us, the prescription that lets us lie down in limbo for a while. No raging here; just a search for quiet and for at least a few moments when life doesn't hurt so much. . .

The next time you reach for that tranquilliser or that drink, ask yourself whether it might not be good to meet the pain or loneliness head-on for a change. . . We have more resources than we usually think; we may never discover them and therefore never discover ourselves fully, if we do not enter the pain and suffering that tests our depths and tests them true.

There is a place in life for the experience of pain, not for its own sake, but because it burns the dross off. . . in a way that nothing else can. . . Those who never learn to live with pain only make themselves more vulnerable to it. . . They miss the self-identity that emerges when we truthfully confront the real challenges of living. . . People are ordinarily afraid that they will miss the meaning of life if they miss one of its possible pleasures; they run a far greater risk of missing its meaning when they shy away from its sufferings. . . so rage a little against the real suffering in your life. . .

Eugene C. Kennedy, *The Pain of Being Human*

'My friend', [said Father Vincent]. . . 'sorrow is better than fear. For fear impoverishes always, while sorrow may enrich.'

. . .'I have never thought that a Christian would be free of suffering, *umfundisi*,' [Jarvis stated]. 'For our Lord suffered. And I come to believe that he suffered, not to save us from suffering, but to teach us how to bear suffering. For he knew that there is no life without suffering.'

Alan Paton, *Cry the Beloved Country*

[I experienced] a substantial breakthrough in understanding what I think is a theological truth: suffering is *definitely* a part of the Christian's life. It is a part we *hope* will be utterly minimised or, as my positive-thinking friends say, it will turn quickly into joyous experiences, but it is a part of living nevertheless! And often suffering does not grind slowly to a halt, but rather merely grinds on. . . [Many] times it is a *necessary* and *vital* part of God's plan. . .

Actually, suffering is one of the most effective ways God has to make his people — even his own Son — usable. . . How easy it is to ignore the doctrine of suffering in the Bible and to slip on the blinders of denial about the beautiful purposes of suffering.

Joyce Landorf, *Irregular People*

We want not so much a Father in heaven as a grandfather in heaven — whose plan for the universe was such that it might be said at the end of each day, 'A good time was had by all.'

I should very much like to live in a universe which was governed on such lines but, since it is abundantly clear that I don't and since I have reason to believe nevertheless that God is love, I conclude that my perception of love needs correction. . . The problem of reconciling human suffering with the existence of a God who loves is only insoluble so long as we attach a trivial meaning to the word 'love' and limit his wisdom by what seems to us wise. . .

[It] is natural for us to wish that God had designed for us a less glorious and less arduous destiny; but then we are wishing not for more, but for less.

C.S. Lewis, *The Problem of Pain*

Lord give us grace
that we may know that in the darkness pressing round
it is the mist of sin that hides thy face;
that thou art there
and thou dost know we love thee still.

Gilbert Shaw

It's dark now —
And I'm flying low,
Cold.
But deep within me
I remember
A darkness like this
That came before.
And I remember
That after that hard dark —
That long dark —
Dawn broke.
And the sun rose
Again.
And that is what I must
Remember now.

Ken Walsh, *Sometimes I Weep*

A Benediction
And the God of all grace, who called you to his eternal glory
in Christ, after you have suffered a little while, will himself
restore you and make you strong, firm and steadfast. To him
be the power forever and ever. Amen.

1 Peter 5: 10–11, NIV)

40

For those who have been sinned against

I called on your name, O Lord, from the depths of the
pit. You heard my plea. . . you came near when I
called to you and you said, 'Do not fear.' O Lord, you
took up my case; you redeemed my life. You have seen,
O Lord, the wrong done to me. Uphold my cause.

I call on you, O God, for you will answer me, give
ear to me and hear my prayer. Show the wonder of
your great love, you who save by your right hand those
who take refuge in you from their foes. . . hide me in
the shadow of your wings from the wicked who assail
me.

Since you are my rock and my fortress, for the sake
of your name lead and guide me. Free me from the
trap that is set for me, for you are my refuge. . . I will
be glad and rejoice in your love, for you saw my affliction and knew the anguish of my soul. . . Praise be to
the Lord, for he showed his wonderful love to me when
I was in a beseiged city.

I will praise the Lord, who counsels me; even at night
my heart instructs me. . . Because he is at my right hand,
I shall not be shaken. Therefore my heart is glad and
my tongue rejoices; my body also will rest secure.

You are my hiding place; you will protect me from
trouble and surround me with songs of deliverance. The
Lord's unfailing love surrounds the one who trusts in
him.

I sought the Lord, and he answered me; he delivered
me from all my fears. Taste and see that the Lord is

good; blessed is the one who takes refuge in him. The Lord is close to the broken-hearted and saves those who are crushed in spirit.

The salvation of the righteous comes from the Lord; he is their stronghold in time of trouble. The Lord helps them and delivers them. . . from the wicked and saves them, because they take refuge in him.

In all their distress he, too, was distressed and the angel of his presence. . . saved them. In his love and mercy he redeemed them; he lifted them up and carried them all the days of old.

Guide me in your truth and teach me, for you are God my Saviour and my hope is in you all day long.

And the God of all grace, who called you to his eternal glory in Christ, after you have suffered a little while will himself restore you and make you strong, firm and steadfast.

'For I know the plans I have for you,' declares the Lord, 'plans to prosper you and not to harm you, plans to give you hope and a future. Then you will call upon me and come and pray to me, and I will listen to you. You will seek me and find me when you seek me with all your heart. I will be found by you,' declares the Lord, 'and bring you back from captivity.'

Rejoice in the Lord always. I will say it again: Rejoice!

(Lamentations 3: 55–59; Psalm 17: 6–9; Psalm 31: 3–4, 7 and 21; Psalm 16: 7–9; 32: 7,10b; 34: 4, 8 and 18; 37: 39–40; Isaiah 63: 9; Psalm 25: 5; 1 Peter 5: 10; Jeremiah 29: 11–14; Philippians 4: 4 — all NIV)

'One out of every four girls and one out of every ten boys are victims of sexual abuse.' These are now reliable statistics. I am one of those people, but I was thirty years old before I faced the fact that I had a very painful childhood. I had blocked those hurting memories behind a thick wall.

If anyone had asked me, I would have denied it all and been convinced I was telling the truth. It was only as my own children grew that I began to have sudden flashes of memory which frightened me enormously. I remained silent, building that emotional wall even thicker. I believed I was an upright Christian woman and to admit this would be against my whole image of a coping, 'all together' person, active in my church and work.

But the memories kept coming. Eventually I was forced to look at those painful years. I felt so ashamed, guilty, dirty and hurt, painfully hurt by the past. The sense of guilt was excessive. I had a tendency to blame myself for things which were clearly not my own fault. My memories stopped my capacity to grow and act, to develop my self-esteem.

Blame was another feeling. 'Whenever bad things happen to good people, there is likely to be the feeling that we might have prevented the misfortune if we had acted differently,' writes Harold Kushner. If I blamed myself, I wanted to hurt myself for what I had messed up — and so came anger. If one pushes the anger down, it resurfaces as depression.

Looking at those painful memories required enormous courage from me. For a number of years I had believed God was always with me — my Saviour, my comforter, my deliverer, my strength in adversity. Although I knew this cognitively, I could not feel it emotionally. What I knew in my mind to be true qualities of God, I could not feel or understand. My view of God was distorted and confusing, as I tried to marry the truths of scripture with my own emotions.

Tentatively, I began to share some of these worries with my pastor whom I trusted completely. Gently, ever so quietly, I began also to share some of those memories. I had a great fear of disapproval, disbelief — and I felt completely worthless, humiliated, embarrassed to share my story. But my pastor was accepting and showed compassion, grief and understanding. He helped me to move from the abyss of inaccessible, shut-off memories and gradually helped me to integrate the memories into increasing wholeness.

I learnt much about God during this traumatic, overwhelming time. The Bible became very precious to me. I underlined many of the passages which affirm the compassion of God, and I prayed and pleaded that I might learn to *feel* what the Bible said. There needs to be a desperation to reach wholeness, a persistence to change my reactions to many of my lifestyle behaviours and willingness to face my memories for what they are. The love of the Holy Spirit enfolded me as I began this process.

God has truly been my refuge, my 'strong tower', as I have begun to work through some of the hurts of my life. The grief of what I had missed out on in my early years was strong. My understanding, through many months and years, eventually led me to the belief that God had suffered with me through every hour and every tear. This vital fact helped change my life. With every sadness, every grief, God had been there for me. Jesus had died for my sins, but he had also died for the sins of those who had sinned against me. Christ the illuminator shone deeply into my heart and helped me understand that, as he had forgiven those who had caused harm to me, I also needed to forgive those people.

Forgiveness is an act of one's mind. Emotions may come along with it, but not always. I found that as I chose as an act of my will to forgive them, Jesus performed a miracle in my life to help me feel that forgiveness. It came very gradually, as I handed more and more of my hurts to my Lord.

Throughout all this, one thing remained and helped me more than any other. That was hope: a vital, living hope in a God of surprises and good things. When I was at my very lowest, hope sustained me and carried me through. Another wonderful help was the belief that the future would see me more whole, more together. My broken spirit began to become infused with hope and the certainty of a good future promised to me by my Saviour.

Another important issue was *listening* — my listening to God, God listening to me, and a very few other caring, confidential people who made themselves available to listen to me. Listening is wonderfully therapeutic.

There are still many questions, many puzzling memories,

yet I am able to relax, knowing that the whole truth lies in God's heart and he fully understands and knows all about me. I thank him constantly for the illumination he has given me, and wait for the fullness and the wholeness that will come in the years ahead.

❧❦❧

I see your hands,
not white and manicured,
but scarred and scratched and competent,
reach out —
not always to remove the weight I carry,
but to shift its balance, ease it,
make it bearable.
Lord, if this is where you want me,
I'm content.
No, not quite true. I wish it were.
All I can say, in honesty, is this:
If this is where I'm meant to be,
I'll stay. And try.
Just let me feel your hands.
And, Lord, for all who hurt today —
hurt more than me —
I ask for strength and that flicker of light,
the warmth, that says you're there.

Eddie Askew, *Many Voices, One Voice*

What do we do with our anger when we have been hurt? The goal, if we can achieve it, would be to be angry at the situation rather than at ourselves, or at those who might have prevented it or are close to us trying to help us, or at God who let it happen. Getting angry at ourselves makes us depressed. Being angry at other people scares them away and makes it harder for them to help us.

Being angry at God erects a barrier between us and all the sustaining, comforting resources of religion which are there to help us at such times.

But being angry at the situation, recognising it as being something rotten, unfair and totally undeserved — shouting about it, crying over it — permits us to discharge the anger which is a part of being hurt, without making it harder for us to be helped.

Harold S. Kushner, *When Bad Things Happen to Good People*

The tragedy. . . lies in the fact that sexually abused children are often too ashamed to tell their story, even years later as adults, and their secrets eat away at their souls. . . Abuse frequently happens in a child's own home, which makes it even more devastating. Much of it goes un-reported. Some parents refuse to admit, even to themselves, what they suspect or even know is happening. The abused child feels doubly betrayed and may blame him or herself for what is happening. . . Furthermore, there is usually a fear or terror implanted in the mind of the abused child to stop him or her telling anybody.

Dick Innes, *A Child Betrayed*

Hope allows us to embrace the future and draw it into our present. If hope has died, the future has died with it. Without hope, we are restricted to the legacy of the past and the circumstances of the present.

Lack of hope closes the door. Nothing is envisaged. But the person who hopes looks to God, who is always ahead of us. Christ has gone before. He is the leader who has opened up a new future and whose Spirit brings that future into our present. . .

For the one who lives in hope, there is no closure on any situation, for no final earthly word has yet been spoken. . .

The person who lives in hope has open hands and looks to God. This frees us from the tyranny of the present and releases us to do God's will. . .

The one who hopes can afford to wait, persevere and pray. We will not call God into question. We do not need to make things happen and to force things. . .

Hope places God at the centre of our life and action as we look for his kingdom and his Spirit to guide and empower us.

Charles Ringma, 'The Transforming Power of Hope'

Our hurt, frightened inner children need someone to trust. Someone who will not condemn. Someone who will listen, accept and believe their pain. Someone to weep with them and love them. That someone can be our adult selves. No matter how much love our supporters give us, wonderful as this is, it can never compensate for our own lack of personal accepting love. Eventually we have to begin to love and accept ourselves and to believe that God loves us, too.

To love ourselves brings the nurture we did not receive as a child to our whole being. Slowly I'm learning it's not wrong to love my inner child, the inner me. That's what she needed most: to be loved — and she was not.

Cathy Ann Matthews, *Breaking Through*

Very likely the hurting child within us is still suffering from the trauma of abuse and is affecting our adult lives. God wants to bring support and comfort both to the grown adult and our little child. Rather than putting limits on God and allowing only a small space in me for his activities, I have chosen to follow the steps to open myself further to recovery. Over the years I have sensed that as my child was reaching out to me, I was reaching into her. I asked God to come into that fear-filled place and he has entered my deepest pain, my hurting place, and is working to heal the ache in me.

Cathy Ann Matthews, *Breaking Through*

[Child], it is not I, your God, who has willed suffering, it [is the creatures I have made].
They have brought it into the world in bringing sin,
Because sin is disorder and disorder hurts.
There is for every sin, somewhere in the world and in time, a corresponding suffering.
And the more sins there are, the more suffering.
But I came and I took all your sufferings upon me, as I took all your sins,
I took them and suffered them before you.
I transformed them, I made of them a treasure.
They are still an evil, but an evil with a purpose,

For through your sufferings, I accomplish redemption.

Michel Quoist, *Prayers of Life*

The act of love — extending oneself — as I have said, requires the moving out against the inertia of laziness (work) or the resistance engendered by fear (courage). Let us turn now from the work of love to the courage of love. When we extend ourselves, our self enters new and unfamiliar territory, so to speak. Our self becomes a new and different self. We do things we are not accustomed to do. We change.

The experience of change, of unaccustomed activity, of being on unfamiliar ground, of doing things differently, is frightening. It always was and it always will be. People handle their fear of change in different ways, but the fear is inescapable if they are in fact to change. Courage is not the absence of fear; it is the making of action in spite of fear, the moving out against the resistance engendered by fear into the unknown and into the future. On some level, spiritual growth, and therefore love, always requires courage and involves risk.

M. Scott Peck, *The Road Less Travelled*

FOR THOSE WHO SUFFER

O Thou who understandest the frailty of the human heart, hear our prayer for those who have been unfortunate in life and bruised in spirit. Those who have endured with no outside encouragement. Those who are lonely in heart. For them we know not what to ask, but thou knowest, O Lover of Souls. Amen.

Jim Bishop, *Go With God*

Lord,
it is hard for us
to see your love
in the places of our tragedy, pain and grief.
It is hard to believe
that your love is greater than our evil.
Just give us grace

to keep looking
and believing
in the most impossible circumstances
and, as we do what little we can,
keep giving us the vision
of the height, depth, length and breadth
until we do see
and cannot help believing,
and our love, refined by yours,
rises above
sorrow, fear, guilt and shame
and we shine, your light
for good and bad alike,
through cross to resurrection,
with Jesus Christ our Lord.

Alan Gaunt, *New Prayers for Worship*

O Almighty and Everlasting God, we praise thee for teaching us through the cross and resurrection of thy Son that suffering can be a creative force. Grant, we pray thee, that as his humiliation won glory and life, so the sufferings and endurance of those who follow him may be used to bring his presence and his power into a needy world, through the same Jesus Christ our Lord.

George Appleton, *One Man's Prayers*

A Benediction

Almighty God, have mercy on all that bear me evil, will and would harm, and their faults and mine together, by such easy, tender, merciful means as thine infinite wisdom can divine, vouchsafe to amend and redress. Make us saved souls in heaven together where we may ever live and love together with thee and thy blessed saints, O glorious Trinity, for the bitter passion of our sweet Saviour Christ.

Thomas More

Moved to care

Just then a lawyer stood up to test Jesus. 'Teacher,' he said, 'what must I do to inherit eternal life?' He said to him, 'What is written in the law? What do you read there?' He answered, 'You shall love the Lord your God with all your heart, and with all your soul, and with all your strength, and with all your mind; and your neighbour as yourself.' And he said unto him, 'You have given the right answer; do this and you will live.'

But wanting to justify himself, he asked Jesus, 'And who is my neighbour?' Jesus replied, 'A man was going down from Jerusalem to Jericho and fell into the hands of robbers, who stripped him, beat him and went away, leaving him half dead. Now by chance a priest was going down that road; and when he saw him, he passed by on the other side. So likewise a Levite, when he came to the place and saw him, passed by on the other side.

'But a Samaritan while travelling came near him; and when he saw him, he was moved with pity. He went to him and bandaged his wounds, having poured oil and wine on them. Then he put him on his own animal, brought him to an inn and took care of him. The next day he took out two denarii, gave them to the innkeeper, and said, "Take care of him; and when I come back, I will repay you whatever more you spend." Which of these three, do you think, was a neighbour to the man who fell into the hands of the robbers?'

He said, 'The one who showed him mercy.'

Jesus said to him, 'Go and do likewise.'
(Luke 10: 25-37, NRSV)

'What moved the Good Samaritan to help the wounded traveller?' This question, seemingly quite clear, was part of the confirmation course at the Aboriginal Mission Community where I was ministering. Next week, back came one lad's answer: 'The donkey moved the Good Samaritan. . .' Such are the gaffes that highlight cross-cultural communication.

Yet didn't the donkey play its part in this scenario of our Father's love and care for his hurting people? While it is hardly flattering to be compared with such an animal, and bordering on an insult to be called an ass or a donkey, yet hasn't this humble animal been honoured both in our biblical heritage as well as in our more recent Australian cultural formation?

One of Australia's most revered national remembrances is Anzac Day. There at Gallipoli we remember the bravery of those Australian and New Zealand soldiers making an heroic stand in the face of overwhelming odds. Highlighting this picture of war, slaughter and suffering is the memorable story of Simpson and his donkey moving those wounded diggers to a place of relative safety where they could receive badly needed help. Now every year we award an Anzac Peace Prize to someone making a significant contribution to world peace. It features a relief of Simpson and his donkey.

But it is the tradition, that reaches back almost two thousand years, of the virgin Mary 'being great with child' on the back of a donkey, that captures the imagination of young and old, of rich and poor, of the caring and hurting, as we celebrate the birth of the Christ Child.

On Palm Sunday, it was at Jesus' request that the donkey was chosen to play its role in the moving drama of our Lord entering the city of peace and the stirring of the crowd as they welcomed him with the words: 'Hosanna! Blessed is he who comes in the name of the Lord!'

The humble donkey, in contrast to the war horse, is an animal of peace. Jesus comes to bring peace between us and our Father, to move us to goodwill towards each other. And he uses an ordinary animal to achieve his purposes. That seems to be his way. He associated with ordinary people. He chose ordinary people of no education to be his disciples, to bear witness of his resurrected power in a hostile, but suffering world.

God likes ordinary people. That's why he made so many of us! So often, when ordinary people are moved to care for those who are hurting, there is an overflow of thanks and praise to God.

If you look closely, you can see the donkey has the markings of a cross imprinted on its back, which is said to highlight its honour. But you don't have to look closely at those around you to realise they are marked with the image of God. Instinctively you know it. And it's that which moves you to care for them.

Well, isn't that the way the God of love works through us?

❧❧

I have a particularly vivid memory of worshipping. . . one Sunday morning in Bethel, near Bielfeld in Germany, where there is a large Lutheran settlement for mental cases of all kinds. The service was held under the trees, where an altar, a pulpit and seats are arranged for outdoor worship when weather permits. Most of the congregation were inmates, the epileptics wearing leather headgear like footballers in case they fell while the service was in progress. An inmates' band accompanied the singing, which was spirited but erratic; through the sermon and the prayers there were occasional broken shouts and much twitching and turning.

Yet I had a sense of great devotion; it was all very beautiful and uplifting. Walking away afterwards, I saw two white-haired deaconesses seated on a bench with some of the inmates considered to be unfit to attend the service. Under the direction of the deaconesses, they were all joyously singing together, reminding me of Bunyan's description in *Grace Abounding* of how, before he was converted, he heard some women singing on a Sunday morning in Bedford. I dare say the notes were somewhat cracked, but I think I never heard such beautiful singing and wondered whether any more acceptable songs of praise rose to heaven that Sunday morning. It was a place, I decided, where Jesus would have been very much at home.

Malcolm Muggeridge, *Jesus*

The lawyer's question has been turned around. It is no longer, 'Who is my neighbour?', but 'To whom am I a neighbour?' And Jesus adds pointedly, 'Go and do likewise.' Merely knowing the commandment to love our neighbour is not enough. Talking about it is not enough either, no matter how eloquent we are. Nor is it enough to wait until a 'worthy' neighbour turns up, someone on whom we can have compassion without losing our dignity or getting our hands dirty. The commandment to love our neighbour is in effect *now*, regardless of time, place or circumstance. 'To whom am I a neighbour?' means 'Where is someone who needs my help?'

Heinz Vonhoff, *People Who Care*

Therefore Christians must have strong shoulders and mighty bones, that they may bear flesh — that is, the weakness of their brethren: for Paul says that they have burdens and troubles. Love therefore is mild, courteous, patient, not in receiving, but in giving; for it is constrained to wink at many things and to bear them.

Martin Luther, *Commentary on Galatians*

It is wonderful how much time good people spend fighting the devil. If they would only expend the same amount of energy loving other people, the devil would die in his own tracks of ennui.

Helen Keller, *The Story of My Life*

This is a truly Christian life, here faith is truly effectual through love — that is, it issues in works of the freest service cheerfully and lovingly done, with which we willingly serve another without hope of reward, and are satisfied with the fullness and wealth of our faith. . .

Why should I not therefore freely, joyfully, with all my heart, and with an eager will, do all things which I know are pleasing and acceptable to such a Father, who has overwhelmed me with his inestimable riches? I will therefore give myself as a Christ to my neighbour, just as Christ offered himself to me.

Martin Luther, *Treatise on Christian Liberty*

People who are conscious that their lifespan is over — you can have that consciousness either through being old or you can have it in other ways, through having some incurable disease — for them, leaving this world is enormously helped by being surrounded by loving care, and that is the sort of thing, for instance, Mother Teresa does in Calcutta.

She brings in — what in terms of our utilitarian medicine or welfare notions is a perfectly crazy thing — she brings in from the streets people who are dying in order that they may have perhaps just five minutes in the presence of a loving Christian face, and she considers, and I agree with her, that this is infinitely worthwhile, that they should leave this world with an image of love and not with a sense of — alas, as so many human beings have when they come to the end of their days — of simply being rejected, of being unneeded, of being derelict.

Malcolm Muggeridge, *Some Answers*

Many churches are more concerned about what happens inside their doors than outside. Members will help the poor and needy as long as they don't have to dirty their own hands to do it. Admittedly, it's easier to organise fellowship suppers and church picnics than it is to reach out to the sick and suffering in the community. Caring, after all, takes time and personal involvement.

Charles Colson, *Against the Night*

In effect, the world is saying to the church, 'If you people have anything, show it. Don't come quoting scripture or mouthing words. I want to see a demonstration of what you say.

'You say that Christ transforms people. You believe that Christ can take a man who in his business is grasping, greedy and selfish, and transform him and make him into a person who loves people more than money, who is more concerned about the welfare of those in need than he is about grasping and getting more money.

'You say that Christ can transform people like that? Show me!'

I don't see this in business where it seems that church people are just as grasping and greedy as the people not in the church. The world says to us, 'You speak glibly about the love of God. But if you really want us to understand the love of God, then you be an expression of the love of God. You love us; you care for us; you enter into our lives, our concerns, our hurts as you say God does. Unless you do, your words mean nothing.'

Findley B. Edge, *The Greening of the Church*

I read about a Christian who was walking down the street in the slum area of one of our major cities. He saw a man, apparently struck by a car, lying in the gutter. If this had been in biblical times, the Good Samaritan would have bound up his wounds and taken him to the hospital. But today it is against the law to move an injured person on the city streets. So the Christian did what the law allowed; he telephoned for an ambulance and waited with the injured man. The ambulance service, being what it is in that particular city, especially in the slum area, took an hour to get there. The man died on the way to hospital.

In such a situation what are Christians to do? Do they simply stand by injured people waiting for the ambulance to come? No! If people want to be Christian in this kind of civilisation, they must work to improve the ambulance service!

Findley B. Edge, *The Greening of the Church*

The Sunday morning communion service ended with the familiar words: 'Go forth into the world in peace. . .' I've heard them many times, taking them sometimes as comfort, sometimes as a ritual ending, sometimes only half hearing because I'm already trying to remember which pocket my car keys are in. This time they came as a challenge: my role as a Christian is not simply — if it is simple — to live with Christ's peace in my heart. It is to live that peace in the world, not for my benefit, but for the world's. To do that positively in my relationships isn't to practise the doormat humility of the weak, letting others walk over me out of fear and then dressing it up as Christian meekness. It is a creative force stemming from a real understanding of Christ's purposes for humankind.

Eddie Askew, *No Strange Land*

We who lived in concentration camps can remember the men who walked through the huts comforting others, giving away their last piece of bread. They may have been few in number, but they offer sufficient proof that everything can be taken from you but one thing: the last of the human freedoms — to choose one's attitude in any given set of circumstances.

Victor Frankl, *Man's Search for Meaning*

Thank you, Father, for life and for all that makes life worthwhile — not only the pleasures but also the hardships, the tears as well as the cheers. You are a wonderful God; you have not only given life, but all that gives meaning to life. And you have given your Son to bring the real significance of life that begins here and continues on into eternity.

You have also given me neighbours to share it with. Thank you, Father. Some are fit and well, others are lonely and hurting; some are living in relative luxury, others are unemployed and dejected. But you love them all. Enable me to show this love in a way which meets their need and brings glory to your name. Thank you for the chance to do this.

In the name of Jesus, your Son, who demonstrated such love among us. Amen.

A Benediction
God, our Father, be merciful to us and open our eyes to see the hurting and the lonely around us.

Jesus, our Lord, fill our hearts with love and move us to care with hands touched by a divine impulse.

Holy Spirit, our Comforter, transform our selfish inhibitions into becoming compassionate neighbours. Amen.

Dying

For everything there is a season. . . a time to be born and a time to die.

Even though I walk through the valley of the shadow of death, I fear no evil, for you are with me. I trust in you O Lord; I say, 'You are my God.' My times are in your hand.

Who will separate us from the love of Christ? Will hardship, or distress. . . or peril or sword? No, in all these things we are more than conquerors through him who loves us. For I am convinced that neither death nor life. . . nor anything else in all creation will be able to separate us from the love of God in Christ Jesus our Lord.

I know that my Redeemer lives. . . and after my skin has been destroyed, then in my flesh I shall see God.

For to me, living is Christ and dying is gain. . . My desire is to depart and to be with Christ, for that is far better. I have fought the good fight, I have finished the race, I have kept the faith. From now on there is reserved for me the crown of righteousness, which the Lord, the righteous judge, will give me on that day.

'Father, into your hands I commend my spirit.' Having said this, he breathed his last.

(Ecclesiastes 3: 2, NRSV; Psalm 23: 4, NRSV/NASB; Psalm 31: 14–15; Romans 8: 35 and 37–39; Job 19: 25–26; Philippians 1: 21 and 23; 2 Timothy 4: 7–8; Luke 23: 46 — all NRSV)

We learn much from the dying of our Lord Jesus. As he came to the end of his life, he left the crowds for the company of those dearest to him in the upper room. Judas had left and, later, he went to the Garden of Gethsemane with his disciples, choosing the three closest to be with him in his crisis.

'Father, if it be possible, grant that this cup may pass from me, nevertheless not my will but thine be done.'

What that cup held was not just death, but a death that was in some mysterious sense the punishment of God on all humanity's sin.

Returning to his disciples, he asked with sorrow, 'Could you not watch with me?' (As we visit or stay at the bedside of those we are to lose, we are not asked to intervene — but they, like Jesus, will ask us, 'Could you not watch with me?').

In the time of struggle before his death, Jesus had separated from the crowds, from Judas, from the eight, asking only his dearest friends to be with him in his crisis. He did not want sympathy, he did not want counsel, he did not want activity; he merely wanted them to be there, watching, alert, available — and his closest friends failed him. . .

In Gethsemane, Jesus was beginning to die our death, suffering the desolation, the weight of the world's sin. Following the death of Christ, we find the disciples gathered together in the upper room, confused and fearful. Thomas, seeking reality, confronts the disciples: 'I cannot believe.' Two others, on their way home to Emmaus and speaking to their unknown companion, describing the death of Jesus, said, 'We had hoped that it was he who would have redeemed Israel.'

Like many confronted with death, their hopes, their aspirations, their world were shattered. . .

But Jesus died to remove the fear of death from us. So what death did to Jesus is much, much less than what Jesus did to death. In our dying, we can be 'safe in the arms of Jesus'. For an atheist, death is the end; for a believer, the beginning. (As a Jewish proverb put it, 'The day of death is when two worlds meet with a kiss: this world going out, the future world coming in.')

Humans are the only animals that contemplate their

death. And we die as we have lived. To live well and to die well is a glorious privilege. Death is not the greatest loss — the greatest loss is what dies within us while we live. (How sad to die at thirty, but be buried at sixty!)

Erich Fromm once wrote, 'To die is poignantly bitter, but the idea of having to die without having lived is unbearable.'

'I came from God,' said George Macdonald, 'and I'm going back to God, and I won't have any gaps of death in the middle of my life.' So let us endeavour so to live, suggests Mark Twain, that when we come to die even the undertaker will be sorry!

Some of us do not know what to do with our lives here and now, yet we want another one that will last forever.

> *Tomorrow we shall meet, death and I,*
> *and death shall thrust his sword into one*
> *who is wide awake,*
> *but in the meantime; how grievous the memory*
> *of hours frittered away.*

The awesome truth is that we live forever, and we take beyond death the raw material we have made of our lives before that curtain rings down and the next act begins. And death, as the old saying has it, cancels everything but truth. In life, we can set our house in order, prepare provisions abundantly while we are still able. The journey is very long. . .

Everything we do will be done forever. Everything we say will be said forever. Everything we think will be thought forever. So life ought to be lived earnestly and death prepared for seriously.

'What is life all about?' the dying patient asked his doctor. 'I am searching for meaning. I look at my life and ask, "What have I lived for?" My family, my work, my interests — yes, all of these are important; they did give me purpose. Yet somehow it is not enough.

'I have been looking for more as I looked inside me and waves of emptiness have been flowing through me. I want more. . . I want to find the meaning of my life.'

'So,' the Christian doctor recounted later, 'I offered myself to help him in his search. For me, faith gives meaning. I find meaning as I commit myself in faith to the God of love.'

Another man underwent surgery, but the cancer had spread widely. Speaking with him the next day, his doctor outlined the nature of the tumour, its inoperability and incurability — and the likely future outcome.

'Thank you,' he replied. 'I do understand. I have about twelve months to live, but this gives me time to see what I want to see, do what I want to do, to set my affairs in order and to make my peace with God. This is a unique privilege.'

Life is to be measured in its enjoyment and its effectiveness, not in its length.

Visiting a seriously ill patient in a hospital, the pastor was told that he was 'pre-terminal' — evidently not quite terminal, but expected to be so. The pastor wondered, 'Can't that be said of everyone? Aren't we all "preterminal"?'

❧

O death in life, the days that are no more.

Tennyson

Death, the gate of life.

John Milton

I think of death as a glad awakening from this troubled sleep which we call life — as an emancipation from a world which, beautiful though it be, is still a land of captivity.

Lyman Abbott

Meanwhile, where is God?

This is one of the most disquieting symptoms. When you are happy, so happy that you have no sense of needing him, so happy that you are tempted to feel his claims upon you as an interruption, if you remember yourself and turn to him with gratitude and praise, you will be —

or so it feels — welcomed with open arms.

But go to him when your need is desperate, when all other help is vain, and what do you find? A door slammed in your face and a sound of bolting and double bolting on the inside. After that, silence. You may as well turn away. The longer you wait, the more emphatic the silence will become. . . What can this mean? Why is he so present a companion in our time of prosperity and so very absent a help in time of trouble?

. . .The same thing seems to have happened to Christ: 'Why hast thou forsaken me?' Does that make it easier to understand?

C.S. Lewis, *A Grief Observed*

'Lazarus is dead.' . . .Jesus began to weep.

John 11: 14 and 35

In that final moment of surrender,
when the last, laboured breath is stilled;
a cry of triumph echoes from a distant land.
A proud galleon with sails unfurled
sets forth across the still waters
to carry the weary traveller home.
Faces from bygone days gather to make welcome.
Trumpets sound the victory song;
Sweet voices soar in harmonic splendour,
as perfumed breezes fill the air.
The ship has arrived;
the traveller steps out into the beyond
and soars with ecstasy, as all pain is gone.
Withered limbs become strong and straight;
confused thoughts clear,
to comprehend the glory that is eternity.
The moment of honour has begun.
Suffering is sanctified.
The earthly life but a distant memory.
The joy of the present filling all senses,
as heaven is revealed in all its beauty.

Helen Keyte

Death is nothing at all. I have only slipped away into the next room. I am I, and you are you. Whatever we were to each other, that we still are. Call me by my old familiar name, speak to me in the easy way which you always used. Put no difference in your tone, wear no forced air of solemnity or sorrow. Laugh as we always laughed at the little jokes we enjoyed together.

Pray, smile, think of me, pray for me. Let my name be ever the household word that it always was. Let it be spoken without affect, without the trace of a shadow on it. Life means all that it ever meant. It is the same as it ever was; there is unbroken continuity. Why should I be out of mind because I am out of sight? I am waiting for you, for an interval, somewhere very near, just round the corner.

All is well.

Harry Scott Holland

Afraid? Of what?
To feel the spirit's glad release?
To pass from pain to perfect peace?
The strife and strain of life to cease?
Afraid — of that?
Afraid? Of what?
Afraid to see the Saviour's face,
To hear his welcome and to trace
The glory gleam from wounds of grace?
Afraid — of that?
Afraid? Of what?
A flash — a crash — a pierced heart;
Darkness — light — oh, Heaven's art!
A wound of his a counterpart!
Afraid — of that?
Afraid? Of what?
To enter into Heaven's rest,
And yet to serve the Master blest,
From service good to service best?
Afraid — of that?
Afraid? Of what?
To do by death what life could not,

Baptise with blood a stony plot,
Till souls shall blossom from the spot?
Afraid — of that?

E.H. Hamilton

'Kenneth, do you remember when you were a tiny boy
how you used to play so hard all day that when night
came you were too tired even to undress and you'd tumble
into your mother's bed and fall asleep? That was not
your bed; it was not where you belonged. You would
only stay there a little while. Much to your surprise, you
would wake up and find yourself in your own bed in
your own room. You were there because someone had
loved you and taken care of you. Your father had come
with big strong arms and carried you away.

'Kenneth, darling, death is like that. We just wake up
some morning to find ourselves in the other room. Our
room where we belong, because the Lord Jesus loved us
and died for us.'

The lad's shining face looking up into hers told her that
the point had gone home and there would be no more
fear, only love and trust in his little heart as he went to
meet the Father in heaven. He never questioned again.

Several weeks later he fell asleep just as she had said
and Father's big, strong arms carried him to his own room.

Peter Marshall

I don't think you need to be afraid of life. Our hearts are
very frail and there are places where the road is very steep
and lonely, but we have a wonderful God. And as Paul
puts it: 'What can separate us from his love?' 'Not death,'
he writes immediately. No, not death, for standing in the
roaring Jordan, cold with its dreadful chill and, conscious
of its terror, of its rushing, I, too, like Hopeful in Pilgrim's
Progress, can call back to you who one day in your turn
will have to cross it, 'Be of good cheer, my brother, my
sister, for I feel the bottom and it is sound.'

A.J. Gossip, 'When Life Tumbles In, What Then?',
a sermon preached the day after his wife died

Death is the supreme festival on the road to freedom.

Dietrich Bonhoeffer

Although all of life is a dying, thank you, Lord, that every exit is also an entrance. When I was born, I exited a safe warm place and was painfully projected into this unknown world of time and space. And when I die I may undergo a similarly frightening experience. But, Lord, you've been through it and come back: thank you for the firm assurance that death has lost its sting because you have annulled its fearfulness, if not the mystery of the process we call dying.

Although tears may accompany my exiting, trumpets will welcome my arriving. Oh, that will be glory for me!

So, Lord, here I come! Deathless life, here I come! Celestial immortality, here I come! Unbroken calm and unimaginable eternity of surprises, here I come!

A Benediction

As you walk through the valley of the shadow of death, never fear. The Lord is with you. He has been there before and he knows the way. As you calmly trust him, may you experience the comfort of his love, and hear his excited summons, 'Brother/sister, welcome home!'

43

Good grief

For godly grief produces a repentance that leads to salvation and brings no regret, but worldly grief produces death.

But he knows the way that I take; when he has tested me, I shall come out like gold.

Where can I go from your spirit? Or where can I flee from your presence? If I ascend to heaven, you are there; if I make my bed in Sheol, you are there. If I take the wings of the morning and settle at the farthest limits of the sea, even there your hand shall lead me, and your right hand shall hold me fast.

Indeed, you are my lamp, O Lord. The Lord lightens my darkness. By you I can crush a troop and by my God I can leap over a wall. This God — his way is perfect; the promise of the Lord proves true; he is a shield for all who take refuge in him.

Remember your word to your servant, in which you have made me hope. This is my comfort in my distress, that your promise gives me life.

He was despised and rejected by others; a man of suffering and acquainted with infirmity; and as one from whom others hide their faces he was despised, and we held him of no account.

Not that I am referring to being in need; for I have learned to be content with whatever I have. I know what it is to have little and I know what it is to have plenty. In any and all circumstances I have learned the secret of being well-fed and of going hungry, of having plenty and of being in need. I can do all things through him who strengthens me. In any case, it was kind of you to share my distress.

But he said to me, 'My grace is sufficient for you, for power is made perfect in weakness.' So I will boast all the more gladly of my weaknesses, so that the power of Christ may dwell in me.

And remember, I am with you always, to the end of the age.

(2 Corinthians 7: 10; Job 23: 10; Psalm 139: 7–10; 2 Samuel 22: 29–31; Psalm 119: 49–50; Isaiah 53: 3; Philippians 4: 11–14; 2 Corinthians 12: 9; Matthew 28: 20b — all NRSV)

At a time when I was struggling to keep a positive perspective on my lot in life, I copied each of these little reminders on a small card. I placed the cards where I would be sure to come across them through my day. I now don't recall the original author, but I am very thankful for this contribution to my growing!

In everything give thanks: for this is the will of God in Christ Jesus concerning you. . .

It is not always possible to thank God *for* the experience, but it is essential to thank God *in* the experience.

When faced with the unexpected, you create your own emotional state by either griping or giving thanks.

You are never tested above your ability to endure. You may be tried beyond your desires, but God knows your mettle. He diagrams your future and knows exactly what you need. So instead of griping and groaning and feeling sorry for ourselves, we are advised to 'count it all joy'.

Do not expect your triumph over self-pity to be a miracle of God's grace without your cooperation.

Albert Schweitzer has written:

Christ comes to us today as he came to those men of old by the lakeside. He speaks the same words, 'Follow me' and sets us to the tasks he has to fulfil in our time. He commands and those who obey, learn, in their own experience, through toils and conflicts and sufferings, who he is. . .

Good grief begins with truly feeling the sorrow and freely expressing it. There is nothing particularly Christian about bottlingup our grief. The Bible speaks much about weeping when tragedy comes and we should never reject the therapy of tears through any false sense of shame. But good grief is more than the relief of tears. No matter how rebellious we feel at the time, there comes again the life to be lived and much depends on the spirit in which we take it up.

A good grief will have sensitised the soul. We shall be more compassionate with others in their time of trouble. We shall have gained an insight and perhaps a spiritual depth we never had before.

Above all, if we have in any way, during the agony, known something of the presence of the crucified, we shall know eventually that the terrible experience was not sheer loss.

If God could turn the greatest grief the world has ever known into a triumph of his love, there is nothing that can come our way which we cannot use for our good in bringing us closer to him and to our neighbour.

❈

The spiritual life is not something we possess, but something which possesses us. It is the search for that which has eternal value.

It is not measured by our estimate of the worth of what we now hold dear. Rather it is measured by the extent to which we are willing to let all we hold dear be lost, in order that we might gain it.

It is a hunger in the heart, not a full storehouse.

It is not measured by the achievements of our searching, but by our persistence; and by our insistence that this is not our life's true goal.

It is a journey anticipated and longed for, rather than a road already travelled.

This is the teaching of Jesus.

Peter Evans

As I read the scriptures through the lens of my own pain and sense of having lost touch with God, I saw many things I'd never seen before. I was afraid to find out the source of the enormous energy and anxiety that I had hidden from myself, like a great black beach ball I'd pushed out of sight in my unconscious.

But I also learned something else, as I came back to Christ and read the scriptures — something which had been there all along, but which I hadn't been ready to see before: the God of the Bible is not primarily interested in our 'evangelism' programs, in our 'small groups' or even in our 'piety'. He's evidently not really even very interested in religion. But he is passionately interested in people, people in pain — all kinds of pain, things like hunger, cold, sickness and poverty — as well as in our experiences of sin, anxiety and lostness!

As a matter of fact, Jesus said that he was going to be so immersed in people's pain and hunger and loneliness that we will meet him personally as we contact the hungry, thirsty or sick person (Matthew 25: 35–36). If that's true, then witnessing and small groups are important only as God can use them as doorways through which he and we can come to meet the people and heal the pain and separation in the world!

And I began to see that the concrete helping of people where they live is the sacrament — the outward and visible sign — of the passionate love of Jesus I have been hoarding in my own heart. The call I had felt to love him had led me at last to consider meeting him, where he works, in the pain of other people.

Keith Miller, The Passionate People

To the person who asks, 'What good is God? Who needs religion, if these things happen to good people and bad people alike?' I would say that God may not prevent calamity, but he gives us the strength and the perseverance to overcome it. . .

Life is not fair. The wrong people get sick and the wrong people get robbed and the wrong people get killed in wars and accidents. Some people see life's unfairness and decide, 'There is no God; the world is nothing but chaos.'

Others see the same unfairness and ask themselves, 'Where do I get my sense of what is fair and what is unfair? Where do I get my sense of outrage and indignation, my instinctive response of sympathy when I read in the paper about a total stranger who has been hurt by life? Don't I get these things from God? Doesn't he plant in me a little bit of his own divine outrage at injustice and oppression, just as he did for the prophets of the Bible? Isn't my feeling of compassion for the afflicted just a reflection of the compassion he feels when he sees the suffering of his creatures?'

Our responding to life's unfairness with sympathy and with righteous indignation, God's compassion and God's anger working through us, may be the surest proof of all of God's reality.

Harold S. Kushner, *When Bad Things Happen to Good People*

VALLEY FERN

Under the trees and mid the tangled undergrowth I
    see you
Standing a little apart.
Your soft refreshing beauty does not catch the eye
    as the springtime wildflowers.
You sit quietly, clinging among the rocks,
    fronds gently drooping,
And as the marbled sunlight catches the dew drops
    caressing your green, I see a star-shine of
    reflected light.
Peace.
Serenity.
The soft movement of your fronds to touch the
    world around you.
But I have known the valley in a storm
when the peaceful trickle at your feet has become a
    raging flood. . .
when the eddy pool which reflects your patient
    stance becomes a swirling mass of destructive debris!
    You cling to that rock,
Laid flat.
Battered.

It is only those roots which have found a stronghold
    and your tenacious will that keeps your centre
    anchored.
The storm abates.
Your immediate world is changed. . .
Bare somehow. . .
Exposed.
What is left of you just now does not seem a thing of
    beauty.
You cannot hold up your head.
The mud of the deluge clings to you.
Disaster.
Devastation.
. . .But the roots are holding and that central tangly
    fragment that is your life-spring is intact.
To what purpose the clinging roots, Valley Fern?
Does it all seem a waste?
Who cares?
Time passes, and I watch a miracle.
The soft curl of new life emerges.
Tentatively. . .
Then, opening out in a freshness and vibrance of
    green. . .
changing the landscape,
bringing hope of new beauty.
A new beginning!
The browned edges of the past are memories only.
The storm has swept away the clutter, leaving
    potential for more serenity and beauty than before.
Yes, you are still vulnerable, but I look with
    thankfulness at the lessons your tenacity
    has taught.
Persistence.
The stabilising power of the Rock.
And, that peace and beauty need not be destroyed
    by the deluge, but somehow renewed, changed,
    refocused.
When I walk in the valley I can look at you,
    Valley Fern. . . and be blessed!

Corry Skilbeck

How can we really know what you have been through in the loss of such wonderful friends? We sorrow with you and we try to realise something of the new era you have entered in the last few weeks, with a conglomerate of adjustments to be made by everyone.

Given the circumstances and accompanying strain, each of you will surely be in need of added wisdom, love, tolerance and strength — a mountain, the top of which is shrouded with mist; and yet to be climbed. There *must* be some wildflowers growing on your 'mountain' and you will find them. Rocks also, probably, to trip over! But views unsurpassable.

I guess, in a way, routines of living from day to day can help us — they keep life flowing no matter what prevails and I want to join with you in praying that the Lord will provide a wellspring to meet your needs as you attempt to create those new routines.

Our hearts, prayers and love are open towards you.

A letter from a close friend

Dear Lord, we love you and we long to know you better — to know you with us day by day, and in us more and more. In spite of everything, Lord, this is a wonderful world. We see you in all around: in the love of family and friends, in the kindness of those who serve us and visit with a smile.

And the greatest lover of all was Jesus. When he died, you died for us, Lord, and we died. Now we have nothing to fear: the past is forgiven; the future is a wonderful promise.

Thank you, Lord, for all the blessings that have been ours and the blessings we have here, too.

But some of us are still sad today and we pray for each other. We pray that today a little joy and gladness may break through to ease the burden that's troubling us. Above all, give us the peace and patience to bear all our aches and pains, and for the courage to smile even when we are hurting inside.

Help us to be your children, Lord, and to feel your loving arms around us both when we wake and when we go to sleep. Amen.

Lou Evans

Almighty God and Father of us all,
Have mercy on this troubled world of ours.
We are pilgrim people, made from clay,
Captives of our own greed and frailty,
And yet. . .
We are the work of your hands,
You have made us in your own image
And we bear within us your Spirit of life,
The seeds of immortality.
Give us, we pray, a stronger faith,
So that we may walk joyously into the unknown,
an unshakable hope,
so that we may comfort the despairing,
And a love as vast as all the oceans,
So that we may hold all mankind in our hearts.
All-powerful God,
Look in your love upon us, your pilgrim people,
As we struggle towards you.
Be our food for the journey,
Our wine for rejoicing,
Our light in the darkness,
And our welcome at the journey's end.

Sheila Cassidy, *Prayer for Pilgrims*

A Benediction

May the Lord, who himself suffered grief and sorrow and who
carries your griefs and sorrows, comfort you, strengthen you,
sustain you and give you peace. Amen.

44

Growing together in community

Since you have accepted Christ Jesus as Lord, live in union with him. Keep your roots deep in him, build your lives on him, and become stronger in your faith as you were taught. And be filled with thanksgiving.

Your life in Christ makes you strong and his love comforts you. You have fellowship with the Spirit and you have kindness and compassion for one another. I urge you then to make me completely happy by having the same thoughts, sharing the same love and being one in soul and mind. . . The attitude you should have is the one that Christ Jesus had.

Christ is like a single body, which has many parts. . . there is no division in the body, but all its different parts have the same concern for one another. If one part of the body suffers, all the other parts suffer with it; if one part is praised, all the other parts share its happiness.

So when each separate part of the body works as it should, the whole body grows and builds itself up through love.

You are the people of God; he loved you and chose you for his own. So then you must clothe yourself with compassion, kindness, humility, gentleness and patience. Be tolerant with one another and forgive one another whenever any of you has a complaint against someone else. You must forgive one another just as the Lord has forgiven you. And to all these things add love which binds all things together in perfect unity. The peace that Christ gives is to guide you in the decisions you make; for it is to this peace that God has called you together in one body. And be thankful.

Be wise in the way you act towards those who are not believers, making good use of every opportunity you have. Your speech should always be pleasant and interesting, and you should know how to give the right answer to everyone.

(Colossians 2: 6–7; Philippians 2: 1–2; 1 Corinthians 12: 12 and 25–26; Ephesians 4: 16b; Colossians 3: 12–15; 4: 5–6 — all GNB)

According to teacher and counsellor, John Powell, the five steps that lead to the fullness of life are: (1) to accept oneself, (2) to be oneself, (3) to forget oneself in loving, (4) to believe, (5) to belong. Each one, he suggests, builds upon the previous accomplishment.

In step 5, a person will discover the reality of community. A community is a union of persons who share in mutuality their most precious possession — themselves.

Sharing ourselves always involves risk. For all of us there have been injuries to trust along the way that need to be healed by acceptance and forgiveness. When we are able to let down our defences and be known in our human frailty, we find that there are no big people in community, only little people of all ages and in all stages of growth.

In community, each person feels carried by the others and in turn carries them. Only in community, where we are supported by the whole body of Christ, will we have the capacity to welcome the poor and the outcast, to care for the deeply distressed. We will also welcome those who are different from us because we need their gifts in order to become whole.

What about the conflict of 'being me and loving you'? Sometimes my individuality and desire for personal growth vie with God's call to commitment to the group. Yet I am convinced that my inner freedom and fulfilment is ultimately found in community.

James Fowler maintains the community of faith plays a vital role in the development of Christian maturity, for it is in community that we discover our vocation to become partners in God's redemptive work in the world.

If faith community is founded in forgiveness, it is completed in celebration. As a family, we share in the celebrations that make life meaningful and joyful, breaking bread together in anticipation of the eternal wedding feast, the great celebration of life with God.

❧❦❧

The church's vocation is to be the world's spinal column because it is a human and divine community and announces the kingdom of heaven by fulfilling it already here below. In looking at the church, the world should see something it desires and feels the need of — something which helps in the establishment of the secular city itself. The church is the body of Christ, the perfect community formed of communities, all animated by the Holy Spirit.

Max Delespesse, *The Church Community: Leaven & Lifestyle*

Community is a place where our heart can put down roots, a place where we are at home. The roots are not there to comfort us or turn us in on ourselves. Quite the opposite: they are there so that each of us can grow and bear fruit for humanity and God. We put down roots when we discover the covenant among people who are called to live together, and the covenant with God and with the poor.

Community is there not for itself, but for others — the poor, the church and society. It is essentially missionary. It has a message of hope to offer and a love to communicate, especially to those who are poor and in distress.

Jean Vanier, *Community and Growth*

Let the one who cannot be alone beware of community. . . Let him or her who is not in community beware of being alone. . . Only in the fellowship do we learn to be rightly alone and only in aloneness do we learn to live rightly in the fellowship.

It is not as though the one preceded the other; both began at the same time — namely, with the call of Jesus Christ.

Dietrich Bonhoeffer, *Life Together*

Community is not made up of the same kind of people. . .
God did not organise the church on the basis of sameness.
True, there is the element of unity emphasised within the
church, but sameness is never valued as the foundation
of the church. . . I am in community with you because
God has called both of us to discipleship in Christ. The
same Spirit who called you has also whispered in my heart
the same message, 'Jesus is Lord!' And he is the one who
has made us brother and sister to each other in a way no
earthly birth could have done.

William Clemmons, Discovering the Depths

The prayer of our heart can grow strong and deep within the
boundaries of the community of faith. The community of
faith, strengthened in love by our individual prayers, can lift
them up as a sign of hope in common praise and thanksgiving. Together, we reach out to God beyond our many
individual limitations while offering each other the space for
our own most personal search. . . God has called us away
from the darkness of our illusions into the light of his glory.

Henri Nouwen, Reaching Out: The Three
Movements of the Spiritual Life

The first sphere of this great movement into unity is the
achievement of wholeness within ourselves. . . Once we
begin the journey, we receive so many strengths. The
greatest strength is that the journey attracts fellow
travellers. One who begins alone will be joined by others.
In that mystery of communion, the church is reborn and
rekindled in many quiet corners of the earth.

John Main, The Joy of Being

The fellowship of the Lord's Supper is the superlative
fulfilment of Christian fellowship. As the members of the
congregation are united in body and blood at the table of
the Lord, so will they be together in eternity. Here the
community has reached its goal. Here joy in Christ and
his community is complete. The life of Christians together
under the word has reached is perfection in the sacrament.

Dietrich Bonhoeffer, Life Together

The transformation of a group from a collection of individuals into genuine community requires little deaths in many of those individuals. But it is also a process of group death, group dying. . . The whole group seems to writhe and moan in its travail. Individuals will sometimes speak for the group: 'It's like we're dying. The group is in agony. Can't you help us? I didn't know we'd have to die to become a community. . . '

When its death has been completed, open and empty, the group enters community. . . An extraordinary amount of healing and converting begins to occur — now that no-one is trying to convert or heal. And community has been born.

M. Scott Peck, *The Different Drum:*
Community Making and Peace

Community life is there to help us not to flee from our deep wound, but to remain with the reality of love. It is there to help us believe that our illusions and egoism will be gradually healed if we become nourishment for others. We are in community for each other, so that all of us can grow and uncover our wound before the infinite, so that Jesus can manifest himself through it.

Jean Vanier, *Community and Growth*

Thank you, Father, for providing companions for my faith journey: sisters and brothers to encourage me when I falter, support me when I stumble, draw me back when I wander too far off the track.

Thank you, Father, for the shared times of celebration around a common table, for the comfort of being part of a family in times of dislocation and change, for the love and affirmation I receive when I start to reveal how vulnerable I am.

Father, I find that the tension of being 'me' and also part of a group of unlikely people is not easy. In order to grow into community, I have to give something of myself up — to go through little deaths, to feel the pressure of a cross. And I don't like it. Sometimes the solution to this unbearable tension seems to be to escape from it all and become an island, free from the hassles, blind spots and constant demands of other people.

Then, Lord, you pour out your gentle Spirit to renew my spirit, and I find again the right rhythm of solitude and communion, desert and marketplace. When you call me back, Lord, I find that my sisters and brothers are inseparable from you. Each one has a gift to bring to me when I become childlike enough to receive it.

That we all may be one, Lord Jesus, as you and the Father are one. Amen.

A Benediction
Father, guide us as you guide creation,
according to your law of love.
May we love one another
and come to perfection
in the eternal life prepared for us.
Father, give me the heart and mind of Jesus
to reflect him to the people within my faith community
and those in the larger community.
As I avail myself of your gracious hospitality
around the table of Christ,
let it flow on to others.

The Twenty-Fifth Ordinary Sunday,
An Australian Prayer Book

45

Radical friendship

Friends should be kind to the despairing person,
or they will give up faith in the Almighty;
but my friends disappoint me like a stream,
like mountain brooks that overflow their banks,
swollen and dark with ice, with melting snow,
but vanishing when they are scorched,
and disappearing in the summer's glow.

I still rebel and complain against God; I can't hold back my groaning. How I wish I knew where to find him. . . I would state my case before him and present all the arguments in my favour. . . he would listen as I spoke.

The Lord will make you go through hard times, but he himself will be there to teach you and you will not have to search for him any more. If you wander off the road to the right or the left, you will hear his voice behind you saying, 'Here is the road. Follow it.'

I need only say, 'I am slipping',
and your love, Yahweh, immediately supports me;
and in the middle of all my troubles
you console me and make me happy.

Praise the Lord, who carries our burdens day after day; he is the God who saves us.

Don't worry over anything whatever; tell God every detail of your needs in earnest and thankful prayer, and the peace of God, which transcends human understanding, will keep constant guard over your hearts and minds as they rest in Christ Jesus.

You can throw the whole weight of your anxieties upon him, for you are his personal concern.

(Job 6: 14–15; 23: 1–6 — both GNB; Isaiah 30: 20-21; Psalm 94: 18–19 — both JB; Psalm 68: 19, GNB; Philippians 4: 6–7; 1 Peter 5: 7 — both J.B. Phillips)

God often has a host of well-meaning but less than helpful defenders. They are the people who meet us, in our moments of deepest distress and need, with a rush of words in which they seek to explain what has happened to us and to defend God. They come out with platitudes like, 'God doesn't make mistakes', or 'God knows best' — all of which, while true, are not particularly helpful. All too often, having given us their pat pronouncements, they hurry off.

Why do they do it? Perhaps it is a mixture of awkwardness and obligation. Awkwardness, because our need distresses them and they would prefer to shut it out of their minds. Obligation, because they feel they have to say something and that it ought to be 'spiritual'.

What have they done? They have filled what was, for them, an uncomfortable silence with their words. They might even convince themselves that they have achieved something. Perhaps, for that very reason, what they have done is to help themselves handle their own discomfort. What they could have given, and failed to bestow, was the gift of themselves; just being there, feeling something of our hurt along with us. All we wanted was someone to be there, who just in doing so, could assure us that a hurting was there, too. That is the gift of radical friendship. What we wanted was someone who would share our pain — not someone who would try to explain it or defend it.

That was where Job's friends failed him. While they sat in silence and shared his distress, they helped him; it was when they tried to refute his expressions of anger and bewilderment that they let him down. Job was looking for friends and found theologians! He wanted sympathy and was given doctrine instead. The Lord's self-appointed defenders were on the job again. In the end, Job could contain himself no more and burst out,

'What a help you are to poor God! What a support to his failing powers!' (Job 25: 1, Moffatt). Distress drove the sufferer to exclaim, 'Oh that I knew where to find God!' His despairing 'Why?' was not answered, but in the end he discovered that God had been there all the time. The radical friend was there!

Nowhere is this more true than in the cross of Christ. Jesus experienced the worst that humankind could do. He was humiliated. He knew what it was to be abandoned, not just by his friends, but even by God. He suffered powerlessness and helplessness — which we need. On the cross, more than anywhere and above all else, he was still Immanuel — God with us.

❧

The ministry of friendship is not judged by our capacity to explain God's ways or defend God's teachings, but by our ability to stand with an alienated human against the insidious forces of our world, and to believe, at all costs, in that person. . .

Once Job breaks his silence and launches into tirades against his birth and his God (Job 3), the friends leap to the defence of the Almighty. The poet transforms the patient Job of tradition into the angry victim of tragic reality. Likewise, he exposes the idealised friends of legend as defensive proponents of orthodox religion. . . His friends feel compelled to justify God before his creatures. . .

To be a friend is to be cohuman in a dehumanised situation where those who are despairing have lost their religion as a source of inner support. . .

Job is not satisfied with accusing his friends of unwarranted cowardice; he challenges them to be honest. . . [to] shed their masks of religious jargon and confront him with specific sins he has committed (6: 24-26). He longs for the straight talk of those who speak from their heart instead of a handbook of theological truisms (v.25). The friends are trapped in their own pride; they are driven to dispute rather than empathise with Job. . .

Job forces us to consider friendship as a radical option

for life in an age of increased anonymity and contrived
sensitivity. . .

Trusting a friend without reservation in the face of an
alien world is a major concern of Job. Our temptation is
to assume that we could be a loyal friend to others in
need; the greater problem is our inability to trust anyone
to be a radical friend. We have lost faith in trust.

Norman Hable, 'Only the Jackal Is My Friend'

For God, the master and maker of the universe, who made
all things and determined the proper place of each, showed
himself to be long-suffering as well as our true friend.
But in fact he always was and is and will be just this. . .

Letter to Diognetus

The first service that one owes to others in the fellowship
consists in listening to them. . . Christians, especially ministers, so often think they must always contribute something when they are in the company of others, that this
is the one service they have to render. They forget that
listening can be a greater service than speaking.

Many people are looking for an ear that will listen.
They do not find it among Christians, because these Christians are talking where they should be listening. But if
you can no longer listen to others, you will soon be no
longer listening to God either; you will be doing nothing
but prattle in the presence of God, too.

This is the beginning of the death of the spiritual life,
and in the end there is nothing left but spiritual chatter
and clerical condescension arrayed in pious words. One
who cannot listen long and patiently will presently be
talking beside the point and be never really speaking to
others, albeit not being conscious of it. Anyone who
thinks that their time is too valuable to spend keeping
quiet will eventually have no time for God and others,
but only for themselves and for their own follies.

Dietrich Bonhoeffer, Life Together

I have just hung up; why did he telephone?
I don't know. . . Oh! I get it. . .

I talked a lot and listened very little.
Forgive me, Lord, it was a monologue and not a dialogue.
I explained my idea and did not get his;
Since I didn't listen, I learned nothing,
Since I didn't listen, I didn't help,
Since I didn't listen, we didn't communicate.
Forgive me, Lord, for we were connected
and now we are cut off.

Michel Quoist, *Prayers of Life*

I have a few very close and confidential friends. . . These
men hold our relationship in highest regard and great
trust.   They view our times together (as I do) as exceed-
ingly important occasions.   We talk.   We think.   We
evaluate decisions.   We share our struggles.   We pray.   We
invest these hours with the realisation that God uses us
in each other's lives.   We are available and we are in
touch.   Our goal is to strengthen and help one another in
any way we can.
   By being accountable and vulnerable in our times
together, we are able to get to the heart of the issue without
the standard smokescreens and fog that frequently cloud
friendships.

Charles R. Swindoll, *Dropping Your Guard*

I can remember, during my student years in Edinburgh,
walking home one frosty midnight from a philosophical
discussion on the existence of God and stopping in my
walk to gaze up into the starry sky.   Into those deep
immensities of space, I hurled my despairing question, but
it seemed to hit nothing and no answer came back. . . I
did not indeed expect or desire to hear anything with the
ear of flesh. . . but I wanted something more than an
argument. . .
   I believe a great many people have that sort of complaint
to make against God.   If God really exists, they say, why
does he not declare himself more plainly?   Why does he
not grant us a more unmistakable revelation?   Why does
he not make one quite certain sign, a sign that those who
run may read, a sign that would forever put an end to

doubt and afford us what we call 'foolproof' evidence — not only of his existence, but of his will for us all?

The best comment I can pass on all these questionings is to say how I have now come to feel about my own early questionings. We ask for an unmistakable sign. *What sign would we accept?*. . . I therefore put the question. What more can he do, whether for our enlightenment or for our salvation, than he did and does in Jesus Christ?

John Baillie, *The Idea of Revelation in Recent Thought*

Psychologically speaking, the one who believes is not simply satisfied; the heart still remains a 'restless thing', the ebb and flow of feeling and emotion, the sense of exaltation and impotence, the sense of confidence followed by reaction, the oscillations between hope and fear, happiness and depression do not cease. The state of the Christian is one of 'confident despair'.

But this despair is *confident*. All these inner moods and feelings as they rise and fall toss like the waves of the sea over an immovable sheet of rock, upon which these words are clearly inscribed: 'I belong to Christ in spite of everything. In spite of myself, in spite of my moods and feelings, in spite of all my experience of my own impotence, even in the sphere of faith. I belong to Christ not because I believe in him, but because of what Christ has said through the Word which God has spoken to me in him, the Mediator.'

Emil Brunner, *The Mediator*

The church stands, not at the boundaries where human powers give out, but in the middle of the village.

The Bible directs us to God's powerlessness and suffering; only the suffering God can help.

Dietrich Bonhoeffer, *Letters and Papers from Prison*

When the signs of age begin to mark my body (and still more when they touch my mind); when the ill that is to diminish me or carry me off strikes from without or is born within me; when the painful moment comes in which I suddenly awaken to the fact that I am ill or growing old; and above all, at that last moment when I feel that I am losing hold of myself and am absolutely passive within the hands of the great unknown forces that have formed me; in all those dark moments, O God, grant that I may understand that it is you (provided only my faith is strong enough) who are painfully parting the fibres of my being in order to penetrate to the very marrow of my substance and bear me away within yourself.

Teilhard de Chardin, *Le Milieu Divin*

Give us, O Lord, a steadfast heart, which no unworthy affection may drag downwards; give us an unconquered heart, which no tribulation can wear out; give us an upright heart, which no unworthy purpose can tempt aside. Bestow upon us also, O Lord our God, understanding to know you, diligence to seek you, wisdom to find you and a faithfulness which may at last embrace you; through Jesus Christ our Lord.

St Thomas Aquinas

My Lord and God:
I thank you that Jesus said to his followers,
'I have called you friends.'
Thank you for the privilege of being a friend of Jesus.
Thank you for the radical friendship that he gives me:
  a friendship which stands by me when other friends fail;
  a friendship which keeps on believing in me;
  a transforming friendship which, in love, seeks to make me
  more like him.
Help me, as one who confesses him as Lord,
to be an agent of his radical friendship in the lives of others.

A Benediction
May the God of steadfastness and encouragement
grant you to live in such harmony with one another,
in accord with Christ Jesus,
that together you may with one voice
glorify the God and Father of our Lord Jesus Christ.

Romans 15: 5–6, RSV

WEEK

46

Looking to Jesus

Let us run with perseverance the race that is set before us, looking to Jesus, the pioneer and perfecter of our faith, who for the sake of the joy that was set before him endured the cross, disregarding its shame, and has taken his seat at the right hand of the throne of God.

A disciple is not above the teacher, but everyone who is fully qualified will be like the teacher. . . I am among you as one who serves.

You know that among the Gentiles those whom they recognise as their rulers lord it over them and their great ones are tyrants over them. But it is not so among you; but whoever wishes to become great among you must be your servant, and whoever wishes to be first among you must be slave of all. For the Son of Man came not to be served but to serve, and to give his life a ransom for many.

I am the good shepherd. The good shepherd lays down his life for the sheep. . . I have set you an example, that you also should do as I have done to you.

This is my commandment, that you love one another as I have loved you. No-one has greater love than this, to lay down one's life for one's friends.

Let the same mind be in you that was in Christ Jesus who, though he was in the form of God, did not regard equality with God as something to be exploited, but emptied himself, taking the form of a slave, being born in human likeness. And being found in human form, he humbled himself and became obedient to the point of death — even death on a cross.

Christ also suffered for you, leaving you an example,

so that you should follow in his steps. . . When he was abused, he did not return abuse; when he suffered, he did not threaten; but he entrusted himself to the one who judges justly.

(Hebrews 12: 2; Luke 6: 40; Luke 22: 27; Mark 10: 42–45; John 10: 11; John 13: 15; John 15: 12–13; Philippians 2: 5–8; 1 Peter 2: 21–23 — all NRSV)

As a boy I used to belong to Crusaders, a British union of boys' Bible classes, which had as its motto: 'Looking unto Jesus.' There is no finer motto for the Christian life than that. It makes a difference if each of us consciously looks to Jesus — not only in the quiet moments of spiritual discipline at the beginning of the day, but throughout the day's hustle and bustle — and gains inspiration afresh from the example he has set us.

In our church, there was a senior deacon who, as far as I was concerned, was 'way out' theologically. An old-fashioned liberal, he saw Jesus primarily in terms of a 'leader', one whose example was to be followed. To my shame, I was somewhat dismissive of his stance at the time and was far more concerned at his views on the virgin birth and on the atonement. And yet as I reflect on him, I realise that he patterned his life on his 'leader' far more than most. Indeed, although an eminent professor, he it was who visited an incontinent old lady and took home her soiled sheets to wash. There was a Christlike quality to his life. And yet I with my evangelical rectitude was more concerned for his theology.

How deluded we can become! Are there not times when *orthopraxis* is more important than *orthodoxy?* How does God view the lovelessness of certain 'Bible-believing' Christians in Ulster or in the southern states of the USA? How for that matter does God view my own lovelessness? James was right: 'Faith without works is dead' (James 2: 26).

Jesus has said, 'I have set you an example, that you also should do as I have done for you' (John 13: 15). How seriously do we take these words of Jesus? In the church

today, there is much talk about leadership — and rightly
so. The church of God needs leaders who will have the
courage to lead. But leadership must never be confused
with lordship. Leadership must always be patterned on
that of the 'Servant-King'. As the great New Testament
scholar, T.W. Manson, once put it: 'In the kingdom of
God, service is not a stepping-stone to nobility: it *is*
nobility, the only kind of nobility that is recognised.'
Church leaders take note!

Jesus set an example not only of service, but also in the
way in which his whole life was geared to please his
Father. Obedience to the Father's will was a hallmark of
his life, whatever the cost. Here too we need to look to
Jesus. Alas, time and again we are more eager to compare
ourselves with others than to follow him. In ministry, the
constant temptation is to look at others and to see how
they are doing. Not surprisingly, then, it has been said
that the besetting sin of ministry is jealousy.

In such a situation the words of the risen Jesus to Peter
are important: for when Peter was tempted to make a
comparison with the other disciple, Jesus dismissed all
comparisons: 'If it is my will that he remain until I come,
what is that to you? Follow me!' (John 21: 22). Jesus
challenges us all to follow him, wherever the path,
whatever the cost — and in this way please the Father,
as Jesus did.

In a church all too often marred by conflict and dissent,
Jesus sets us an example, too. 'When he was abused, he
did not return abuse; when he suffered, he did not
threaten; but he entrusted himself to the one who judges
justly' (1 Peter 2: 25). Whether the conflict be inside or
outside the church, the attitude of Jesus is still normative.

Time and again, church life plumbs the very depths of
bitterness because the protagonists are so convinced of the
righteousness of their cause. Sadly, the ultimate casualty
of such conflicts is the cause of Christ. If only the people
concerned had looked to Jesus, and entrusted their cause
to him!

Consider the holiness of Christ's nature and the holiness of Christ's life. . . Christ's inward beauty would ravish love out of the devils, if they had but grace to see his beauty; yea, he would lead captive all hearts in hell, if they had but eyes to behold his loveliness. . . The saints in glory now 'see the face of Christ' (Revelation 22: 4). They see all the dignity, beauty that is in Christ; and they are so taken with this sight that they do nothing else but stare, and gaze, and behold his face for ages — and yet they are never satisfied with beholding; suppose they could wear out their eyes at the eyeholes in beholding Christ, they should desire to see more.

Isaac Ambrose, *Looking Unto Jesus*

I come as a learner, with no policy to advocate, no plan already formed to follow. But I come with one burning desire: it is that in all our activities, sacred and secular and ecclesiastical and social, we should help each other fix our eyes on Jesus, making him our only guide. . . Pray for me, I ask you, not chiefly that I may be wise and strong or any such thing, though for these things I need your prayers. But pray for me chiefly that I may never let go of the unseen hand of the Lord Jesus and may live in daily fellowship with him. It is so that you will most of all help me to help you.

William Temple, on the occasion of his enthronement as Bishop of Manchester

Keep ever before you the likeness of Christ crucified. As you meditate on the life of Jesus Christ, you should grieve that you have not tried more earnestly to conform yourself to him.

Thomas à Kempis, *The Imitation of Christ*

But God does not neglect his lost creature. He plans to recreate his image in us, to recover his first delight in his handiwork. . . but there is only one way to achieve this purpose and this is [that] God, out of sheer mercy . . .must become like the image of [us]. But this restoration of the divine image concerns not just a part, but the whole of human nature. It is not enough for us simply to recover right ideas about God, or to obey his will in the isolated actions of our lives. No, we must be re-fashioned as a living whole in the image of God. . . Such is God's purpose and destiny for us. . . an image needs a living object, and a copy can only be formed from a model. Either we model ourselves on the god of our own invention, or the true and living God moulds the human form into his image.

Dietrich Bonhoeffer, *The Cost of Discipleship*

The stress on the example of Jesus is so widespread in the New Testament because the imitation of his example is theologically crucial in terms of the renewal of the image of God in all of us.

Michael Griffiths, *The Example of Jesus*

It is probable that the idea of the *imitatio Christi* had more to say than is commonly recognised by critics in the selection of incidents from the life of Jesus for record in the Gospels.

C.H. Dodd, *The Johannine Epistles*

Discipleship, as Jesus conceived it, was not a theoretical discipline of this (i.e. the rabbinical) sort, but a practical task to which the disciples were called to give themselves and all their energies. Their work was to study by practice. Fishermen were to become fishers of others, peasants were to be labourers in God's vineyard or God's harvest field. And Jesus was their Master not so much as a teacher of right doctrine, but rather as the master craftsman whom they were to follow and imitate. Discipleship was not matriculation in a rabbinical college, but apprenticeship to the work of the kingdom.

T.W. Manson, *The Teaching of Jesus*

This is our God, the Servant King,
He calls us now to follow him,
To bring our lives as a daily offering
Of worship to the Servant King.

Graham Kendrick, *The Servant King*

Teach us, good Lord, to serve you as you deserve:
To give and not to count the cost,
To fight and not to heed the wounds,
To toil and not to seek for rest,
To labour and not to ask for any reward
Save that of knowing that we do your will,
Through Jesus Christ our Lord.

Ignatius Loyola

Lord Jesus:
You amaze me. My mind struggles with the thought that you, the Lord of glory, should have emptied yourself of all that was rightfully yours in order to become one with us. Indeed, Lord, you became one not with the high and the mighty, but with the weak and lowly. The mystery of your incarnation is beyond my mind's comprehension — and yet not beyond my heart's devotion. Jesus, I worship you. I give myself to you. I will follow you, today and all the remaining days of my life.

Lord Jesus:
If I am to follow you, then I must focus upon you. And as I look, I am amazed again — the life you lived, the death you died, defy comparison. And yet they call for imitation. So help me, Lord, to look to you today and all the days that will follow. . .

By your Spirit's power:
help me to live as you lived — serving not with an eye on the main chance, but rather with the interests of others at heart. And if you call me ever to go the way of misunderstanding and rejection, help me to follow your example, entrusting myself and my reputation to the God who judges justly.
 Lord Jesus, hear my prayer and answer the desires of my heart. Amen.

A Benediction
Grow in the grace and knowledge of our Lord and Saviour Jesus Christ. To him be the glory both now and to the day of eternity. Amen.

2 Peter 3: 18

47

In the beginning was the sermon

He appointed twelve. . . that he might send them out to preach.

And this gospel of the kingdom will be preached in the whole world as a testimony to all nations.

Let us go somewhere else. . . so I can preach there also. That is why I have come.

The Spirit of the Lord is on me because he has anointed me to preach good news to the poor.

At once he began to preach in the synagogues that Jesus is the Son of God.

And how can they hear without someone preaching to them?

Preach the word; be prepared in season and out of season.

(Mark 3: 14; Matthew 24: 14; Mark 1: 38; Luke 4: 18; Acts 9: 20; Romans 10: 14; 2 Timothy 4: 2 — all NIV)

The highly popular Australian television program 'Fast Forward' always includes a sketch of a rather sanctimonious parson delivering his latest useless sermon in one minute flat. The humour lies not so much in what he says, but in what he is, because he reminds us of so many preachers that we have known personally.

The public regard for preaching is now so low that any distasteful or irritating conversation is repelled by the cry, 'Stop preaching at me.'

Nor were things that different one hundred years ago. In his classic whale tale, *Moby Dick*, Herman Melville described 'the solemn churches that preach unconditional inoffensiveness by all to all'.

Across the Atlantic, in Victorian England, Oscar Wilde wrote of 'the successful men in any of the learned professions. How perfectly hideous they are. Except, of course, in the church. But then in the church they don't think. A bishop keeps on saying at the age of eighty what he was told to say when he was a boy of eighteen; and as a natural consequence he always looks absolutely delightful.'

If preaching is in the sorry state that these wits allege, then the greatest grief must be felt by the spirits of the Reformers, for their attitude to preaching was of the most zealous and noble kind. Melancthon regarded preaching as 'the very greatest, holiest, most needful, highest service of God'. Luther wrote, 'Therefore we should know that God hath so ordered that none should come to knowledge of Christ or acquire forgiveness through him or receive the Holy Spirit without external public means, but hath put such treasure in. . . the preaching office.'

In the twentieth century, a chorus of voices has cried out for the word of preaching. 'Preaching is the riches and poverty of the church,' wrote Dietrich Bonhoeffer. 'Proclamation is human language in and through which God himself speaks,' declared Karl Barth.

> What do I seek? I seek the word
> that shall become the deed of might
> whereby the sullen gulfs are stirred
> and stars begotten on their night.

Thus wrote the poet Christopher Brennan. And a triumphant defence of preaching was offered by the Afro-American writer, James Baldwin, who once said: 'Nothing that has happened to me. . . equals the power and the glory that I sometimes felt when, in the middle of a sermon, I knew that I was somehow, by some miracle, really carrying. . . the word.'

I myself remember an occasion at a Christian youth convention when Archbishop Desmond Tutu spoke to three thousand of us about the burden of South Africa. I have an indelible memory of the extraordinary feeling that came over me during that address — a feeling of what I call utter transfiguration. For once, my eyes had seen the glory of the coming of the Lord.

In Robert Burns' day, preaching was not only a high art, but a popular entertainment as well. 'Holy Fairs' were organised at which the public could enjoy a continuous open-air feast of preaching by the best in the country. Burns wrote a lengthy, comical and irreverent account of one such fair. In so doing, he nevertheless confirmed the pre-eminence of the art.

What follows is my own parody of the Burns poem, which I dedicate to all lovers of the craft of preaching:

> The people on the holy hill
> Had come to hear some preaching;
> Perhaps they'd find a man of skill
> And hope their 'call' would reach him.
> Before they launched into the fair
> To help parson selection,
> Longsufferers showed they didn't care,
> But practised mass defection
>   On each first day.
> Old snarling Billy started off
> Athumpin' and ablarin',
> 'Till stifled by his smoker's cough
> He left the pulpit swearin'.
> He cursed the day free enterprise
> Was added to the system,
> Nor would he ever realise
> That no-one ever missed him.
>   He'd had his day.
> Hark now, the tent has changed its tone —
> There's peace and rest no longer —
> A morals man is casting stones,
> The groans are getting stronger.
> 'Please bring the young Rev. on,' they cried,
> 'At preaching he's quite handy!
> His heart is full of love divine,
> The rest are full of brandy
>   The livelong day.'

> While some were thinking on their sins
> Or comforting the ladies,
> The young Rev. got them on their pins
> To take the war to Hades.
> The ones who'd gone for Auld Lang Syne
> From half-filled jars and barrels
> Returned to find the foulest swine
> Were drunk on hymns and carols
> Until next day.

The first thing is to know that the Christian community should never come together, except where God's very word be preached and prayer made. . . Therefore where God's word is not preached, 'tis better people should neither sing, nor read, nor come together. . .

Martin Luther

'Tis a right excellent thing, that every honest pastor's and preacher's mouth is Christ's mouth, and his word and forgiveness is Christ's word and forgiveness.

Martin Luther

First, Christian preaching should be true to the discernible revelation of God in Jesus Christ. . . Second, Christian preaching should be both intelligible and pertinent to its present audience: these two qualities are demanded by the claim that the Christian message is indeed a 'revelation' and a revelation of universal importance.

Geoffrey Wainwright, *Doxology*

Teach, stir the mind, afford enjoyment.

Ezra Pound

The men of old wanting to clarify and diffuse throughout the empire that light which comes from looking straight into the heart and then acting, first. . . established order in their own families; wanting order in the home, they first disciplined themselves; desiring self-discipline, they rectified their own hearts; they sought precise verbal definitions of their inarticulate thoughts and, in order to attain precise verbal definitions, they set to extend their knowledge to the utmost.

Confucius

The story is told of a young Japanese poet who was apprenticed to an old master. Day after day he laboured to produce a poem that would satisfy the demands of his teacher. At last, he finished his work. It was a simple poem about a plum tree in a field on the twigs of which snow had fallen.

When the master studied the poem, he said, 'Too many twigs; you only need one twig.'

Herman Hesse, My Belief

Your voice surprised me.
It came not like a summer bird
fulfilling the expectations
of the holiday-maker,
but like good news
to those who sit upon the rock
patiently,
expecting nothing.
I beg you, don't deny it me.

Dimitri Tsaloumas, The Observatory

Lord Jesus, Eternal Word of God:

In my busy world, there is so much noise: computer blips, department store music, street buskers, idle chatter, tram bells and roaring engines. I take it all for granted as the background score of my life. But I long for a sound like the sound of a foreground soloist: a sound that is richly meaningful to me. Your word is always like that. Your word is your voice, your laughter, your command. It is:

. . .like a water-melon, split open by August
to quench a muleteer's thirst
on a steep climb —
such freshness
I have never tasted in my life.

(Tsaloumas)

I pray for all those whose great calling it is to preach your word. Grant them the passion and the power to make the most wonderful sound in the world, the sound of your voice. And Lord. . . give me ears to hear. Amen.

A Benediction
May God bless you with the hearing of his word, so that you may be a doer of his word.

48

Second last words and the last word

The voice of one crying in the wilderness: Prepare the way of the Lord, make his paths straight. Every valley shall be filled, and every mountain and hill shall be brought low, and the crooked shall be made straight, and the rough ways shall be made smooth; and all flesh shall see the salvation of God.

Behold, I send my messenger to prepare the way before me, and the Lord whom you seek will suddenly come to his temple; the messenger of the covenant in whom you delight, behold, he is coming, says the Lord of hosts.

. . .And he will go before him in the spirit and power of Elijah, to turn the hearts of the fathers to the children and the disobedient to the wisdom of the just, to make ready for the Lord a people prepared.

. . .And you, child, will be called the prophet of the Most High; for you will go before the Lord to prepare his ways.

For by grace you have been saved through faith; and this is not your own doing, it is the gift of God — not because of works, lest anyone should boast. For we are his workmanship created in Christ Jesus for good works, which God prepared beforehand, that we should walk in them.

. . .justified by his grace as a gift, through the redemption which is in Christ Jesus.

For he says to Moses, 'I will have mercy on whom I have mercy, and I will have compassion on whom I have compassion.' So it depends not upon our will or exertion, but upon God's mercy.

(Luke 3: 4–6; Malachi 3: 1; Luke 1: 17 and 76; Ephesians 2: 8–10; Romans 3: 24; 9: 15–16 — all RSV)

Have you ever found yourself under pressure to carry out God's work — to proclaim his good news to different people, to lead particular people through to faith in Christ? Have you ever felt that someone's future depended on your ministry, your guidance, your presence?

What a burden we place on ourselves! How can we live with such expectations? Well, the good news is that we don't have to. We ought never to be in the business of saying 'last words' to people! God is the one who does that. He is the one who takes the initiative as he reaches out to people with his words of grace and life.

The past, the present and the future are all in his hands. He is the author and finisher of all things and we are able to rest in that knowledge. Nothing we can do will earn our — or anyone else's — salvation. It is all of God — by grace alone. We, and others, simply respond to God's loving approaches and trust him for everything.

Now it may well be that we find ourselves involved in a power game when we step into the lives of others. It is so much easier to be in control than to allow God to be sovereign and for us to fall into a secondary role — and be content with second last words.

However, to believe that God always has the last word takes a tremendous weight off our shoulders. We who seem to be such good 'messiah' material can with much relief leave the work of salvation to God. Recognising that we are totally inadequate to take God's place, we can begin to settle into the process of saying '*second* last words' in preparation for God's last word.

Saying second last words can take many and varied forms. They may be said in the offering of a cup of cold water, some food, clothing and shelter to refugees, a shoulder for someone to cry on or a listening ear to someone in trouble. Or they may be offered in relating some of our faith story or telling the good news of Jesus Christ. All of these actions fall into the category of second last words: they prepare the way for God's last word, the great event of justification by faith.

A striking illustration of this process comes from Bangladesh at the time of the 1971 war. About ten million people fled to the borders of India and Burma, there to be helped by Christian aid organisations. Food and clothing were given in the name of Jesus. Returning home later that year, many of those people were wide open to the challenge of the gospel: God's last word to them. Since then, the churches have witnessed a number of these people respond to God's grace. Second last words prepared the way for God's *last* word.

❧

The origin and the essence of all Christian life are [found] in the one process or event which the Reformation called justification of the sinner by grace alone. The nature of the Christian life is disclosed not by who we are in ourselves, but by what we are in this event. The whole length and breadth of human life is here compressed into a single instant, a single point. The totality of life is encompassed in this event. . . We are free for God and our brothers and sisters.

We become aware that there is a God who loves us, that others are standing at our side whom God loves as he loves us and that there is a future with the triune God, together with his church. We believe. We love. We hope. The past and the future of our whole life are merged in one in the presence of God. The whole of the past is [found] in the word 'forgiveness'. The whole of the future is in safekeeping in the faithfulness of God.

But the justifying word of God. . . is always preceded by something penultimate, some action, suffering, movement, volition, defeat, uprising, entreaty or hope — that is to say, in a quite genuine sense by a span of time, at the end of which it stands.

What is this penultimate? It is everything that precedes the ultimate, everything that precedes the justification of the sinner by grace alone, everything which is to be regarded as leading up to the last thing when the last thing has been found. . . The penultimate does not determine the ultimate; it is the ultimate which determines the penultimate.

Preparing the way for the word: this is the purpose of everything that has been said about the things before the last.

Dietrich Bonhoeffer, *Ethics*

The next-to-the-last word, the word which prepares the way for divine-human encounter, may be implicitly communicated in a private relationship or explicitly proclaimed from a pulpit. It may be communicated sacramentally or scientifically. The way may be prepared through one's participation in marital conflict or marital bliss, through the work of the world or through worship, through disease and impending death, or through the recovery of health and restoration of life.

No-one has the last word; yet everyone may have the next-to-last word. No method of ministry fences the way by which God comes to us. No human words, not even the recital of scriptures, necessarily communicates the divine Word. Although no one form of ministry is in itself ultimate, all forms of ministry may be penultimate.

Ed Thornton, *Theology and Pastoral Counseling*

I know that thou art the author and finisher of faith,
that the whole work of redemption is thine alone,
that every good work or thought found in me
is the effect of thy power and grace,
that thy sole motive in working in me to will and to do
is for thy good pleasure.

Puritan prayer

And so it is essential for us to look entirely outside ourselves to see the splendour of God's plan of deliverance. Salvation is not so much a matter of doing as of *appreciating what God has done*. God wants us to be free from thinking about ourselves long enough to consider what his love has done. After all, to be fully reassured, to be free from the suspicion that we are fooling ourselves and working up faith in nothing more substantial than our own wishful thinking, we need to have our attention fixed on Jesus the Messiah.

Richard Lovelace, *Renewal as a Way of Life*

Our highest activity must be response, not initiative. To experience the love of God in a true and not an illusory form is therefore to experience it as our surrender to his demand, our conformity to his desire.

C.S. Lewis, *The Problem of Pain*

There is a voice that cries in the wilderness,
the prophetic word demanding change:
'Prepare the way of the Lord;
fill in the gullies, level the ridges,
straighten the crooked, move the mountains.
God's glory shall be revealed
and every eye shall see it.'
Smooth the rough places,
move the mountains;
let God's glory be displayed!. . .
In the wilderness of our religions
where theological fashions come and go,
buildings and crowds persist as status-symbols,
and pomp and circumstance are high on the ratings,
where evangelism can be considered poor taste,
prayer and sacrifice as optional extras,
and even Jesus is feared as 'extremist':
Prepare the way of the Lord.
Smooth the rough places,
move the mountains:
let God's glory be displayed!

Bruce Prewer, *Australian Psalms*

. . .You are Christian only so long as you look forward to a new world, so long as you constantly pose critical questions to the society you live in, so long as you emphasise the need of conversion both for yourself and for the world, so long as you in no way let yourself become established in a situation of seeming calm, so long as you stay unsatisfied with the *status quo* and keep saying that a new world is yet to come. You are Christian only when you believe that you have a role to play in the realisation of this new kingdom, and when you urge everyone you meet with a holy unrest to make haste so that the promise might soon be fulfilled.

Henri Nouwen, *With Open Hands*

I pray that this will be my ministry: to join people on their journey and to open their eyes to see you. Many people are searching. Often they are studying, reading, discussing, writing and performing to find an answer to their most intimate questions. But many remain groping in the dark. Give me the courage to join them and say to them as Philip did (to the Ethiopian), 'Do you understand what you are reading?'

Henri Nouwen, *A Cry for Mercy*

Messiahs do not have the ability to save other people.

It is time to stop this pretense, time to grieve for all the children, the elderly, the sick, the hungry, the homeless, the needy we will never be able to save. Messiahs cannot keep fathers from drinking, mothers from contracting breast cancer, brothers from dying in wars, sisters from being raped or children from abusing drugs. We simply do not have the power.

Not only do we not have the power to save other people; we do not even have the power to save ourselves. . . Pretending to be powerful does not make one so.

Carmen Berry, *When Helping You Is Hurting Me*

What makes the temptation of power so seemingly irresistible? Maybe it is that power offers an easy substitute for the hard task of love. It seems easier to be God than to love God, easier to control people than to love people, easier to own life than to love life.

Henri Nouwen, *Seeds of Hope*

I think that it is important to say that this conviction that helplessness could be an integrating theme (in terminal care) arose out of reflection on my own experience. In a chaplain's role particularly I had found myself involved with dying people or their families in situations where there was 'nothing more to do', in which we were all helpless. I had found also that, paradoxically, if I was prepared to stay in these situations, accepting my feelings of helplessness, then these were some of the times I was most helpful as a pastor.

Bruce Rumbold, *Helplessness & Hope*

Father:
How often I lose sight of the fact that you are the initiator in all matters of grace and that the world — and my life — are constantly in your hands.
Forgive me when I:
> *try to take over my own salvation,*
> *come to have too great an idea of my importance,*
> *develop messianic tendencies in my ministry with others*
> *and forget that you are the only one who is able to offer 'last words'.*
Help me:
> *to offer my presence with 'no strings attached',*
> *to be prepared to listen without pontificating,*
> *to touch people at their point of need without*
> *feeling that I have to solve their problem,*
> *to speak about the good news without needing to*
> *press for a definite response,*
> *to leave the last word always with you.*
Thank you for the great sense of relief that such an approach brings to me.
Thank you that I don't have to understand how you work in my life — or the lives of others.
Thank you for the knowledge that you do come to me — and others — in your own way and in your own time.
You are to be praised and worshipped. In Christ's name. Amen.

A Benediction
May the great triune God make himself known this day:
  the Father, to surround you with his love,
  the Son, to assure you of redemption,
  and the Spirit, to impart wisdom and insight. Amen.

Then Jacob woke from his sleep and said, 'Surely the Lord is in this place and I did not know it!' And he was afraid and said, 'How awesome is this place! This is none other than the house of God, and this is the gate of heaven.'

Moses was keeping the flock of his father-in-law Jethro, the priest of Midian; he led his flock beyond the wilderness and came to Horeb, the mountain of God. There the angel of the Lord appeared to him in a flame of fire out of a bush; he looked and the bush was blazing, yet it was not consumed. . . When the Lord saw that he had turned aside to see, God called to him out of the bush, 'Moses, Moses!' And he said, 'Here I am.' Then he said, 'Come no closer, for the place on which you are standing is holy ground.'

When they told Mordecai what Esther had said, Mordecai told them to reply to Esther, 'Do not think that in the king's palace you will escape any more than all the other Jews. For if you keep silence at such a time as this, relief and deliverance will arise for the Jews from another quarter, but you and your father's family will perish. Who knows? Perhaps you have come to royal dignity for just such a time as this.'

Once while Jesus was standing beside the lake of Gennesaret and the crowd was pressing in on him to hear the word of God, he saw two boats there at the shore of the lake; the fishermen had gone out of them and were washing their nets. He got into one of the boats, the one belonging to Simon, and asked him to put out a little way from the shore. Then he sat down and taught the crowds from the boat.

Peter turned and saw the disciple whom Jesus loved following them; he was the one who had reclined next to Jesus at the supper and had said, 'Lord, who is it that is going to betray you?' When Peter saw him, he said to Jesus, 'Lord, what about him?' Jesus said to him, 'If it is my will that he remain until I come, what is that to you? Follow me!'

One night, the Lord said to Paul in a vision, 'Do not be afraid, but speak and do not be silent; for I am with you and no-one will lay a hand on you to harm you, for there are many in this city who are my people.' He stayed there a year and six months, teaching the word of God among them.

I have learned to be content with whatever I have. I know what it is to have little and I know what it is to have plenty. In any and all circumstances I have learned the secret of being well-fed and of going hungry, of having plenty and of being in need. I can do all things through him who strengthens me.

(Genesis 28: 16–17; Exodus 3: 1–2,4–5; Esther 4: 12–14; Luke 5: 1–3; John 21: 20–22; Acts 18: 9–11; Philippians 4: 11b–13 — all NRSV)

There's a lovely children's hymn which says:

> God who put the stars in space,
> Who made the world we share,
> In his making made a place
> For me, and put me here.

Norman and Margaret Mealy

A place for me! The hymn celebrates the providential care of God in putting us each in our own place. It invites the thought that our place is where God puts us, to serve his purpose. Each person has his or her place; I have my place.

We usually acknowledge that people have their place.

Often the benefit of hindsight helps us see it; something happens and suddenly, looking back, we can see how God has prepared the way, creating openings, preparing someone by gifts or experience or temperament to be the right person at the right place and at the right time.

We notice God doing this especially when the situation is some blessing we enjoy or something pleasant that happens providentially for people we know. We might not always be willing to acknowledge the providence so readily when it leads to an opportunity for service or when we have to put ourselves on the line to seize the God-given opportunity.

The situation of Esther is a case in point. The people of Israel were living in exile in Persia, but she had attained a privileged position as queen to King Ahasuerus. When the Prime Minister, for personal reasons, attempted to destroy the Jews, Esther's guardian tried to enlist her help. Now this involved some danger to her life: self-interest dictated that she lie low and do nothing, but the situation was desperate. So Mordecai then said to her: 'Who knows whether it is not for a time like this that you have become queen?'

What might this mean for us and our place? It would mean that we are to take the fact that we are particular people by gift, temperament and opportunity, and use that in the particular places we are and among the particular people we encounter. Simon Peter is a good example: Peter's place was the lake, where he was a fisherman. Once, his boat became a pulpit for Jesus. By being himself and being in his place, Peter gave service to Jesus.

Now there are opportunities like that for most of us every day of our lives. Whatever our place, it can also be the place where we serve God. Our place, our location is not just a geographical accident: it is the place where God intends that we should be and we should offer service in his name.

In his discussion of 'the congregation as hermeneutic of the gospel', Lesslie Newbigin reminds us that in the New Testament, the church is only spoken of in two ways. Either it is the church of God (or Christ), or it is the church in some specific place — Rome, Corinth, Galatia and so on. That fact is significant: it means the local church is 'God's embassy in a specific place'.

❧❦❧

It is no superstition to seek out the spots where God has come down to visit his people. It is not that God is any more there, or is any more likely to return there; but we are better prepared to meet with him there. And God comes to those who are ready to meet with him wherever they are. There is no respect of places with God. And nothing draws God down to any place like a heart like his own.

Alexander Whyte, Bible Characters, Old Testament

God put me in this situation and God means it, with all its problems and its difficulties, to make for my happiness and usefulness in time, and for my joy and peace in eternity. This is meant for my joy and peace in this world and in the world to come.

William Barclay, The Letters to Philippians,
Colossians, Thessalonians

[Dick Shepherd] often told the story of an artist who could clearly remember the first occasion he deliberately turned his back on the kingdom of God. A schoolboy home for the holidays, he was out walking alone when a small girl, to whom he was a hero, ran out of a cottage to give him a bunch of faded flowers. He ignored her and walked on. Later he looked back and saw the child in tears and the flowers scattered on the road.

This story meant a lot. 'It is my deepest conviction,' he said, 'that at least once in every twenty-four hours the offer of the kingdom of God is still made in some simple and straightforward way to everyone. It may be only in the form of a faded bunch of flowers to be accepted with gentle courtesy, or it may be as a cross set on a height which we must storm with infinite courage, but whatever the offer looks like, it is, I believe, a summons to us to give love the pre-eminence and to allow it to prevail.

We may accept this daily offer or reject it; we may pass it by, as most often happens, not recognising it for what it is, but I am utterly convinced that the offer itself and our attitude towards it are the most important facts in human existence.'

Carolyn Scott, *Betwixt Heaven and Charing Cross*

George MacLeod in industrial Glasgow has called social action 'the earthing of God'. But then he had not pulled out the plug from the other end, disconnecting the heavenly power.

Rhys Miller, *Calling and Recalling*

I beg you do not look on Dortmund as a steppingstone, but rather say: here I shall stay as long as it pleases God; if it be his will, until I die. Look upon every child, your confirmands, every member of your congregation as if you will have to give account for every soul on the day of the Lord Jesus. Every day commit these souls from the worst and weakest of hands, namely, your own, into the best and strongest of hands. Then you will be able to carry on your ministry not only without care, but also with joy overflowing and joyful hope.

Friedrich von Bodelschwingh, to his son
as minister in his first parish.

Commitment, courage and a consecrated imagination: these must be the marks of a twentieth-century evangelist. . . We have to provide a deliberate Christian presence in the community. Our absenteeism is our greatest sin. *Being there* is what counts. Being there, not necessarily because you want to be there, but for God. Being there, in good times and in bad. Being there, as points of acceptance and warmth and love. Being there, waiting patiently, praying silently, alert and positive, serving the days of your apprenticeship and earning the right to speak. Being there, ready for the encounter in which your Lord will come.

No reproach will deflect the evangelist who has taken the cue from his or her Lord. In the fullness of time and moved by the divine love, Christ plunged from the heart of the Godhead into the icy turbulence of this crazy, sin-torn, wonderful world, with all its suffering and with all its tenderness.

Jack Burton, *The Gap*

1949 had been a great year but Alan [Walker] viewed it with some concern.

'Once again God pulled me back towards the centre of things,' he wrote in his diary in October. 'With a quiet house. . . concern over some recession at Waverley and my own inner discontent, I thought with myself.

'After a bad night, I rose early, opened my Bible at random and found the 34th chapter of Ezekiel. In a moment, I was reading the words, "Woe to the shepherds of Israel that do feed themselves! Should not the shepherds feed the flock?"

'From the book came the clear challenge that I had been thinking too much of my own satisfaction, too little of the "flock" given me at Waverley.

'I heard, too, the challenge to prayer and Bible study, both of which have suffered so badly since the pressure of going to Amsterdam came on. But then towards the end of the chapter came the promise: "I delivered them out of the hands of those that served themselves. . . there shall be showers of blessing."

'Then it was that God led me to a re-dedication to the task at Waverley. This is where my first responsibility lies and whatever happens elsewhere is dependent on a strong witness here and the power which God will lend me for this task.

'Thus again I believe God arrested me as so often before and drew me back to the centre of things. If there is a slackening here at Waverley, it has begun in a slackening in my own heart and loyalty — and the recovery must begin there — and this glad morning has witnessed the beginning in God, who can remake all things anew.'

Harold Henderson, *Reach for the World*

But God *everywhere* can become God *nowhere*; God in *all*

things can lead to God in *nothing*: specific times and places are important. *Worship* is the mortar which binds together our doctrines, our personal discipleship and our social vision. It should be the chief source of our spiritual nourishment, providing an ethereal counterpoint to daily involvement in the life of the world. . . In worship, we still attempt to express our response to the mystery, our commitment to the way of love, and our longing for new energy and power. It should be an essentially joyous activity, where awe and reverence blend with warmth and acceptance, where we are 'touched with loving sympathy' and where 'silence heightens heaven'.

But when worship ends, we have to return again to our task. Serious discipleship imposes great responsibilities, for which only a full-hearted commitment will suffice. Battles lie ahead, in which few of the decisive encounters will take place on church grounds. The work is urgent, the dangers are real, yet our hearts should be filled with hope.

'Almost thou persuadest me to be a Christian!' Across the gap, that ancient exclamation can still be prompted (in the unlikeliest quarter) by a selfless and compassionate Christian presence. However, a witness of such challenging authority only becomes possible when other transactions, of an intensely personal nature, have taken place earlier. . .

Jesus looks at us as he looked at Simon Peter, long ago, and asks the same simple question: *Lovest thou me?*

Jack Burton, *The Gap*

Living God:
From this place where you have set me, I lift my heart and mind to you in prayer and praise. Let me be still and open to the sense of your presence now in my prayer. You are the God beyond all space and time, you are eternally present in each and every place, yet in your miracle of love and grace you are willing to draw near and receive from me the love of my poor heart.

In this place where you have set me, I believe that you are present, working to achieve your will. Work in me and work through me to advance the kingdom of your love. I pray for all with whom I share this place, all with whom I share my life: for family and loved ones, friends and colleagues and neighbours. Thank you for the gifts you give through them. I ask that I may be the channel of your grace to them.

In this place where you have set me, let me live and serve and give myself in the pattern of my Lord's example. In every challenge, difficulty and opportunity, let me know that he is near, in all his power to bless. Let me walk in his light, act in his strength and live in his love.

Through Jesus Christ our Lord. **Amen.**

A Benediction
God be with us where we are;
God go with us where we travel;
God remain with us where we rest,
until we rest in him eternally.
And the grace of the Lord Jesus Christ be with us,
and with all for whom we pray,
now and evermore. **Amen.**

50

There's a track winding back

Then the man and his wife heard the sound of the Lord God as he was walking in the garden in the cool of the day, and they hid from the Lord God among the trees of the garden. But the Lord God called to the man, 'Where are you?' He answered, 'I heard you in the garden and I was afraid because I was naked; so I hid.'

So the Lord God banished him from the Garden of Eden to work the ground from which he had been taken. After he drove the man out, he placed on the east side of the Garden of Eden cherubim and a flaming sword flashing back and forth to guard the way to the tree of life.

For those blessed by the Lord shall inherit the land, but those cursed by him shall be cut off.

Thomas said to him, 'Lord, we don't know where you are going, so how can we know the way?' Jesus answered, 'I am the way and the truth and the life. No-one comes to the Father except through me.'

Now that same day two of them were going to a village called Emmaus, about seven miles from Jerusalem. They were talking with each other about everything that had happened. As they talked and discussed these things with each other, Jesus himself came up and walked along with them; but they were kept from recognising him.

And beginning with Moses and all the prophets, he explained to them what was said in all the scriptures concerning himself. As they approached the village to which they were going, Jesus acted as if he were going further. But they urged him strongly, 'Stay with us, for it is nearly evening; the day is almost over.' So he went to stay with them.

When he was at the table with them, he took bread, gave thanks, broke it and began to give it to them. Then their eyes were opened and they recognised him.

Blessed are those whose strength is in you, who have set their hearts on pilgrimage.

(Genesis 3: 8–9, NIV; Psalm 37: 22, NRSV; John 14: 5–6, NIV; Luke 24: 13–16 and 27–31, NIV; Psalm 84: 5, NIV)

The first track was made not for travel or exploration, but for the enjoyment of walking through the bush in the company of good friends. It was a track made by God and each evening 'in the cool of the day' he would walk with Adam and Eve. The first result of human sin was that the guilty pair found they could no longer walk that track with God.

The second track was made by Adam and Eve as they left the garden. It led away from greenness and away from the Tree of Life and the Tree of Knowledge — and from that track every other human track was branched. One early branch was the track of their son Cain who made his own way 'to be a restless wanderer on the earth'.

Some people have had a deep 'yearning just to be returning' to that original track where humans enjoyed the company of God. Enoch found it and never came back. People with clay feet like Abraham, Jacob and Elijah may not have arrived like Enoch, but they followed an inner restlessness that made them wanderers on a pilgrimage looking for 'a city whose builder and maker is God'. Part of that search for God was a yearning for greenness.

For some like Job, the pilgrimage was in the mind and the tracks were in the form of intellectual questioning, but it was still a journey with changing landscapes and the counterplay between sunshine and shadow.

The important thing is to be on the move — walking, moving, 'on pilgrimage' to respond to a restlessness created by God so that 'we might find rest in him' (Augustine). God's highest points of revelation were not given in church or in colleges, but to people on the road, to nomads — the children of Israel, the returning exiles from Babylonia, the disciples. Many of the Psalms celebrate pilgrimage and were written to be sung on the move.

The first theological dissertation of the resurrection was given on the road to Emmaus as they walked along. It's a tradition only that these two are thought of as male disciples. If, as I like to think, it was a husband and wife (they did, after all, invite him to their home), then the Garden of Eden scene is recreated and the resurrection means that God walks again with the man and wife. The road to Emmaus then becomes symbolic of that first track and that 'yearning to be returning' can now be fulfilled. In any case, every track has the potential of leading back to that first one.

But not all find the way. If the restlessness is not recognised as having a divine origin, then it leads to wandering, but not pilgrimage. For many it is a wandering in the pleasant fields of indulgent materialism which feeds the restlessness, but never satisfies its hunger. These become tourists, but not pilgrims.

Others, like the poet Christopher Brennan, make the journey into the human dimension as an escape from God — this track is called Cain Way. Its philosophy is the wandering on the way to one's self. But the poet is honest enough to say that it leads nowhere and has a 'foredoom'd disastrous' end:

> The wanderer of the ways of all the worlds,
> to whom the sunshine and the rain are one
> and one to stay or hasten, because one knows
> no ending of the way, no home, no goal.
>
> *The Wanderer*

In contrast to Cain Way, there is one track that goes all the way back to the Garden. It's a track that began in Galilee and then spread to Jerusalem. From Jerusalem it spread to Judea, Samaria and then finally to the uttermost parts of the earth. And when people ask 'Show us the way', it is Jesus Christ alone who can say with authority: 'I am the way.'

There's a track winding back to an old-fashioned shack
. . .That's why I am yearning
Just to be returning.

O'Hagan, 'Along the Road to Gundagai'

The more I read, the more convinced I became that nomads had been the crankhandle of history, if for no other reason than that the great monotheisms had, all of them, surfaced from the pastoral milieu.

Bruce Chatwin, *Songlines*

Above all, do not lose your desire to walk: every day I walk myself into a state of well-being and walk away from every illness; I have walked myself into my best thoughts and I know of no thought so burdensome that one cannot walk away from it. . . but by sitting still, and the more one sits still, the closer one comes to feeling ill. . . thus if one just keeps on walking, every-thing will be all right.

Sören Kierkegaard, letter to Jette

Body and soul contain a thousand possibilities out of which you may build many I's. But in only one of them is there a congruence of the elector and the elected. Only one — which you will never find until you have excluded all those superficial and fleeting possibilities of being and doing with which you toy out of curiosity or wonder or greed, and which hinder you from casting anchor in the experience of the mystery of life and the consciousness of the talent entrusted to you, which is your I.

Dag Hammarskjöld, *Markings*

Shortly after Christ's death on the cross, two men were walking along the road to Emmaus, a village some seven or eight miles distant from Jerusalem. . . As they walked along they naturally talked about the crucifixion and its aftermath; so absorbed in their talk that they scarcely noticed when a third man drew alongside and walked with them. . .

He accepted their invitation [to stay with them]. When they sat down to eat, and he broke bread and blessed it, they recognised him at last. He was no stranger, but their Saviour. Then he disappeared. Cleopas and his companion. . . hurried back full of joy and hope to Jerusalem, along the road they had so lately travelled, to tell the others of their marvellous experience. On every walk. . . whether to Emmaus, Wimbledon or Timbuktu, there is the same stranger waiting to accompany us along the way, if we want him.

Malcolm Muggeridge, *Jesus Rediscovered*

Lord:
So much of our faith was shaped by pilgrim people — people on the move, on the road. It was a faith tested by thought and measured along the tracks of life and experience.

Forgive us that we have changed the scene of the road into a lounge room, a church building, an air-conditioned study, a learning hall. Forgive us that every time we 'do Christianity' we seem to be sitting down, listening, sharing, singing songs to one another — yes, there is a place for that, but we still need the movement of the pilgrimage, we need that sense of being on a track that leads somewhere.

Thank you for that love of green that lies deep within as a reminder that there is a place to return to — a place that creates a 'yearning, just to be returning'. Thank you for people who stand up for green — maybe without knowing its significance.

Help me to accept that the track that winds back to green at some point passes through desert landscapes, whose wide horizons spill over into eternity and whose barrenness strips away at our pride. Help me to learn the message of the desert 'that humankind shall not live by bread alone, but every word that proceeds from the mouth of God'.

Lead me to walk through the bush — I need the exercise for my body and I need the release that comes from physically walking. May these walks become part of my spiritual experience. . .

A Benediction
And may you find tracks that lead back to that original path where God and the first part of human creation walked in harmony. Amen.

51

Commitment and cost

We. . . have been chosen. . . to be obedient to Jesus Christ.

If you love me, you will keep my commandments. If you continue in my word, you are truly my disciples; and you will know the truth, and the truth will make you free. Everyone then who hears these words of mine and acts on them will be like a wise man who built his house on rock. If any want to become my followers, let them deny themselves and take up their cross and follow me. For those who want to save their life will lose it, and those who lose their life for my sake will find it. For what will it profit them if they gain the whole world, but forfeit their life?

The Lord your God you shall follow him, him alone you shall fear, his commandments you shall keep, his voice you shall obey, him you shall serve, and to him you shall hold fast.

I have chosen the way of faithfulness; I set your ordinances before me. I run the way of your commandments, for you enlarge my understanding. Teach me, O Lord, the way of your statutes and I will observe it to the end. Give me understanding that I may keep your law and observe it with my whole heart. Lead me in the path of your commandments, for I delight in it. Turn my heart to your decrees and not to selfish gain. See, I have longed for your precepts; in your righteousness give me life. I will keep your law continually, forever and ever. This blessing has fallen to me, for I have kept your precepts.

Teach me your way, O Lord, that I may walk in your truth.

The precepts of the Lord are right, rejoicing the heart; the commandment of the Lord is clear, enlightening the eyes.

I will give them one heart and put a new spirit within them. . . so that they may follow my statutes and keep my ordinances and obey them. Then they shall be my people and I will be their God.

Do you not know that if you present yourselves to anyone as obedient slaves, you are slaves of the one whom you obey, either of sin, which leads to death, or of obedience, which leads to righteousness. But thanks be to God that you, having once been slaves of sin, have become obedient from the heart to the form of teaching to which you were entrusted.

Now that you have purified your souls by your obedience to the truth so that you have genuine mutual love, love one another deeply from the heart. Like obedient children, do not be conformed to the desires that you formerly had in ignorance. Instead. . . be holy.

We take every thought captive to obey Christ. For the love of Christ urges us on. . . he died for all, so that those who live might live no longer for themselves, but for him who died and was raised for them.

(1 Peter 1: 2; John 14: 15; 8: 31–32; Matthew 7: 24; 16: 24–26; Deuteronomy 13: 4; Psalm 119: 30, 32-36, 40, 44 and 56; Psalm 86: 11; 19: 8; Ezekiel 11: 19–20; Romans 6: 16-17; 1 Peter 1: 22; 1 Peter 1: 14–15; 2 Corinthians 10: 5; 5: 14 and 15 — all NRSV)

Christians throughout history have ranged in commitment from cold to hot. (Even Jesus was tempted — he really was — to be other than a suffering Messiah.) The earliest of his followers were generally (though not exclusively) at the warmer end of the temperature scale. Some went around with Jesus to watch his amazing miracles or get some free food. Others were prepared to risk their lives and reputations for him.

And post-Easter Christians followed someone who had been executed: the prospect of an early or violent death does something to your commitment-level!

A young first-century church, at Antioch, was visited by one of the most committed Christian leaders in the first century, Barnabas. In his first preaching to these new converts he urged them to 'be faithful and true to the Lord with all your hearts' (Acts 11: 23). As Australians would say, 'Get fair-dinkum!' Don't be a half-hearted Christian! Be committed!

Commitment involves change, growth, fervour, enthusiasm. 'Enthusiasm' comes from two Greek words — *en* (in) and *theos* (God), so the word means 'one possessed by God (or the gods)'. Enthusiasm literally means being full of God.

Christian enthusiasts are concerned above everything else with what God wants (Matthew 6: 33). Being a Christian is the most exciting thing in all the world!

Charles Schwab, the American industrialist who rose from poverty to put the US Steel Corporation together, said, 'You can succeed at almost anything for which you have unlimited enthusiasm.' Emerson said, 'Nothing great was ever achieved without enthusiasm.' And here's another quote from my desk calendar: 'Years wrinkle the skin, but lack of enthusiasm wrinkles the soul.' Which reminds me of Thoreau's 'None are so old as those who have outlived enthusiasm.'

Most people get enthusiastic about something, as you will discover at a football grand final, in a disco or at a political convention. However, as Billy Graham once said, 'It is very strange that the world accepts enthusiasm in every realm but the spiritual.' Those who have achieved great things for God have been people of infectious zeal and unquenchable enthusiasm.

John the Baptist was one of these. Jesus said he was a bright and shining light, a light that blazed and shone. But John the Baptist had earlier said that Christ would baptise with the Holy Spirit and with fire.

How do we get on fire for God?

The earliest Christians were people on fire for God. 'We can't help speaking,' they said, 'of the things we have seen and heard.' Jeremiah was like that. He could not keep

God's message to himself. It was like a fire burning deep within him. He'd tried to hold it back, but could not (Jeremiah 20: 9).

Generally speaking, we get from those who follow us the level of commitment we expect. Quintilian laid it down as a first principle of rhetoric that the orator who wishes to set the people on fire must himself be burning. Because church-people are in a sense a pastor's employers, there's a temptation for the pastor to soften the prophetic side of ministry, opting to pitch the commitment-level within people's 'comfort zone'. Where ecclesiastical wineskins are bereft of new wine, the church becomes stale, lifeless.

There may be order but, as British Anglican David Watson used to say often, it's the orderliness of the cemetery. The oyster may be there, but the pearl has gone.

Now there's another side to all this. 'Dead churches are afraid of enthusiasm': that's true, but enthusiasm has a history that justifies this fear to some extent. 'Enthusiasts' were sometimes people who had plenty of heat, but not too much light. They got all excited about minor things. Fanatics are enthusiastic, but such enthusiasm can sometimes lead to stupidity or even violence. Paul said that before he was a Christian, he was zealous. But his zeal was misdirected: he persecuted the church.

W.B. Yeats, in his poem 'The Second Coming', says 'the best lack all conviction' while 'the worst are full of passionate intensity'. We must search for the dividing line between enthusiasm and fanaticism — being inspired by God or the devil. A person without judgment is like a car without brakes; but a person without enthusiasm is like a car without a motor.

The Presbyterian preacher James Stewart once said: 'The supreme need of the church is the same in the twentieth century as in the first: it is people on fire for Christ.' As the hymn says:

> O Thou who camest from above,
> The pure celestial fire to impart,
> Kindle a flame of sacred love
> On the mean altar of my heart!

A cold church is like cold butter: it doesn't spread very easily. A selfish church is like a glee club: existing for the benefit of its members rather than those outside it. Other churches through their preaching offer all sorts of goodies like a trouble-free or sickness-free life — which is foreign to the teaching of the New Testament.

So it is possible to become a Christian for the wrong reasons. Faith in Christ is not an insurance policy against 'the slings and arrows of outrageous fortune'. Never forget, Jesus promises you three things: constant trouble and constant joy and constant presence with you!

Certainly, it is worthwhile to be a Christian for the side-benefits, including eternal life! This is expressed in the saying, 'You are no fool if you give up what you cannot keep, to gain what you cannot lose.' The prayer by Cardinal Newman sums up this motivation: 'Teach me, dear Lord, frequently and attentively to consider this truth: that if I gain the whole world and lose [you], in the end I have lost everything. Whereas, if I lose this world and gain [you], in the end I have lost nothing.'

But the greatest incentive to complete commitment to Jesus Christ is his love, shown ultimately in his death for us. 'Love so amazing, so divine demands my soul, my life, my all!'

✄

There is strong support among Christians for the notion that an individual is free to do whatever they please, as long as it does not hurt others. Two out of five Christians maintain that such thinking is proper, thus effectively rejecting the unconditional code of ethics and morality as taught in the Bible. Three out of ten Christians agree that nothing in life is more important than having fun and being happy. . . One out of four believers thinks that the more you have the more successful you are. The fact that the proportion of Christians who affirm these values is equivalent to the proportion of non-Christians who hold similar views indicates how meaningless Christianity has been in the lives of millions of professed believers.

George Barna, The Disciple-Making Pastor

A true disciple of Christ is one [who] follows him in duty and shall follow him to glory. [A true disciple] follows Christ as the sheep after the shepherd, the servant after the master, soldiers after their captain, aiming at the same end that Christ aimed at, the glory of God. . . All the followers of Christ must deny themselves. It is the fundamental law of admission into Christ's school, and the first and greatest lesson to learn in his school. . . They take up their cross: [this] should reconcile us to troubles and take the terror from them; they are what we bear in common with Christ. And many a life is lost for Christ's sake in doing his work, by labouring fervently for him. . . by choosing rather to die than to deny him or his truths and ways. Christ's holy religion is handed down to us, sealed with the blood of thousands. . .

Matthew Henry, *Commentary on the Whole Bible*

The need for devotion to something outside ourselves is even more profound than the need for companionship. If we are not to go to pieces or wither away, we all must have some purpose in life; for no one can live for themselves alone.

Ross Parmenter

A disciple is one who knows God personally and who learns from Jesus Christ, who most perfectly revealed God. . . Obedience to God's will is the secret of spiritual knowledge and insight. . . You will know as much of God, and only as much of God, as you are willing to put into practice.

Eric Liddell, *The Disciplines of the Christian Life*

But Saint Francis, faithful guardian of the secrets of God, when he judged that Master Bernard was fast asleep, in the deep stillness of night rose from his bed. With face turned to heaven and hands and eyes lifted to God, in complete surrender and with the warmest devotion he prayed, saying: 'My God, my All.' These words he groaned out to God with copious tears, again and again

with solemn devotion until dawn: 'My God, my All' —
no more. So said Saint Francis, worshipping God's majesty, which seemed to stoop to the imperilled world and
provide a remedy for the salvation of the poor through
his own Son. Enlightened by the spirit of prophecy, for-
seeing the mighty deeds God was about to do through
his own Order, and considering in the same spirit's teaching his own insufficiency and poverty of virtue, he was
calling on God to do himself what he was unable to do.
Without such aid, [all our] frailty is powerless. Hence his
words: 'My God, my All.'

The Little Flowers of St Francis

Since. . . Francis, along with his companions, had been
called by God to bear the cross as much as to preach it,
he and the pioneers of his Order seemed, as indeed they
were, men truly crucified. Bearing the Crucified in dress,
food and in all their doings, desiring rather the reproach
of Christ than the empty things of the world and its
treacherous blandishments, they rejoiced in sufferings and
held honour in contempt. They went through the world
like pilgrims and strangers, carrying nothing with them
but Christ. . .

Thus it happened that, in the early days of the Order,
Saint Francis sent Brother Bernard to Bologna, that there
he might produce fruit for God. . . Some children saw
him in his unusual and miserable dress and began to
heap insults on him. Brother Bernard, true saint that
he was, not only bore them patiently, but even suffered
them with deepest joy, because he was a true disciple
of Christ who became 'the scorn of the crowd and
shame. . .' For the love of Christ, he deliberately placed
himself in the market-place of the city, where he could
be the greatest object of the people's ridicule.

One tugged at his hood from behind, another from the
front, one threw dust, another stones. They pushed him
this way and that. Bernard endured all this violence
joyfully and patiently, without resistance in word or deed.
What is more, in order to endure such persecution day
after day, he would deliberately return to the same place.

Whatever violence was heaped on him by them, he remained calm in spirit and with joyous face. . .

The Little Flowers of St Francis

[When] the martyr in Tibet, Kartar Singh. . . went to preach the gospel, the people said: 'Keep quiet, we don't like to hear about Christ.' He was the son of very wealthy people and gave up everything to preach the gospel in Tibet. His experience was that wealth cannot give peace and satisfy the soul; only Christ can satisfy.

When I was in Tibet, they told me how this man was killed. He was taken to the top of a hill, sewn up for three days in a wet skin and exposed to the sun. When that man told me about the martyrdom of Kartar Singh, I noticed that his face was shining with joy and I was rather surprised.

'You are telling me something sad and you seem happy.'

'It is not sad — I tell you about his death, but there was no death, but life, wonderful life. He was three days in that skin, hungry and thirsty, and when asked, "How do you feel now?" he replied, "I thank God for this great privilege to suffer for him", but he did not suffer. He had such joy that I wish people could realise it; then they would agree with me that to live with Jesus Christ is heaven on earth. The people took sharp iron nails and thrust them into his body; the blood was flowing out of him, but he had such wonderful joy, a joy that cannot be expressed.

'Everybody left him. He said: "Everyone has left me, but not my Saviour; he is with me and not only with me, but within me. In this skin, I am really in heaven. I thank God for this privilege."'

Sadhu Sundar Singh, *Life in Abundance*

It may be easy for good Christians to die for Christ; it may be easy to be a martyr to be killed at once. But it is difficult to live for Christ because, if we live for him, then we have to die daily. The real secret of life is that we should know how to die daily.

Christianity is not a religion, not a society, but Christianity is Christ himself.

I have seen many seekers after truth who only used their head; the result was agnosticism and atheism. But when they used their heart, they found something and were satisfied.

Sadhu Sundar Singh

Each day before I leave my study I ask God to 'wear me like a garment.' My clothes are nothing in themselves — they are inanimate and, when I take them off, they can't stand up, walk or do anything on their own. They collapse. I want to be like that in relation to Christ. I want my only animation to be Christ who lives in me, who thinks his thoughts, desires his will and loves his love through me (see Galatians 2: 20).

Richard Halverson, 'Wear me like a Garment'

Therefore it becomes us to spend this life only as a journey towards heaven, as it becomes us to make the seeking of our highest end and proper good the whole work of our lives; to which we should subordinate all other concerns of life. Why should we labour for or set our hearts on anything else, but that which is our proper end and true happiness?

Jonathan Edwards

Meister Eckhart in particular keeps on reminding us that we must grasp God in everything. . . We must be completely detached about all circumstances, external and internal; we must even be detached about detachment. The truly spiritual person does not even seek tranquillity (of whose importance Eckhart elsewhere speaks in emphatic terms), because he is in no way hampered by lack of it.

So all possible answers we might give to the question, 'What shall I do to inherit eternal life?' are declared irrelevant and counter-productive; we are given no encouragement at all to entertain our feeling that if only we did not get these headaches, if only we had nicer neighbours, if only we knew how to pray, if only we were more humble, everything would go swimmingly.

Simon Tugwell, 'The Beatitudes'.

He [a church official] was one of those grim-looking men who sometimes hold office in the church. (Nobody doubts their integrity, but nobody wants to be like them.) All the lines of his face seemed to run down at acute angles, as though he lived all the while with an unpleasant odour under his nose. . .

It is an undoubted fact that many people outside the churches think that if they become Christians they will become miserable. They think that life in Christ is less and less rather than more and more. They think that it is giving up most of the things which make glad our hearts. . . Who could help being radiant with God living in them? The best Christians have surrendered their wills and their minds to Christ.

W.E. Sangster, *The Secret of Radiant Life*

Jesus was a deeply serious man. He was tremendously in earnest. . . He was so serious that there were times when his face was wet with tears. There were times that he sobbed as only the brokenhearted sob. Naturally many have come to think of him as one who could never laugh and whose face was seldom if ever lighted by a smile.

But. . . in spite of his seriousness — and because of this fact! — he was the most joyful of people. The artists have done Jesus a great injustice by picturing him as one whose life was one long sob. He did sob, but he also sang.

He could laugh. . . In fact, he was so glad that many of his day who looked on religion as a bit of a kill-joy did not think that Jesus was religious at all. . . Those too serious to laugh generally major on minors.

Clovis Chappel, *If I were young, I'd avoid being half-baked*

O most merciful Lord, grant to us your grace, that it may be with us and labour with us and persevere with us even to the end. Grant that we may always desire and will that which is most acceptable and dear to you. Let your will be ours and our wills follow yours in everything. . . Grant to us, above all that can be desired, to rest in you and to have our hearts at peace with you. You are the true peace of the heart and its only rest; outside of you all things are hard and restless.

O Father and God of our risen Lord, like the would-be followers then, we now tend to follow Christ at a distance. It just seems safer that way: no threat of being called fanatic or faint-hearted. O God, empower us to walk close with him, to learn of him, to be like him, to serve with him. From him may we know how to forget self, but never forget you. May we learn of him the power of gentleness, the grace of humility, the greatness of servanthood, the freedom found in service to you. O Master, let us walk with you. . .

William M. Johnson

Hold my faith steady when I cannot see the road ahead. May I always know I am loved. Protect me this day from evils seen or unseen. May I expect little and so be less prone to be disappointed.

It's a tough decision, Lord. Should I surrender completely to your will? But what will I have to give up? My commercial culture teaches me to think like this, Lord. I pay a price — and what do I get in return? Is the value worth it all?

But then, when I think of your love for me, it's not a question of giving up anything, but rather of living a truly worthwhile life. Any relationship involves surrender of some independence, in return for the great benefits of friendship, a listening ear, a reassuring touch when things go wrong, the promise of companionship into the future. . .

Help me, Lord, to believe the testimony of thousands through the centuries: once we are really committed to you, sacrifice is not an issue. No-one can outgive God. And after all, when I gave myself to you, I promised you everything. I promised to be yours to the end.

May I see the superficiality of merely being religious. Help me to do what is right because I love you, not to earn your love. Help me to serve you from gratitude for all you have given to me, rather than for any reward. You sacrificed your life for me: may I learn to hate the things that cost you your life. May I sacrifice whatever will hinder your grace operating through me.

Save me from the disillusionment of trusting anyone or anything but you.

Teach us, good Lord, to serve you as you deserve, to give and not to count the cost, to fight and not to heed the wounds, to toil and not to seek for rest, to labour and to look for no reward save that of knowing that we do your will through Jesus Christ our Lord.

Ignatius Loyola

A Benediction
May the Lord bless and strengthen you; may you always remain faithful to him who gave you life and his life, who loves you. May you freely choose to offer him everything: your love, your obedience, your relationships, your time, talents and possessions — even your own life. For the glory of Jesus Christ our Master. Amen.

52

Strive for greatness: be a servant

Come, bless the Lord, all you servants
   of the Lord,
who stand by night in the house of
   the Lord!
Praise the Lord!
Praise, O servants of the Lord;
   praise the name of the Lord.
Let steadfast love become my comfort
   according to your promise to your servant.
Remember these things, O Jacob,
   and Israel, for you are my servant;
I formed you, you are my servant;
   O Israel, you will not be forgotten by me.
Here is my servant, whom I uphold,
   my chosen, in whom my soul delights;
I have put my Spirit upon him;
   he will bring forth justice to the nations.
You are my witnesses, says the Lord,
   and my servant whom I have chosen,
so that you may know and believe me
   and understand that I am he.
Before me no god was formed,
   nor shall there be any after me.

But get up and stand on your feet; for I have appeared
to you for this purpose, to appoint you to serve and
testify to the things in which you have seen me and to
those in which I will appear to you. Of this gospel I
have become a servant according to the gift of God's
grace that was given me by the working of his power.

I became its servant according to God's commission that was given to me for you, to make the word of God fully known. What then is Apollos? What is Paul? Servants through whom you came to believe, as the Lord assigned to each. For we do not proclaim ourselves; we proclaim Jesus Christ as Lord and ourselves as your slaves for Jesus' sake. . . and made us to be a kingdom, priests serving his God and Father, to him be glory and dominion forever and ever. Amen. If you put these instructions before the brothers and sisters, you will be a good servant of Christ Jesus, nourished on the words of the faith and of the sound teaching that you have followed.

Whoever serves me must follow me, and where I am, there will my servant be also. Whoever serves me, the Father will honour. Whoever wishes to become great among you must be your servant. Moreover, it is required of stewards that they be found trustworthy. Submit yourselves therefore to God. He has graciously granted you the privilege not only of believing in Christ, but of suffering for him as well. Do not lag in zeal, be ardent in spirit, serve the Lord. Render service with enthusiasm, as to the Lord and not to men and women. . . since you know that from the Lord you will receive the inheritance as your reward; you serve the Lord Christ. . . by purity, knowledge, patience, kindness, holiness of spirit, genuine love. . .

Whoever speaks must do so as one speaking the very words of God; whoever serves must do so with the strength that God supplies, so that God may be glorified in all things through Jesus Christ. To him belong the glory and power forever and ever. Amen.

Preserve my life, for I am devoted to you;
   save your servant who trusts in you.
   You are my God.
I am your servant; give me understanding,
   so that I may know your decrees.

(Psalm 134: 1; 113: 1; 119: 76; Isaiah 44: 21; 42: 1; 43: 10; Acts 26: 16; Ephesians 3: 7; Colossians 1: 25; 1 Corinthians 3: 5; 2 Corinthians 4: 5; Revelation 1: 6; 1 Timothy 4: 6; John 12: 26; Mark 10: 43; 1 Corinthians 4: 2; James 4: 7; Philippians 1: 29; Romans 12: 11; Ephesians 6: 7; Colossians 3: 24; 2 Corinthians 6: 6; 1 Peter 4: 11; Psalm 86: 2; 119: 125 — all NRSV)

Our aim in life is simply to be like Jesus. He was a 'Servant King', as a popular Christian song puts it. You have the privilege — what an honour! — to be a servant of the King of all kings and to serve him as you meet him in others.

Success, in Jesus' terms, is not being boss, lording it over others, but to be a servant. James and John were two of Jesus' followers who learned this the hard way. They wanted privileged thrones in Jesus' kingdom: one of them on the left side and the other on the right. The other disciples, naturally, were furious with them. Tempers flared and there were angry exchanges.

But Jesus said, 'You know that in the world those who are thought to be "successful" are those who "get to the top". They have power over others. But it's not to be like that with you. Whoever wants to be great must be your servant; whoever wants to be number one must be the slave of all. I did not come to be served, but to serve — and to give my life for others' (Matthew 20: 25-28). (And those on the right and left of the Lord in the moment of his greatest triumph were two crucified thieves!)

Later, these fellows revealed that they were very slow learners at this point. When they gathered to celebrate the Passover, none of them wanted to do the slave's chore and wash the dirty feet of his friends. So Jesus gave them — and us — an object-lesson in greatness. He removed his cloak, took a towel, filled a basin with water and started to move slowly around the group, washing their feet and wiping them with the towel. Amazing: in Hebrew culture only slaves washed others' feet.

In that dramatic silence, only the embarrassed breathing and the trickle of water could be heard. Here is God incarnate, stripping himself to wash the feet of his proud friends!

Ultimately, the cross itself was the supreme symbol of his servanthood. He served by giving his life for his friends (and that includes us!).

> When I survey the wondrous cross,
> On which the Prince of glory died
> My richest gain I count but loss,
> And pour contempt on all my pride. . .

Jesus did not give his followers a blueprint about how the church should be run; there is no specific organisational model for the institution of the church in the New Testament. But there is a dynamic one: servanthood! Greatness in the kingdom of Jesus is to be a slave of others. The Chinese have a proverb: the tallest bamboo bends the lowest.

The best Christians have learned this lesson well. A theological seminary built a new office block. The president insisted his faculty take all the spacious new offices, while he took a crowded old office in a back wing. The action was both sincere and symbolic and made a profound impression on the students. Peter Drucker, the management expert, once wrote: 'The greatest time-waster for most executives is a decision that has to do with someone's status. A move into new offices, for example, stirs up guerilla warfare as to who gets which office.'

Effective Christians are not merely those who know a lot about Christian doctrine or the Bible, but who are willing to serve others. Effective leaders are not merely those who have a following, but who humbly serve those they lead, helping them become the best they can be (even if that means they do 'greater works' than the leader!). In serving, we become more like Jesus Christ.

Your calling is not to exalt yourself, but to exalt Christ. Theologian James Denney once wrote: 'You cannot bear witness to yourself and Jesus Christ at one and the same time. You cannot, at one and the same time, convey the impression that you yourself are clever and that Christ is mighty to save.'

The ideal Christian may not be a great orator, a charismatic prophet, a generous benefactor or a giant of faith. The ideal Christian, to paraphrase 1 Corinthians 13, is patient and kind, not envious, boastful, arrogant or rude. The ideal Christian does not insist on his or her own way, is not irritable or resentful, does not rejoice in wrongdoing, but rejoices in the truth. He or she is longsuffering, a true believer, is hopeful and endures anything.

Whatever your titles or accomplishments or outstanding gifts, they are all passing away. Only faith, hope and love will last forever. And they are the marks of a true servant.

❧

I am like James and John
Lord, I size up other people
    in terms of what they can do for me;
    how they can further my program,
      feed my ego,
      satisfy my needs,
      give me strategic advantage.
I exploit people,
    ostensibly for your sake,
    but really for my own sake.
Lord, I turn to you
    to get the inside track
    and obtain special favours,
      your direction for my schemes,
      your power for my projects,
      your sanction to my ambitions,
      your blank cheques for whatever I want.
I am like James and John.

Kent and Barbara Hughes, Liberating Ministry from
the Success Syndrome

Jesus taught a lot about service by washing his disciples' feet. In our highly urban culture where we wear closed shoes and socks and drive in automobiles, washing feet is not an especially effective way to express service. We read about what Jesus did; we get the basic insight that it is important to serve others and then we try to interpret that in our culture. Maybe we read to an old person or mow somebody's lawn. For me, 'washing feet' might be to prepare coffee for my wife each morning.

Richard Foster

Radical servanthood does not make sense unless we introduce a new level of understanding and see it as the way to encounter God himself. To be humble and persecuted cannot be desired unless we can find God in humility and persecution. When we begin to see God himself, the source of all our comfort and consolation, in the centre of servanthood, compassion becomes much more than doing good for unfortunate people.

Radical servanthood, as the encounter with the compassionate God, takes us beyond the distinctions between wealth and poverty, success and failure, fortune and bad luck. Radical servanthood is not an enterprise in which we try to surround ourselves with as much misery as possible, but a joyful way of life in which our eyes are opened to the vision of the true God who chose the way of servanthood to make himself known. The poor are called blessed not because poverty is good, but because theirs is the kingdom of heaven; the mourners are called blessed not because mourning is good, but because they shall be comforted.

McNeil, Morrison and Nouwen, Compassion :
a Reflection on the Christian Life

In an interview in the October 1983 issue of *Northwest Orient* magazine, Andre Soltner of 'Lutece' in New York, one of the world's premier restaurants, puts it this way: 'I am more than thirty years a chef. I know what I am doing and each day I do my absolute best. I cook for you from my heart, with love. It must be the same with service. The waiter must serve with love. Otherwise, the food is nothing. Do you see?

'Many times, I will leave my kitchen and go to the tables to take the orders myself. It starts right then and there. The feeling the customer must have is relaxation. If not, then his evening is ruined. Mine, too, by the way. How can he love, if he's not relaxed? People ask me all the time what secrets I have. I tell them there is nothing mysterious about "Lutece". I put love in my cooking and love in the serving. That is all.'

Tom Peters and Nancy Austin, *A Passion for Excellence*

We must face the modern situation honestly. The biblical image of servant is not popular. In the face of much bondage, much sickness and much sorrow, there are many professionals who are eager to offer their services for a dear price and from the protection of a status lifted far above those served. . . Is there still a place for the servant? I fear that if there is not, our lofty civilisation will swiftly degenerate. The social and economic proofs seem too powerful to deny. . . Agents of healing and deliverance are those who do not lord it over others, but identify with others in their joys and sorrows, successes and losses, recoveries and setbacks.

But we have learned from our biblical heritage that such identification and servanthood does not grow out of heroic decisions, but out of personal deliverance from false gods and integration into the community, finding true freedom in acknowledgment of the sole sovereignty of God. The hero reaches down to save and further demeans the one in bonds. The servant of Christ experiences his or her solidarity with the one in bondage, a solidarity based on the awareness of God's love embracing both.

The Pastor as Servant, Earl E. Shelp &
Ronald H. Sunderland (eds)

If it is true that people can grow, expand their capacities, jump higher, run harder and compose greater music, that means that the ultimate leadership is servant leadership, for we will produce followers who will surpass us. Runners will become coaches — to train other athletes who will break their records. Executives will hire subordinates and motivate them so well that they may become their superiors. It is not easy to adjust to such a view of the development of leaders.

So, when some people get to the top, they pull up the ladder with them. They cannot tolerate the ambition of the young and see every subordinate as a potential rival. Such executives hang on by their fingernails in organisations until the last possible moment and give their attention to fighting off rivals rather than nurturing successors. It is a foolish way to lead, inasmuch as we are always within one generation of extinction.

Alan Loy McGinnis, *Bringing Out the Best In People*

- Servants lead out of relationships, not by coercion. Servants don't demand obedience or submission. They meet their followers at the point of need. Servants have a common touch, maintain living contact and demonstrate consistent concern for their followers.

- Servants lead by support, not by control. Servants give from themselves rather than take for themselves. They love and lift others rather than manipulating them.

- Servants lead by developing others, not by doing all the ministry themselves. Servants, whether clergy or laity, recognise that the kingdom of God calls for the full participation of all believers. All spiritual gifts are given by God for service to Christ's body (Ephesians 4: 11-13).

- Servants guide people, not drive them. Volunteer organisations like churches require selfless leaders rather than selfish bosses or bullies.

- Servants lead from love, not domination. Authority, in part, grows out of 'the consent of the governed'. Peter sounded this theme clearly: 'Tend the flock of God that is your charge, not by constraint but willingly, not for shameful gain but eagerly, not as domineering over those in your charge but being examples to the flock' (1 Peter 5: 2-3).

- Servants seek growth, not position. Servants aren't

ambitious. They keep the growth and spiritual health of others paramount. Unlike Diotrephes, an ambitious leader in the early church who preferred to 'put himself first' (3 John 9), servants put others first.

Robert D. Dale, *Pastoral Leadership*

Field-Marshal Montgomery reckoned there were seven key ingredients necessary in a successful leader in war and all of them are applicable to spiritual warfare as well. The leader must:

1. Be able to sit back and avoid getting immersed in detail.
2. Not be petty.
3. Not be pompous.
4. Be a good picker of [assistants].
5. Trust [subordinates] and let them get on with their job without interference.
6. Possess the power of clear decision.
7. Inspire confidence.

Ian Dobbie, 'The Leader'

It has been said of some religious leaders that they have an unusual ability to be able to strut sitting down.

Richard Lovelace, *Dynamics of Spiritual Life*

Lord, make us strong enough to do what we should do
  calmly,
  simply,
  without wanting to do too much,
  without wanting to do it all ourselves.
In other words, Lord, make us humble
  in our wish and our will to serve.
Help us above all to find you in our commitments,
  For you are the unity of our actions;
  You are the single love
    in all our loves,
    in all our efforts.
You are the wellspring,

And all things are drawn to you.
So, we have come before you, Lord,
to rest and gather our strength.

Michel Quoist

O thou who hast so graciously called me to be thy servant, I would
hold myself in readiness today for thy least word of command.
Give me the spirit, I pray thee, to keep myself in continual
training for the punctual fulfilment of thy most holy will.
Let me keep the edges of my mind keen:
Let me keep my thinking straight and true:
Let me keep my passions in control:
Let me keep my will active:
Let me keep my body fit and healthy:
Let me remember him whose meat it was
to do the will of him that sent him.

John Baillie, *A Diary of Private Prayer*

Eternal God, the light of the minds that know you, the joy of
the hearts that love you, and the strength of the wills that serve
you; grant us so to know you, that we may truly love you, and
so to love you that we may fully serve you, whom to serve is
perfect freedom, in Jesus Christ our Lord.

St Augustine of Hippo

Kings lord it over their subjects, but with us the highest must
be like the lowest, the chief like a servant.
Who is greater — the one who sits at table or the servant
who waits? Surely the one at table. Yet Jesus is among us
like a servant. He came not to be served but to serve, and to
give his life as a ransom for many.
So when we have done all that we have to do, we shall simply
be servants who have done our duty.
Come to Jesus, all those whose work is hard, whose load is
heavy, and you will be renewed.

A New Zealand Prayer Book

Lord, teach me to be generous.
Teach me to serve you as you deserve;
to give and not to count the cost,

to fight and not to heed the wounds,
to toil and not to seek for rest,
to labour and not to ask for any reward save that of knowing
that I do your holy will.

O divine Master,
grant that we may not so much
seek to be consoled as to console;
to be understood, as to understand;
to be loved, as to love.
For it is in giving that we receive;
it is in pardoning that we are pardoned;
it is in dying that we are born to eternal life.

A New Zealand Prayer Book

A Benediction
May the Lord Jesus Christ, who became one of us to serve us
and to die for us, so enrich you with his example and his love,
that you may serve and love him until your dying breath. . .

   May his love, mercy and peace remain with you always.
Amen.

Postlude

Prayer of the forsaken

To come to the pleasure you have not you must go by a way which you enjoy not.

St John of the Cross

There is no more plaintive or heartfelt prayer than the cry of Jesus: 'My God, my God, why hast thou forsaken me?' (Matthew 27: 46b, KJV). Sometimes God seems to be hidden from us. It feels as if we are 'beating on heaven's door with bruised knuckles in the dark', to use the words of George Buttrick.

Christians down through the centuries have had the same experience. St John of the Cross named it 'the dark night of the soul'. An anonymous English writer identified it as 'the cloud of unknowing'. Jean-Pierre de Caussade called it 'the dark night of faith'. George Fox said simply, 'When it was day I wished for night, and when it was night I wished for day.' Be encouraged – you and I are in good company.

St John of the Cross says that two purifications occur in the dark night of the soul. The first involves stripping us of dependence upon *exterior results*. We find ourselves less and less impressed with the religion of the 'big deal' — big buildings, big budgets, big productions, big miracles. Not that there is anything wrong with big things, but they are no longer what impress us.

The second purifying involves stripping us of dependence upon *interior results*. Like a frightened child, we walk cautiously through the dark mists that now surround the Holy of Holies. We become tentative and unsure of ourselves. Nagging questions assail us with a force they never had before. 'Is prayer only a psychological trick?' 'Does evil ultimately win out?' 'Is there any real meaning in the universe?' 'Does God really love me?'

Through all this, paradoxically, God is purifying our faith by threatening to destroy it. Our trust in all exterior and interior results is being shattered so that we can learn faith in God alone.

Wait on God. Wait, silent and still. Wait, attentive and responsive. Learn that trust precedes faith. Firmly and deliberately say, 'I do not understand what God is doing or even where God is, but I know that he is out to do me good.' And as we wait for the promised land of the soul, we can echo the prayer of Bernard of Clairvaux: 'O my God, deep calls unto deep' (Psalm 42: 7). The deep of my profound misery calls to the deep of your infinite mercy.'

Excerpts from the chapter 'Prayer of the Forsaken', in Richard Foster, *Prayer: Finding the Heart's True Home*, Hodder & Stoughton, 1992, pp.17ff.

Abbreviations

Abbreviations of versions of the Bible used in this book

AMP: *Amplified Bible*, Zondervan, 1987

GNB: *Good News Bible*, the Bible in Today's English Version, The American Bible Society, 1976

JB: *Jerusalem Bible*, Darton, Longman & Todd, 1968

KJV: *The Holy Bible*, King James Version, 1611

LB: *The Living Bible*, Tyndale House, 1971

Moffatt: *The Moffat Translation of the Bible*, Hodder and Stoughton, London, 1982

NEB: *The New English Bible*, OUP/CUP, 1970

NIV: *Holy Bible, New International Version*, International Bible Society, 1973

NKJV: *New King James Version*, Thomas Nelson, 1991

NRSV: *New Revised Standard Version Bible*, OUP, 1991

Phillips: J.B. Phillips, *The New Testament in Modern English*, MacMillan, 1958

REB: *Revised English Bible*, OUP/CUP, 1989

RSV: *Revised Standard Version*, Thomas Nelson, 1952

RV: *Revised Version*, OUP, 1895

Bibliography

Other sources used in weekly readings

WEEK 1

Eddie Askew, *Many Voices: One Voice*, The Leprosy Mission International, 1985
Jon Black, in *Everyday with Jesus*, Richard K. Carlson (arr.), Waverley Abbey House, 1987
John Court and Dorothy O'Neil, *Rainbows through the Rain*, Lutheran Publishing House, 1989
Charles Hart, Lyrics for 'Phantom of the Opera'
Selwyn Hughes, *Every Day with Jesus*, Waverley Abbey House
C.S. Lewis, *Miracles*, Macmillan, 1947
Henri J.M. Nouwen, *A Cry for Mercy*, Doubleday, 1981

WEEK 2

Sheila Cassidy, *Good Friday People*, Darton, Longman and Todd, 1991, pp.83, 184, 186
Iona Community Worship Book, Wild Goose Publications, 1988, pp.56, 85, 106
Stuart Jackman, *The Davidson Affair*, Faber and Faber, 1966, p.168
Jürgen Moltmann, *The Power of the Powerless*, Harper and Row
Nancy Ann Smith, *Winter Past*, Inter-Varsity Press, 1977, p. 120
Margaret Spufford, *Celebration*, Collins Fount, 1989, pp.92, 117–119
Thomas Turnbull, 'The Birth', in *New Christian Poetry*, Collins, 1990, p.146
Philip Yancey, *Where Is God When It Hurts?*, Marshall Pickering, 1991, p.134

WEEK 3

George Carey, in a sermon preached at St Paul's, February 1991
John Chryssavgis, 'The Spirituality of the Desert', in *The Desert is Alive*, G. Ferguson and J. Chryssavgis, JBCE, 1990, p.111
Ross Kingham, *Surprises of the Spirit*, Barnabas Communications, 1991, p.12
George A. Maloney, *Broken But Loved*, Alba House, 1981, pp.30–31
Virginia Stem Owens, in *Christianity Today*, 19 January, 1979, p.469
Joseph of Panepho, quoted by John Chryssavgis, 'The Spirituality of the Desert', in *The Desert is Alive*, G. Ferguson and J. Chryssavgis, JBCE, Melbourne, 1990, p.117
M. Scott Peck, *The Road Less Travelled*, Rider, 1988, p.77
Abbe de Tourville, *Letters of Direction*, Mowbray, 1939, p.81

WEEK 4

Anthony de Mello, *Wellsprings: A Book of Spiritual Exercises*, Gujarat Sahitya Prakash, 1983, pp.136–137
Geoffrey Dutton, *Kenneth Slessor*, Penguin, 1991, pp.118–119
Charles Elliott, *Praying through Paradox*, Collins, 1987
David L. Fleming, *The Spiritual Exercises of Saint Ignatius*, The Institute of Jesuit Sources, 1978, pp.207–211

John Henry Newman, in Ian Ker, *John Henry Newman: A Biography*, Oxford University Press, 1988, pp.490–491

WEEK 5
Jerry Bridges, *Trusting God*, Navpress, 1989, p.195
Stephen Brown, *When Your Rope Breaks*, Kingsway Publications, 1988, p.134
V. Raymond Edman, *The Disciples of Life*, Van Kampen Press, 1948, pp.20 and 197
Fay Inchfawn, *Having It Out*, Lutterworth Press, 1960, p.88
Guy H. King, *A Belief that Behaves*, Marshall Morgan & Scott, 1956, p.16
C.S. Lewis, *Prayer: Letters to Malcolm*, Collins, 1964, p.117
J.B. Phillips, *The Young Church in Action*, Collins, 1968, p.11
Joseph M. Stowell, *The Dawn's Early Light*, Moody Press, 1990, p.100

WEEK 6
Charles Dickens, *David Copperfield*, Collins, c.1900, p.772
Fynn, *Mister God this is Anna*, Collins Fount, 1974, pp. 188–189
D.H. Gresham, *Lenten Lands*, Collins, 1988
D.H. Gresham, 'Letter to the Producers'. This was written in 1991 for the program for the West End production of the play 'Shadowlands' by William Nicholson, and has been subsequently reprinted in programs for this play all over the world.
C.S. Lewis, *The Great Divorce*, Geoffrey Bles, 1946
Katherine Paterson, *Bridge to Terabithia*, Puffin, p.128

WEEK 7
Harold Bauman, *Living through Grief*, Lion, 1980, pp.44, 45
Joseph Bayley, in Ingrid Trobisch, *Learning To Live Alone*, Inter-Varsity Press, 1985, preface xii
Donald Howard, *Christians Grieve Too*, AIO, 1986
Catherine Marshall, *To Live Again*, Peter Davies, 1957
Daisy Newman, *I Take Thee, Serenity*, Robert Hale, 1977, pp.277, 286
Hannah Whitall Smith, *The God of All Comfort*, Moody, 1956, p.11

WEEK 8
Robert Bridges, *The Baptist Hymn Book*, Psalms & Hymns Trust, 1962, p.572
Mary Craig, *Blessings*, Hodder & Stoughton
Joni Eareckson in Philip Yancey, *Where Is God When It Hurts?*, Marshall Pickering, 1991, p.134
Hildegard of Bingen, *Illuminations*, Matthew Fox (ed.), Bear & Co, 1985, p.49
Grahame Kendrick, *Let's Praise*, No.120
Lord Longford, *Suffering and Hope*, Harper/Collins, 1990, pp.24, 131
G.D.R. McLea (trans.), *Poems of the Western Highlands*, SPCK
Phillip Yancey, *Where is God When It Hurts?*, Marshall Pickering, 1991, p.134

WEEK 9
Barry Chant, *How to Live the Kind of Life You've Always Wanted to Live*, House of Tabor, 1987, p.102
Kim Hawtrey, *Life After Debt*, Albatross, 1991, pp.117–118
Thomas R. Kelly, *A Testament of Devotion*, Hodder and Stoughton, 1943, p.104
G.H. Morling, *The Quest for Serenity*, Word, 1989, p.51
Stephen Neill, *Christian Holiness*, Lutterworth Press, 1960, p.42
Frank R. Tillapaugh, *Unleashing Your Potential*, Regal Books, 1988, pp.152–153
Paul Tillich, *The New Being*, SCM, 1963, p.77

WEEK 10
George Appleton, *Journey for Soul*, Collins Fount, 1981, p.98
Bernard of Clairvaux, *On the Song of Songs, sermon 9: 7* (Cistercian Fathers Series) I, 56
Geoffrey Bull, *When Iron Gates Yield*, Hodder & Stoughton, 1976, p.188
Dawn through Darkness, Giles Harcourt (ed.), p.123
Samuel Johnson, *Rasselas, Poems and Selected Prose*, Bertrand H. Bronson (ed.), 3rd edition, Rinehart and Winston, 1971, pp.35–36
Leunig, *A Common Prayer*, Collins Dove, 1990
Mothers' Union Prayer Book
Brother Roger of Taizé, *Praying Together in Word and Song*, Mowbray, London and Oxford, 1988, p.32
Richard Sibbes, *The Bruised Reed and Smoking Flax*, in *Works*, Alexander Grosart (ed.), 1862–1864, I, 85–86
Paul Tillich, *The Eternal Now*, Charles Scribner and Sons, 1963
Evelyn Underhill, in George Appleton, *Journey for a Soul*, Collins Fount, 1981, p.20

WEEK 11
Ethel Barrett, *Will the Real Phony Please Stand Up?*, Regal Books, 1969, p.23
Robert Bloch, *That Hell Bound Train*, Venture SF, Mercury Press, 1958
Joy Davidman, *Smoke on the Mountain*, Westminster, 1954, pp.30, 31, 33
D.H. Gresham, unpublished article
C.S. Lewis, *The Great Divorce*

WEEK 12
Ray S. Anderson, *The Gospel According to Judas*, Helmers and Howard, 1991, pp.18–19, 88–89
Dietrich Bonhoeffer, 'Night Voices in Tegel', *Letters and Papers from Prison*, Macmillan, 1972, pp.349–355
John Bradshaw, *Bradshaw On: Healing the Shame that Binds You*, Health Communications, Inc., 1988
Frederick Buechner, *A Room Called Remember*, Harper and Row, 1984, pp.44–45
Annie Dillard, *Holy the Firm*, Harper and Row, 1977, pp.56–57, 73
Craig Dykstra, 'Family Promises: Faith and Families in the Context of the Church', in *Faith and Families*, Lindell Sawyers (ed.), The Geneva Press, 1986, pp.137, 143
C. Norman Kraus, *Jesus Christ our Lord — Christology from a Disciple's Perspective*, Herald Press, 1987, pp.207, 211
Michael Polyani, *Personal Knowledge*, Routledge and Kegan Paul, 1958, p.322
Ronald Gregor Smith, 'J.G. Hamann and the Princess Gallitzin', *Philomathes*, Robert Palmer and Robert Hammerton–Kelly (eds), Martinus Nijhoff, p.339
Ronald Gregor Smith, 'Preparing for the Ministry', *Collected Papers*, University of Glasgow (unpublished), August, 1938

WEEK 13
Anonymous, in *A Guide to Prayer for Ministers & Other Servants*, Rueben P. Job and Norman Shawduck (eds), The Upper Room, 1983, p.265
Charles Cummings, *The Mystery of the Ordinary*, Harper and Row, 1982, pp.129–131
Gerard W. Hughes, *God of Surprises*, Darton, Longman & Todd, 1988, pp.129–130
George MacDonald in *George MacDonald An Anthology*, C.S. Lewis (ed.), Macmillan, 1978, p.95
G. Matheson, in *Churches of Christ Hymn Book*, Wilke & Co. Ltd.,

1976, No. 348
Hannah Whitall Smith, *The God of All Comfort*, Moody, 1956, pp.38, 40
Marilee Zdenek & Marge Champion, *God is a Verb!*, Word, 1980, p.84

WEEK 14
Karl Barth, *Church Dogmatics IV.1*, T. & T. Clark, 1956, pp.246–247
John Donne, in *The Oxford Authors*, John Carey (ed.), Oxford, 1990, pp.175–176
T.S. Eliot, 'Little Gidding' in *Collected Poems 1909–1962*, Faber & Faber, 1963, pp.221–223
Eberhard Jüngel, *God as the Mystery of the World: On the Foundation of the Theology of the Crucified One in the Dispute between Theism and Atheism*, T. & T. Clark, 1983, pp.62–63, 219–220
John and Charles Wesley, *Selected Writings and Hymns*, Paulist Press, 1981, p.197

WEEK 15
Gerard W. Hughes, *God of Surprises*, Darton, Longman and Todd, 1988, pp.48-49
Victor Hugo, *Les Misérables*, Penguin Books, 1982, pp.117–118
Brother Lawrence, *The Practice of the Presence of God*, Hodder and Stoughton, 1985, p.29
Sally Magnusson, *The Flying Scotsman*, Quartet Books, 1982, p.104
Henri Nouwen, *In the Name of Jesus*, Darton, Longman and Todd, 1989, pp.31–32
J.I. Packer, *Knowing God*, Hodder and Stoughton, 1975, p.265
David Watson, *Discipleship*, Hodder and Stoughton, 1985, p.119
Words for Worship, Christopher Campling and Michael Davis (eds), Edward Arnold, 1986, Item 620

WEEK 16
Cavan Brown, unpublished ms.
George Essex Evans, 'An Australian Symphony', in Walter Murdoch, *A Book of Australian Verse*, 1945, pp.60–61
Dag Hammarskjöld, *Markings*, Faber, 1964, p.83
Mother Teresa, in Malcolm Muggeridge, *Something Beautiful for God*, 1977, p.48
Patrick White, 'Flaws in the Glass', *Bulletin*, 29 June 1980, p.151
J.G. Whittier, 'Dear Lord and Father of Mankind', *The Hymnal*, Aylesbury Press, 1980, No.410

WEEK 17
Meister Eckhardt, in *Meister Eckhardt*, Ursula Fleming (ed.), Collins, 1988, pp.40–41
Charles de Foucauld, *Cry the Gospel with Your Life*, Dimension Books, (undated), p.114
Thomas à Kempis, *The Imitation of Christ*, Leo Sherley-Price (tr.), Penguin, 1952, p.30
George A. Maloney, *Inscape*, Dimension Books, 1978, p.183
Thomas Merton, *A Vow of Conversation*, The Lamp Press, 1988, pp.188–189
Thomas Merton, 'In Silence', *Collected Poems*, New Directions, 1977, p.280
Teresa of Avila, in Matthew Fox, *Original Blessing*, Bear & Co., 1983, p.134
Mother Teresa of Calcutta, in *The Communion of Saints*, Horton Davies (ed.), Eerdmans, 1990, p.14

WEEK 18
Anonymous woman in a radio interview, in Margaret Hebblethwaite, *Finding God in All Things*, Collins, 1990, p.151
Frederick Buechner, *Wishful Thinking*, Collins, 1973, p.69
John R. Claypool, 'Living by the Sword', a sermon published by the Crescent Hill Baptist Church,

2800 Frankfort Avenue, Louisville, Kentucky, 40206, Vol. 8, No.9, 10 May 1970

St Francis of Assisi in *War, Peace and the Bible*: a discussion and study guide prepared for the Baptist churches in Victoria, Australia, 1986, p.7

John Garvey, *Modern Spirituality: an Anthology*, Darton, Longman and Todd, 1985, p.xiii

Genghis Khan, 1226

Dawn Longenecker, Sojourners Peace Ministry, in *War, Peace and the Bible*: a discussion and study guide prepared for the Baptist churches in Victoria, Australia. Revised edition, 1986, p.7

A New Zealand Prayer Book, Collins, 1989, p.109

Origen (185–254), in *War, Peace and the Bible*: a discussion and study guide prepared for the Baptist churches in Victoria, Australia, 1986, p.7

John Stott, in a sermon preached in All Souls' Church of England, Langham Place, London, 1979

David Suzuki, *Inventing the Future: Reflections on Science, Technology and Nature*, Allen and Unwin, 1990, p.87

Kallistos Ware, 'The Spiritual Father in Orthodox Christianity', *Modern Spirituality: An Anthology*, John Garvey (ed.), Darton, Longman and Todd, 1985, p.43

WEEK 19

Dietrich Bonhoeffer, *Letters and Papers from Prison*, SCM, 1971, pp.360–361

Cavan Brown, *Pilgrim through This Barren Land*, Albatross, 1991, pp.219-221

The Desert is Alive, Graeme Ferguson and John Chryssavgis (eds), Joint Board of Christian Education, 1990, pp.13–15

Jürgen Moltmann, *The Crucified God*, SCM, 1974, p.205

Jürgen Moltmann, *The Way of Jesus*

Christ, SCM, 1990, pp.176–177

M. Scott Peck, *The Different Drum: Community Making and Peace*, Simon and Schuster, 1987, pp.102–103

H.A. Williams, *The True Wilderness*, Collins Fontana, 1979, pp.52–53

WEEK 20

Dietrich Bonhoeffer, *The Cost of Discipleship*, Macmillan, 1963, p.60

John Calvin, *Institutes of the Christian Religion*, John T. McNeill (ed.), Westminster Press, 1960, Vol. I, p.367

Peter W. Ensor, 'Worship', in *Ministry in the Local Church*, Howard Belben (ed.), Epworth Press, 1986, p.44

Richard J. Foster, *Celebration of Discipline*, Harper & Row, 1978, p.148

Andrew Murray, *With Christ in the School of Prayer*, Revell, 1953, p.22

Thomas F. Torrance, *The Mediation of Christ*, Eerdmans, 1983, p.97f.

Robert E. Webber, *Worship is a Verb*, Word, 1985, p.29

WEEK 21

Roy Chapman and Donald Hilton, *Prayers for the Church Community*, National Christian Education Council, 1978, No.121

John Donne, in *The Minister's Prayer Book*, John Doberstein (ed.), Collins, 1986, p.130

Kevin Yelverton, unpublished article

WEEK 22

Fr Andrew, in *The Pan Book of Religious Quotations*, Pan Books, 1889, p.325

Donald Bloesch, *The Struggle for Prayer*, Harper and Row, 1980, p.98

Robert Browning, in *The Pan Book of Religious Quotations*, Margaret Pepper (ed.), Pan Books, 1989, p.325

John Bunyan, *ibid*

Carlo Carretto, *ibid*

Corrie ten Boom, *ibid*

Hubert Van Zeller, *ibid*
WEEK 23
G.B. Caird, in *Holy Thoughts on Holy Things*, Rev. E. Davies (ed.), Ward, Lock and Bowden, p.382
Giles Fletcher, in *The World's Great Religious Poetry*, Caroline Miles Hill (comp.), Macmillan, 1938, p.323
Alexander McLaren, in Mrs Charles E. Cowman, *Streams in the Desert*, Lakeland, 1925, Vol.I, p.197
George Mueller, in Mrs Chas E. Cowman, *Streams in the Desert*, Lakeland, 1925, Vol.I, p.197
A.B. Simpson, *Days of Heaven on Earth*, Francis Ashbury, 1984, July 15
Charles H. Spurgeon, in *Devotions and Prayers of Charles H. Spurgeon*, Donald E. Demary (comp.), Baker, 1960, p.44
J. Hudson Taylor, in Mrs Chas E. Cowman, *Streams in the Desert*, Lakeland, 1925, Vol.I, p.47

WEEK 24
Augustine of Hippo, in *Selections from Augustine*, William R. Cannon (comp.), The Upper Room, 1950, pp.33–34
Karl Barth, *The Humanity of God*, John Knox Press, 1960, pp.46–47
George Arthur Buttrick, 'The Presence of God in an Alien World', in Clyde E. Fant, Jr, *20 Centuries of Great Preaching*, Word Books, 1971, pp.268, 271
Derek Prince, *Faith to Live By*, Servant Books, 1977, p.13
Martin Rist, 'The Revelation', in George Arthur Buttrick, *The Interpreter's Bible*, Abingdon Press, 1957, p.543
Charles H. Spurgeon, in *Devotions and Prayers of Charles H. Spurgeon*, Donald E. Demaray (comp.), Baker, 1960, p.88
James Cowden Wallace, in *The World's Great Religious Poetry*, Caroline Miles Hill (comp.), Macmillan, 1938, pp.135–136

WEEK 25
Carl Jung, in Peter O'Connor, *Understanding Jung, Understanding Yourself*, Methuen, 1985, p.173
Morton Kelsey, *Dreams: A Way to Listen to God*, Paulist Press, 1978, pp.76, 9, 1, 101, 76
Morton Kelsey, in Catherine Marshall, *Something More*, Hodder and Stoughton, pp.118–119, 113, 118, 128
Louis M. Savary, Patricia H. Berne and Strephon Kaplan Williams, *Dreams and Spiritual Growth*, Paulist Press, 1984, pp.28, 69, 72, 29, 68, 22–24, 23, 24, 68, 72

WEEK 26
Joseph Conrad, *Heart of Darkness*, Penguin, 1983, pp. 121, 28, 113, 52, 113, 70, 67, 69, 66, 111, 68, 112–113, 108, 103, 97
Sören Kierkegaard, *Gospel of Sufferings*, James Clarke & Co.
C.S. Lewis, *Poems*, Walter Hooper (ed.), Harvest / HBJ Books, 1977, pp.124
C.S. Lewis, *George MacDonald, An Anthology*, Bles, 1974, p.23
Paul Tyson, unpublished article

WEEK 27
Karl Barth, *Dogmatics in Outline*, SCP, 1949, p.28
Dietrich Bonhoeffer, *The Cost of Discipleship*, SCM, 1948, pp.197–198
The Cloud of Unknowing, Ira Progoff (tr.), Laurel, 1983, pp.61, 90
Esther de Waal, *A World made Whole: Rediscovering the Celtic Tradition*, Fount, 1991, pp.77, 112
Gordon Dicker, *Faith with Understanding*, Unichurch, 1981, p.182
David L. Fleming, *A Contemporary Reading of the Spiritual Exercises: A Companion to St Ignatius' Text*, Institute of Jesuit Sources, 1980, pp.xiv, 57
Francis Ridley Havergal, 'Take my life and let it be consecrated', *The Australian Hymn Book*, Collins,

1977, No. 520
Gerard W. Hughes, *Walk to Jerusalem in Search of Peace*, Darton, Longman and Todd, 1991, p.240
William James, 'The Varieties of Religious Experience', in Leslie D. Weatherhead, *Discipleship*, SCM, 1934, p.16
George MacLeod, *The Whole Earth Shall Cry Glory: Iona Prayers*, Wild Goose Publications, 1985, pp.10, 21
Bruce D. Prewer, *Australian Psalms*, Lutheran Publishing House, 1979, p.98
Louis J. Puhl, *The Spiritual Exercises of St Ignatius*, St Paul, 1975, p.88
Wendy Robinson, *Exploring Silence*, SLG, 1979, p.21
Uniting in Worship: Leader's Book, Uniting Church Press, 1988, p.74
Uniting in Worship: People's Book, Uniting Church Press, 1988, pp.219–220
Leslie D. Weatherhead, *Discipleship*, SCM, 1934, pp.17–18

WEEK 28
David Augsburger, *Seventy Times Seven: The Freedom of Forgiveness*, Moody, 1970, p.19
W. Howard, *Groups That Work*, from chapter by O. Hobart Mowrer, Zondervan, 1967, p.106
H.D. MacDonald, *Forgiveness and Atonement*, Baker, 1984, p.69
Jared P. Pingleton, *The Role and Function of Forgiveness in the Psychotherapeutic Process*, Journal of Psychology and Theology, Vol.17, No.1, p.35
Corrie ten Boom, *The Hiding Place*, Hodder & Stoughton and CLC, 1971, pp.220–221
P. Tournier, *Guilt and Grace*, Harper and Row, 1962, p.191

WEEK 29
F.W. Boreham, *The Tide Comes In*, Epworth Press, 1958, p.15
John R. Claypool, *Learning to Use Our Troubles*, unpublished

sermon, 21 January 1979
Daily Mass Book, Lent 1991–1992, The Liturgical Commission, p.170
Alan Gaunt, *New Prayers for Worship*, John Paul the Preacher's Press, 1978, p.5
E. Stanley Jones, *A Song of Ascents: A Spiritual Biography*, Abingdon, 1968, p.48
Peter Kreeft, 'Seven Lessons from the Saints about Suffering', in John Winter (ed.), *Equipping the Saints*, Vol.II, No.1, Winter 1988, p.6
A New Zealand Prayer Book, Collins, 1989, pp.116, 119, 133–135
M. Scott Peck, *The Road Less Travelled*, Simon and Schuster, 1978, pp.15, 16
E. Lea Phillips, *Prayers for Worship*, Word, 1979, p.136
Ken Walsh, *Sometimes I Weep*, SCM, 1973, p.112

WEEK 30
Victoria Barclay, 'Can You Take as Good as You Give?', *Panorama*, August 1987, p.48
F.W. Boreham, *The Tide Comes In*, Epworth, 1958, pp.21–22
Manning Clark, *The Puzzles of Childhood*, Penguin, 1990, p.135
Manning Clark, *The Quest for Grace*, Penguin, 1990, p.139
Leslie D. Greenberg and Susan M. Johnson, *Emotionally Focused Therapy for Couples*, The Guildford Press, 1988, p.20
Martin Marty, 'Gencon', *The Christian Century*, September 4–11, 1991, p.831
David Tracy in Martin Marty, 'Gencon', *The Christian Century*, September 4–11, 1991, p.831
Dennis Waitley, *Seeds of Greatness*, Revell, 1984, pp.131, 183
John Wimber, 'Why I Don't Respond to Criticism', in *Equipping The Saints*, Vineyard Ministries International, Summer 1988, p.15
Robert Winderlich, 'Tame that

Tongue', Lutheran Hour address 82: 36/37, Lutheran Publishing House, 1982

WEEK 31
Ethel Barrett, *Will the Real Phony Please Stand Up?*, Regal GL Publications, 1969, p.199
Joni Eareckson Tada, *A Step Further*, Zondervan, 1978, p.17
Tony Campolo, *20 Hot Potatoes Christians are Afraid to Touch*, Word, 1988, pp.16–17
David Seamunds, *Healing for Damaged Emotions*, Victor, p.41
Lyle Dorsett, *And God Came In*, Macmillan, 1983, p.113

WEEK 32
Ascension Day prayer of the Church in Wales
Anonymous, in Peter Brierley, 'Priorities, Planning and Paperwork', MARC Europe, 1992
Phillips Brooks, in *The Prayer Manual*, F.B. Macnult (ed.), A.W. Mowbray, 1957
'Little Things Mean a Lot', *Christopher News' Notes*, No. 323, 1989
King George VI in his Christmas Day broadcast to the British Empire in 1939
Bill Hybels, *Too Busy Not to Pray*, IVP, 1988
International Evangelical Lutheran Church, Helsinki, Finland, *News*, April, 1989
Myron Rush, *Burnout*, Scripture Press, 1989, p.13
John Wesley, in *The Prayer Manual*, F.B. Macnult (ed.), A.W. Mowbray, 1957
Janice Wise, 'Needed: Grace for Growing Old', *Decision* Magazine, August 1990
Kay You, Sports Coach, 'I reached a dream', in *Decision* Magazine, February 1990, p.5

WEEK 33
William Abraham, *The Logic of Evangelism*, Eerdmans, 1989, pp.38, 170
Tom Allan, *The Face of My Parish*, p.70
Myron Augsburger, *Mastering Outreach and Evangelism*, p.17
David Bosch, *Theological Currents and Cross-currents Today*, International Bulletin of Missionary Research, Vol. II, No.3, July, 1987
Harvey Conn, *Doing Justice and Preaching Grace*, p.80
Jim Elliott, in *The Journals of Jim Elliott*, Elizabeth Elliott (ed.), Revell, 1978
Eusebius, *Ecclesiastical History*, 3: 372
St Francis in *Sebastian Temple*, Franciscan Communications, 1967
Alan Goodson, *Prayers for Today's Church*,
Lesslie Newbigin, *The Gospel in a Pluralistic Society*, Eerdmans/ WCC, 1989, p.116
J.I. Packer, *Fundamentalism and the Word of God*, p.135
Pope Paul VI, *On Evangelization in the Modern World*, Apostolic Exhortation, Evangelii Nuntiaandi, 8 December, 1975, Publications Office, United States Catholic Conference, 1976
Calvin Ratz, *Mastering Outreach and Evangelism*, p.29
Michael Saward, *Prayers for Today's Church*, Dick Williams, (comp.), CPAS Publications, 1972
Charles Wesley, *Baptist Praise and Worship*, OUP, 1991, No.76

WEEK 34
Robert R. Blake, Jane Srygley Mouton, Robert L. Allen, *Spectacular Teamwork*, John Wiley & Sons, 1987, p.6
David Cormack, *Team Spirit*, Marc Europe, 1987, pp.19, 20, 203, 216

WEEK 35
Philip Adams, in John Smith, *Advance Australia Where?*, Anzea

Publishers, 1988, p.216
Theodore P. Bornhoeft, *Prayers Responsively*, Concordia Publishing House, 1984, p.207
Charles Colson, *Who Speaks for God?*, Crossways Books, 1985, p.71
George W. Forell, *The Augsburg Confession: A Contemporary Commentary*, Augsburg Publishing House, 1968, p.38
Richard Foster, *Celebration of Discipline*, Hodder and Stoughton, 1980, p.140
Mahatma Gandhi, in Michael Green, *Evangelism through the Local Church*, Hodder and Stoughton, 1990, p.79
Michael Green, *Evangelism through the Local Church*, Hodder and Stoughton, 1980, p.103
Martin Luther, *Luther's Large Catechism*, Friedemann Hebart (tr.), Lutheran Publishing House, 1983, Part II, pp.51, 52
Martin Luther, *Smalcald Articles*, The Lutheran Book of Concord, Fortress Press, 1959, p.150
Robin Mann, in *May We Be One*, Lutheran Hymnal, Lutheran Publishing House, 1989, No. 800, verse 3
Henri Nouwen, *Clowning in Rome*, Doubleday, 1975, p.38
Edward Hayes Plumptre, *Thy Hand O God Has Guided*, The Australian Hymn Book, Collins, 1977, No. 389, verse 1
Bob Slosser, *Miracle in Darien*, Logos International, 1979, p.87
Howard Snyder, *New Wineskins*, Marshall Pickering, 1987, p.201
Geoff Strelan, in *One Family, We're Together*, Lutheran Hymnal, Lutheran Publishing House, 1989, No. 802, verse 4
Peter Wagner, *Your Church Can Be Healthy*, Abingdon, 1979, p.121

WEEK 36

John Claypool, 'Forgive us our Trespasses', unpublished sermon preached at Northminster Baptist Church, Mississippi, 23 March 1980
Jean-Pierre de Caussade, *Abandonment to Divine Providence*, Image Books, 1975, p.36
The Cloud of Unknowing, in *The Pan Dictionary of Quotations*, Margaret Pepper (ed.), Pan Books, 1989, pp.129, 404
T. S. Eliot, *East Coker III*, in William Johnston, *The Mysticism of the Cloud of Unknowing*, Anthony Clarke, 1980, p.175
King George VI in his Christmas radio broadcast 1939
Abraham Heschel, *The Prophets*, Harper & Row, 1962, p.193
St John of the Cross, *The Dark Night*, 5, in Philip Seddon, *Darkness*, Grove Books, 1983, p.18
Tony Kelly, 'Free to Forgive', *National Outlook*, February 1984, p.18
Noel Dermot O'Donoghue, 'The Jonas Experience' in *Modern Spirituality: An Anthology*, John Garvie (ed.), Darton, Longman and Todd
Eugene Peterson, *Five Smooth Stones for Pastoral Work*, John Knox Press, 1975, p.110
Alex Rebello, *Broken Stillness*, St Paul Publications, 1988, p.17
Rumi, in *The Pan Dictionary of Quotations*, Margaret Pepper (ed.), Pan Books, 1989, p.272
Philip Seddon, *Darkness*, Grove Books, 1983, pp.12, 13, 20, 21
C.H. Spurgeon, in *Day by Day with Spurgeon*, Al Bryant (comp.), Word, 1985, p.7
Miguel Unamuno, in Colman McCarthy, *Inner Companions*, Acropolis Books, 1975, p.227
Rowan Williams, 'Dark Night, Darkness' in *A Dictionary of Christian Spirituality*, Gordon Wakefield (ed.), SCM, 1983, pp.104–105

WEEK 37

J.M.G. Barclay, in Ronald T. K. Fung, *The Epistle to the Galatians*, *The New International Commentary* on the New Testament, Eerdmans, 1988, p.269

Robert Browning, Epilogue, from The Oxford Book of Nineteenth Century English Verse, John Hayward (ed.), Oxford University Press, 1964, p.350

John Bunyan, Pilgrim's Progress and Holy War, W.P. Nimmo and Co., 1884, pp.61, 62

Amy Carmichael, in Elizabeth Elliot, A Chance to Die, The Life and Legacy of Amy Carmichael, Revell, 1987, pp.264 and 379

Elizabeth Goudge, The Joy of the Snow: An Autobiography, Hodder and Stoughton, 1976, p.229

Joaquin Miller, in Streams in the Desert, Mrs Chas E. Cowman (comp.), Oriental Missionary Society, 1925, pp.47,48

John Mason Neale, based on Stephen the Sabaite (725–94) in Christian Praise, The Tyndale Press, 1957, p.278

Edith Schaeffer, Affliction, Hodder and Stoughton, 1978, pp.147, 148

Colin Sterne, in Redemption Hymnal, Elim, 1951, No.793

WEEK 38

Glenn Clark, The Soul's Sincere Desire and Two or Three Gathered Together, CFO International, 1953, pp.111–112

Glenn Clark, Windows of Heaven, Purnell, 1955, p.22

Glenn Clark, I will Lift up Mine Eyes, Harper and Row, 1984 pp.55–90

Djiniyini Gondarra, Father, You Gave us the Dreaming, Bethel Presbytery, Northern Synod, Uniting Church in Australia, 1988, pp.1, 4, 5

I Have a Dream. The Story of Martin Luther King in Text and Pictures, Time-Life Books, 1968, p.57

Catherine Marshall, Adventures in Prayer, Hodder & Stoughton, 1975, pp.49–51, 53, 55, 58–59

Jürgen Moltmann, The Theology of Hope, SCM, 1967, pp.22–23

Anne Pattel-Gray, Through Aboriginal Eyes, WCC Publications, 1991, pp.4, 6

Robert H. Schuller, Move Ahead with Possibility Thinking, Doubleday, 1967, pp.43–44, 157–158, 166, 167, 181

Myrtle Williamson, CFO Sings, Association of Camps Farthest Out, Minnesota, 1982, p.68

WEEK 39

Dietrich Bonhoeffer, in The Steps of Bonhoeffer: A Pictorial Album, J. Martin Bailey & Douglas Gilbert (eds), Pilgrim Press, 1969, p.86

Kahlil Gibran, The Prophet, William Heinemann, 1980, pp.61–62

Thomas à Kempis, Of the Imitation of Christ, Whitaker House, 1981, p.47

Eugene Kennedy, The Pain of Being Human, Image Books, 1974, pp.232–234

Joyce Landorf, Irregular People, Balcony Publishing, 1982, pp.126–128

C.S. Lewis, The Problem of Pain, Collins, 1957, pp.28–31

George Matheson, The Australian Hymn Book, Collins, 1977, p.615

Alan Paton, Cry, the Beloved Country, Jonathon Cape, 1957, pp.102, 208

Adrian Plass, View From a Bouncy Castle, Harper Collins, 1991, p.78

Gilbert Shaw in Tony Castle, The Hodder Book of Christian Prayers, Hodder & Stoughton, 1986, p.238

Alexander Solzhenitsyn, in Philip Yancey, Where Is God When It Hurts?, Marshall Pickering, 1991, pp.22, 73

Charles Haddon Spurgeon, in Day By Day With Spurgeon, Al Bryant (comp.), Word Publishing, 1985, pp.63–64

George Wald, in Philip Yancey, Where Is God When It Hurts?, Marshall Pickering, 1991, p.41

Ken Walsh, *Sometimes I Weep*, SCM, 1973, p.109

Philip Yancey, *Where Is God When It Hurts?*, Marshall Pickering, 1991, pp.22, 73

WEEK 40
Eddie Askew, *Many Voices, One Voice*, The Leprosy Mission International, 1985, p.39

Jim Bishop, *Go With God*, McGraw-Hill, 1958, p.183

Alan Gaunt, *New Prayers for Worship*, John Paul the Preacher's Press, 1978, p.22

Dick Innes, 'A Child Betrayed', *Encounter*, June, 1991, Vol.22, No.6, p.3

Harold S. Kushner, *When Bad Things Happen to Good People*, Pan, 1981, pp. 115–116, 149,

Cathy Ann Matthews, *Breaking Through*, Albatross, 1990, pp.196, 205, 221–222

Thomas More, in Tony Castle, *The Hodder Book of Christian Prayers*, Hodder & Stoughton, 1986, p.263

Michael Quoist, *Prayers of Life*, Gill and Son, 1963, p.66

Charles Ringma, 'The Transforming Power of Hope', *On Being*, August 1988, Vol.15, No.7, p.17

WEEK 41
Eddie Askew, *No Strange Land*, Leprosy Mission International, 1987, pp.38, 75

Charles Colson, *Against the Night*, Hodder & Stoughton, 1990, pp.103–104

Findley B. Edge, *The Greening of the Church*, Word, 1976, pp.46, 89

Victor E. Frankl, *Man's Search for Meaning: An Introduction to Logotherapy*, Ilse Lasch (tr.), Hodder and Stoughton, pp.65, 66

Helen Keller, *The Story of My Life*, Hodder and Stoughton, 1958, p.306

Martin Luther, *Commentary on Galatians*, 1535, Phillip S. Watson (tr.), James Clarke & Co., 1961, p.540

Martin Luther, 'Treatise on Christian Liberty', in *Works of Martin Luther*, Baker, 1982, Vol.II, pp.336, 337

Malcolm Muggeridge, *Jesus*, Collins, 1975, pp.90, 91

Malcolm Muggeridge, *Some Answers*, Michael Bowen (ed.), Methuen, 1982, p.29

WEEK 42
Lyman Abbott, in *Living Quotations for Christians*, Sherwood Eliot Wirt and Kersten Beckstrom (ed.), Hodder and Stoughton, 1974, p.49

Dietrich Bonhoeffer, in *The Penguin International Thesaurus of Quotations*, Penguin, 1976, p.217

A.J. Gossip, 'When Life Tumbles In, What Then?', in James S. Hewitt, *Illustrations Unlimited*, Tyndale House, 1988, p.140

E.M. Hamilton, 'Afraid — of What?', source unknown

Harry Scott Holland, source unknown.

Helen Keyte, 'Distant Shores', unpublished poem

C.S. Lewis, *A Grief Observed*, Faber and Faber, 1971, p.9

Peter Marshall, in James S. Hewitt, *Illustrations Unlimited*, Tyndale House Publishers, 1988, p.140

John Milton, 'Paradise Lost', in *A Dictionary of Quotations*, P.H. Dalbiac (ed.), Thomas Nelson and Sons, n.d., p.58

Jim Schembri, in the *Age*, Melbourne, 1991

Alfred Lord Tennyson, 'The Princess Ida', in *A Dictionary of Quotations*, P.H. Dalbiac (ed.), Thomas Nelson and Sons, n.d., p.185

WEEK 43
Sheila Cassidy, *Prayer for Pilgrims*, Collins, 1980, p.191

Lou Evans, unpublished prayer

Peter Evans, unpublished sermon
Harold Kushner, *When Bad Things Happen to Good People*, Pan, 1982, p.149
Keith Miller, *The Passionate People*, Word, 1979, p.25
Corry Skilbeck, 'Valley Fern', unpublished poem

WEEK 44

Dietrich Bonhoeffer, *Life Together*, SCM, 1954, pp.67, 112
William Clemmons, *Discovering the Depths*, Broadman, 1976, p.107
Max Delespesse, *The Church Community: Leaven & Lifestyle*, Ave Maria Press, 1968, p.126
James W. Fowler, *Becoming Adult, Becoming Christian*, Harper & Row, 1984, pp.86–92
John Main, *The Joy of Being*, Darton, Longman and Todd, 1987, pp.9, 10
Henri J.M. Nouwen, *Reaching Out: The Three Movements of the Spiritual Life*, Collins, 1976, p.145
M. Scott Peck, *The Different Drum, Community Making and Peace*, Touchstone, 1987, pp.102, 103
John Powell, *Fully Human, Fully Alive: A New Life through a New Vision*, Argus Communications, 1976, p.23
Jean Vanier, *Community and Growth*, St Paul Publications, 1979, pp.251, 252

WEEK 45

St Thomas Aquinas, in Selina F. Fox, *A Chain of Prayer Across the Ages*, John Murray, 1956, p.13
John Baillie, *The Idea of Revelation in Recent Thought*, Oxford, 1956, pp.138–140
Dietrich Bonhoeffer, *Letters and Papers from Prison*, SCM, 1971, pp.282, 361
Dietrich Bonhoeffer, *Life Together*, SCM, 1954, p.75
Emil Brunner, *The Mediator*, Lutterworth Press, 1934, p.526
Teilhard de Chardin, *Le Milieu Divin*, Collins, 1960, pp.89, 90
Normal Hable, '"Only the Jackal Is My Friend" — On Friends and Redeemers in Job', *Interpretation*, Vol XXXI No.3, July 1977, pp.227–236
Michel Quoist, *Prayers of Life*, Gill and Son, Logos, 1963, p.15
'The So-Called Letter to Diognetus', *The Library of Christian Classics — Volume I Early Christian Fathers*, SCM, 1953, p.220
Charles R. Swindoll, *Dropping Your Guard*, Hodder and Stoughton, 1983, p.107

WEEK 46

Isaac Ambrose, in Michael Griffiths, *The Example of Jesus*, Hodder and Stoughton, 1985, p.38
Dietrich Bonhoeffer, *The Cost of Discipleship*, SCM, 1959, pp.269ff.
C.H. Dodd, *The Johannine Epistles*, Hodder and Stoughton, 1946, p.85
Michael Griffiths, *The Example of Jesus*, Hodder and Stoughton, 1985, p.45
Thomas à Kempis, *The Imitation of Christ*, XXV
Graham Kendrick, *The Servant King*, Thank you Music, PO Box 75, Eastbourne, 1983
T.W. Manson, *The Teaching of Jesus*, CUP, 1945, pp.239, 240
William Temple, in John Perry, *Christian Leadership*, Hodder and Stoughton, 1983, p.10

WEEK 47

Dietrich Bonhoeffer, *Christology*, Fontana, 1974, p.52
Confucius, 'The Unwobbling Pivot and the Great Digest', in Hugh Kenner, *The Poetry of Ezra Pound*, Bison Book Edition, 1985, p.37
Herman Hesse, *My Belief*, Cape, 1976, p.220
Martin Luther, in Karl Barth, *Church Dogmatics*, Vol. 1. 1, T. & T. Clark Ltd, 1969, p.107
Ezra Pound, in David Heymann,

The Last Rower, Faber, 1976, p.215
Dimitris Tsaloumas, *The Observatory*, University of Queensland Press, 1983, p.31
Geoffrey Wainwright, *Doxology*, Epworth Press, 1980, p.177-178

WEEK 48
C Berry, *When Helping You Is Hurting Me*, Harper & Row, 1988, pp.79–80
D Bonhoeffer, *Ethics*, SCM, 1955, pp.79, 83, 91–92, 93
C.S Lewis, *The Problem of Pain*, Fontana, 1957, p.39
R Lovelace, *Renewal as a Way of Life*, IVP, 1985, p.115
Henri J.M. Nouwen, *A Cry for Mercy*, Gill & McMillan, 1982, p.99
Henri J.M. Nouwen, *Seeds of Hope*, Darton, Longman & Todd, 1989, p.56
Henri J.M. Nouwen, *With Open Hands*, Ave Maria, Notre Dame, 1972, pp.114, 126
Bruce Prewer, *Australian Psalms*, Lutheran, 1979, p.84
B. Rumbold, *Helplessness and Hope*, SCM, 1986, p.23
Ed Thornton, *Theology and Pastoral Counselling*, Fortress, 1964, pp.40–41
The Valley of Vision, A. Bennett (ed.), Banner of Truth Trust, 1975, p.4

WEEK 49
William Barclay, *The Letters to Philippians, Colossians, Thessalonians (The Daily Bible Study)*, The St Andrew Press, 1959, p.30
Friedrich von Bodelschwingh, in *A Minister's Prayer Book*, John Doberstein (ed.), Collins, 1964, p.210
Jack Burton, *The Gap*, SPCK/Triangle, 1991, pp.48, 131–132
The Church Hymnary, OUP, 1973, No.155
Harold R. Henderson, *Reach for the World: The Alan Walker Story*, Discipleship Resources, 1981, pp.82–83
Rhys Miller, *Calling and Recalling*, Uniting Church Press, 1984, p.117
Lesslie Newbigin, *The Gospel in a Pluralist Society*, Eerdmans, 1989, p.229
Carolyn Scott, *Betwixt Heaven and Charing Cross*, Robert Hale, 1971, p.25
Alexander Whyte, *Bible Characters, Old Testament*, Oliphants, 1952, p.95f

WEEK 50
Bruce Chatwin, *The Songlines*, Picador, 1987, p.21,
Dag Hammarskjöld, *Markings*, Faber, 1964
Soren Kierkegaard, letter to Jette, in Bruce Chatwin, *The Songlines*, Picador, 1987
Malcolm Muggeridge, *Jesus Rediscovered*, Fontana, 1969, p.89
Jack O'Hagan, 'Along the Road to Gundagai', *A Treasury of Australian Songs*, Therese Radic (comp.), Curry O'Neil, 1983, p.32

WEEK 51
George Barna, *The Disciple-Making Pastor*, Revell, 1988, p.21
Clovis Chappell, *If I were young I'd avoid being half-baked*, Abingdon-Cokesbury, 1945, pp. 96–97
Jonathan Edwards, in *Basic Writings*, Ola Elizabeth Winslow (ed.), New American Library, 1966, p.142
Richard Halverson, 'Wear me like a Garment', in *Practical Christianity*, LaVonne Neff et al (eds), Tyndale House, 1988, p. 59
The Little Flowers of St. Francis, E.M. Blaicklock & A.C. Keys (tr.), Hodder and Stoughton, 1985, pp. 16–17
Matthew Henry, *Commentary on the Whole Bible*, Hendrickson, 1991, p.1698
William M. Johnson in *Ministers*

Manual (Doran's), James Cox (ed.), Harper & Row, 1990, pp. 26, 85

Eric Liddell, *The Disciplines of the Christian Life*, Triangle/SPCK, 1986, pp. 27, 28

Ignatius Loyola, in *Praying with the Saints*, Veritas Publications, 1989, p.46–47

Ross Parmenter, in *The Pan Dictionary of Religious Quotations*, Margaret Pepper (ed.), Pan, 1989, p.95

Sadhu Sundar Singh, *Life in Abundance*, Christian Literature Society, 1986, pp. 41–42

W.E. Sangster, *The Secret of Radiant Life*, Hodder & Stoughton, 1957, pp.58–63

Sadhu Sundar Singh, in Alys Goodwin, *Sadhu Sundar Singh in Switzerland*, Christian Literature Society, 1989, p.39

Simon Tugwell, 'The Beatitudes' in *Modern Spirituality: an Anthology*, John Garvey (ed.), Darton, Longman and Todd, 1985, p.66

WEEK 52

St Augustine of Hippo, cited in Tony Castle, *The Hodder Book of Christian Prayers*, Hodder & Stoughton, 1986, p.18

John Baillie, *A Diary of Private Prayer*, OUP, 1963, p.81

Robert D. Dale, *Pastoral Leadership*, Abingdon Press, 1986, pp.34-35

Ian Dobbie, 'The Leader' in *Bash: A Study in Spiritual Power*, John Eddison (ed.), Marshalls, 1982, p.70

Richard Foster, in *Practical Christianity*, La Vonne Neff et al (eds), Tyndale House, 1988, p.295.

Kent and Barbara Hughes, *Liberating Ministry from the Success Syndrome*, Tyndale House, 1988, p.49

Richard Lovelace, *Dynamics of Spiritual Life*, Intervarsity Press, 1981, p.248

Alan Loy McGinnis, *Bringing Out the Best in People*, Augsburg, 1985, p.181

McNeil, Morrison and Nouwen, *Compassion — a Reflection on the Christian Life*, Image Books, 1983, p.31

A New Zealand Prayer Book, Auckland: Collins, 1989, pp.109 & 117

The Pastor as Servant, Earl E. Shelp & Ronald H. Sunderland (eds), The Pilgrim Press, 1986, pp.17-18

Tom Peters and Nancy Austin, *A Passion for Excellence*, Collins, 1985, p.289

Michel Quoist, in *100 Contemporary Christian Poets*, Gordon Bailey (comp.), Lion, 1983, p.136

Contributors

Personal profiles of contributors

Ray S. Anderson is Professor of Theology and Ministry at Fuller Theological Seminary. He and his wife Mildred live in Huntington Beach, California, where he is pastor of Harbour Fellowship. Recent books published include *Christians who Counsel* (Zondervan, 1990) and *The Gospel According to Judas* (Helmers and Howard, 1991).

Gerry Ball is the pastor of Gordon Baptist Church in Sydney. A pharmacist, he trained and served as a missionary in East Pakistan, has pastored churches in South Australia and New South Wales and was for sixteen years Principal of Burleigh College, the South Australian Baptist Theological College. He is married to Denise and they have six children and three grandchildren.

Paul Beasley-Murray is an English Baptist minister who has served as a missionary in Zaire, a pastor in Altrincham, Cheshire, and was until recently Principal of Spurgeon's College, London. He is author of a number of books, is married to Caroline, and they have four children.

David Bell is a Uniting Church minister in team ministry in rural Victoria. David's special interest is in poetry and its potential for shaping and controlling preaching. He is married to Julie and they have four young children.

Bryden Black is the recently appointed Director of the Department of Evangelism & Church Growth in the Anglican Diocese of Melbourne. He and his family returned to Melbourne four years ago after Bryden completed doctoral studies in the UK. Previously they lived in Harare, Zimbabwe, where Bryden was vicar of two Anglican parishes and Cathy, his wife, a medical doctor. They have four children.

Peter Brierley has been, until recently, Director of MARC Europe, a World Vision-sponsored leadership training organisation headquartered in London. Peter is one of England's leading statisticians. He worships at an Anglican church in Kent.

Cavan Brown was born in rural Western Australia and since 1969 has been a Baptist pastor in three rural churches and two city churches. He is currently pastor of Geraldton Baptist Church.

Greg and Maryanne Brown worship at East Toowoomba Uniting Church. They are involved in leadership and lay training, conduct a free community counselling service, and operate a support ministry to Christian leaders and manse families. They juggle work and ministry with parenting their two sons, Christopher and Adrian.

Ruth Bunyan is Principal of Strathcona Baptist Girls' Grammar School in Victoria. She has taught mathematics at secondary and tertiary levels at a number of educational institutions in Melbourne. She is married to Peter and they have three children.

Bill Carter has had nearly four decades of diverse ministry in three states of Australia. During the last two decades he has been concerned about issues of world poverty and disarmament. He is married to Margaret and has an extended family of eight children.

Feline Chin is the mission and evangelism staffworker of Georgetown Baptist Church, Penang, Malaysia. She is also currently a student of the Baptist Theological Seminary, Penang.

Ross Clifford is a lecturer at Morling Theological College, Sydney, before which he was Baptist pastor at Gymea in Sydney's southern suburbs. Prior to entering the ministry, he practised as a solicitor and barrister in Sydney and the Northern Territory. He has completed graduate study in apologetics, and Church and State. Ross and Beverley have two children.

John Court is still at heart a resident of Adelaide, where he taught at Flinders University and was president of the Bible

College of South Australia. He and his wife are currently living in Pasadena, California, where he is Professor of Psychology in the Fuller Theological Seminary Graduate School of Psychology.

Rowland Croucher has pastored churches in New South Wales, Victoria and Canada. For the past ten years he has ministered to clergy, church leaders and their spouses, first with World Vision, now with John Mark Ministries. He is also convenor of a ministry and research project among ex-pastors. He and Jan are a 'clergy couple' with four children.

Christine Dyer was a secondary school teacher with the Victorian Education Department. Since taking early retirement, she has been studying theology.

Keith Farmer is married to Margaret and they have three adult children. Keith is the principal of the Churches of Christ Theological College in New South Wales and lecturer in Pastoral Studies. Prior to this work, Keith was involved for twelve years in local church pastoral ministry.

Eddie Gibbs was ordained in the Church of England over thirty years ago and worked with the South American Missionary Society. Then, during his time with the Bible Society, he led seminars in church growth and was National Training Director for Mission England. In 1984, he joined the faculty of Fuller Theological Seminary where he occupied the Chair of Evangelism and Church Renewal. In July 1993, he joined the pastoral staff of All Saints Episcopal Church, Beverley Hills, California.

Douglas Gresham was born in the USA to parents who were both writers. After their divorce, with his mother, Joy Gresham, and brother, he lived in England, where Joy married writer C.S. Lewis. The story of their four years of happiness before her death in 1960 is well-known. Douglas, his wife Merrie and their three sons and two daughters have lived in Perth and Tasmania, before recently returning to Europe where they live now in Eire. He is the author of *Lenten Lands*.

John Helm was a pastor to Baptist churches in New South Wales and South Australia for thirty-two years until he joined Burleigh College, the Baptist College in South Australia, in 1988. He carries responsibilities in pastoral studies, spirituality and field education and has undertaken training as a spiritual director. He and his wife Cathy have three married daughters.

Peggy Jones has been a librarian at Whitley Baptist College in Melbourne, Victoria and, more recently, secretary/research assistant with Compassion, a child-development mission. She is currently working towards a BA, majoring in English. She and Don have four children.

Chua Soon Kent was born in 1961 in Sandakan, Malaysia, and is currently a final year student at the Baptist Theological Seminary, Penang. He is married to Wong Ling Kee, a former schoolteacher, a gifted pianist and musician. His callings are to preaching, personal evangelism and music.

Bryan Z. Kile is a Presbyterian minister. He recently received his Doctor of Ministry degree from Fuller Theological Seminary in California. He recently moved from Shelford, Victoria back to the USA with his wife Linda and her daughter, Allison.

Ross Kingham is a minister of the Uniting Church in Australia, and currently director of Barnabas Ministries Incorporated, an ecumenical ministry of encouragement and renewal for Christian leaders. He is married to Valmai, a medical practitioner who for some years has been working with people needing psychiatric care. They have three children and live in Duffy, ACT, Australia.

Wanda Nash has studied at the universities of Sydney and Southampton, has worked with the terminally ill at St Christophers' Hospice, London and with children with severe physical handicaps. She is chair of the International Stress Management Association, based in the UK, and has written a number of books on stress. She and her clergyman husband, Trevor, run such courses as 'Towards Wholeness'.

Carmen Nelson grew up in Sydney and became a Presbyterian deaconess. She teaches Religion at the Canberra Girls' Grammar School, is a lay reader and pastoral assistant in an Anglican parish in the ACT and is active in the Movement for the Ordination of Women. She is married to Ray, and they have two sons.

David Nicholas is manager of the Christian Television Association of NSW. He graduated from the NSW Baptist College in 1959, completed Masters studies in journalism and radio/television in the USA and has been a Baptist pastor for 34 years. He and his wife Judith have three adult children.

Alan Nichols has been an Anglican priest for thirty years and has held pastoral, communications and supervisory roles in the dioceses of Sydney and Melbourne. He was Archdeacon of Melbourne from 1986 to 1991 and recently completed a period of service, with his wife Denise, with the Jesuit Refugee Service Asia Pacific, based in Bangkok, with a special responsibility for face-to-face work with refugees from Burma. He now works with World Vision. He has written many books, of which the most recent is *David Penman*.

Howard Pohlmer, a Lutheran minister, has worked in Alice Springs and among the Guugu Yimidhirr Aborigines at Hope Vale, near Cooktown, where he authored a book on their history, *Gangurru* (from which comes the word 'kangaroo'). He has served in the Fassifern Valley, southeast Queensland and now is involved in a team ministry on the Sunshine Coast. He is married to Ora.

Edward Keith Pousson, from South Louisiana, joined Reserve Christian Fellowship in 1975 and worked as a missionary in Haiti, West Africa and Malaysia, returning home in 1982 to be ordained by his home church and placed on staff as a Bible teacher and missions director. After further training at Fuller Theological Seminary in church growth, he now teaches at the Tung Ling Bible School, Singapore. Edward is married with two sons.

Norman Pritchard ministered in two Scottish parishes before coming to Australia to become the senior minister at the Scots Church, Melbourne. He is married to Joan and they have two children.

Bronwyn Pryor is a trained infants teacher, with subsequent studies in Arts and Theology. She concentrates on children's ministry, especially as an enabler in the use of puppets. Bronwyn is currently the Victorian chairperson of Camps Farthest Out, an international ecumenical retreat movement.

Robin Pryor, a Uniting Church Presbytery Minister in Maribynong, Melbourne, leads seminars on vocational stress in ministry and has edited *Open to God: Discovering New Ways to Pray*. Formerly a demographer in Australian universities and with the United Nations, he is married to Bronwyn, and they have three young adult children.

Frank Rees pastored Baptist churches in Melbourne before pursuing doctoral studies at the University of Manchester on the relationship of doubt and faith in the Christian journey. Then followed seven years as a pastor of the Hobart Baptist Church in Tasmania. He is now professor of systematic theology at Whitley College, Melbourne. He is married to Merilyn and they have three children.

Julie Renner lives in the southern foothills of Melbourne's Dandenong Ranges with her husband and three university-age children where she is a deacon in their local church. Her commitment to wholism and training expresses itself in ministry that empowers people in many contexts, particularly those who have been marginalised.

Lawrence Simpson is a leading Australian cardio-vascular surgeon. He has been president of the Christian Medical Fellowship, chairman of elders of his local Baptist church and is chairman of John Mark Ministries. He and his wife Margaret have three married daughters.

Corry Skilbeck, a teacher, specialises in assisting helpers of the disabled. With her husband Peter, she leads a 'Crossroads' program for disabled people at her local Baptist church.

Peter Thamm, a former schoolteacher, is pastor at Everton Hills Lutheran Church, Queensland, having served previously in Sydney and Alice Springs. He is married to Mavis and has three teenage children. He is interested in photography and writing and has had four stories published. He is convenor of MERGER marriage growth seminars in Queensland and is active on the Congregational Life Committee of his district.

Paul Tyson has studied politics, philosophy, theology and education and is teaching in a Christian school in Cairns, Queensland.

Claire Wilkinson has been a primary schoolteacher for many years. She retired early to coordinate her church's counselling and healing centre and bookroom before being called to serve as a pastor in Knox Baptist Church in Victoria. She and her recently deceased husband have five children.

Kevin Yelverton is now the pastor of a Baptist church in Geelong, Australia, after ministering in New Zealand. He currently serves as secretary of the Baptist World Alliance Commission on Christian Leadership. Maried to Cherry, they have two children.